AF385816

SONS OF RAGNAR

VIKING WARRIORS WHO TERRORISED BRITAIN AND IRELAND

PAUL HARPER

Pen & Sword

MILITARY

AN IMPRINT OF PEN & SWORD BOOKS LTD.
YORKSHIRE – PHILADELPHIA

First published in Great Britain in 2026 by
Pen & Sword Military
An imprint of
Pen & Sword Books Ltd
Yorkshire – Philadelphia

Print ISBN 978 1 03610 559 4
ePUB ISBN 978 1 03610 561 7
ePDF ISBN 978 1 03610 563 1

A CIP catalogue record for this book is available from the British Library.

Typeset by SJmagic DESIGN SERVICES, India.

Printed and bound in the UK by CPI Group (UK) Ltd.

Pen & Sword Books Limited incorporates the imprints of Archaeology,
Atlas, Aviation, Battleground, Digital, Discovery, Family History, Fiction,
History, Local, Local History, Maritime, Military, Military Classics, Politics,
Select, Transport, True Crime, After the Battle, Air World, Claymore Press,
Frontline Publishing, Leo Cooper, Remember When, Seaforth Publishing,
The Praetorian Press, Wharncliffe Books, Wharncliffe Local History, Wharncliffe
Transport, Wharncliffe True Crime and White Owl.

For a complete list of Pen & Sword titles please contact

PEN & SWORD BOOKS LIMITED
George House, Units 12 & 13, Beevor Street, Off Pontefract Road,
Barnsley, South Yorkshire, S71 1HN, England
E-mail: enquiries@pen-and-sword.co.uk
Website: www.pen-and-sword.co.uk

or

PEN AND SWORD BOOKS
1950 Lawrence Rd, Havertown, PA 19083, USA
E-mail: uspen-and-sword@casematepublishers.com
Website: www.penandswordbooks.com

CONTENTS

Introduction vi

Chapter 1   Brotherhoods 1
Chapter 2   Ragnar Versus St Germain 10
Chapter 3   Ironside 23
Chapter 4   The Dark Foreigners 35
Chapter 5   The Great Frisian Army 52
Chapter 6   A Tale of Lagertha 62
Chapter 7   The Eagle's Claws 71
Chapter 8   House of Munsö 81
Chapter 9   The Martyr and the Wolf 92
Chapter 10   The Fall of Alt Clut 103
Chapter 11   The Raven's Fort 115
Chapter 12   Warrior Bishop 126
Chapter 13   Winter Camp 132
Chapter 14   King of the Norse 140
Chapter 15   Ivar's Howe 148
Chapter 16   The Madness of Halfdan 158
Chapter 17   Ubbe and Cynuit 171
Chapter 18   Dawn of England 185
Chapter 19   Siege of Paris 200
Chapter 20   Warrior of the Valkyries 215

Acknowledgements 228
References 229
Index 265

INTRODUCTION

I desire my death now. The disir [Aesir] call me home, Herjan [Odin] hastens onwards from his hall to take me. On the high bench, boldy, beer I'll drink with the gods. Hope of life is lost now – laughing shall I die!

Ragnar Lothbrok's final words in 'Krákumál',
author and date unknown[1]

As snakes sunk their fangs into his flesh after the Northumbrian King Aella ordered his death, Ragnar warned: 'How the piglets would grunt now if they knew what the old boar suffers.'[2]

Before setting off, Randalin, also known as Aslaug, feared Ragnar's plan was 'careless' as he was taking too many longships and risked capture if there was a shipwreck because he had only two smaller vessels. But Ragnar responded there would be no 'glory' with a large fleet and how England had been captured by crews in two boats, referencing Anglo-Saxon foundation tales. Envious of his sons' growing fame, as their recent Mediterranean raid made them notorious, Ragnar did not heed the warnings and was determined to embark on the foolhardy voyage from Scandinavia while his sons were still away.

When departing, Ragnar asked: 'What does the ring breaker (king) hear, come from the rocks howling, that the flinger (king) of hand-fire (gold), must forsake his sea-serpents (ships)?'[3]

After he was shipwrecked, Ragnar was soon confronted by Northumbrian forces. Fearing it was Ragnar Lothbrok himself, King Aella urged his men not to harm him as his 'sons will never leave us alone if he falls'. After proving almost unstoppable on the battlefield, Ragnar was eventually pressed down with shields as his army was heavily defeated. King Aella threatened to 'cast him into an enclosure of serpents' if he didn't reveal his identity and would drag him out instantly if he was Ragnar.

Despite being thrown in with the snakes, they refused to attack Ragnar, and Aella's men believed he must be 'mighty' because weapons did not injure him either. Stripped of his 'hallowed tunic', which Randalin had made to protect him, the snakes began attacking Ragnar as he recounted his 'splendid feat' of fifty-one battles and warned of the piglets' vengeance.[4]

The death of Ragnar Lothbrok in the snake pit – murdered by King Aella. (Hugo Hamilton/ WikiCommons)

It finally dawned on Aella he was Ragnar Lothbrok. Soon after, Ragnar was dead, and Aella's fate was sealed.

This is a simple story of family vengeance, a blood feud, of loyalty and honour, but it has proved remarkably enduring. There was arguably no greater Old Norse legend spoken of than Ragnar Lothbrok and his five most famous sons, Ivar the Boneless, Bjorn Ironside, Ubbe, Hvitserk (Halfdan) and Sigurd Snake in the Eye.

My fascination began after watching the thrilling siege of Paris in the *Vikings* TV series around a decade ago and learning there was a historical Ragnar who raided the French city but then suffered humiliating divine justice and disappeared from record. As someone who loves mysteries, I was instantly hooked. With its incredible casting, including actor Travis Fimmel as Ragnar, the *Vikings* series ensured the story remains as captivating as ever.

Numerous references to the potential real-life Ragnar and his sons can be found throughout ancient texts, written down between a year to many hundreds of years later. They range from brief accounts to elaborate stories composed by monks or later Scandinavian writers with vivid imaginations.

Tales backed up by historical accounts are conflated with mythological figures and implausible claims. Saga traditions have often been confused, the deeds of similarly named famed Vikings jumbled up and repackaged into an even more elaborate yarn. Future dynasties desiring to bolster their prestige and ancestry concocted suspicious genealogies tracing them back to the Ragnar Lothbrok dynasty to bask off their glories.

The people of Scandinavia, who would be the best source, were using an ancient language at the time and carving their messages into stone inscriptions. Christian institutions subjected to the Viking wrath were telling the traditional written story. Old Norse tales emerged some 300 years later in a world of monsters, goblins and gods as real as the person next to them.

The main sources are two Icelandic sagas by unknown authors that will be referenced frequently and featured in the book *The Sagas of Ragnar Lothbrok*, which was translated by Ben Waggoner. The first one, known in Old Norse as *Ragnars saga loðbrókar* and dated to around the late 1200s, will be called 'Ragnar's Saga'. This epic saga, which reveals little of Ragnar's actual deeds and is focused more on his love life, expanded on another text called the *Skjoldungatal* from Iceland dated to the early-thirteenth century.

Another Icelandic saga called *Ragnarssona þáttr* emerged decades later and improves on the earlier saga and avoids some questionable aspects. It will be known as the 'Tale of Ragnar's Sons'.

An elaborate third, key, thirteenth-century text composed by Saxo Grammaticus known as the *Gesta Danorum* (*Deeds of the Danes*) recounts a roll call of epic feats related to Ragnar and his sons but clearly mixes legend and history. A twelfth-century poem known as the 'Krákumál' presents itself as Ragnar retelling his famous feats just before death.

One thing for certain is the term 'Viking' either stemmed from the Old Norse word *Vikingr*, meaning a person raiding away from home or related to the ancient southern district of Viken in Norway. The Anglo-Saxon word *Wicing* related to a group engaged in piratical activity but not necessarily from Scandinavia. At the time, the 'Vikings' were called ' 'Northmen', 'Danes' and 'heathens'. The Irish called them 'gentiles', which means 'heathens' or 'gaill', i.e. 'foreigners'. Modern-day Norway, Sweden and Denmark were not yet in existence.[5]

Our understanding of the Viking Age through archaeology has grown immensely in the past century, but the historicity of famous names, none more so than Ragnar himself, continue to be endlessly debated. While not all questions can and perhaps will ever be answered, this is a determined attempt to uncover the real story behind Ragnar's sons.

Places that weathered the Viking storm, from rural Devon to the northern Irish coast and a Scottish volcanic plug are highlighted. Their history will be touched upon and the reason they became unlikely centre stages in this conflict. Chaotic raids in Paris led first by Ragnar and potentially his son Sigurd Ragnarsson forty years later in many ways begin and end the story. Exciting research reveals the true story of a climactic battle between Ubbe and the Saxons. Mysterious 'dark foreigners' in Ireland who are synonymous with sons of Ragnar are probed. And there's a focus on the origin of the Great Heathen Army led by Ragnar's sons, which invaded Anglo-Saxon realms to avenge the death of their father as later Scandinavian tales claimed.

The question of whether warrior shield-maidens were real and ultimately whether a female warrior like Lagertha could have existed will be tackled. Bjorn's notorious Mediterranean raid and links to a Swedish dynasty, centred around a huge mound, are featured, along with claims Ivar was also buried in a huge coastal barrow to warn off invaders.

There's an investigation into a memorable character from the *Viking* series called Bishop Heahmund and the location of a famous battle that launched one of Britain's 'great' monarchs. One chapter on the Viking camps reveals the life of the army, while another explores an infamous martyrdom. 'Ragnar's Saga' and the infamous acts associated with him from his nickname to grisly ending are also investigated.

The nature of his death is, of course, questionable, but the 'piglets' were very real. And according to legend they heard him loud and clear.

Chapter 1

BROTHERHOODS

My mother said to me, that they would buy for me, a ship and lovely oars, to go away with the Vikings, standing in the stern, steering the glorious ship, then putting into ports, killing a man or two.

> Egil Skallagrimsson, 6, looks forward to
> life as a Viking, tenth century[1]

It was a winter that lasted so long that its devastation echoed through the ages, signalling the apocalypse known as Ragnarök, the demise of the gods and humanity before the world was reborn. This became known as the 'Fimbulwinter', from the Old Norse *Fimbulvet*, i.e. the 'mighty, awful winter'.

Much of the fascinating mythology that drove beliefs in Scandinavia was revealed in the *Prose Edda*, a thirteenth-century Old Norse text by Icelandic scholar Snorri Sturluson. It spoke of the 'Weirds of the Gods', which prophesied that a chilling winter would strike before the gods clashed in Ragnarök with calamitous results. When the mythical king Gylfi enters the hall of the gods (who are known as the Aesir), he asks three men seated at a table what they know of Ragnarök, one replies:

> *'Great tidings are to be told of it and much. The first is this, that there shall come that winter which is called the Awful Winter, in that time snow shall drive from all quarters, frost shall be great then, and winds sharp, there shall be no virtue in the sun. Those winters shall proceed three in a session, and no summer in between but first shall come three other winters, such that all over the world there shall be mighty battles.'[2]*

The 'Fimbulwinter' appears a mythical retelling of the catastrophic climate in the sixth century, when a huge volcanic blast spewed sulphur, bismuth and other substances into the atmosphere, which created a dust veil that reflected the sun's light back to space and cooled the planet, severely impacting daylight.

The aerosols, which can stay in the atmosphere for up to three years, were transported over long distances in 536 by winds across the northern hemisphere. Another unprecedented volcanic eruption occurred three years later and then the world's first bubonic plague, the Justinian Plague, named after the serving Eastern Roman emperor, broke out in 541, fuelled by the desolate conditions.

A study by the National Museum of Denmark of tree ring growth from 654 wooden samples from archaeological excavations between 300 and 800 found that for 536 and 539 there was a 33 per cent and 53 per cent growth reduction respectively when compared to 535. Other studies suggest a drop in global temperatures of more than three degrees.[3]

Scholar Morten Fischer Mortensen said research found a 'sharp decline in grain production' and areas 'simply abandoned by people' and forests spread over the deserted fields:

> *'When the trees couldn't grow, there was nothing that could grow in the fields. In a society where everyone lives from agriculture, this has had catastrophic consequences. I almost get chills from seeing these small, narrow tree rings, because I know how much grief, death and misfortune they represent.'*[4]

In Scandinavia, the impact was profound because the period from 536 to 550 may have wiped out half of the population, which is truly incomprehensible.[5] Scandinavia was particularly vulnerable to the lack of harvest, with the already drastic difference in climate, landform and seasonal conditions across a vast and unique geographical landscape. Most of the fertile and level areas lie in the south, particularly in Denmark, which contains the lower-lying ground and rich soils filled with lakes, bogs and marshes. Swedish provinces such as Uppland and the lands around Oslofjord in Norway where the great Viking Age trading emporiums of Birka and Kaupang respectively emerged, and became centres of power, held richer farmland.

A coastal region stretching between central and western Norway from Stavanger to Trondheim was much better suited to agriculture and was where its kings had their large royal farms. Northern Sweden and Norway are generally taken up by mountains and often inhospitable.

More than 60 per cent of Sweden is covered by the Norrland (Northland), which stretches east onto the plains of Siberia and is covered in rolling hills and coniferous forests with the cultivated land in the north restricted to riverbanks. With its vast mountainous terrain and great fjords, just 3 per cent of the land is available for farming in neighbouring Norway, but its extensive coastline is some 1,600 miles long and teeming with marine life.[6]

Traces of the 'Fimbulwinter', which lasted for up to eighteen months from 536, can be seen in the 'Völuspá' ('Prophecy of the Seeress'): 'The Wolf shall swallow the sun, and this shall seem to men a great harm…the Midgard Serpent shall blow venom so that he shall sprinkle all the air and the water.'[7]

These prophecies appear to recall the solar darkness and volcanic debris as the future generations made sense of such terrifying unexplained events alongside their mythological beliefs. Its nightmarish aftermath before a gradual return to normality evolved into an apocalyptic tale. 'The terrible Fimbulwinter must have lived long in Northern folk memory, and been retold, sung and embellished with mystical interpretation,' said scholars Neil Price and Bo Gräslund.[8]

The Vikings' fascinating mythology featured gods, giants, dwarves and monsters, which took influences from Christianity but centred around nature. Often depicted as a menacing old man with a long grey beard, Odin was the chief god, who along with his brothers Vili and Vé were the sons of Borr (the son of Búri who was created from salt) and the giantess Bestla. The brothers had killed the giant Ymir and created the world from his body as his flesh became the earth, his blood the water and the top of the skull formed heaven.[9]

Ymir's gigantic children lived on in Utgard, where they were constant enemies of the gods. Giants and the known world were separated by a sea in which lay a great serpent called Jörmungandr, the nemesis of Odin's famous son Thor, which had a tail so long it encircled the world.

In Old Norse mythology, there were two groups of deities – the Aesir and the Vanir. While the Vanir embraced the giant Mimir, the Aesir received Njord and his children Freyr and Freya. The Aesir lived in Asgard, where Odin's hall Valhalla (Valhǫll in Old Norse meaning 'hall of the slain') welcomed warriors killed in battle.[10] Asgard was connected to Midgard (the earth), where humans resided, via a massive rainbow bridge called Bifröst. There was believed to be nine mythological worlds surrounding a sacred tree called the Yggdrasil (world tree).

The Vikings who shared these beliefs lived in a strictly class-based society, with the unfree, free and their rulers. At the bottom were 'thralls', i.e. slaves, who suffered a bleak existence. Many were taken from the Slavic regions bordering Scandinavia so much so that the name Slav (*Scalvus*) became confused with the medieval Latin term *scalvus* for slaves.

Above the thralls, were the freemen, the free, peasant farmer, known as the *bóndi* who owned land but were still dependent on their master from the noble class, which included the *jarls* who ruled a particular region. Freemen farmers formed the backbone of society, and they could be many things alongside, including a sailor, a trader, a Viking overseas and those who lived in the northern areas with its harsher climate survived as fishermen and hunters to supply the west's incessant demand for furs, walrus ivory and reindeer hides.[11]

Scandinavia was extremely well connected and resourceful. The list of goods traded included whetstones (for sharpening blades), slaves, weapons, furs (from bears, marten, sables and squirrels), malt, wine, fruit, sea ivory, ship cables (from walrus and seal hide), ornaments, silks, woollens, fish, reindeer antler (for combs), fish products, millstones (for grinding flour), hacksilver (fragments of silver cut from larger objects such as ingots and used as currency), pots and coins.[12]

In the mid-eighth century, the Viking trade network expanded significantly as new trading emporiums, beginning with Ribe in southern Denmark followed by Birka in Sweden, were opened. Suddenly, the western world's weakness and wealth became apparent.

A warrior culture, which emerged after the 'Fimbulwinter' and carried out of a land grab of deserted settlements, spawned ambitious local chieftains and kings with sworn followers, who sought control of the trade and quickly realised how religious sites and coastal towns and villages in the west were poorly defended and easy targets.

Many factors ultimately led to the Viking Age, but a revolution in sea travel in Scandinavia from the mid-eighth century with the development of a keel capable of supporting a mast was the key component, which these kings and chiefs used to devastating effect.[13]

Long and narrow warships known as 'longships' (*langskip* in Old Norse) proved crucial to their success when raiding. Fearsome looking longships boasted intricately carved dragon heads or snake heads on the high bow posts. As they neared the shore, rows of brightly painted shields were often hung on outboard racks along each side of the hull, and the massive woollen sails were also decorated with colourful stripes.

Longships were clinker built, which meant the lower edge of each hull plank, or strake, overlapped the upper edge of the one below. Sharp bows enabled the longships to easily cut through the sea, and reduced resistance when force was applied to the hull via the sail or oars. As one writer observed, the vessels were 'centuries ahead of their time', and the boats rested on the water 'like a duck'.[14]

The essential component of a ship's speed and ability to turn was a good sailcloth, which required a large and skilled workforce, and this was primarily a role for women, many of whom would be slaves and worked in cramped sunken-floored weaving huts found in abundance on settlements and around halls in Scandinavia, which often had next to no light. The years spent trying to pick out the different threads and different vegetable dyes would have ruined their eyesight.[15]

It was an incredibly extensive and long-winded task to make a sail with the wool collected from an estimated 27,000 to 30,000 Viking Age sheep farms in Norway. It took 20 hours to weave one metre of sailcloth and almost 3,200 hours to make the 157 metres needed for such a sail. The cloth was woven in 16 or 17 different pieces, which were then sewed together to create a sail of 90 square metres. In total, spinning and weaving took 8,000 hours or four and a half modern working years. This does not include the time needed for harvesting the wool or the finishing processes, such as fulling, which thickens and compacts wool through heating.[16]

And this was led, managed and executed primarily by women. As the historian Dr Eleanor Barraclough, author of *Embers of the Hands*, pointed out 'if you take away women, you end up with essentially naked blokes in rowing boats because there are no sails, there are no clothes for sea voyages, there are no clothes at all'.[17] Women also made the food that was cooked, preserved and stored for the journey, Barraclough added.[18]

More than 90 trees on average were needed to construct the vessel, along with 285 pieces of naturally curved oak, 600 horsetails for cordage, three tons of ore to produce 400–450kg of iron rivets and 100kg of wool from 100 sheep.[19] Viking fleets were often connected to a hinterland, where they had a community producing the material for ships on an industrial scale. Raiding grew into its own economy. In good weather, it took a week to sail from Norway to Ireland, around 1,350km, with a stop en route at the Shetland Islands. Crews could sail nonstop on the open ocean and could travel 150km to 190km daily at speeds of around 12 knots under sail, while the oars were deployed upriver.[20]

When there was no established harbour, they beached the longships because they were so lightweight, which helped with the regular portages, where the vessels were carried or rolled down stream or to a point where they could rejoin the river. There were side effects from the low weight, and the vessels needed an experienced and seasoned sailor in charge when conditions were rough. Lost ships and crew were common during the Viking Age, and sagas frequently speak of shipwrecks, including one involving Bjorn Ironside. A skilled sea expertise was crucial, the captain and fleet calculated their position and journey using cloud formations, the colour of water, marine creatures and birds, driftwood, the feel of a wind, currents, weeds and notable landmarks.[21]

Old Norse sagas even refer to a fabled *solarsteinn* ('sunstone'), a transparent crystal made from calcite or Icelandic spar, which could calculate the sun on cloudy days, but its existence has never been convincingly proven.[22]

In 1880, almost exactly 1,000 years after it was built based on tree-ring dating, one of the best-preserved Viking vessels was uncovered in a huge burial mound in the Sandefjord region of Norway. Known as the Gokstad Ship, the excavation revealed a clinker-built ship, made largely from oak with remarkably thin wooden strakes, which measured 23.8m (78ft) long and 5.10m (16ft 8in) wide. The vessel was built to carry a crew of thirty-six, who sat on private sea chests with sixteen oar stations on either side. The dead man inside, who was aged roughly 40 years old and around 5ft 9in to 6ft, suffered a violent death, judging from the cut marks on the skeleton. Decorated with gold-embroidered tapestries, the grave chamber included luxurious eating and drinking utensils, a sleigh, six beds, a chest, a saddle, gilt harness, sixty-four shields, twelve horses, eight dogs and two peacocks.[23]

As the Vikings set out on their quest to trade, exploit, plunder and populate the worlds to the west, it set them on a collision course with the most powerful state in

Vikings used vessels such as the Gokstad Ship at the Viking Ship Museum in Oslo with devastating effect. (Sergey Ashmarin/CC BY-SA 3.0)

the last 300 years since western Rome. The Carolingian Frankish realm included modern-day France, Germany, the Low Countries, Italy, Switzerland, Austria and parts of Spain, Slovenia, Hungary and the Czech Republic.[24]

During his reign, Emperor Charlemagne ruthlessly forced Saxons to convert to Christianity and outlawed paganism, which alarmed pagan Scandinavia because the neighbouring West Slavic people, the Obotrites, were allies of Charlemagne and he awarded them land in conquered Old Saxony territory on their border around the River Elbe, which runs through Germany to the North Sea. In the unfathomable Massacre of Verden, named after the confluence of the Elber and Weser rivers where the mass slaughter occurred, Charlemagne's forces beheaded all 4,500 Saxon prisoners in one day to subdue the rebellious region.

Despite his pre-eminence, a biography written around 70 years after his death by Notker the Stammerer, a scholar and Benedictine monk at the Abbey of Saint Gall, tells of how Charlemagne was gripped with fear about the north. When looking out of a window overlooking the port of Narbonne in southern France, a fleet 'filled with our fiercest enemies' turned up, which Charlemagne recognised instantly as Northmen. When they realised the king was present, who they knew as Charlemagne the Hammer, they feared being 'smashed to pieces' and withdrew. Their mere presence had supposedly reduced Charlemagne to tears:

'Do you know why I weep so bitterly, my true servants? I have no fear of those worthless rascals doing any harm to me; but I am sad at heart to think that even during my lifetime they have dared to touch this shore; and I am torn by a great sorrow because I foresee what evil things they will do to my descendants and their subjects.'[25]

One Danish king, called Godfred, rose to prominence, who amassed incredible wealth through taxation in Hedeby, where he could launch pirate expeditions and conquests. Hedeby is now part of Germany and located around 3 miles from Schleswig, deliberately situated at the end of a navigable channel called the Scheli. Surrounded by a huge semi-circular rampart, encompassing around 60 acres, this became the key Viking trading town in Jutland and the centre of power. It was the real life Kattegat depicted in the *Viking* series, which is the name of the sea strait between Sweden and Denmark. Goods that flowed into Hedeby included ceramics, glassware and Frankish swords from western Europe, millstones of Basalt from the Rhineland, Norwegian pots and dishes of soapstone, Slavic slaves and Baltic furs.[26]

In 808, Godfred, who had succeeded Sigfred, destroyed the competing Slavic emporium of Reric and transferred its merchants to Hedeby. Fearing retribution from the Franks and Slavs, the Danish king then dramatically increased the Dannevirke; a series of earthworks, including trenches, ramparts and walls, which stretch for 30km from Hedeby to the west of the peninsula. The River Eider's northern bank was surrounded by a rampart except for one gate for which chariots and horsemen could enter and leave.[27] Godfred's increasing power extended to Vestfold in Norway.

Two years after destroying Reric, Godfred launched an ambitious raid with 200 ships on Frisia, a coastal region of northern Netherlands and north-western Germany inhabited by a West Germanic people known as the Frisians, which included the empire's key trading settlement of Dorestad. According to the *Royal Frankish Annals*, which recorded the state of the monarchy from 741 to 829, Godfred was victorious after three battles with the Frisians and imposed a tribute on his conquered foe of 100lbs of silver. The devastating attack infuriated Charlemagne, who called up armies, but the fleet departed, and Godfred himself was killed before he could face retribution by his own son for abandoning his mother and taking another woman. His death sparked a succession crisis that would dominate Viking royal politics.[28]

Francia also became embroiled in its own succession crisis around twenty-five years after the death of Charlemagne involving his grandsons, Charles the Bald, Lothair and Louis the German (also known as Louis II), who were the surviving sons of Louis the Pious. At the Battle of Fontenay in June 841, Lothair, who succeeded his father, was defeated in a brutal conflict against Charles the Bald and

Louis the German, which haunted the Franks for generations. Two years later, in the Treaty of Verdun, the empire was divided with West Francia (which evolved into France) being taken by Charles, Middle Francia (the Low Countries and Italy) going to Lothair and East Francia (largely modern Germany) handed to Louis II.

The civil warfare in the Frankish empire did not go unnoticed. In the *Annals of St Bertin*, a contemporary account from the abbey of the same name in Saint-Omer, France, the Latin text refers to Vikings raiding in 861 as *'suas sodalitates'*, which could equate to 'their companies', 'their teams', 'their sworn gangs' or 'their bands of comrades'.[29] These groups, who swore oaths of loyalty, are also commonly known as 'brotherhoods', skilled warriors and craftsmen, bound to fight for their chiefs and rewarded lavishly.

Viking armies were often a coalition of smaller units, some tied to a particular region of Scandinavia, which merged to form a larger force led by a chieftain or king in his own right who would join expeditions.[30] Frankish authorities saw the Vikings as illegal gatherings, and worst of all pagans, bound by sworn oaths rather than kingship, who would merge with other gangs and then return to their original form when they had been either defeated or gained sufficient plunder. Viking fleets could be a mixture of not only Scandinavian warriors, but also Finnish, Frisians and from Baltic countries such as from modern-day Latvia, Estonia, Poland, Belarus and Lithuania.[31]

One woman uncovered at the famous Repton burial site had grown up in the Baltic continent while two other men buried were from Sweden and the west coast of Denmark respectively. The same is true of a later 10th century mass grave discovered in Dorset, in which the dead had come from across northern Europe, including modern Russia, the southern Baltic and north of the Arctic Circle. Some gangs may have even been turncoat Franks, Irish and Anglo-Saxons along with slaves and frustrated peasants.[32]

Research into the strontium and oxygen isotopes of Viking skeletons at Weymouth, Oxford and Repton revealed diverse origins and they were not from one geographical location but had lived together for the past few years.[33]

These multi-national brotherhoods were soon turning up nearly every year in Ireland, Francia and Britain. Academic Frank Stenton said the Frankish conquest of Frisia in the late-eighth century left them exposed to Viking raiders because they never had a powerful fleet to protect the coastline. Britain and the Frankish empire were 'at the mercy of any Danish expedition strong enough to overcome resistance at its landing place'.[34]

The shallow draught of Viking vessels enabled them to be sailed along rivers and water systems much further than ever before at depths as shallow as 1m.

Suddenly, fleets could travel further inland and attack without warning. Francia, with the major navigable rivers of the Seine, Loire and Garonne, was particularly vulnerable to the Northmen.

In 841, the Vikings first made their presence felt in the Seine, which was critical to West Francia's wealth and power. The city of Paris, founded by the Parisii tribe around 250 BC, would become a frequent target for the Vikings during the ninth century. As the important Roman city of Lutetia, it was concentrated around the Île de la Cité, an island in the Seine, which houses Notre-Dame cathedral.

Amid increasing pressure from Germanic tribes in the third century, the island was turned from a trading port into a large walled fortress for troops of military campaigns, protected by a rampart. After the Romans left, the Franks took over Gaul, but the city retained its prominence. While the Franks were Germanic, as they were powerful confederates for Rome who provided military service in exchange for land, they became heavily influenced by Roman culture

The Merovingian Dynasty, which united the tribes of Franks and Gallo-Romans, made Parisii its capital. By the ninth century, the city featured four great monasteries – St Denis, St Genevieve and the two St Germain's (l'Auxerrois and des Pres) – along with the royal palace, and so it inevitably became a lucrative prospect for Viking fleets.

One fleet turned up in 845 and extracted the largest tribute ever and were led by arguably the most famous Viking of them all. His name was Reginherus (Ragnar).

Chapter 2

RAGNAR VERSUS ST GERMAIN

*Animals die, friends die, likewise you die yourself. But what's said
about you, never dies, if you get a noble reputation.*

Hávamál, tenth to eleventh century[1]

The end of the Viking Age in the eleventh century is tied to the Christianization of Scandinavia but efforts to convert the pagan far north began 200 years earlier. Anskar, the Archbishop of Hamburg-Bremen, made a dangerous sea journey in 829 in which he was robbed on route by Vikings with his companion Witmar. Eventually, they reached a port called Birka, later known as Byorko, around 18 miles north-west of Stockholm.

Anskar consecrated his nephew Gautbert as the bishop of Sweden and he carried out missionary work for several years, where many secret local Christians were willing converts. This mission, however, ended abruptly when other locals began to persecute Gautbert and besieged his house.[2] Fuelled with hatred, they killed Nithard, a brother of the priest Erimbert, who accompanied Anskar on his return trip to Sweden, and bound Gautbert and his companions, plundering the house before chasing them away with insults and abuse.[3] This tale was relayed in the *Vita Anskarri*, a biography of St Anskar written by his successor Rimbert between the years 869 and 876.

An influential local man's son who helped ransack the house and stored the booty in his father's house suffered 'divine vengeance' and died along with his wife and son. In desperation, his father, who was now left with one son, consulted a soothsayer to find out which gods he had offended. After carrying out ceremonies, the soothsayer told him: 'Christ has ruined you. It is because there is something in your house which has consecrated to him that all the evils you have suffered have come upon you, nor can you be freed of them as long as this remains in your house.'[4]

He desperately discovered the item was a book and fearing the consequences fixed it to a post outside his home. While a Christian collected the book, which ended the religious curse, the others did not escape retribution. Rimbert claimed, 'the rest were punished, either by death or plague, or by the loss of property' and received 'due punishment from our Lord Jesus Christ'.[5]

In the next decade, Anskar's mission would eventually succeed in opening churches at Birka, Hedeby and Ribe in Scandinavia. Dramatic tales of divine retribution were a feature among religious sources that suffered from repeated Viking raids. Many accounts had clearly been exaggerated or made up entirely but reenforced the Christian faith.

The *Vita Anskarri* may just contain the first ever reference to the historical Ragnar. The figure who could be Ragnar, called 'Raginar' in the text, had been awarded land in modern Torhout, Flanders, by the West Francia king Charles the Bald around 841 but had later fallen out of favour with the emperor and was disposed of his territory. Rimbert mentions how 'Raginar' was 'well known' to his religious audience and had taken control of the monastery.[6]

Despite poverty, St Anskar would not abandon the monastery and continued to live with a handful of people. The bishop, however, became distressed because Raginar took some of the rescued Danish and Slav boys earmarked for a life of service from the monastery and sent them out as servants.

In a vision, the archbishop Anskar said he found King Charles and Raginar at a house and confronted them because he wanted the boys to be trained for the service for the almighty lord. In response, Raginar lifted his foot and kicked his mouth:

> *'When this happened, he thought that the Lord Jesus Christ stood by him and said to the king and to Raginar "To whom does this man whom ye treat so shamefully belong? Know that he has a master and because of this you will not go unpunished." When he said this, they were terrified and affrighted, whereupon the bishop awoke. The divine vengeance which overtook Raginar showed how true was the revelation. For a little later he incurred the displeasure of the king and lost the monastery and everything that he had received from the king, nor did he ever regain his former favour.'[7]*

It is far from certain this was the real Ragnar. There was a contemporary Raginar, a bishop of Amiens, but this religious figure fought for Charles the Bald three years later and continued as the bishop until his death in 849. Torhout is around 30 miles from the River Scheldt, which was closely linked to Ragnar's sons.

Academic Simon Coupland believes it is 'highly unlikely' to be Ragnar because Rimbert never associates him with the later Paris attack, and it was a common Frankish name in the ninth century.[8] However, scholar Peter Sawyer believed that it is the same Ragnar, suggesting the raid on Paris was carried out in revenge.[9]

Accounts of the Paris raid emerged from a monk of the benedictine monastery of St-Germain-des-Prés targeted by Ragnar's forces. The monk Aimoin wrote *De miraculis sancti Germani* (*On the Miracles of Saint Germain*) between 874 and 881, and he said it was based on two earlier accounts including one called the

Translatio of Sancti Germani (*Translation of St Germain*) written by an unknown monk, around 846; a year after the raid.

Viking raiders 'pierced the Christian's frontier' and advanced up the Seine, encountering little Frankish resistance and then set about committing 'innumerable sins and grievous crimes against the Christian people there.'[10]

Sailing south from Denmark, the fleet would have reached the Seine estuary in less than a week.[11] Ragnar's fleet first sacked Rouen and then Carolivenna (Chaussy), around 9 miles from the wealthy Abbey of St-Denis, targeting religious sites and no doubt spreading fear and panic in Paris.

On the Miracles of Saint Germain describes how the Vikings captured men and women slaves and 'burned and plundered' monasteries, towns and churches, which were left depopulated. Vikings found 'no one resisted them in fighting' and were filled with 'complete ignorance and pride' as they headed to Paris on foot.[12]

The fleet numbered 120 ships with a crew of around 30 to 40 men each, totalling around 3,600 to 4,800. As rumour spread that Ragnar's men were about to occupy the monastery of St-Germain-des-Prés itself, after they got as far as Carolivenna, the monks resolved to flee and take their precious relics and the saint's bones.

Aerial view of the Île de la Cité (city island) in modern-day Paris, which was once besieged by Ragnar's fleet of Vikings. (Eric Salard/CC BY-SA 2.0)

Monks packed up the relics and headed to shelter at Combs-la-Ville, about 20 miles south-east of Paris. Other monks at the nearby St-Denis also fled but without valuables due to the personal intervention of Charles as he arrived in the north of the city with his forces. Christian defenders, better equipped than the 'naked and almost clumsy' Northmen, were abandoned by their God on account of their unworthiness and 'were put to flight, some fleeing to mountain passes, some to valley hollows, some through open fields, and others to the murkiness of forests.'[13]

In response, Charles the Bald summoned the kingdom's entire military force but not everyone answered the call. His army gathered on two banks of the Seine to confront the Northmen, but the plan backfired disastrously because Ragnar simply concentrated his men on the smaller contingent of Franks on the south bank.

Franks were brutally cut down as their allies watched helplessly from the other side of the river. In a truly shocking act, the Vikings singled out 111 survivors and hung them on trees, stakes and houses as a tribute to Odin in front of the horrified Franks to gain fortune in the battle ahead. Other fleeing soldiers were chased through villages and slaughtered.[14]

Charles the Bald hastily retreated to the Abbey of St-Denis, which he was determined to protect at all costs. The next morning, on Easter Sunday, the Vikings ransacked Paris, which had been largely deserted of terrified inhabitants. According to *On the Miracles of Saint Germain*:

> *'the unbelieving and proud people of the Normans, pretending that they were superiors and thinking that their men might seize the kingdom by the suddenness of the Christians, rushed to Paris on the very Sabbath of the Paschal festival. In the early morning, when the sun shone bright rays and illuminated the entire world, they broke out of the ships with great speed, and took the city of Paris, empty for fear of the people, and without any soldiers.'[15]*

Merchants and bargemen of Paris did little themselves to defend their homes or their shrines. Almost completely unopposed, Vikings poured into the city on 29 March 845.

Inhabitants and clergy had been given enough warning of the impending danger and taken away their money and valuables. Frustrated, the Vikings sent envoys to Charles in the monastery to ask for payment in return for leaving the city. The detail of a tribute was added by Aimoin in his later account but not mentioned in the original *Translation of St Germain*.[16]

However, the contemporary *Annals of St Bertin*, which recorded the Viking raid of '120 ships of Northmen' who were 'laying waste to everything', said the offer of tribute was made by the Franks when Charles realised 'his men couldn't possibly win'.[17]

A depiction of the Viking siege of Paris in 845 led by Ragnar and his fleet of 120 warships. (WikiCommons)

Despite reservations, Charles had seen his small contingent destroyed by Ragnar and was persuaded to sue for peace by counts who may have been bribed. West Frankish nobles were seen to be narrow, selfish and unpatriotic, and tribute would have been the most satisfactory way to remove the Vikings. The king agreed to the Viking terms, which included a massive payment of 7,000lbs in silver and gold, along with the provision they left the city and never returned unless as friends or allies. Northmen would also be allowed to sail away from the city unmolested and presumably keep their existing spoils.[18]

This tribute payment to the Vikings to get them to leave called Danegeld, effectively 'Dane Money', remained the second largest of twelve such payments to Northmen in the ninth century.[19] A general tax would have been levied by the king on the impacted population in Neustria and Burgundy, western and east-central regions in the kingdom respectively. Magnates of the king would have collected this money from large landholders, who in turn would have obtained this money by demanding extraordinary taxes from peasants and anyone else subjected to their authority.[20]

The tax for the Viking took two months to collect, and they did not depart until around June or July of 845. While waiting around Paris, dysentery broke out among the Vikings in a supposed act of holy retribution after they ransacked sacred religious sites. They entered the monastery of the St-Germain-des-Prés, where they found monks celebrating with the morning prayer and all but one of the monks escaped. After the Vikings entered the monastery, dedicated to the Bishop of Paris who had died nearly 300 years earlier, the account speaks of a mysterious fog which engulfed the invaders:

> *'Therefore, while the most holy oratory itself was being violated by the most cruel and impious crowd [Vikings], it was suddenly filled with such a dense fog, and the same obscene violators were so struck by the blindness of the divine judgement, that, wishing to leave it, so terrified by fear and trembling.'*[21]

On the Miracles of Saint Germain describes how the Northmen were 'afflicted with dysentery and so many kinds of various diseases' and they were 'dying every day'. Vikings became 'struck with fear' of St Germain's spirit because so many of their brethren died, but the Christians managed to survive.

After returning to the court of Horik I, who was the ruler of the Danes and son of King Godfred, Ragnar boasted of his great victory, immense wealth, the weakness of the Franks and placing the entire kingdom under tribute. When Horik I doubted the story, Ragnar displayed prizes captured in Paris, which included a beam from the monastery of St-Germain-des-Prés and a lock from the city gate. He bragged about the rich and fertile land of the Franks but how its people were 'fearful and trembling to fight' and remarked 'among the land of the Christians, the dead had more valour than the living'.[22]

Ragnar would, however, soon face divine judgement. The unnamed monk who wrote the original account around 845/46 learned of Ragnar's supposed punishment through Count Cobbo, who had been present at the court of King Horik I as part of a diplomatic embassy sent by King Louis the German who ruled East Francia, which bordered the Danish realm and was a more immediate threat. Afterwards, Count Cobbo had visited St-Germain-des-Prés and relayed Ragnar's dramatic downfall when he mentioned the bravery of Germanus.[23] Ragnar was 'struck down' at Horik I's feet when telling how 'the only person in Francia to resist was an old man called Germanus'; the saint who died more than 250 years earlier.[24] According to the original *Translation of St Germain*:

> *'Just as he said this, he [Ragnar] falls to the ground tremulous and fearful and begins to cry in an unnatural voice that Germanus [St Germain] in person stood there and wielding a stick in his hand, was scourging him grievously. Then the king and all the chief men of his who were present there were astonished, struck with excessive terror*

> *by what had occurred. In truth, the same Ragenarius [Ragnar],*
> *blasphemer of God and all the saints, was taken to his own house by*
> *the hands of others, humbled and disturbed and stoutly scourged by*
> *the most holy Germanus [St Germain].*
>
> *'Afflicted and suffering the greatest torments for three days, he*
> *orders a golden statue to be made and taken to Germanus by an*
> *envoy of King Louis who was now present there when the aforesaid*
> *blasphemer was struck by that same holy man. And with an oath be*
> *also promised to become a Christian and to worship the God of the*
> *Christians, leaving aside other gods.'*

Desperate pleas to appease St Germain with a golden statue were rejected, and Ragnar died a miserable death when his bowels burst.[25] He 'cracked in half and all his entrails spilled on the ground. Thus, the most miserable one ended his life.'[26] Aimoin later claimed the statue was meant to represent St Germain himself. The fate of Ragnar's crew was equally bleak as they too were crippled with dysentery and then massacred by a terrified King Horik I.

> *'The others who remained, died every day, and not only they, but*
> *everyone whose body was stricken down with intestinal disease.*
> *But the aforesaid king of the Normans [Horik I], fearing he himself,*
> *like the others, should perish by a terrible death, ordered all those*
> *who remained to be beheaded, and their heads to be delivered to the*
> *Christian people.'[27]*

Among Vikings 'who had invaded the borders of the Christians, no one was left behind like those who fled in flight, whom we believe escaped the exile even after death.'[28]

The earlier *Translation of St Germain* claims four of Ragnar's crew escaped but 'not the destruction of death' soon afterwards.[29] These claims are naturally suspicious as Ragnar's raiding party may have exceeded 4,000 men.

In the same year, Horik I had sent 600 ships up the River Elbe in Germany against Louis the German, but the Saxons had emerged victorious, and the Vikings departed and sacked a 'civitas of the Slavs' on the way home.[30] Presumably, Horik I was now looking to make peace with Louis, but the idea he beheaded thousands of Northmen from Ragnar's crew, who likely had his permission in the first place, can be dismissed.

Despite dysentery being highly contagious, incredibly only the pagans were struck down with the disease. As the record arose from the very monastery targeted by the Northmen, there are other reasons to doubt this elaborate demise of Ragnar and his entire crew. Some monks targeted by the Vikings killed off their enemies with humiliating stories. Ragnar's demise has parallels with the Swedes who chased out the Christian congregation in the same year and recorded around twenty years later.

Literary tales of death and disease that befell Vikings who raided holy places in Paris would be repeated just 20 years later when Northmen who sacked St-Denis monastery in Paris in 866 suffered a terrible fate as 'some went mad, some were covered in sores, some discharged their guts with a watery flow through their arses and so died.'[31]

Charles Francis Keary, author of *The Vikings in Western Christendom, AD 789 to AD 888,* believed the account of Ragnar's death and mass killing of his crew can be easily dismissed, noting other accounts of the 'fatal effects from sacrilegious plunder around the same time'.[32] Keary said:

> *'By this time there could scarcely have been a single living Viking who had not borne a part in the plundering of some shrine; had the effects of sacrilege been everywhere so sweeping, half of the Scandinavian race must have incontinently perished. If the Ragnar of the Paris siege was the Ragnar Lodbrok of tradition he certainly did not die, then and in that way.'*

The *Annals of St Bertin* doesn't mention Ragnar and neither does the *Annals of Fulda,* which is more concerned with East Frankish affairs, but still records the attacks:[33] 'The Northmen ravaged Charles's kingdom, came up by boat on the Seine as far as Paris and having received a great sum of money both from him and the inhabitants of the region, departed in peace.' The *Annals of Fontenelle,* compiled contemporarily at the Abbey of St Wandrille on the banks of the Seine, mention Ragner but not his death:[34] 'Ragneri [Ragnar], dux of the Northmen, arrived with his fleet, came all the way to Paris, and on the vigil of Holy Easter, that is, on 28 March, entered that same urb.'

There may, however, have been a degree of truth in the sickness that plagued Ragnar's men because the *Annals of St Bertin* recounts how the fleet had continued to raid and plunder on their way back but were struck down:

> *'When they were going away in ships loaded with booty from a certain monastery which they had sacked and burned, they were struck down by divine judgement either with blindness or insanity, so severely that only a few escaped to tell the rest about the might of God.'*[35]

Another contemporary source known as the *Annals of Xanten* recounts the same sickness recording Ragnar himself died from the disease.[36] It revealed how 600 of the Viking crew had died during the raid on Paris but in a slant against Charles recorded:

> *'Owing to his indolence, Charles agreed to give them many thousands of pounds of gold and silver if they would leave Gaul, and this they did. Nevertheless, the cloisters of most of the saints were destroyed, and many of the Christians were taken captive. Thereafter the robbers were afflicted by a terrible pestilence, during which the chief sinner among them, by the name of Reginheri [Ragnar], who had plundered the Christians and the holy places, was struck down by the hand of God.'*

The *Annals of Xanten* adds the remaining Vikings returned their spoils to the god of the Christians on the advice of one of their Christian prisoners after deciding which gods they should seek for safety. Horik I and all the 'heathen people' refrained from meat and drink for fourteen days and when the 'plague ceased' the king sent back all their Christian prisoners.

Notably, the annals use an Old Norse name 'Reginheri' and include details of the king fasting, which is not included in the *On the Miracles of Saint Germain* account suggesting they got their information from a Scandinavian source.[37] While an interesting facet, the language 'struck down by the hand of God' shows influence

A view of the Île de la Cité from the Pont Neuf in Paris that was the centre of the chaotic siege of 845.

from the monastery's tales. Another translated version claims Ragnar died after he was 'beaten by the Lord'.[38]

Dysentery plagued medieval warriors, including the future English king Henry V, who died from the disease in 1422 after Agincourt. The killer disease causes inflammation of the large intestine and symptoms include vomiting and fever but worst of all debilitating diarrhoea, sparking severe dehydration and death. Those riddled with the disease were incapable of fighting. In bleak medieval war camps, the contagious disease could spread through poor sanitation, contaminated food and water as well as through infected persons.[39]

Outbreaks were especially common among forces besieging fortified towns in makeshift and poorly constructed camps, which Ragnar's troops faced as they waited for the tribute. Remedies ranged from opium to numb the pain and more complicated therapies involving cut bramble-roots in addition to simple fasting and resting. Less conventional methods involved reciting Psalm 56 three times and Our Father nine times, highlighting the connection between the disease and religion.

The fact Ragnar is never mentioned again in Frankish annals is seen as proof he died, but Viking leaders didn't renegade on tribute agreements. Danegeld was paid to Ragnar on the promise he would never return, and it seems he kept his end of the bargain. The same is true of the notorious Godfred in 853, Ragnar's own son Bjorn in 858 and Weland in 862 after they were paid considerable sums to leave. 'There is indeed no suggestion in contemporary sources that any of the armies which took tribute from Charles the Bald returned to the West Frankish realm,' said academic Simon Coupland.[40]

More than twenty-five raids where the names of Viking chiefs were absent are recorded in the *Annals of St Bertin* in the twenty years after the Paris siege. Monks who composed the annals were often focused only the devastation wrought. There was a caveat because the agreement seemed to apply to the emperor until their death rather than a kingdom, so the Vikings could return and extract tribute from the new ruler. In Charles the Bald's case, he reigned for another thirty-plus years.

Clearly, the Ragnar who terrorised the Franks was of some considerable standing and connected to Scandinavian royalty, either as a king's chief henchman or relation. Old Norse sagas and texts state Ragnar Lothbrok's father was Sigurd Ring, but no ruler of this name is known. Some scholars believe Sigurd Ring is a conflation of two documented Danish kings – Sigfred and Anulo – killed in a famous battle in the early-ninth century over the throne.[41]

Sigfred, who was often mixed up with Sigurd in medieval texts, was likely a brother or nephew of the earlier King Godfred. After the death of Godfred, his nephew Hemming ruled for two years from 810 until his own death, which sparked a succession crisis. When Sigfred launched his bid for Danish kingship, he was challenged by Anulo, the son of King Harald, from a competing royal lineage. Harald appears to have ruled briefly before or immediately after Godfred's predecessor Sigfried.[42]

Royal Frankish Annals said both Sigfred and Anulo were killed in a brutal battle in which a staggering total of 10,940 perished. This exceptionally high figure, which is clearly exaggerated, suggests a far-reaching civil war. Anulo's party was victorious and his brothers Harald Klak and Ragnfred began to rule as joint rulers, but their initial reign was short-lived.[43] Two years later, five sons of Godfred removed them from the throne, and then Ragnfred was killed in 814. The other son, Harald Klak, survived and later ruled again from 819 to 827. The two royal factions from the lineage of Godfred and Harald warred for the next 40 years.

Hundreds of years later when later chroniclers such as Saxo studied the Danish king lists they would have seen Sigfred and Anulo listed side by side. The unusual name 'Anulo' was frequently misinterpreted in Danish medieval literature because of its likeness to the Latin word 'annulus' meaning 'ring'.[44] This in turn created 'Sigurd Ring' in the later legend as a Swedish king who fought in a famous civil war against his uncle Harald Wartooth, the king of Denmark, in the legendary Battle of Brávellir. While documented in various sources, the battle appears legendary and based on the civil wars.

There was a rule in ninth-century Denmark in which the eldest member of the entire royal family stood to inherit the throne next. Moreover, there was an ancient Germanic tradition of a special relationship between an uncle and a nephew, and a deceased uncle's name being passed onto their nephew. Godfred's nephew referred to as Reginoldus or Ragnfred was killed in 808 during a siege against the Obotrites, a group of West Slavic tribes in what is now northern Germany. This Reginoldus was described as the 'foremost in the kingdom next to the king' in the *Chronicle of Moissac*, which was compiled in an abbey of the same name in south-western France in the tenth century.[45]

Academic Rory McTurk believes Reginoldus was Sigfred's brother and that his name was passed on to Sigfred's son Ragnar. Therefore, the Ragnar who attacked Paris was of the royal line and related to Horik I as his first cousin, once removed, or they were cousins if Sigfred and Godfred were brothers.

A fascinating contemporary poem supports the association of Sigfred as Ragnar's father – from possibly the oldest Skaldic verse. While questions persist whether Ragnar ever existed, it is intriguing that a possible contemporary poem from renowned Skaldic poet Bragi Boddason mentions such an individual. Bragi is believed to descend from a noble family in south-western Norway, and to have lived between 835–900.[46]

Bragi Boddason composed *Ragnarsdrápa* during the ninth century, which translates as the *Long Poem with a Refrain for Ragnarr*. It contains twenty verses that describe four different mythological stories, told by Bragi as if he is viewing them upon a wooden shield given to him by Ragnarr.[47]

The line repeated twice reads: 'Ragnarr gave me the Ræ's [sea-king[chariot's [ship] moon [shield] and a multitude of stories with it.' The father of 'Ragnarr' was called Sigurd: 'Unless in such a way that the famous son of Sigurðr (Ragnarr) should want good recompense for the resounding boss-hubbed wheel of the maid of Hǫgni.' Four myths Bragi recounts are: the attack of Hamdir and Sorli against King Jormunrekr, the never-ending battle between Heðinn and Hǫgni, Thor's fishing for Jǫrmungandr [the Midgard Serpent] and Gefjun's ploughing of Zealand from the soil of Sweden.[48]

The poet was transferring the symbolic power of the carvings on the shield, including the objects, to Skaldic poetry. Bragi uses complex kennings, which feature heavily throughout Old Norse sagas, often describing pagan myths and that use additional words to describe a common term.[49]

A kenning also works as a figure of speech to explain something not normally associated with, such as a camel is the 'ship of the desert' because the animal is the normal mode of transport in the desert and the ship is the equivalent on the sea. Names of gods and goddesses could also be used as the base words in kennings to represent men and women, such as 'sword-Odin'.[50]

Fabulous examples of kennings include 'valkyrie of the headdress' (married woman), 'gazelles of the storm' (ships) 'witches mount' (wolves) and 'sun of the sea' (gold). Sometimes men and women were imagined as trees and then associated with weapons for men or jewellery for women.

Academic Sydney Knell translated the famous poem and highlighted various kennings, which include, for example, phrases such as *'byrjar drösla'*, which means 'sailing wind horse' (i.e. 'ship') or *'rymregin þremja'*, which equates to 'gods of the noise of sword-edges' (i.e. 'warriors') and *'inda munnlaug'* equalling 'hand basin of wind' (i.e. 'sky').[51]

Interestingly, Bragi supposedly served Bjorn at Haugi (Bjorn of the Barrow) in Sweden, which will be studied in more detail in Chapter Eight. Some historians believe the 'Ragnarr' of *Ragnarsdrápa* must be another Ragnar, but this seems questionable because there are no obvious alternatives.

Another element of note is the reference to a 'ýða stillir landa vanr', meaning 'people ruler without lands', i.e. 'sea-kings'. These famous sea-kings could begin to offer an explanation on the real Ragnar Lothbrok and why he achieved notoriety. In Old Norse sources, a *sakonungr*, translating as a 'sea-king', was a raider who had gained enough wealth and power to be recognised as a king. Snorri's *Ynglinga saga* remarks how 'many sea-kings who commanded large troops and had no lands'.[52]

Archaeologist Neil Price, author of *The Children of Ash and Elm*, said sea-kings often had 'warlord manors', such as at Avaldsnes in Norway, with hinterlands that provided food and drink for the warriors and the raw materials to maintain ships, while the farmlands could supply men for emergency defence and crews for the fleets of raiders.

The power of the sea-kings grew in the Norwegian Midlands from around the 720s when they secured control over the long-distance trade of valuable Arctic raw materials and products such as furs, walrus ivory and whetstone. At this time, 'things', which were assemblies of free men that served as both courts and parliaments, where disputes were resolved and political decisions made, fell out of favour in Rogaland county, the area around Avaldsnes. This suggests power was becoming centralised with kings rising in stature. As Price observed, the emergence of sea-kings such as Ragnar were 'crucial to the beginnings of the Viking Age', sparked by their bid for increased power and control over trade and populations along the coasts.[53]

Legends of a heroic Viking leader called Ragnar, Ragnall or Lothbrok, who had very famous sons, are remarkably persistent throughout medieval literature. The first time the full name 'Ragnar Lothbrok' emerged was in the first history of Iceland text, the *Íslendingabók*, which was written by its most famous medieval chronicler Ari Thorgilsson between 1120 and 1133, with Sigurd and Ivar mentioned as his sons.[54] Over the next 200 years, the legend grew beyond all imagination.

Historian Charles Francis Keary believes Ragnar was an exiled or adventurous royal who set out on sea voyages to get fame and fortune and returned to his homeland with a massively improved standing and wealth: 'We should have Ragnar standing in rather the ideal position of the Viking leader, close to the throne yet with no acknowledged claim to succession – a person whom both the rival parties in the kingdom would have had an interest in pressing to leave it.'[55]

When Horik I came to the throne, Ragnar had 'no better prospect of succession than before' and, therefore, sought riches and power through raiding. Keary continued: 'This is a possible explanation of Ragnar's pre-eminence in Norse tradition. He may have been one of the first of the royal stock who devoted himself wholly to Viking life.' Keary added the fact Ragnar had been 'devoted to the adventures of a sea-king, we may suppose this was the life of Ragnar Lodbrok. This might account for his popularity in northern tradition.'[56]

After Paris, there are no further contemporary references to the historical Ragnar Lodbrok besides the potential *Ragnarsdrapa* verse. The scholar Rory McTurk said that while the story had been clearly exaggerated and embellished 'unless really convincing evidence is found' the Ragnar who led the Seine expedition must have died in 845.[57] Another historian, Elisabeth Ashman Rowe, who wrote a comprehensive book *Vikings in the West: The Legend of Ragnarr Loðbrók and His Sons*, charting all the historical sources, also believes Ragnar died from dysentery after raiding Paris.

The Ragnar of later Old Norse tales, however, must have survived for at least another fifteen years after the raid on Paris. For the later saga writers, he was a famed warrior and king, but they provide little detail of his actual conquests, aside from Saxo Grammaticus.

While the fate of Ragnar remains in question, the picture is clearer regarding his infamous five sons. Their exploits over the next forty-five years following Paris were incredibly well documented and their impact would be felt from the Irish coast all the way to the Mediterranean and as far as Africa.

Chapter 3

IRONSIDE

On the appointed day, the ships are put to sea, the knights rush in haste, the banners are raised, the sails are swollen by the winds, and the devouring wolves go and tear the Lord's sheep to pieces, shedding sacrifices of human blood in honour of their god Thur [Thor].
William of Jumièges, eleventh century

Madjus (Vikings) in 'sixty-two ships' appeared in 859 off the north-west coast of Spain wrote the historian Ibn Idhari, from the Maghreb region of North Africa around the late thirteenth to fourteenth century.[1] This notorious expedition, which became famous around large parts of the world, was led by the historical prototype of Bjorn Ironside and potentially other sons of Ragnar.

Idhari and other later authors appear to have based their accounts on lost texts by tenth-century Muslim scholars. The Vikings were referred to as 'Madjus' or 'Majus' by the Muslims, which could mean 'magician, worshipper of many gods and heathen' but possibly related to fire worship and their practise of burning the dead. Their religious customs may have reminded them of the Persian Magians, who were ancient priests associated with astrology and magic.[2]

Bjorn's crew embarked on a chaotic journey into the Mediterranean. Never had a Northman fleet ventured so far and carried out such an audacious campaign of raiding. The fleet was mentioned in the ninth-century *Chronicon Sebastiani Salmanticensis,* composed in Oviedo in the Christian Asturias kingdom and named after its supposed author Sebastian of Salamanca, which told of how 'Lordomani' (Northmen) attacked in Galicia, a region of north-west Spain, for the second time and then 'murdered, burnt, and plundered everywhere, harrying all the coasts'.[3]

While the Vikings exploited the weak coastal defences in Francia and Anglo-Saxon England with ruthless efficiency, in this uncharted territory, they immediately faced fierce resistance. 'Lordomani [Northmen] that came for the second time, were slaughtered off the coast of Galicia by count Pedro,' recorded the *Albeldense Chronicle*, which was also compiled at Oviedo during the late-ninth century reign of Alonso III and attributed to Dulcidio, a cleric who was close to the king. It placed the victory during the time of his predecessor Ordoño, who ruled between 850 and 866.[4]

Despite the defeat, Bjorn's fleet progressed along the coast in the hunt for slaves and riches. At the time, a dynasty from the powerful Umayyad Caliphate had established the Muslim Emirate of Córdoba and ruled most of the modern-day Iberian Peninsula, which makes up modern Spain and Portugal. The region was known as 'al-Andalus' to Muslims, who were called Moors by Europeans.

Idhari described how the Vikings found Galicia well-guarded by fleets from the caliphate.[5] 'Two of their ships, the vanguard of the others, were hunted by the guardships and taken in a harbour in the province of Beja,' retold Idhari. 'Silver, gold, prisoners, and provisions were found in them.' After the capture, there were still sixty ships remaining, and they had no intention of turning back from Beja, a city in southern Portugal.

Instead, the Viking fleet, which may have boasted 2,000 men, sailed further along the Algarve towards the mouth of the river at Seville. An army under the banners of Hadjib (a high-ranking official) Isa-ibn-Hasan, drove them off and blocked access to the river of Guadalquivir, which would have taken Bjorn's Northmen deep into the al-Andalus kingdom.[6] They may have been looking to target Córdoba, more than 130 miles inland along the same river, which was the biggest city of western Europe at this time with its market filled with the silks and spices of the Orient, slaves, gold, Frankish swords and armours.[7]

Northmen had been based around Seville in late 844 for more than two months, looting the nearby towns before they were destroyed by the Emirate of Córdoba, who torched 30 ships from their fleet and hung the heads of slain Vikings on palm trees, and sent another two hundred heads of the 'noblest Madjus warriors' to a tribe in Tangier, Morocco.[8]

The fleet which arrived fourteen years later must have known about the devastating defeat. Given the horror that transpired, it was a marker of their fearlessness as they continued towards Gibraltar after running into the caliphate's forces again. Idhari told of how they sailed to Algeaciras (Algeciras) and burned down the grand mosque.[9]

After reaching Algeaciras, a port city near the strait of Gibraltar, the Vikings made camp and set their sights on Africa. For fellow Vikings, this became a heroic feat of adventure and daring but for the many who suffered untold misery it must have been a campaign of grotesque and sustained piracy.

Norman chronicler William of Jumièges, in his *Gesta Normannorum Ducum* (*The Deeds of the Dukes of the Normans*), composed between 1050 and 1070, promoted the heroic tale of Viking ancestors of Norman dukes when Roger I was seeking to conquer Sicily. Recalling Bjorn's infamous ninth century raids, William said:

> *'At that time, the pagans, pouring forth from the lands of the Norse and Danes, with the son of their king Lothroc [Lothbrok], named Bier of the Iron Rib (Bjorn Ironside), and with Hastings [Hastein],*

the most wicked of all the pagans, who led this expedition, afflicted the inhabitants of the seashores with all manner of calamities, overthrowing cities and burning abbeys. We shall tell you shortly who this Lothroc [Lothbrok] was and from what lineage he descended.[10]

According to the text, Biers (Bjorn), portrayed by Swedish actor Alexander Ludwig in the *Vikings* TV series, was forced from his homeland and launched the expedition as a protege of Hastein, who wanted to make him famous.

'When King Lothroc, [Lothbrok] of whom we have already spoken, came of succeed his father. This king, recalling the laws of his ancestors, forced his son named Bier [Bjorn], of the iron rib, to leave his kingdom, with an immense retinue of young men and with Hastings [Hasteins], his governor, a man filled with wickedness in every way, that, going into foreign countries, Bier might conquer by arms a new residence. This Bier was called iron rib, not that he covered his body with a shield, but because, marching into battle without weapons, he was invulnerable and defied the efforts of all weapons, his body having been violently rubbed by his mother with all kinds of poisons.[11]

This was the first reference to 'Lothbrok', i.e. 'shaggy breeches', but frustratingly despite William of Jumièges saying he would discuss his lineage, there are no further mentions of Lothbrok. However, it does suggest Lothbrok was still alive and a powerful figure in Scandinavia more than a decade after the raids on Paris in 845.

Magic features in various sources for the Ragnar Lothbrok legend, as it did in this tale, with special powers attributed to his unnamed daughters who weave a prophetic raven banner and with Ubbe described as a sorcerer.

Arab traveller Ibn Fadlan met the 'Rus' Vikings on the Volga River in 922 and infamously recounted a disturbing cremation boat ritual of a chieftain in which a young slave girl is voluntarily sacrificed alongside. She was raped and stabbed to death in a ceremony conducted by a menacing 'Angel of Death' woman. Before her death, the slave girl had been lifted above a wooden frame and claimed to see her dead relatives and then her 'master in a green and beautiful paradise'. As Ubbe was also hoisted up high to use his sorcery, it indicates the symbolic act granted special powers and a connection to the afterlife.

Ibn Fadlan, who was on a diplomatic mission from the Abbasid Caliphate in Baghdad, then the world's leading intellectual and cultural city, demonstrated the fascination with the cremation aspect of Viking culture, remarking how the boat was reduced to ashes by a great wind within an hour. 'You Arabs are fools,' one Rus told him. 'You put the men you love most into the earth, and the earth and insects eat them, but we burn them in an instant so at once and without delay they enter paradise.'[12]

The claim that Lothbrok was a king also remains a mystery because the only Danish rulers in the Frankish annals named around this time were Horik I until 854 and Horik II afterwards, but the Franks were focused solely on the key realm of Jutland, which bordered their territory. Based on a later chronicle of around 1137 from the Roskilde Cathedral in Zealand, there were other kings on the Danish islands of Zealand and Funen, Skane in the southernmost part of Sweden and Viken in eastern Norway. The same chronicle was the first in Scandinavia to associate sons of 'Lothpardus' (Lothbrok) with the Great Heathen Army campaign and to describe how Ivar 'lacked bones'.[13] Roskilde is just 7 miles from Lejre, where the biggest Viking Age royal hall was discovered and where Ivar ruled from according to the 'Tale of Ragnar's Sons'.

Zealanders were always aligned with Ragnar in Saxo Grammaticus' *Deeds of the Danes* written in the early-thirteenth century, and this may just be the region of Scandinavia where sons of Ragnar's sons hailed and possibly ruled from. While the only known accounts have Ragnar dying from dysentery soon after raiding Paris, it is fascinating that William of Jumièges named Lothbrok as a king with no obvious source and calls into question the claim that he died in dramatic circumstances after raiding Paris, eleven years before Bjorn's raiding began.

The nickname of 'Ironside' is not found elsewhere in the Old Norse texts, which suggests the real-life Bjorn may well have held this nickname. Equally, it could have been inspired by the eleventh-century English king Edmund Ironside, who was also famed for his prowess in battles.[14] The 'Ironside' moniker was also used by Saxo Grammaticus, but he claimed that Bjorn gained it through his bravery on the battlefield against King Eysteinn: 'Biorn, having inflicted great slaughter on the foe without hurt to himself, gained from the strength of his sides, which were like iron, a perpetual name (Ironsides).'[15]

The journey of Bjorn's fleet can be picked up in the historical record before it reached the Mediterranean. The *Annals of Fontenelle* reported how a 'very large Danish fleet' under Sigtryggg (Sidroc) on the River Seine came as far as Pitres in Normandy where they made camp on the specific date of 18 July 856:

> *'Then, after thirty-three days, that is, on 19 August, the Northman Bern [Bjorn] arrived with a powerful fleet. Thereafter, having united their forces, they caused a great deal of carnage and destruction as far as the forest of Perche. In this place, King Charles and his army met up with them, and inflicted a great defeat upon them.'*[16]

Danes travelled up the Seine and 'ravaged' everything unchecked, according to the *Annals of St Bertin*. They attacked Paris, where they burned the church of SS-Peter and Geneieve and all the other churches except for the cathedral of St-Stephen, the church of SS-Vincent and Germain and St-Denis which paid a 'great ransom to save these churches being burned.'

Bjorn's fleet of Vikings began overwintering and set up camp on the island of Oissel further north along the Seine close to the city of Rouen.[17] The commune of Jumièges is just 17 miles from Rouen along the same river, which may explain why the story emerged here.

William of Jumièges based his text on an earlier version by Dudo of Saint-Quentin called *Historia Normannorum* (*History of the Normans*), composed between 996 and 1015, which failed to mention Bjorn and centred the raid around Hastein. Although, unlike Hastein, a Viking chieftain called Bjorn was documented in the Frankish annals at the time, which implies William of Jumièges was improving on the earlier tale.

The *Annals of St Bertin* recorded a Viking chief called Bjorn meeting with King Charles the Bald in 858: 'Bjorn, chief of one group of the pirates on the Seine, came to Charles at the palace of the Verberie [a commune in northern France] and gave himself into his hands and swore fidelity after his own fashion.'[18] Vikings on Oissel were later 'hemmed in by King Charles [the Bald] with a naval blockade' in 858 but a rebellion led by his brother Louis the Younger forced him to abandon the siege, claims the same source.[19]

While it is not recorded, Bjorn would have most likely received a large ransom from Charles the Bald to leave. A letter from the West Francia bishops in November of that year to Louis the German mentions a tribute being raised to pay Vikings.[20] After a tribute payment, chiefs and dukes such as Bjorn would have departed and sworn not to attack Charles the Bald's realm in West Francia again. In the early spring of 859, the duo of Bjorn and Hastein set their course for the northern coast of modern Spain.

Months later from their base in Algeciras, the fleet led by Bjorn and Hastein 'crossed over to Africa, and plundered the inhabitants of that country,' according to Idhari.[21] Vikings landed in Nekor in modern-day Morocco, which was then part of a region called Mauretania along the North African coast. Nekor was surrounded by a wall of coarse brick and possessed a large mosque, with a roof supported by pillars of thuya (a rare type of wood that was abundant in the region), along with prosperous markets, gardens and orchards of pears and pomegranates.[22]

Al-Bakrī, an eleventh-century historian in the Iberian peninsula who like other Muslim medieval scholars uses the Islamic calendar that begins in 622 when the prophet Muhammad led his followers from Medina to Mecca, places the landing in the year 244, which corresponds with Gregorian calendar dates of 19 April 858 to 7 April the following year. Bakri places the raids in 858, but the contemporary *Annals of St Bertin* says the Viking crew departed a year later. Vikings spent eight days in the city and captured women from the Salihid dynasty, which had founded the Emirate of Nekor in the eighth century, wrote al-Bakrī: 'They took the city, plundered it, and made its inhabitants slaves, except those who saved themselves by flight. Among their prisoners were Amaarrahman and Khanula, daughters of Yakif ibn-Motacim ibn-Salih. Mohammed ibn-Abdurrhaman (the ruler of al-Andalus) ransomed them.'[23]

The same story is told by tenth-century scholar Ibn al-Qutiyya, who relays how Bjorn's men captured the grandfather of Ibn-Salih, the local ruler, but the Emir Abdurrhaman ibn-Hakam ransomed him and 'out of gratitude' the dynasty had remained friends with the Umayyad Caliphate ever since. Al-Qutiyya mistakenly attributes the ransom payment to Emir Mohammed's predecessor Abd ar-Rahman II, son of Al-Hakam.

Many captured residents of Nekor endured a lifetime of slavery based on an eleventh-century text called the *Fragmentary Annals of Ireland*, which is featured in the next chapter.[24]

Evidence of this Mediterranean raid may have emerged from an unlikely source. A study of 44 house mice from the Madeira Archipelago, which includes the islands of Madeira, Porto Santo and Ilhas Desertas, found that they share the same DNA as rodents from Scandinavia and northern Germany. The similarities with the molecular structure between those in Madeira and northern Europe were described as 'striking' and suggested they derived from a single source.

One or two Vikings ships, possibly among Bjorn's fleet when they were heading to or leaving Nekor, may have been blown off course and accidentally introduced the European mice to the islands, which are located around 600km off the coast of northern Africa. The study, however, cautions that further tests are needed of house mice in Portugal to rule out the country as a source area.[25]

Al-Nuwayri, a fourteenth-century Egyptian historian also drawing from earlier sources, told of how the Vikings returned to Spain and 'seized the fort of Orihuela' on the south-east coast, around 40 miles from Alicante. Troops of Todmir, which was the Muslim name for the region of Murcia, fled in their wake, said al-Nuwayri.[26] Vikings were likely based around the Rio Segura, as the fort of Orihuela could be found 7 miles along the same river. They built a fortified base with a defensive rampart and palisade in the modern-day Ebro Delta Natural Park on the coast of Catalonia, directly across from the Balearic Islands, which were soon targeted by Bjorn's forces, who 'attacked the isles of Majorca and Minorca' records *Chronicon Sebastiani Salmanticensis*.[27]

Mediterranean raiders led by Bjorn were tracked in the *Annals of St Bertin*, starting in 859, a year after he met Charles the Bald: 'Danish pirates made a long sea voyage, sailed up the straits through Spain and Africa and then up the Rhone. They ravaged some civitates and monasteries and made their base on an island called Carmague.'[28] The contemporary Frankish account tallies with Muslim chroniclers such as al-Nuwayri, who said they advanced to France's borders and took 'much booty and many prisoners'. Bjorn's fleet overwintered during 859/60 on the marshy delta of the River Rhone in the south of France known as the Camargue, most likely around the capital city Saintes-Maries-de-la-Mer, raiding a monastery near Roussillon in south-eastern France on route. In the spring, Northmen sailed up the River Rhone for more than 100 miles targeting the cities of Arles, Nîmes and Valence within Middle Francia, so the promise to Charles the Bald who ruled Western Francia was not impacted, highlighting the strategic nature of the raiding. Danes on the Rhone got as far as Valence 'ravaging and destroying everything' and then returned to the island of Camargue, reported the *Annals of St Bertin*.[29]

At this point, perhaps the most famous aspect of the Mediterranean raid unfolded as the Vikings cast their eyes on Rome.[30] According to William of Jumièges:

> *'Hastings [Hastein], wishing to raise his lord [Bjorn] to a higher fortune, began with a troop of accomplices to aim more seriously at the imperial diadem. At last, after holding counsel, these men launched their sails into the sea, resolved to go and attack the city of Rome unexpectedly and to take it for themselves.'*

Travelling along the French Riviera, the Vikings were blown off course and ended up in the city of Luni (called Luna by the Romans). When the Viking fleet arrived at Luni, with its grand yet decaying former structures and white marble buildings, Hastein believed this was the imperial city, but Luni is, in fact, around 300km (187 miles) further north.

Seeing their arrival, the residents of Luni prepared for battle by barricading their gates and fortifying their ramparts. Deciding the city could not be captured by arms, the wily Hastein sent messengers to the city's bishops to say that he was 'overwhelmed with a mortal illness' and begged them to 'be good enough to make him a Christian' and allow him to be baptised. Despite their fearsome reputation, the Vikings were allowed to enter the city and Hastein was carried to the church, where he was baptised with the holy oils and then brought back to his ship. Pretending to be dead, Hastein was carried back to the church in a coffin, where the bishop began carrying out a ceremony. Suddenly, Hastein leapt out of the coffin and killed the bishop and the count of Luni with his sword. His followers began killing the congregation and ransacked the city as chaos ensued. This scene was mirrored in the *Viking* series, but it was Ragnar who faked his death to enter Paris after the failed siege.

Naturally, this tale is questioned as similar deceptions to enter hostile territory were attributed to other Norman dukes, such as Robert Guiscard and Roger I of Sicily. Cunning was clearly valued as much as bravery and skill of arms among noble warriors, with writers such as William of Jumièges seeking heroic Viking figures to inspire Norman equivalents.[31]

Given the first contemporary reference to Hastein as a Viking leader around the mouth of the River Loire was dated to 867, by the chronicler Regino of Prüm based at an abbey of the same name in modern Germany, who calls him 'Hasting', it seems likely he had been involved.[32] Remarkably, thirty years later, Hastein led a massive army across England when presumably in his mid-fifties.

According to contemporary Frankish sources, the only time Luni was raided was in 849 and by Moors and Saracens, which suggests Dudo and William of Jumièges mistakenly conflated the raids.[33] Viking fleets, which often scouted cities extensively and knew of political situations, Roman roads, river routes and religious festivals, are also unlikely to have mistaken Luni for Rome.

In 861, Bjorn and Hastien's raiders captured Pisa and other cities, which they plundered and 'laid to waste', recorded the *Annals of St Bertin*. Given Pisa is just 35 miles away from Luni along the same coastline it is entirely feasible that they targeted both. Excavations of Luni by British archaeologist Bryan Ward Perkins failed to discover evidence of the destruction by Bjorn and Hastien's men, but he believed they reached the city.[34] Ceccardus of Luni, a ninth-century bishop, was thought to have been martyred by the Vikings and is celebrated with a feast day on 16 June.[35]

Both the main sagas include the sons of Ragnar, without naming the specific sons, raiding Luni when they were trying to conquer Rome. 'Ragnar's Saga' claims they encountered a poor beggar at Luni, who they asked how far it was to Rome. The traveller had replied that his old iron shoes and other broken shoes on his back were new when he set off and he had been 'on the journey ever since', so Ragnar's sons abandoned plans to reach Rome.[36]

While Ivar was active in Ireland and Sigurd is described as much younger than his brothers, possibly Ubbe and particularly Halfdan had accompanied Bjorn as rookie Vikings. It would explain their rise as the later leaders of the Great Heathen Army given its infamy, which coupled with the increased wealth would have made

A stunning panoramic shot of the Gibraltar straits, where Bjorn's fleet ran into the forces of the Umayyad Caliphate. (Mihael Grmek/CC BY-SA 3.0)

them famous throughout Scandinavia and able to attract fellow brotherhoods to the invasion of Anglo-Saxon England. They were probably ruling in a Scandinavian kingdom, most likely Zealand, based on William of Jumièges describing Lothbrok as a 'king'.

The *Chronicon Sebastiani Salmanticensis* and the tenth-century writer Ibn al-Qutiyya told of how the crew also stopped in the famous Mediterranean port city of Alexandria in Egypt. This was the end of a lucrative two- to three-year expedition, but the Vikings still had to make their way back through the dangerous narrow Strait of Gibraltar, which is just 9 miles wide, and the caliphate was waiting for them.[37] Al-Nuwayri told of how:

> *'On their way back they met the fleet of the Emir Mohammed, began a battle with it and lost four of their ships, two of which were burnt. What was in the two others fell into the hands of Moslem. Then began Madjus to fight furiously, and a great multitude of Moslem died as martyrs.'*

Idhari claimed the Vikings had 'already lost more than forty of their ships' in a storm before they faced the emir off the coast of Sidona in Lebanon and then 'lost two others, laden with great riches'.

Naval battles were a frequent occurrence in the Viking Age, and it was the custom to rope together ships to form a floating platform, with the best-manned ship presumably led by the leaders in the middle. The main tactic was simply to row against and board the enemy ship and sometimes cut it loose if it also formed a platform. Masts were lowered and the crew relied solely on oars. As they approached, they held their shields overhead so closely it covered their entire body. Stones were launched onto enemies from high-sided vessels.[38] The fierce battle between the fleets of Bjorn and the caliphate suggested such a scenario.

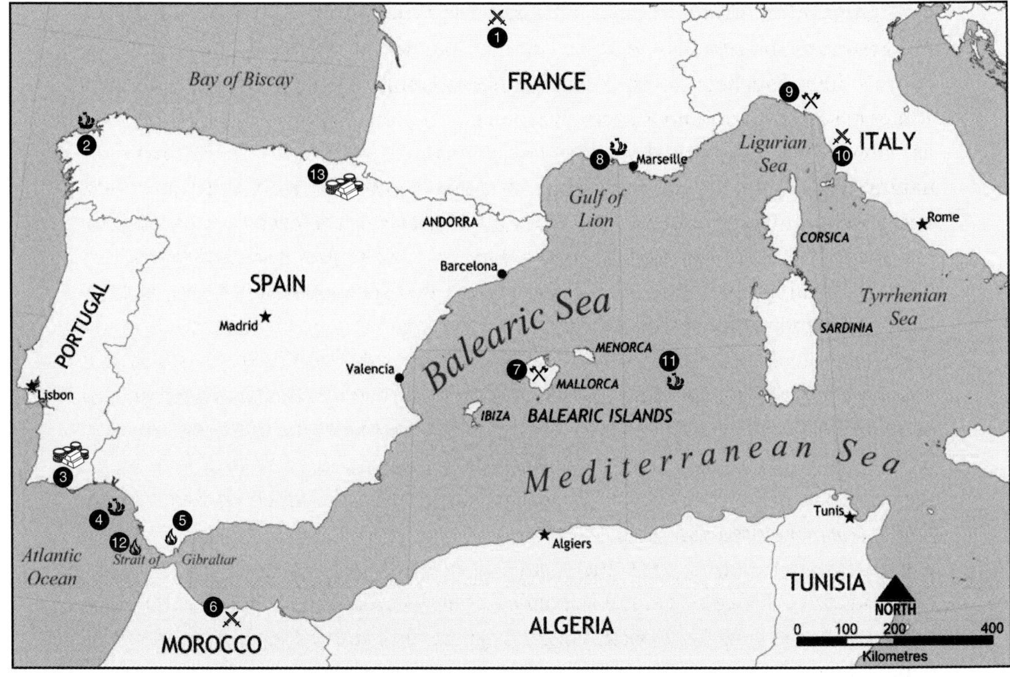

The infamous journey of the fleet of Bjorn and Hastein around the Mediterranean.

KEY TO MAP

1. Attacks on Paris churches in summer 857 before overwintering on Oissel in 857/58, where Viking groups remained for several years
2. Some of Bjorn's crew slaughtered in spring 859 by count Pedro's force in Galicia, northwest Spain
3. Umayyad Caliphate fleet capture silver, gold and prisoners in two ships of Bjorn's fleet near Beja, Portugal
4. Bjorn and Hastein blocked from entering Guadalquivir river to Córdoba
5. Viking raiders led by Bjorn burned down grand mosque in Algeciras, Spain
6. Northmen fleet raids Nekor in Morocco, capturing hostages including local ruler
7. Mallorca and Minorca raided from base on Catalonian coast
8. Bjorn and Hastein sail 100 miles up River Rhone, after overwintering at Camargue in 859/60, attacking Arles, Nîmes and Valence
9. Hastein fakes death and Vikings plunder Luni in Italy
10. Northmen attack and capture the city of Pisa in Italy, reports the raiders head as far as Greece
11. Crew shipwrecked at unclear point, possibly in Mediterranean Sea, less than 20 of 60 ships left around 860/61
12. Brutal naval battle with Umayyad Caliphate in Straits of Gibraltar
13. Bjorn's army sacks Pamplona and ransoms King Garcia I for 70,000 gold dinars

Claims of a shipwreck are repeated by William of Jumièges, while the *Fragmentary Annals* also repeat a similar number of destroyed ships. Two of Bjorn's fleet had been torched by flaming catapults launched by the emirate's forces based on an infamous secret weapon used by the Byzantine Empire's known as 'Greek Fire'. This was thought to consist primarily of crude oil, obtained from natural wells in the Middle East, which was mixed with pine resin and animal fats, and possibly other additives such as quicklime, calcium phosphide and saltpetre that made it stickier and burn hotter and longer.[39] Byzantines had used Greek Fire with devastating effect through a siphon pump that sprayed enemy fleets, and the lethal substance was copied by Arab naval fleets but launched by catapult because they never mastered the siphoning method. Those who survived the storm and attack by the caliphate, including Bjorn and Hastein, had one final and what proved an extremely profitable card to play. As they returned from the mammoth journey back towards the north coast of Francia, they targeted the city of Pamplona in the small Christian kingdom of Navarre in northern Spain, which borders France, where they captured the local king Garcia I and held him to ransom. The king was released after an extraordinary amount of 70,00 gold dinars, approximately 679 pounds or 308kg of gold, was handed over according to al-Nuwayri. Such an unheard-of sum may have taken weeks to gather and so the king's two sons were kept hostage.[40]

Those who survived in around just eighteen of the sixty-two ships that departed from western Francia were left incredibly rich. No doubt, Bjorn and Hastein were the richest of all. The sum of the misery, destruction and death that they inflicted on the towns, cities and populations of the Mediterranean was not documented. Only the unfortunate residents of Nekor, enslaved and now bound for Ireland, are mentioned. Scores of buildings, lighthouses, guard buildings and mosques must have been destroyed in their trail of carnage.[41]

Nearly a century passed before Vikings attacked the region again, showing it warned off other pirate fleets. While the Vikings were able to reach destinations much further away than Spain, such as Constantinople and Baghdad, they did so by creating safe outposts and established trade routes.[42] Before the Mediterranean, they faced the hazardous Cantabrian Sea, also called the Bay of Biscay, between Brittany and northern Spain, which is known for its strong winds, long swells and unpredictable conditions. Beyond these dangers, they would find a scarce but warlike population and a powerful navy force of the caliphate, which ensured they never had the free license to plunder the coasts for sustained periods as they did in western Europe.

Bjorn's epic voyage would surely have pleased his chief god. Violent, fickle and treacherous, Odin was the god of war, god of the gallows and god of the dead, who welcomed famous warriors to his hall of the slain. Strange and demonic, he possessed unrivalled wisdom, which had been gained through sacrifice and trickery rather than by nature. For a drink from the well of Mimir (the fount of wisdom), he offered up an eye, and for its magic and runes, he hung for nine days on the Yggdrasil, the sacred world tree in Norse mythology, while wounded with a spear.

Unlike his son Thor, however, Odin was not a god for the common man and sought his own gain and knowledge. Those who dealt in policy and power, cast magic and created runes, who knew the ecstasy of creation and chaos of war were favoured.[43] 'Odin is the highest and eldest of the Aesir, he rules all things and mighty as are the other gods, they all serve him as children (who) obey their father,' wrote Snorri Sturluson in his *Prose Edda*.

Known as 'Woden' to the Anglo-Saxons, Odin had many names including 'lord of hosts', 'spear-lord', 'the knower of many things', 'the shaker', 'the burner', 'he that putteth armies to flight', 'the protector' and 'the destroyer'.[44] He owns a proud eight-legged stallion called Sleipner, two snarling wolves called Gere and Freke, and two ravens known as Hugin and Munin. A powerful spear called Gunger, which never misses its mark, was his most trusted weapon. Dwarves had forged him a magical golden ring called Draupner (the dropper).[45]

Bjorn may have soon been welcomed to Odin's famed hall of Valhalla, the hall of the slain, because there are no further contemporary historical references to him. According to William of Jumièges:

> *'Bier [Bjorn] under whose flags these devastations were committed and who was the king of these armies, having wanted to return to his country, suffered a shipwreck, had great difficulty in being received in a port by the English, and was lost by the storm. a large number of his ships. He went to Frisia and died there.'*[46]

The English port may have been Hamwic (modern Southampton), which was a thriving trade market, or Portland in Dorset, where the first-ever band of Viking raiders in the British Isles, from Hordaland in Norway, killed a local reeve in 789.

Although Bjorn may have died soon after the Mediterranean raid, mirroring Ragnar's fate after Paris, he had been immortalised as the ultimate adventurous, warlike and daring Northman; a cult figure in an age where violence, plunder and conquest ruled. As will be featured in Chapter 8, later sagas tell a different story about Bjorn's ending. The story of his brother Ivar the Boneless was only just beginning.

Chapter 4

THE DARK FOREIGNERS

They will tunnel beneath God's oratories; churches will be burned;
men with black, keen spears will blight the fruits of noble rule.
'A Poem of Prophecies', author unknown,
eleventh–twelfth century[1]

Brú na Bóinne (palace of the Boyne) is one of the world's most mythical and famous archaeological places, boasting the largest collection of megalithic art, carvings and sculptures on stone monuments, in western Europe. Featuring the spectacular passage tombs of Newgrange, Knowth and Dowth, it remains synonymous with Ireland's history.

During my visit, the guide, who joked such trips are dependent on Ireland's two favourite words 'weather-permitting', turned off the lights inside the gigantic tomb to show perhaps the most incredible aspect of the construction was how the tiny, cramped passage through the massive boulders had been deliberately aligned with the winter solstice when it was built from around 3,500 BC.[2]

Mimicking the incredible 'roof-box' on top of the entrance, this showed how light could shine through on the winter solstice on 21 December to illuminate the burial chamber inside, where three huge, curved basin stones held remains.[3,4]

Studies have revealed the Neolithic people were astronomers and educators, who used mysterious spirals, zigzags and serpents on the stones to pass on their knowledge to future generations. The 'calendar stone' at Knowth, where 200 individuals have been found cremated or buried, appears to display the cycles of the moon and tidal movements. Such ingenuity challenges all our preconceptions about these ancient civilisations.

Many mysteries still surround Brú na Bóinne and the fascinating artwork, but it is known that this was a special place of ritual and burial ceremonies until around 2,500–2,000 BC, when activity halted for around 2,000 years. When the Vikings set their sights on Ireland, this remarkable site next to the River Boyne, named after the goddess Bóinn, which possibly means 'shining cow' or 'woman of white cows', remained a prestigious venue for the king of northern Brega.[5] Only a few people, such as a priest or shaman, could enter the actual passages with the cremation ceremonies conducted directly outside the spectacular tombs.

The sacred site of Knowth was one of the tombs known to have been raided by the historical prototype for Ivar the Boneless in 863.

In 863, Brú na Bóinne attracted some unwelcome visitors who had no respect for these customs. The historical prototypes for Ivar the Boneless (Ímair in Irish texts), Olaf the White (Amlaíb) and Auisle, the joint Viking rulers of Dublin, together with Lorcán mac Cathail, the king of Mede (Meath), scoured the tombs for riches.[6] The *Annals of Ulster*, believed to be a near contemporary account, reports:

> *'The caves of Achad Aldai [linked to Newgrange], and of Cnodba [Knowth], and of Boadán's Mound above Dubad [Dowth], and of Óengoba's wife, were searched by the foreigners—something which had never been done before.*
>
> *'This was the occasion when three kings of the foreigners, i.e. Amlaíb [Olaf] and Ímar [Ivar] and Auisle, plundered the land of Flann son of Conaing; and Lorcán son of Cathal, king of Mide, was with them in this.'*

Knowth is called Cnogba in Old Irish meaning 'Hill of Bua', who was the earth and sovereignty goddess, while Dowth derives from *dubad* meaning 'darkness' in Irish. A folklore tale grew that a mythical king called Bresil Bodibad summoned the labour of all men in Ireland to build a mound to heaven, but his sister cast a spell so that the day lasted forever. However, the wicked plan backfired as the sun went down, and the workers escaped.[7]

The possible description of Newgrange as Achadh Aldai, 'the field of Aldai' relates to an ancestor of the Tuatha Dé Danann (the folk of the goddess Danu), a race of supernatural gods in Irish mythology often depicted as kings, queens, craftspeople, druids, healers, warriors and bards. For 3,000 years, they ruled Ireland before they were banished to the otherworld after being defeated by the Milesians, who controlled the surface-level world, while the Tuatha Dé Danann remained as fairy people who interacted with their human neighbours at festivals such as Beltane on 1 May and Samhain on 1 November.[8]

The name for Newgrange is Sí an Bhrú, 'the fairy mound of the Bru', and it is debated whether the Vikings had searched the passage tomb.[9] By this point, Ireland had weathered the Viking storm for nearly seventy years, but the act of entering these sacred monuments must have sparked fury among the native Irish. This was demonstrated in the following year when Áed Finnilaith, the High King of Ireland and from the Uí Néill dynasty, captured one tomb raider Lorcán mac Cathail and had him blinded.

Few sites in Ireland, whether religious or sacred, were off bounds for the Northmen on the hunt for plunder. Violence was endemic in Irish society as rival kingdoms jockeyed for power. At the time, Ireland contained more than 150 kingdoms subject to six large regional overlords from Leinster, Munster, Ulster, Connaught, the Southern Uí Néill and the Northern Uí Néill. The latter two were the most powerful and at the top of the ladder was the High King (*ri ruirech*), who had the ultimate authority and held their seat at the Hill of Tara.[10] These kingdoms were often less than 100 square miles and contained a few thousand people.[11]

Written sources describe 26 attacks by Vikings from the first raid in 795 and 820, but a staggering 87 were carried out by the Irish during the same timescale.[12] Vikings became part of the complex internal rivalries because the Irish kings often used them to weaken other kingdoms or profited from the emerging slave trade.[13] However, there were limits, and the phrase 'at the door of the church' was often found in Irish literature, indicating that this was a step too far even for the warring Irish kings who respected the sacred religious cores and avoided damaging shrines. Vikings never abided by the same restrictions in the ninth century, and people who crowded into the vast monastic settlements for protection were easily gathered and taken away as slaves.[14]

The late scholar David Dumville remarked that being a Viking was a 'lifestyle' not an ethnic term that applied to Scandinavia, driven by a desire as evidenced at Brú na Bóinne to get rich quickly by 'robbing tombs, trading slaves or committing massacres.'[15]

During the ninth century, the real life Ivar the Boneless emerged as perhaps the most notorious in an extensive line of notorious pirate kings. Few Northmen

The main Irish kingdoms at the start of the tenth century, with the key towns indicated. (Erakis/WikiCommons)

garnered such a fearsome reputation in the annals of history. This enigmatic figure also had perhaps the biggest impact of all Vikings terrorising Britain and Ireland because his dynasty dominated for years afterwards, with their power centred around York and Dublin, which grew into prosperous trading settlements.

Adam of Bremen, a director of the cathedral school of Bremen, wrote the *Gesta Hammaburgensis ecclesiae pontificum* (*Deeds of the Bishops of the Church of Hamburg*) in the 1070s, which contained a reference to Ivar as son of a Lothbrok with the description '*Inguar filius Lodparchi*':

38

'There were also other kings over the Danes and Northmen, who at this time harassed Gaul with piratical incursions. Of these tyrants the most important were Horic, Orwig, Gotafrid, Rudolf, and Ingvar [Ivar]. The most cruel of them all was Ingvar, the son of Lodbrok, who everywhere tortured Christians to death. This is written in the Gesta of the Franks.'[16]

Bremen's text, which mentioned 'Lothbrok' for only the second time, was clearly influenced by the *Annals of Fulda*, which features three of the above kings and a later account by Abbo of Fleury on Ivar, who is never mentioned in the Frankish annals.

'Ragnar's Saga' tells of how Ivar, who was 'born boneless', was the eldest son who led his siblings on conquests. Portrayed as a complicated character, often wrestling with the dangers of potential conflicts and expressing reservations, Ivar ultimately leads the expeditions and delivers the decisive actions. When Ivar discusses a planned attack on the kingdom of Eysteinn, he fears a 'great cow' called Sibilja 'made so powerful that as soon as men hear the bellowing, his enemies cannot withstand it.' Before battle, Ivar orders his forces to construct a huge bow with arrows to attack the fearsome animal, which quickly begins bellowing on the battlefield and terrifies his warriors. Suddenly, Ivar drew his bow which resembled a 'tiny twig' and fired the arrows:

'His arrows flew as if he had shot them from the strongest crossbow, and so straight that every arrow pierced Sibilja's eyes. She fell down and then tumbled head over heels and her bellows became much worse than before.'[17]

Sibilja survived and charged at Ivar's men, so he ordered them to lift him up high and they threw him on the back of the cow. 'He became as heavy as if a boulder had fallen on her,' told the saga. 'Every bone in her body was broken and she died from this.'[18]

Later, Ivar urges caution in attacking King Aella to avenge the death of his father and seeks to be given compensation instead of warfare, which his brother Hvitserk (Halfdan) refuses to accept. After swearing an oath, King Aella agrees that Ivar can have 'as much of England as could be spanned by the largest ox-hide'. Cunningly, Ivar stretches a hide so much that it covers so much that it covers the size of a large settlement, where a great city was built called 'London Town'. When King Aella's messengers arrive, Ivar sends them away with money, and they promise not to join in any attack, even if their ruler calls for them, which dramatically weakens the army the Northumbrian ruler can muster against Ragnar's sons.[19]

While associated as a son of Ragnar, the parentage and identity of Ivar is disputed. A king called Ímair in Old Irish was a Viking king of Dublin in the decade before the Great Heathen Army invaded what became England, according to later sagas supposedly to avenge the death of Ragnar Lothbrok. This Ivar is then not mentioned in Irish texts between 864 and 870 when the invasion took place, which the tenth-century chronicler Ethelward said was led by the 'tyrant Ivar'. The confusion stems from how the first historical reference in the *Fragmentary Annals*, possibly compiled in the kingdom of Osraige during the eleventh century, describes Ivar as a brother of Olaf the White, or Amlaib Conung (king) in Old Irish, and the son of Gofraid, the king of Norway. This source stated Olaf arrived to collect tribute on behalf of his father and then 'his younger brother Imar came after him to levy the same tribute', which was dated to around 853.[20]

This family connection is repeated when what appears to be an imagined saga story expanding on basic factual detail in 867 tells of how Ivar and Olaf grew jealous of their other brother Oisle (also known as Auisle), and Olaf ambushed his camp and delivered the fatal blow.[21]

Considered a more reliable contemporary source, the *Annals of Ulster* are believed to be a continuation of a hypothesised *Chronicle of Ireland*, which may have begun in Iona in the late-sixth century. While the *Annals of Ulster* refers to Olaf's arrival in 863, it calls him a 'son of the king of Lochlann' and doesn't mention Ivar until four years later.[22] The same annals recorded the death of Auisle in 867, who was 'one of three kings of the Northmen' and was killed by his 'kinsmen in guile and parricide'. The author of the *Fragmentary Annals* may have assumed a biological relationship between Ivar, Olaf and Auisle and composed a romantic story of jealousy and envy to explain the killing of Auisle.[23]

The fact that the *Fragmentary Annals* associate Olaf and Gofraid with Norway but describe the leaders of the Great Heathen Army, which Ivar spearheaded, as 'Danes' supports this conclusion. Norway and Denmark did not exist at the time, but notably the annals place the two groups in different regions.

This matter is confused because Rognvald (Ragnall) Amlaib (Olaf), Gofraid (Gudrod) and Sitruic (Sigtrygg) are recurring names among the grandsons and great-grandsons of Ivar, which suggest they were all members of the same family.[24] The repetition of names does pose the question ultimately whether Ivar was in fact a son of Ragnar, or the relationship was simply dreamed up by later Scandinavian writers to explain the Great Heathen Army's conquest of what became England. However, Ivar and Olaf are never associated as brothers in any contemporary or later texts, besides a muddled account from twelfth-century Anglo-Norman chronicler Gerald of Wales, and it is thought they were brothers in a literal sense, i.e. 'brothers in arms'.[25]

The first raid in Ireland had been recorded in 795 when Rathlin Island (known as 'Rechru' in Old Irish texts), located off the north-west corner of Ireland and the first island seafarers would visit travelling along the west coast of Scotland, was targeted. Viking raids on Ireland occurred with shocking regularity afterwards.

Iona, the birthplace of Christianity in northern Britain, was sacked in 802 and then sixty-eight members of its community were killed four years later. The rich monastic site of Armagh soon became a target of the Vikings, and it suffered three raids in a month in 832. Large churches such as Armagh housed a secular clergy, monks, nuns and a married lay population, who took care of the sick, disabled and unwanted children. In the early-ninth century, they were fast becoming Ireland's first towns and villages.[26]

Monasteries were easy pickings for the Northmen because they were poorly defended and filled with wealth. Vikings were looking for the lucrative relics of dead saints, religious books magnificently decorated with ornate covers and communion vessels, including chalices, bowls and ornate silver-lidded cups. Precious metalwork stolen, such as crosses, pyxes and silver chalices, along with the thousands of coins in France and Britain amassed from plundering, were often quickly melted down and used for jewellery. Gold and silver were used for arm-rings, neck-rings, brooches and particularly ingots, which became a popular form of currency and have been found across ninth-century Viking Age sites in Britain and Ireland.[27]

Outside the church settlements, Ireland was almost entirely rural. Cattle were the prized currency, with the ownership of the animals and ability to loan them often defining status. Settlements were in kin groups, with around 45,000 ring forts, known as raths, dotted around Ireland, while others with more wealth created artificial islands, known as crannogs, or occupied the large hill forts that predate Christianity.[28] Slavery, which will be discussed in Chapter Ten, appears to have fuelled the early Viking raids with fourteen recorded incidents in the 830s and 840s when captives were reported as being taken.[29]

The 'Rus' Vikings, from the Finnish word for Swedes meaning 'Ruotsi' and related to a 'crew of oarsmen' or 'Roslagen' in Swedish, which has the same meaning, began opening eastern trade routes with a base at Staraya Ladoga in the mid-eighth century on the mouth of the Volkhov River in Russia.

The Rus headed along the Dnieper River to the Black Sea and reached Constantinople, then capital of the eastern Roman Empire and home to nearly half a million people, which they called Mikligardr (the great city).[30]

Heading along the Volga River brought the Rus into the land of the Bulgars, a nomadic Turkish tribe, where Arab merchants would buy their slaves, fur, beeswax and honey, Baltic amber and Frankish swords. This route eventually led to the Caspian Sea and Baghdad, the home of the Abbasid Caliphate, which had an insatiable demand for men and women slaves for manual labour and lust.[31]

A vast international network of trade emerged, with the Viking emporiums of Hedeby on the Jutland peninsula in modern Denmark, Kaupang in south-west Norway and Birka in Sweden connected to the burgeoning markets with the Middle East and reaping the rewards from the flow of Arabic silver.

Artist's impression of Dublin c.1000 showing the former black pool where the River Poddle met the River Liffey. (© National Museum of Ireland)

In 840–41, the Vikings overwintered for the first time in Ireland at Lough Neagh and this was followed by the creation of longphorts, which translates as 'ship camps', at Linn Dúachaill (Annagassan, County Louth) in 841 and another at Dublin in the same year.

There may have different settlements in Dublin with one located besides a major ford across the River Liffey called Áth Cliath, meaning 'ford of the hurdles', and the second mentioned in the *Annals of Ulster* on the site of a monastery on the south bank of a tidal inlet called Dubh Linn, meaning 'black pool'. It was formed where the River Poddle, which now runs through a culvert, joined the River Liffey. Remarkably the Dubh Linn lawn at the back of Dublin Castle is likely the exact spot where the first major Viking encampment sprung up.[32]

Viking groups were clearly looking to gain a foothold in the regions where they were profiting from raids and slavery. Dublin's founding may be connected to the emerging Kaupang trading emporium in Vestfold on the shore of the Oslofjord, which appeared from around 800 and flourished for more than 100 years. Research has found that 75 per cent of the Viking age structures in Dublin were labelled as 'Type 1' buildings and share a striking resemblance to a building called 'A200' at Kaupang, which features low post-and-wattle walls,

The Dubh Linn garden at the back of Dublin Castle, where the first major Viking camp sprung up.

a roof supported by two pairs of 103 posts or groups of posts and a centrally located stone-kerbed hearth.[33]

The fascinating discovery of 162 Viking Age Celtic-inspired penannular brooches in Norway, around south-west Norway and Vestfold in wealthy male graves, along with a high number of weapons, horse gear (consisting mainly of bridles and strap ends) and tools hinting at their warrior status, have shown the close cultural ties between the region and Ireland. The brooches, which were produced as copies or versions of Irish originals, made of iron or bronze and glazed with silver or pewter, could be linked to their loyalties and rank in a new power structure with strong ties to Ireland. Historic use of penannular brooches by men is mentioned in the Irish law tracts, *Senchus Mór* and *Críth Gablach*, in which they were tied to different groups in a hierarchical system, from local chiefs to leaders who aspired to control larger regions.[34]

Vikings who arrived in Dublin from Scandinavia were multi-skilled and doubled up as tradesmen. Finds along the modern High Street reveal the presence of leather workers and comb makers, while Christchurch Place may have housed the cobblers. Based on the better-quality homes and number of coin discoveries, Fishamble Street was probably where the merchants lived along with amber workers and possibly woodcarvers.[35] Around 3,000 pieces of amber, which were used in jewellery and valued for its magical properties, have been found in Dublin.[36]

A selection of brooches found in Ireland during the Viking Age. Styles such as penannular, kite and thistle brooches were popular. (© National Museum of Ireland)

Other craftsmen, such as blacksmiths and boatbuilders, who were in high demand may have lived just outside the city. Many of the men discovered at the two largest Viking burial sites in Dublin at Kilmainham and Islandbridge were buried with their tools, such as forge-tongs, pincers, hammers, shears and sickles. Others were merchants as evidenced by their fashioned weights with lead cores and folding bronze scales that weighed precious stones and metal, particularly silver.[37]

Despite Dublin's prosperity, and later sites at Waterford, Cork, Wicklow and Limerick, the Vikings were restricted to the coastal fringes of Ireland. This is starkly evidenced by how of eighty-two graves discovered in Ireland, the largest number west of Norway, a total of 80 per cent were found within 5km of the centre of Dublin and of these 75 per cent were found at Kilmainham and Islandbridge.[38]

The militarised nature of the early Viking settlers in Dublin is displayed by the high number of weapons including bows, arrow heads, axe heads, shield bosses and swords (42 in Dublin) found in the graves, where the ratio of men to women was ten to one.[39]

Irish kingdoms proved worthy adversaries to the Vikings because their guerilla warfare tactics and hit and run raids proved highly effective in disrupting the Vikings. The multitude of small kingdoms also meant it was impossible for the Northmen to deliver a killer blow. One leading Viking chieftain,

The 'Ballinderry Sword' was a Viking Age iron weapon discovered in the bog of the site of a crannog in Ballinderry, County Westmeath. (© National Museum of Ireland)

Turgeis, was drowned in 845 in Lake Owel by Máel Sechnaill, the High King of Southern Uí Néill, who proved a determined opponent.

In the mid-ninth century, a new conflict emerged between two Viking groups known as the *Finngaill* ('fair foreigners') and *Dubgaill* ('dark foreigners') in Irish texts. It has generally been accepted that 'dark' relates to a new group of Vikings, and 'fair' relates to an existing group, which makes sense as the 'dark foreigners' arrived in 851 and destroyed the decade old Áth Cliath (Dublin) settlement. The *Annals of Ulster* reported: 'The dark heathens came to Áth Cliath, made a great slaughter of the fair-haired foreigners, and plundered the naval encampment, both people and property. The dark heathens made a raid at Linn Dúachaill (County Louth), and a great number of them were slaughtered.'[40]

The following year, there was a three-day battle between the rival Viking groups at Carlingford Lough – from the Old Norse *Kerlingfjǫrðr,* meaning 'narrow sea-inlet of the hag' – in which the dark foreigners emerged victorious again.

Amid this conflict Olaf the White arrived in Ireland the following year, and 'the foreigners of Ireland submitted to him, and he took tribute from the Irish.'[41] Scholars have been divided on whether Olaf, the son of the king of Lochlann, headed the dark or fair foreigners because he is never associated with either group specifically.

The events suggest the fair foreigners because they had suffered two heavy defeats in the previous years, and Tomrair, the earl of Lochlann, was slain in 848 along with 200 men in a battle against the forces of Ólchobar mac Cináeda, king of Munster, and Lorcán mac Cellaig, king of Leinster. This implies Olaf was sent to reassert the power of Lochlann, commonly associated with western or south-western Norway, after the setbacks and to press his authority on the rival Viking groups and Irish kings.

When the *Annals of Ulster* records the Viking battle in York in 867 led by Ivar Ragnarsson and his brothers, they are called the 'dark foreigners'. The same battle is recorded in the *Fragmentary Annals* that refers to the Great Heathen Army as the 'Danes', adding: 'It was from that that every misfortune and every harassment of the island of Britain arose.'[42]

In 870, the 'treacherous' death of an Irish king was recorded in the *Annals of Ulster* by 'Ulf the dark foreigner' who appears to be Ubbe, while Viking raiders battling the Picts led by Halfdan five years later are referred to as 'dark foreigners' in the same source.[43] Two years later in 877, Halfdan is also described in this annal as a 'king of the dark gentiles (heathens)' in a clash at Strangford Lough against the fair foreigners. A year earlier, Rhodri Mawr, king of Gwynedd, had escaped under siege from the 'dark heathens' when Ubbe was known to be based in Wales, according to the *Annals of Ulster*. In 917, it refers to Ragnall ua Ímair, the grandson of Ivar, as a 'king of the dark foreigners' and when he raided Waterford in the following year. Scholar Clare Downham believed that the 'king of the dark foreigners' applies to the 'chief member of the family of Ívarr', successive leaders of the 'new' group of Vikings who had arrived in Ireland in the mid-ninth century and waged war on the fair foreigners.[44]

Traces of the 'dark foreigners' may be found in Irish place names such as a bridge near Dublin, which was called Droichet-Dubhghaill in Irish, meaning the 'bridge of the dark foreigners', in the *Annals of the Four Masters* in the year 1112. Baile Dubhghaill (Baldoyle) in County Dublin may also refer to 'dark foreigners' along with those in Baldoyle in County Meath, Ballindoyle in County Wicklow, Ballydoyle in County Cork, Ballydoyle in County Tipperary and Ballydoyle in County Wexford.[45]

The real-life Ragnar may have been a Viking chief terrorising Ireland before plundering Paris in 845, which could explain the 'dark foreigners' later arrival. Ragnar's potential raiding in Ireland was highlighted by thirteenth-century Danish historian Saxo Grammaticus in the *Deeds of the Danes*. Saxo described how Ragnar on his first expedition against Hella (Aella of Northumberland), then went to Ireland and killed its king 'Melbrictus'. It reads: 'Here Ragnar completed a year of conquest, and then, summoning his sons to help him, he went to Ireland, slew its king Melbrictus, besieged Dublin, which was filled with wealth of the barbarians, attacked it, and received its surrender.'[46] This tale of Ragnar could relate to an 831 entry in the *Annals of Ulster*, which reads: 'Conaille (County Lough) was invaded by the heathens, and Máel Brigte, its king, and his brother Canannán, were taken prisoner and taken away to the ships.'[47]

The similarities between the names 'Melbrictus' from the *Gesta Danorum* and the 'Máel Brigte' from the *Annals of Ulster* are striking.[48] Academic Allen Mawer argued 'since Saxo is quite independent of the Irish annals, we may believe that we have here an early incident in the career of the historical Ragnar Lothbrok'.[49]

Saxo tells of how Ragnar also killed a king in the territory of the Scots (Irish) called 'Murial', which evolved into the feminine name Muriel and in Irish would be 'Murigheal'. This may be linked to the wife of the same name of Máelbrighde, King of Leinster, who died in 853 according to the *Annals of the Four Masters*. The name 'Máel Brigte', meaning 'devotee of St Brigid' was reoccurring among Irish and Pictish kings.

Based on Saxo's claims, Ragnar had earlier 'killed the earls of Scotland and of Pictland, and of the isles that they call the Southern or Meridional ['Suðreyjar'] , which seems to link to a battle in 839 described as one of the most important in British history.[50]

The *Annals of Ulster* records: 'The heathens won a battle against the men of Foirtriu, and Eóganán son of Aengus, Bran son of Óengus, Áed son of Boanta, and others almost innumerable fell there.'[51]

Fortriu was a central part of Pictland, which covered the northern and eastern regions of modern Scotland, and its name stemmed from how the Romans called the tribes *Picti* in Latin, i.e. 'painted people'. At the time of the battle, Uuen ruled the Picts, while Áed was a king of Dál Riata, presumably under Pictish overlordship, which covered the western seaboard of modern Scotland, including Argyll. The death of Uuen and Bran ended the line of the Óengus I Pictish dynasty, and the next ruler of Dál Riata, Cináed mac Ailpin in Gaelic, rose to power and became the first king of Scotland after conquering the Picts based on later traditions.

By the time Saxo was writing, the Gaelic kingdom of Alba later known as Scotland had replaced Pictland and all its rulers traced their lineage back to the kings of Dál Riata, which he seems to acknowledge. The Southern Isles comprised the Islands of the Clyde, the Isle of Man and the Hebrides, with the latter under control of the Dál Riata before the Vikings took over.

Notably, the 'Krákumál' was likely composed on the Scottish islands in the twelfth century and features Ragnar raiding locally, but an enemy 'Herthjof' in the Hebrides shares the name of a figure from Norse mythology who features in tales such as Starkad the Old. The 'King Marstan of Waterford' who battled Ragnar is also unidentifiable but may relate to the landscape and stem from the Old English *mersc* (marsh) and *tun* (town).[52]

While Ragnar was never mentioned in contemporary Irish texts, up until 845 when he raided Paris, only one Viking chieftain, Saxolb, had been. Perhaps Ragnar had been named in an albeit muddled genealogy tradition because the *Fragmentary*

Annals claimed that Ivar's father, great grandfather and great-great grandfather were all called Gofraid, which appears dubious, while his grandfather was a 'Ragnall'. It was more custom for Viking nobles to take the name of their uncle or grandfather.

The twelfth-century medieval Irish text *Cogadh Gaedhel re Gallaibh* (*The Wars of the Irish with the Foreigners*) refers to Halfdan as a 'king of the dark heathens' and a 'son of Ragnall', which does appear to link Halfdan and Ragnar. This means that all the five sons, barring Sigurd, have either been associated with a 'Ragnar', 'Ragnall' or 'Lothbrok' in non-Scandinavian sources.[53]

While the *Fragmentary Annals* throw considerable doubt on the tradition of Ragnar Lothbrok and his sons, in another respect it supports the legend. The entry for the year 866 describes how 'two younger sons of Albdan, king of Norway, drove out the eldest son Ragnall for fear he would seize the kingship and so he came with his three sons to Orkney'.[54]

Ragnall has been associated with Rognvald Eysteinsson or Rognvald of More, while 'Albdan' is Halfdan the Black, the father of Norway's founder Harald Finehair. 'Ragnall' is the Gaelic form of the Old Norse 'Rognvaldr' and does not correspond with the Old Norse name Ragnar, but such similar names as 'Ragnall' and 'Ragnar' were often confused in medieval literature, and the possibility these were as well should not be overlooked.[55]

Interestingly, Ivar may have had two famous grandsons with the name Ragnall, including one Ragnall ua Ímair who also ruled in Northumbria briefly until his death in 921. Another potential grandson with this name raided afterwards in Francia in the early 920s and aligned with the deposed emperor Charles the Simple.[56]

Rognvald of More features in the *Heimskringla* collection of sagas by Snorri Sturluson, who claims that he was awarded Orkney by Harald Finehair as compensation after the death of his son Ivar in Scotland. Ivar's grandson Ragnall ua Ímair also had a brother or cousin called Imar who died in a battle in 904 in Fortriu. According to Icelandic tradition, Rognvald of More was also a grandson of Ivar Upplendingjarl. This suggests that later Icelandic writers encountering the story of Ivar's grandson Ragnall equated them with their ancestral figure of the same name to bolster his prestige. Academic Alex Woolf noted it shows a 'great deal about how saga traditions developed'.[57] As both had sons who raided in the Mediterranean and Africa, the Ragnall from the *Fragmentary Annals* tale appears based on the real-life Ragnar:

> *'Ragnall's older sons, however, filled with arrogance and rashness, proceeded with a large army, having mustered that army from all quarters, to march against the Franks and Saxons. They thought that their father would return to Norway immediately after their departure.*

> *'Then their arrogance and their youthfulness incited them to voyage across the Cantabrian Ocean [i.e. the sea that is between Ireland and Spain] and they reached Spain, and they did many evil things in Spain, both destroying and plundering. After that they proceeded across the Gaditanean Straits [i.e. the place where the Irish Sea goes into the surrounding ocean], so that they reached Africa, and they waged war against the Mauritanians, and made a great slaughter of the Mauritanians.'*[58]

This tale is surely significant and related to the Old Norse tradition of Ragnar Lothbrok and his sons because Maurentina included Morocco, which is where Bjorn raided after modern Spain. The mentions of the Franks and Saxons are also intriguing because Bjorn had also targeted Paris, while the Great Heathen Army led by Ivar, Ubbe and Halfdan would later invade the Anglo-Saxon kingdoms. As if providing background, the *Fragmentary Annals* insert this tale in the year before the brothers captured York.

While supposedly based on annals from the eleventh century, the texts were copied around the 1640s from an older fifteenth-century manuscript. The question remains how much-later conflated traditions around Rognvald of More and Ragnar Lothbrok impacted the tale. Given the *Fragmentary Annals* focus solely on the Mediterranean raid, first told by William of Jumièges and connected to Lothbrok's son Bjorn around 1070, it was clearly not influenced by 'Ragnar's Saga', dated to around 1300 but circulating in Scandinavia at least 150 years earlier, which only vaguely described the expedition and visit to Luni.

When his sons are still raiding in the Mediterranean, they hear of Ragnar's perils matching later Old Norse sagas, which place the sons in Italy, according to the *Fragmentary Annals*. One brother says they are 'very foolish and mad to be killing ourselves going from country to country throughout the world, and not to be defending our own patrimony and doing the will of our father, for he is alone now, sad and discouraged in a land not his own.'[59]

The son had a vision that 'Ragnall's other son was slain in battle; and moreover, the father himself barely escaped from that battle – which dream proved to be true.' It describes a fierce battle with the Mauritanian forces in which the Vikings emerge victorious and cut off the king's hand. Afterwards the 'Norwegians devastated and burned the whole land' and brought captives back to Ireland.

Vikings captured 'blue men' i.e. 'black men' who 'remained in Ireland a long time', which is likely a reference to North African slaves captured in Nekor, and Muslim chroniclers also recorded that Vikings had taken hostages. Intriguingly, there is potential archaeological evidence of three potential graves from early-medieval Britain of women with possible African descent. In 2013, a burial was discovered in Fairford, Gloucestershire, which was described as a woman aged between 18 and 24 from Sub-Saharan Africa, and radiocarbon dating suggests she probably died between 896 and 1025.

Another related to a late-Saxon cemetery at Norwich, although the identification is open to questions, and a third related to a woman buried around 1000 in a late-Saxon cemetery at North Eltham in Norfolk. While not in Ireland, this means people from Africa or of African descent living and dying in communities in Britain during the Viking Age.[60]

Notably, the tale remarks how 'hardly one in three of the Norwegians escaped, between those who were slain, and those who drowned in the Gaditanian (Gibraltar) Straits', which tallies with how just under 20 of the fleet of 62 Viking ships, or nearly one in three, managed to return from the expedition.

Ragnar does appear to be the 'Ragnall' described as Ivar's grandfather in the *Fragmentary Annals*, who had some territorial interests or was demanding tribute from local kings in western Britain or Ireland. Later, Ivar arrived to stake his claim on these interests.

Notably, Ivar Ragnarsson turned up in 867 a year after Horm, a 'chief of the dark foreigners', was slain in Wales by Rhodri Mawr, king of Gwynedd, according to the Annales Cambriae, compiled in Dyfed during the eleventh century. Horm led the 'dark foreigners' when they first attacked Dublin in 851 and allied with Cerball, king of Ossory, against the fair foreigners.

In effect, the 'dark foreigners' appear a multinational family dynasty, headed by rulers with links to Danish royalty. A global Viking enterprise, profiting in plunder from raids, slavery, trade and extracting tribute from local kings, with bases in Dublin, Frisia and another one, emerged between 864 and 873 at Hedeby, when

Irishmen oppose the landing of the Viking fleet, one of the murals in Dublin City Hall by James Ward (1851–1924). (WikiCommons)

Sigurd and Halfdan were named as Danish kings and the last ruler Horik II was mentioned. Living off established kingdoms through tribute, when necessary, the 'dark foreigners' deployed armies to defeat local rulers who failed to comply.[61]

When operations were hampered in one area, the 'dark foreigners' sent in reinforcements to uphold their interests. When Ivar Ragnarsson arrived in Ireland amid the complex and ever shifting alliances between Irish and Vikings rulers, he threw his lot in with the powerful Olaf and began a dynasty known as the Uí Ímair, 'the descendants of Ímair', which dominated Viking Ireland for more than 180 years.

In 857, the *Annals of Ulster* records how Ivar and Olaf 'inflicted a rout on Caitil the Fair and his Norse-Irish in the lands of Munster'. Caitil the Fair has been tentatively associated with Ketil Flatnose, portrayed in the *Viking* series by WWE star Adam 'Edge' Copeland, who was a possible ninth-century Hebridean king, whose daughter Aud the Deep Minded married Olaf the White.

The 'Norse Irish', who are known as the Gallgoídil, i.e. 'foreigner Gaels', were Irish who had adopted Scandinavian ways or were the children of Scandinavian settlers who had taken Irish women as concubines.[62] The *Fragmentary Annals* remarks 'they had the customs of the Norse, and had been fostered by them, and though the original Norsemen were evil to the churches, these were much worse'.[63]

Two years after the raid on Munster, Ivar, Olaf and Cerball, king of Ossory, led a 'great army into Mide (Meath)' the territory of the High King Máel Sechnaill, of the Southern Uí Néill, which they raided for three months. In a conference to restore 'peace and tranquillity' in Ireland, Cerball submitted to Máel Sechnaill and turned against his Viking allies.

When Máel Sechnaill died in 862, the *Fragmentary Annals* lamented: 'There is much sorrow everywhere; there is a great misfortune among the Irish. Red wine has been spilled down the valley; the only King of Ireland has been slain.'[64]

The attack on Brú na Bóinne in 863 would be Ivar's last in Ireland for nine years. It was now the turn of the island across the sea to face his wrath.

Chapter 5

THE GREAT FRISIAN ARMY

*Now comes flying, the dragon of darkness, a glittering serpent from
Nithafjoll, it flies over fields and bears its wings, a naked corpse.*
'Völuspá', *Poetic Edda*, author and date unknown[1]

Dubbed *'hæþen here'* in Old English, which means the 'Great Heathen Army' in
the *Anglo-Saxon Chronicle*, a massive Viking fleet appeared off the British coast in
865 and threatened the whole fabric of society.[2]

Regular Viking raids had been a blight on Britain for more than thirty years, but
this new massive coalition were looking to gain a permanent footing. Coupled with
wanting to claim its vast wealth and rich agricultural lands, the Vikings would have
been attracted by the weakened political situation. Northmen sensed an optimum
time to launch a conquest with none of the main Anglo-Saxon kingdoms besides
Wessex capable of offering much resistance.

Many Vikings were seeking wealth and fame from raiding, motivated by the
claim the bravest and toughest fallen warriors would be led by the Valkyrie to
Valhalla. Some were drawn by the promise of rich new pastures, while others
perhaps desired to find a woman with the custom in Scandinavia that kings and
nobles could have multiple wives.[3]

Months of planning went into building this menacing fleet. During the Viking
Age, the conscripted fleet of warships known as *leidang* in Old Norse required
various Scandinavian kingdoms, which were split into ship districts (*skipen*) to
build, maintain, equip, man and provision ships, with the onus on the independent
farmers to provide resources, materials and manpower.[4] This conscription became
set in stone during the mid-tenth century, and it is not known whether it existed
around 865, but populations had to answer calls from Viking leaders or face the
consequences.

Some of the crews would have been professional household Viking raiders
bound to their local lord, chieftain or king by sworn oaths, which became known as
the *hirð* (herd). They were tasked with providing military service and in turn would
benefit from the spoils of plunder. There were also the Viking brotherhoods, known
as the *felag* (fellowship of warriors), which could have varied greatly in size but
may have formed for specific trade or raiding expeditions.[5]

A twelfth-century manuscript illustration of the Great Heathen Army arriving on the shores of England. (Morgan Library, New York/WikiCommons)

Each Viking had to come equipped with either a broad-axe or sword together with a spear and shield. For every second thwart (the rower's seat derived from *thvert* in Old Norse) on the ship, there had to be one longbow and 24 arrows, and noncompliance meant fines.[6] While these Vikings were no doubt skilled in warfare and imposing figures, the most important quality on the ships was simply being able to get along with their crewmates because these were often brutally demanding and harsh journeys. The seats where they ate, slept and manned the oars when called upon were just 73cm wide, highlighting the cramped environments. Brutal winds, lashing rain and cold would have made the conditions at times unbearable.[7]

As ever, the prospect of fame, riches and the oaths of loyalty would have ensured most withstood the grim realities. Meat and fish were brought along and salted, pickled or smoked to last the long trips, but there were no cooking or bed facilities. Vikings on board slept in a *hudfat*, which was a sleeping bag made from animal skin covered by a hide blanket. Lords were provided with shelter in the form of a collapsible tent.

Remarkably, at the Great Heathen Army cemetery site at Heath Wood, Derbyshire, a study of the strontium (which builds up in food and teeth) and isotope ratio of three people and three animals, namely a horse, dog and a possible pig, found two of the humans had grown up locally and the other person was non-local, but the animals were believed to have travelled with the army.[8] At the time, the horse was about the size of a modern pony (about 4 feet 10 inches high), and there may have been space for one or two on the longships.[9]

Halfdan surely set off at some stage from the Danish realm, most likely from Hedeby between 865 and 870, with his herd of loyal warriors to join the Great Heathen Army in Britain. Asser, Alfred the Great's biographer, said the Great Heathen Army had come from *de Danubia* (the Danube), and he is believed to have confused *Dacia*, where the river is located, with *Dania* (Denmark).[10]

A large part of this force, which was between 2,000 and 4,000 strong, arrived from Ivar's base in Dublin or modern-day Francia, while some were seemingly already entrenched in Britain. A Viking army had overwintered on the Isle of Thanet in 864/65 and caused havoc after breaking an agreement to remain peaceful. According to Asser, the 'heathen, after the manner of foxes, burst forth with all secrecy from their camp by night, and setting at naught their engagements, and spurning the promised money – which they knew was less than they could get by plunder – they ravaged all the eastern coast of Kent.'[11]

This was an army of convenience rather than a traditional army made up of groups attached to ships, with their own leaders. Viking armies were constantly changing in composition, leadership and location with new elements arriving and leaving all the time.[12]

One of the largest army contingents arrived from Frisia, which extended along the Wadden Sea tidal zone between the north Netherlands and north-western Germany and included the former thriving market town of Dorestad, which went into rapid decline after the Viking raids.

The *History of St Cuthbert* states 'the army which Ubbe duke of the Frisians and Healfdene (Halfdan) king of the Danes had led into England'. These annals were compiled in the tenth or eleventh century in Chester-le-Street or Durham but could be based on texts that began as early as the eighth century. This text calls the leaders the *Scaldingi*, associated with the River Scheldt in Frisia, which was known as the *Scald* in Old English and *Scaldis* in Latin showing obvious likeness.[13] It has also been linked to the *Scyldings*, a Danish royal house that features in the *Beowulf* poem, but Ubbe's distinction as a Frisian duke makes the association with the *Scald* more compelling.

The same source tells of how 'the *Scaldingi* slew nearly all the English in the southern and the northern parts [of England]'.[14]

The twelfth-century *Annals of Lindisfarne* also calls Ubbe a 'duke of the Frisians' who led a 'great army of Danes' into York. A large portion of the army most likely hailed from a base on Walcheren Island, within the River Scheldt estuary, because this region wouldn't have been mentioned without it being an important area.[15] This same phrasing was also used in the *Annals of St Bertin* to describe Vikings from Vestfold raiding in Francia during 843 as *Westfaldingi*.[16]

Saxo Grammaticus described Ubbe, portrayed by Jordan Patrick in the TV series, as an illegitimate son fighting against his father before he makes peace and is restored to favour. He also tells of an earlier warrior called Ubbe the Frisian, showing the connection between the region and this name, now linked to the modern Frisian variant Obe. Some scholars believe Ubbe was ethnically a Dane but became powerful in Frisia, or his mother hailed from the region, which was plausible given his depiction as a half-brother.[17]

The links between Ragnar's sons and the Frisian realm extended beyond Ubbe because the Norman cleric William of Jumièges wrote Bjorn had died in Frisia after his infamous raids. The real-life Sigurd appeared to have a connection to Frisia, possibly heading an offshoot of the Great Heathen Army, which fought on the River Scheldt in 880 and where Northmen had 'long been settled' according to the *Annals of Fulda*. This group may have had a fortified base camp locally because they were described a year later in the same source as raiding in large numbers on horseback.[18]

Frisian bases potentially connected to Ubbe emerged at the start of the twentieth century. Excavators working in Middleburg, the capital of Zeeland in the Netherlands, discovered that the city's medieval circular street pattern followed the outline of a former earth rampart and bank in 1902. Around thirty years later, the Dutch historian Johan Huizinga uncovered other coastal settlements with the same layout between the rivers Somme and the Scheldt, including Oostburg, Oost-Sourburg, Middelburg, Domburg and Burgh in Zeeland.

The 'burgh' place name element means 'fortification, stronghold' and all five Zeeland sites, referred to as *ringwalburgen* (ring fortresses) featured a massive outer circular rampart and moat with settlements inside. Oost-Sourburg measured some 144m (472ft) in diameter and threw up several timber houses on raised platforms with its imported pottery suggesting 'wide-ranging and long distance' contacts. These imports included red deer antler for combs and quartz phyllite rock to make whetstones from the Telemark area in Norway.[19]

The coastal Domburg (meaning 'dune fortress') on Walcheren was the largest of the five with its outer rampart having a diameter of 265m (869ft). It was a mile away from a known trading site, sometimes referred to as Walichrum (the old name for the modern Walcheren region), in the north-east, with a population of up to 1,000 people and was a hub for wool trade. More than 100 sceattas (early pennies) produced in England, Frisia and Jutland during the Anglo-Saxon period have been found on Domburg, dated to between 814 and 875, with most minted on the island or Dorestad.[20]

Discoveries during Domburg excavations of cubic weights with six dots on a beaded rim on both sides, dirham fragments and various pieces of hack silver have been taken as evidence of a bullion economy and trade with an international network. Some finds at Domburg, such as a necklace and a silver toilet set with parallels in Scandinavia, suggest a Viking presence.[21]

The other potentially Viking-related artefacts have included a late-ninth century decorated D-shaped buckle of copper alloy in the Borre-style, which typically features cat-like heads or beasts gripping borders. This design has clear similarities with a buckle found in the great Gokstad Ship burial in Norway. Domburg excavations also led to the discovery of a horse harness mount, which was a copper-alloy triangular-shaped one with the Borre-style design.[22]

These Zeeland sites could have been Viking strongholds to impose their power on the local population, trade and manufacture goods, and launch raids because there are clear similarities with the tenth-century ring fortresses in Denmark dating from the reign of Harald Bluetooth, known as Trelleborgs after one of the strongholds, which could translate as 'slave forts'.[23,24]

Oost-Sourburg had the same dimensions as a Trelleborg-type fort with four main streets and two entrances at right angles to each other.[25] Excavations at Ghent in Belgium, which is also situated on the River Scheldt and served as a Viking Great Heathen Army winter camp in 879–90, showed a ninth-century enclosure forms the layout for the city's semicircular street plan. Antwerp, which is linked to the same raiding, has also shown evidence of an early-medieval or D-shaped enclosure and an array of similar finds to the ones at Oost-Souburg.[26]

Since 841, this region of Frisia had been officially under Viking control when Walcheren was first granted by Lothar to either the deposed Danish ruler Harald

Remarkable aerial view of the Trelleborg ring fort near Slagelse in West Zealand, built during the reign of Harald Bluetooth around 980, which resembled the Viking forts on Walcheren. (Thue C. Leibrandt/CC BY-SA 3.0)

Klak or his nephew Harald the Younger, both of whom were dead by 552, which infuriated the *Annals of St Bertin*: 'This was surely a detestable crime that those who had brought evil on the Christians should be given power over the lands and people of the Christians and the very churches of Christ and that Christian folk should have to serve men who worshipped demons.'[27]

Harald the Younger's brother Rorik was awarded the declining Dorestad and Utrecht to defend against other Vikings and held sway over most of Frisia for more than twenty years but is never specifically associated with Walcheren.

Ubbe must have taken over Walcheren in the decade before the Great Heathen Army arrived, ruling independently or paying tribute to Rorik. Alongside the proximity to Britain, the island of Walcheren had huge strategic value guarding the mouths of the rivers Scheldt and Meuse, and it was easily defensible on a high ridge behind dunes via a creek connected to the Scheldt and surrounded by tidal marshlands and the sea. It was just the kind of place Vikings would set up a permanent or temporary base, next to a bustling North Sea international market.

Many of Ubbe's Viking gang could have grown up in Frisia from as early as the 840s and have spoken a West Germanic dialect that is almost identical to Old English, so they could have been efficient translators and explain the army's success in negotiating with local rulers, albeit at the barrel of a gun.[28]

Some Frisian individuals and tribal groups could have fought alongside Vikings willingly or been forced but still benefited from the plunder. A series of Frisian land laws written up around 1200 includes one that states locals abducted by Northmen and forced to join their raids could still come back and claim possession of land provided they had not taken part in the looting, rape of women and burning of villages. If they had been involved, the Frisians would have to pay a penalty from the plunder captured by the Norse but were exempt if they were not given any.[29]

Later Frisian settlement in England is evidenced by place names with the element 'Frys', 'Fris' and often with 'ton', the Old English word for 'enclosure or settlement' and 'by' from Old Norse, which means 'farmstead' or 'settlement'. These include Frisby on the Wreake, Old Frisby in Leicestershire, Firsby (earliest form Frisobea) in Yorkshire and Firsby (earliest form Frisby) and Friesthorpe (earliest form Frisatorp) in Lincolnshire, along with others such as Friston in East Suffolk and Freasley in Warwickshire.

Six of the eight place names with the Frisian element and Old Norse compound at the end occur in the Five Boroughs that the Vikings took over in modern-day Midlands. In total, sixteen of the twenty-four place names associated with Frisians, identified by the academic Rolf Bremmer, fall within the later Danelaw territory, where the laws of the Vikings held sway.[30,31]

Amid the ruins of Roman Britain, migrants from the North Sea, including from Frisia, arrived in the fifth century on the east coast as largely farming families as well as confederates who provided military muscle for warlords in exchange for land. According to Northumbrian monk Bede, writing in the eighth century, the bulk

Mid- to late-ninth-century Viking hoard found in the Dutch village of Westerklief on the former island of Wieringen, which included six silver bracelets, a necklace, sixteen silver ingots and 78 silver coins. (National Museum of Antiquities, Leiden)

of the Germanic incomers came from three 'powerful' tribes from Anglen (Angles), Saxony (Saxons) and Jutland (Jutes), originating from northern and north-western Germany and Denmark. The Saxons dominated the south-east, hence Wessex (West Saxons), Essex (East Saxons) and Sussex (South Saxons), while Mercia, Northumberland and East Anglia were occupied by Angles, and the Jutes settled in Kent and on the Isle of Wight. Many Britons gradually adopted the culture and customs of their new immigrant neighbours. Several early kings of Mercia and

Wessex, including Cerdic, Ceawlin, Caedwalla, Creoda, Pybba and Penda, appear to have Brittonic names, and the conflict was often regional rather than solely fought on ethnic terms as local bigwigs took over former civitates of the Roman empire.[32]

By the time Ragnar's sons turned up, this was an overwhelmingly Anglo-Saxon and Christian realm, but they still revered Odin, whom they knew as Woden and named a huge ditch, the Wansdyke (Woden's Dyke), after him. Norse gods were honoured with the days of the week – Tuesday (Tyr), Wednesday (Woden) and Thursday (Thunor, which was the Old Norse spelling of Thor). Rulers of all the Anglo-Saxon kingdoms, barring Essex, claimed descent from Woden.

Anglo-Saxons, including also Alfred the Great in his translation of Boethius' *The Consolation of Philosophy*, also paid homage to sinister Germanic mythological figures such as the cunning blacksmith Wayland Smithy, who is associated with the Neolithic long barrow in Oxfordshire, where legend says your horse will be magically reshoed if you leave a coin.

According to 'Völundarkviða', Wayland killed three sons of a king in revenge and fashioned goblets from their skulls, jewels from their eyes and a brooch from their teeth before raping and impregnating his daughter. Darker aspects such as tales of rape, mutilation and violence by Wayland, Norse deities and cremation burials were part of a pagan past the Anglo-Saxons had never properly come to terms with even as they denounced the 'heathen' ways of the Vikings.[33]

As well as the unsettling aspects of their own pre-Christian culture, the intentions of this terrifying Viking fleet must have sent shockwaves across the Anglo-Saxon realms. They were well versed in fighting the Northmen, but the prospect of the pagan raiders settling must have caused deep alarm for this Christian society, which had been expressing their concerns dramatically about the Viking dangers for decades. Lightning and flying dragons, terrible portents in the sky and mysterious fogs were supposedly seen before the Vikings targeted Lindisfarne in 793, which marked the traditional start of the Viking Age, according to the *Anglo-Saxon Chronicle*. Monks would frequently blame plagues and invasions on the population for what they saw as failing to live as God intended as well as looking back and linking comet sightings around the time as a sign of the Lord's displeasure. Vikings were seen as an instrument of God's fury and only repentance from the masses could prevent further attacks.

In 839, the Wessex ruler Egbert wrote to his West Frankian counterpart Louis the Pious about the disturbing nightmare of a priest who visited a 'wonderful' building where he met young boys writing in blood, which represented the 'various sins' of Christians who were 'utterly unwilling' to follow orders in these divine books.

'If Christian people don't do penance for their various vices and crimes and don't observe the Lord's Day in a stricter and worthier way, then a great and crushing disaster will come upon them. For three days and nights a very dense fog will spread over their land,

The famous Wayland Smithy neolithic monument in Oxfordshire named after a dark figure from Norse mythology.

> *and then all of a sudden pagan men will lay waste with fire and sword and most of the people and land of the Christians along with all they possess.'*[34]

A disastrous clash of gods known as Ragnarök, which sparked an apocalypse, also defined Viking mythology. In the 'Völuspá' ('Prophecy of the Seeress') from the *Poetic Edda*, the fearsome wolf Fenrir would break free from its fetters, the Midgard Serpent would rise from the ocean spewing poison and the Naglfar, the ship of the dead, would escape its moorings in Hel as the fire giants, led by Surt, destroyed the rainbow bridge that connected the realm of the gods, Asgard, to the human world of Midgard.[35]

After summoning the gods, Odin led them to the battlefield, but he was devoured by Fenrir, and then, Odin's son Vidar quickly avenged his father after killing the beast by stabbing its heart. Thor kills his nemesis Jörmungandr but succumbs to its poison shortly afterwards: 'The sun is darkened; earth sinks in the sea. From heaven turn, the bright stars away. Rages smoke with fire, the life-feeder. High flame plays against heaven itself.'[36]

Soon a new world emerges, as the earth rises from the ocean 'green anew, the water falls, on high the eagle flies over the fell and catches fish'.[37] As discussed in Chapter One, Ragnarök and its aftermath appears a mythical retelling of the Volcanic Winter and Justinian Plague. However, the Vikings were focused on another climatic encounter.

England must have been a hugely attractive proposition filled with monasteries, churches and trading settlements, such as Lundenwic around the Strand in central London and Hamwic in modern Southampton, but they fell into decline as the Viking raids increased. At the top of Anglo-Saxon society, below the royals, stood the *ealdorman* who was the king's viceroy of the various shires (districts), a title which became hereditary, and they had responsibility for its administration and justice, for calling up the reservist army or *fyrd* of freemen and leading them into battle. *Thegns* were a separate class, which originated as the king's bodyguard, but they could become rich through land and even elevated to ealdormen. *Ceorls* were simple farmers and freemen who owned land and formed the backbone of the society. At the lowest rank were the 'serfs', 'thralls', 'bondmen' and 'slaves', which were crucial for the Anglo-Saxon economy.[38]

Bishops and nobles held vast tracts of lands and estates on behalf of the king and reaped the rewards of food and goods, rent from farmsteads, and the tolls and rents from seasonal or permanent markets. The affairs of the kingdom, which began in the time of late-eight century Mercian king Offa, would be settled by assemblies of the king, bishops and his nobles, and all the early charters are witnessed by these assemblies when the king granted land and privileges.[39]

Lindisfarne had a powerful effect on the psyche of English nobility, but Viking raiding only became a serious threat shortly before Egbert penned the nightmare prophecy in the final years of reign. In 825, Egbert of Wessex had ended Mercian supremacy with a great victory at Ellandun and subdued other south-eastern kingdoms, such as Kent, Sussex and Surrey, which were never again detached from the Wessex monarchy.[40] Offa and Egbert dreamt of a united English realm for themselves and their descendants, gaining the prestige of an all-powerful *bretwalda* (Britain-wide ruler), and the Vikings would prove both the biggest danger and catalyst for this aspiration.

Egbert's son Ethelwulf had ruled from 839 to 858 but was then followed in a short space of time by Alfred the Great's three older brothers, namely Ethelbald, Ethelberht and finally Ethelred, who ascended the throne in the year when the Great Heathen Army arrived. This couldn't have escaped the attention of the Vikings stalking the Frankish coastline, where it was becoming harder for their fleets to advance deep inland because of bridge building by Charles the Bald on the Seine and Loire.[41]

The much-awaited disaster feared by Anglo-Saxon chroniclers manifested in 865. Ethelward, a tenth-century chronicler, said it was the fleet of the 'tyrant Ivar' from the north and his use of '*Igwares*' proved it had come from an original manuscript of the chronicle.[42] Vikings arrived in East Anglia, possibly staying at either the Red Castle or Thetford Castle in Thetford, after travelling up the River Stour. They were paid off by the region's king Edmund, who supplied them with horses. Anglo-Saxons looked on in terror, but this was the calm before the storm. According to later legend, the piglets had arrived.

Chapter 6

A TALE OF LAGERTHA

There were once women in Denmark who dressed themselves to look like men and spent almost every minute cultivating soldier's skills….
As if they were forgetful of their true selves, they put toughness before allure, aimed at conflicts instead of kisses, tasted blood not lips, sought the clash of arms rather than the arm's embrace.
Saxo Grammaticus, 13th century[1]

With her head resting on a shield, a sword, a spear and an axe placed alongside her body and a horse at the foot of the grave, this Viking woman buried in the Hedmark region of Norway was of high standing. The excavation in Nordre Kjølen in 1900 'appears to testify to the idea that shield-maidens really existed in real life', claimed Norwegian archaeologist Gustav Mørck.[2]

The Old Norse concept of the *skjaldmær* ('shield-maiden'), a Viking warrior woman, remains as captivating today as it did in the thirteenth century when the Danish historian Saxo Grammaticus in the *Gesta Danorum* (*Deeds of the Danes*) featured Lagertha in the Ragnar Lothbrok legend. Romantic notions of a female warrior armed with a sword and shield charging into battle have gripped the public imagination and archaeological finds suggest it was a reality.

Portrayed by Katheryn Winnick in the television series, Lagertha is one of the central characters and famed for her fighting skills, bravery and scheming as she usurps several male rivals to take Kattegat and Hedeby at different points. According to Saxo, she had captured Ragnar's attention when he sought to avenge the death of his grandfather Siward, kings of the Norwegians, and fought against Frey, the king of Sweden. With his army, Ragnar had come to rescue the wives of Siward's kinsfolk in Norway from a brothel. Saxo said:

'Among them was Ladgerda [Lagertha], a skilled amazon, who, though a maiden, had the courage of a man, and fought in front among the bravest with her hair loose over her shoulders. All marvelled at her matchless deeds, for her locks flying down her back betrayed that she was a woman. Ragnar, when he had justly cut down the murderer of his grandfather, asked many questions of his fellow

soldiers concerning the maiden whom he had seen so forward in the fray, and declared that he had gained the victory by the might of one woman. Learning that she was of noble birth among the barbarians, he steadfastly wooed her by means of messengers.[3]

Far from being easily wooed, Lagertha 'spurned his mission' and to guard against Ragnar's amorous intentions, she placed a bear and a dog at the porch of her dwelling so that beasts blocked his way. The lovestruck Ragnar was unfazed and sailed to Gualardale (Gualar Valley in Norway), where he visited the house and quickly killed one creature with a spear and grabbed the other one and wrung its neck. This bravery won Lagertha over, and they married and had three children, two girls and a son called Fridleif, who Ragnar later made an earl of Orkney.

In the two main sagas, Thora is the first wife of Ragnar, and they have two sons – Eirek and Agnar. Described as the daughter of an Earl Herrud from Gautland in modern Sweden, she dies from sickness in both sagas. Notably, Saxo Grammaticus refers to the same figure as a 'Herodd' and as a king rather than an earl. After Thora's death in the sagas, Ragnar marries Aslaug, whose parentage is fictional as she is called the daughter of a heroic figure from Norse mythology, Sigurd the Dragon Slayer, and they have five children – Ivar, Bjorn, Hwitserk (Halfdan), Rognvald (only in the first saga) and Sigurd.

There is no mention of Lagertha in sagas or texts, and Saxo Grammaticus was likely influenced by classical works about Amazonian women and in referencing Lagertha's 'flowing hair' is clearly sexualizing her.[4] Later, Saxo Grammaticus claims Lagertha 'flew round to the rear of the enemy in a battle'[5] to terrify the enemy as the Valkyries act in poetry.

Lagertha's name is likely based on the goddess Thorgerd, who was worshipped and often said to be wed to the tenth-century Norwegian ruler Haakon Sigurdsson in the Old Norse tales *Flateyjarbók* and the saga of Olaf Tryggvason. The jarl Haakon lived at Hlaðir (Lade), which shares obvious similarities to Lagertha's Old Norse name of Hlaðgerðr. The '*gerðr*' was the earliest name by which Thorgerd (Þorgerðr) is known in Skaldic sources. Gaulardal, the Gaular valley, which was where Lagertha lived according to Saxo, is situated nearby and was the centre of Thorgerd's cult and where Haakon's wife Thora resided.[6]

There are often supernatural aspects to female warriors in the Old Norse tales. In the 1260s, Brandr Jónsson, Bishop of Hólar in the north of Iceland, translated a long Latin poem, Walter of Châtillon's *Alexandreis*, into Old Norse in which one episode describes Alexander's meeting with a certain queen: 'Then came to the war-booths of the king, that queen of Amazonia, who is called Kalestris, and 200 of those maidens with her who could well be called "shield-maidens" in the Danish tongue.'[7]

While equating the shield-maidens with Amazonian women, the original Latin text included the term 'virgin maidens', so the *skjaldmær* 'shield-maiden' reference was dreamed up by the bishop. Academic Judith Jesch found references to shield-maidens in the sagas 'do not provide any conclusive evidence for literal shield-maidens, or warrior women in the Viking Age. Indeed, they suggest that in the Viking imaginary, any such creatures were most likely to be foreign or, like the Valkyries, mythological.'[8]

In the famous *Vǫlsunga saga*, the well-known heroine Brunhild once describes herself as a shield-maiden in resisting her lover Sigurd the Dragon Slayer. She tells him: 'We're not fated to share our lives together. I am a shield-maiden, wearing a helmet along with warrior-kings. I help them and I don't find battle distasteful.'[9] Interestingly, Aslaug, who is the mother of Ivar, Halfdan, Bjorn and Sigurd in the saga, is the daughter of Brunhild and joins her sons in battle against King Eysteinn.

In 'Ragnar's Saga', following the death of Agnar and Eirek, Aslaug urged her sons to seek vengeance by defeating Eysteinn. Determined to uphold the family's honour, Aslaug realises the dynasty's success can only be ensured through cooperation. She cries only once and sheds a single tear, as 'hard as a hailstone and blood red', when she learns of their deaths and reminds her biological sons that Eirek and Agnar would have sought similar retribution: 'Had you been first to fall, without fail you would be lying, lacking vengeance half a year later brothers, if Eirek and Agnar, I'll conceal it a little, brethren not born of me, still did live and breathe.'[10]

Changing her name to Randalin (goddess of shields), Aslaug spearheaded land forces as the sons of Ragnar avenged their two brothers and defeated Eysteinn. Even though Saxo doesn't include Aslaug, perhaps because of her fictional parentage, he does seemingly allude to her by having Lagertha also have flowing hair and warlike characteristics.

Ragnar plans to cast off Lagertha for another woman in Thora as he did in the sagas when he left Aslaug for Suanlogha, whose name seems based on Aslaug.[11]

Saxo also describes Ragnar having sex with a low born-woman, mirroring how Aslaug is disguised as a farmhand called Kraka in the saga, but in his version, it is Ubbe's mother, an unknown daughter of a Hesbernus. Saxo could well have had access to an earlier version of the legend.[12]

The possibilities of shield-maidens such as Lagertha cannot be ruled out with the existence of various potential female warrior graves. At least 30 Viking Age graves of women with weapons have been found in Denmark, Iceland, Norway and Sweden, which contain swords, spearheads and shields, along with axe and arrow heads. The grave at Nordre Kjølen in Norway was incredibly preserved given the acidic soil in large parts of Norway often makes it unlikely prehistoric and medieval remains are found so intact. When the farmer excavated the mound, he found the woman, who was aged around 20, was buried on her back facing upwards with a shield that had an iron boss under her head and different weapons placed by her side, including a sword to the left and an axe and spear to the right.

Other grave goods included arrowheads, a large whetstone and a small metal tool, probably a file. A horse that had likely been slaughtered lay at her feet. Intriguingly, the sword was pointed towards her head, which is extremely rare in burials because they are normally pointed in the direction of the feet.[13]

Academic Leszek Gardeła, author of an in-depth book *Weapons and Women in the Viking World*, highlighted how the rulers in the Bayeux Tapestry had their swords pointed up. 'Perhaps the unusual position of the sword intended to communicate that the deceased had some paramount role in the community,' he said, suggesting the sword could be 'an heirloom that legitimised her, and potentially her offspring's power'.[14] Some argued that the size of the sword grip would have been too large for such a 'slender' individual, but training, techniques, skill and determination were surely as important as size in battle, and the sword might not have been made for her.[15]

Another remarkable woman's weapon grave dated to the 10th-century was discovered in Løve near Larvik in Vestfold, Norway, where Kaupang was located. She was also buried with a decapitated horse and found with an axe head, a knife and a suspended necklace with multi-coloured beads that may have held special properties. These beads may have manifested links to the past or claims to power.

Unusual aspects included how the axe was placed next to her head rather than by her legs, and how the horse was laid alongside the woman with its neck by her feet, when normally the animals are placed on an elevated platform at the foot of the grave. An elaborate bridle next to the horse's head showed it had special value, while it was fitted with iron crampons on three of its feet that suggested the mourners thought it was going to a cold part of the otherworld.

Significantly, she was dressed in blue because based on sagas this colour along with red was often associated with people of higher rank, while in general people of lower-social status such as slaves wore darker clothing.

A special Viking Age iron rattle, known as a rangle, which was most likely used for religious purposes, was placed on the animal's chest in the Løve burial, next to an early-Bronze Age stone circle showing a desire to connect with the past. Gardeła believes the Løve woman was a 'ritual specialist capable of seeing into the past and the future'.[16] Such women, known as seeresses or völvas, were potentially among the Viking settlers in Dublin because an object resembling a wand was discovered at Kilmainham.[17]

Buried axes could be signs that the women were ritual specialists because they were often used for magic purposes, such as healing rituals in folklore in Scandinavia, Finland and central Europe. In the *Ljósvetninga* saga, an Icelandic sorceress named Torhild (Þórhildr in Old Norse), who dressed in typical male attire of trousers and a helmet, waded into the fjord with an axe. The saga's main character Gudmund (Guðmundr in Old Nose), a chieftain in Iceland in the tenth century, wanted to know if himself or his son would face reprisals in future. During

Artistic reconstruction by Mirosław Kuźma of a female grave from Nordre Kjølen, Hedmark, Norway. (Leszek Gardeła/Mirosław Kuźma)

a ritual ceremony, Torhild struck the water with her axe, and with no visible change in the lake, she assured Gudmund that 'no man would take up vengeance against him', and he could keep his honour. When Gudmund asked if his sons would survive unharmed, Torhild went into the shallows and struck the water again with a loud crash, and suddenly the water turned bloody. 'I think Gudmund that the blow will fall close to one of your sons,' she warned.[18]

Other fascinating burials include a probable woman buried in a mound at Lake Dalstorp in Västergötland, Sweden, who was cremated with ten knives, and the human cremation remains were mixed with other objects to form a thin oval-shaped layer. Afterwards, five spears that were not affected by the fire were driven vertically into the layer. One theory suggests the spears acted to keep the woman from rising and that order would be maintained in the community.[19]

At Bogovej on Langeland in Denmark, 49 graves were discovered but the only person buried with a weapon, an axe head near their right leg, was a 16- to 18-year-old woman. As the grave also included an Arabic dirham of Nuh ibn Nasr (dated to 945) and a piece of steel that could be struck against flint or hard rock to generate a spark, it indicated she was of high social status. Another woman was found buried with a dissected dog and had a slaughtered old stallion horse placed at her feet at Trekroner-Grydehøj in Zealand. After she was buried with a wooden chest, chain and knives, large stones were placed over her head and chest – perhaps in an act of post-mortem stoning.[20]

At Gamla Uppsala, the boat grave of a mysterious but wealthy woman from the ninth century was discovered behind the vicarage garden, buried in expensive clothes sewn with silk from China, finely woven wool and linen. Three men were buried with their horses each in a separate boat alongside. She was laid to rest with a dog and a rooster, which were guardians of the home and would now watch over her grave. While many grave goods were decomposed, a needle case with sewing needles remained as well as a knife with a sheath decorated with a braided silver thread.[21] Around her throat hung an old Arabian coin in an amulet, which depicted the female goddess Freya, the goddess of fertility. Notably, a cat was found among the graves, which was Freya's favourite animal because she owned a carriage that was pulled by two cats as she travelled between worlds.

Freya, the sister of Freyr, had the power over life, death and magic as well as ruling over fertility, love and desire. Her enchanted necklace 'Brisingamen' makes her irresistible to both men and women. Half of the warriors who die in battle end up in the realm of Freya known as Folkvang, along with brave and noble women. Those buried at Uppsala in the boats were clearly intended for Folkvang.[22]

In 2017, a tenth-century Viking Age burial known as Bj 581 sparked worldwide media coverage when it was found at Birka among 3,000 mounds around its perimeter, of which 1,100 were excavated by the late-nineteenth century archaeologist Hjamlar Stolpe, who described this discovery as the 'most remarkable'.[23]

Dressed in 'Eurasian Steppe' clothing, they had been buried in an underground wooden chamber with a mare and stallion horse, one of which was bridled for riding, in a raised platform made from chalk at the chamber's edge. Chamber graves could still be accessed, and some visitors could have been seeking supernatural contact with the deceased, performing magic and collecting family heirlooms.

Grave goods included an iron sword decorated with copper alloy, an axe head, an iron spear, armour-piercing arrows, a battle knife known as a *saexe*, two shield bosses, a spearhead, a quarter of an Arabic silver coin (a dirham of Nasr ibn Ahmad dated 913–33), 28 gaming pieces and three dice made of antler that are associated with battle tactics and traditionally found with high-ranking Viking warriors.[24]

The person aged 30 to 40 wore a distinctive cap linked to Kiev that suggested she was Rus nobility, with an almost identical burial uncovered in Shestovista in Ukraine in 2006. Notably, this burial was also located in a prominent location at the western-most point of Birka on a high rocky promontory overlooking the lake, visible from the lake and water below. This person must have been of massive significance to Birka residents, which was highlighted by how it was only one of three graves where the sword was placed on the left-hand side of the body.

Since the original excavation in the 1880s, this was thought to be a high-status Viking male warrior until DNA testing in 2017 led by Uppsala and Stockholm universities revealed that the buried occupant was lacking a Y-chromosome and was a female. Her ancestry included genetic affinity to present-day inhabitants of Britain (namely England and Scotland), Iceland and Orkney as well as Denmark and Norway and to a lesser extent the eastern Baltic countries of Lithuania and Latvia, demonstrating the wide-ranging connections and cultures at Birka.

The debate has raged ever since about whether this was a female Viking warrior, with many academics cautioning that grave goods are not an automatic indicator of a person's occupation or gender. Moreover, the weapons could conceivably have been put in the graves as gifts by mourners. Her skeleton and bones were 'slender and gracile' despite wielding swords and axes on a regular basis.[25]

With the two shields and spears, this could have been a double grave, with one of the bodies having been removed or having decomposed. Either way, both burials would have been of a similar high status, and one report believed the 'most obvious and logical conclusion' was that she had lived as a professional warrior of high rank: 'The person in Bj 581 was buried in a grave full of functional weapons and war-gear (and little else) in close proximity to other burials with weapons next to a building saturated with weapons outside the gate of a fortress.'[26]

Scholar and archaeologist Neil Price, who co-authored this report into the Birka warrior grave, believes 'there really were female warriors in the Viking Age, including one of command rank, but that they were never numerous'.[27]

Sketch of the excavated grave found and labelled Bj 581 by Hjalmar Stolpe
in Birka, Sweden. (Evalo Hansen/WikiCommons)

Viking Age women could gain considerable standing and acclaim evidenced by the burials at Birka and Nordre Kjølen. While there are no references in the contemporary annals, a Greek historian Johan Skylitzes reported that in 971 women warriors equipped 'like men' were among the dead Rus fighters after a failed attack on Byzantine.[28]

Based on the wealth of sagas and suggestions from weapons burial, it seems unlikely that women were not learning to fight and, in some instances, joining battles in such a militarised society.

The tradition surrounding Ragnar Lothbrok and his sons clearly features a central warrior woman character as his wife or the mother of his children, but how much of this is inspired by the earlier *Vǫlsunga saga* or based on reality is unclear. Many sagas have women playing an active role in equipping their sons with weapons, ships and supplies when they reach fighting age.[29] The weight of evidence from saga references, rich women's graves and those with weapons suggest that women could attain a high rank in society and play an active role in directing preparations for war and raiding. In some cases, they fought on the battlefield. One such real life warrior woman could have inspired the character of Lagertha whose marriage to Ragnar was short-lived, according to Saxo.

Apparently, Ragnar thought 'ill of her trust worthiness'[30] and remembered she had set the 'most savage beasts to destroy him'. This motif is repeated with Ragnar's next love interest, Thora, whose room is guarded by two small snakes, and another woman Alvild, the daughter of a Götaland king, who was given two poisonous serpents that protect her chastity. Strength, fighting skills, cunning and bravery were essential qualities for warriors in the Old Norse sagas on the battlefield and in courtship.

This was not the end of Lagertha's story because she later joined Ragnar in battle as 'her early love still flows deep' against King Harald after the Jutes (from Jutland) and Skanians (from Scania, southern Sweden) had elected him to the throne. With a 'matchless spirit though delicate frame', Lagertha helped Ragnar defeat Harald and returned to her kingdom and with a spear hidden in her gown killed and usurped her husband as the ruler in his kingdom.

Chapter 7

THE EAGLE'S CLAWS

Ælla was Ragnarr's slayer; the crane of battle [eagle] there the company was killed; the ruler's troop destroyed the peace… then the white shield was reddened.

The storm of swords [battle], the shield, the lord's life, than submitted, battle-eager, the boneless in battle fewer, therefore very widely caused the death of Ælla.'

'Hattalykill', author unknown, twelfth century[1]

Thora, the daughter of King Herodd of Sweden, owned snakes which grew so big that they needed a whole ox-carcass to feast on daily. These vipers became such a menace that the king, who had given the snakes to his daughter to raise, declared whoever could kill the beasts would be able to marry her. After divorcing Lagertha, Ragnar desired Thora and embarked on a daring mission to kill the snakes and win Thora's hand.

Heading to the palace alone, Ragnar tied a sword to his side and lashed a spear to his right arm. Two enormous snakes slithered out to face him as the terror-stricken King Herodd and his companions fled. To slay the beasts, Ragnar wore a woollen mantle, a sleeveless garment that is worn over clothes, which had hairy pieces for the thigh to repel the snake bites and then immersed himself in freezing water to harden the shaggy mantle and make it less penetrable. With his shield repelling their teeth and the mantle blocking their poison, Ragnar used a spear to kill the two 'gaping creatures', with his weapon piercing the hearts of both snakes.[2] After slaying the serpents, Ragnar proclaimed: 'I have conquered, cleaving the coiled heath-salmon [snake] to the heart – unless its bale should bite, bringing me sudden death.'[3]

The unusual clothing worn by Ragnar earned him the famous nickname 'Lothbrok', which means shaggy or hairy breeches. Saxo Grammaticus claimed:

'After Ragnar had thus triumphed the king scanned his dress closely, and saw that he was rough and hairy; but, above all, he laughed at the shaggy lower portion of his garb, and chiefly the uncouth aspect of his breeches; so that he gave him in jest the nickname of Lodbrog [Lothbrok].'[4]

In the original saga, Ragnar had worn similar clothing to kill the beasts and romance Thora but boiled them in tar. 'Loðbrók' is clearly a Scandinavian compound word, meaning 'hairy breeches' or 'shaggy trousers', and it is unlikely William of Jumièges invented the nickname because he was not from Scandinavia. The nickname must have stemmed from some lost text or have been an oral tradition in Normandy or England. It is certainly fascinating that this does suggest the nickname became attached to the historical Ragnar.[5]

A simple explanation suggests the name relates to elaborate puffy trousers worn by the real-life Ragnar. During manufacture, weaving techniques called 'roggvar' were used to attach extra fleece to the warp, which were then teased out from the surface to create a tufted effect that would resemble fur. This created an exaggerated and dramatic form of trousers that may have inspired the iconic 'Lothbrok' nickname.[6] Sources such as *Hudud al-'Alam*, by a tenth-century Persian scholar, describe the Rus as wearing extremely large trousers made of cotton fabric that are tucked in above the knee.[7]

Ragnar was believed to be a *sakonungr* (sea-king), meaning a powerful ruler without lands, which were featured prominently in Old Norse sagas and often shared fascinating nicknames. The academic Björn Sigfússon listed these names in the 1930s, which ranged from specific to the individual and occasionally menacing. Some were described by their clothing, which supports the theory that Ragnar gained the nickname through his over-the-top trousers. The sea-kings included:

> *'Atall (fierce, unpeaceable), Beiti (one who manoeuvres), Byrvill (coarse, rude), Eitill (a short, stout fellow), Ekkill (he who sails, fights alone) Geitir (clothed in goat skin) Gorr (little shaver), Horvi (clothed in linen) Hrauónir (destroyer), Reifnir (he who cheers with presents, liberal), Rokkvi (he who goes sails, attacks in the dust).*'[8]

Ragnar boasts of slaying 'eight earls' and 'fifty-one folk battles' before his death at the hands of King Aella in the 'Krákumál'. This epic Skaldic poem also mentions Thora, Herrod and the fall of Eysteinn but other named figures are unidentifiable, and it is unclear if the various conquests in places such as the Hebrides, eastern Baltic and Øresund strait between Sweden and Denmark can be tied to the historical Ragnar.

The *Annals of Xanten* states Ragnar died soon after raiding Paris in 845, but this seems influenced by the monastery of St-Germain-des-Prés, which had been occupied by his forces and produced a highly dubious account of his humiliating death in the aftermath. Saxo's equally elaborate narrative of Ragnar's feats suggests he survived for at least another fifteen years after the Paris raid, which is not mentioned. The account draws parallels with the legendary yarns from Geoffrey of Monmouth, which turned King Arthur into a great conqueror in Britain, at a time when European royal families tried to outdo each other with heroic foundation tales. When writing the *Deeds of the Danes*, Saxo Grammaticus admits his intention was to 'glorify the fatherland'. Monmouth's twelfth-century work is in part based on a Romano-Briton leader called Ambrosius Aurelianus, who fought rebelling Germanic confederates in the fifth century.

Among the numerous conquests, Ragnar avenged the death of his grandfather by killing the Swedish King Fro and was victorious with the Zealanders against Scandinavian rivals from Jutland, Scania and Halland. Ragnar then defeated Harald Klak and the Jutes and eventually drove his rival to Saxony. In 827, Harald Klak was driven from the Danish throne by Godfred's sons, including Horik I, but nothing is known about him until he was killed in 852 by Frisian magnates, where he held Rustringen county, for being a 'potential traitor', according to the *Annals of Fulda*.[9]

Ragnar slew the earls of Pictland and Scotland and handed the provinces of the Southern Isles to Siward (Sigurd) and another son Radbard. Later, Ragnar returned with his sons Bjorn and Eirek and ravaged the Orkney islands and killed a king called Muriel, but his first-born sons with Lagertha, Radbard and Dunwat, according to Saxo Grammaticus, were slain. In Sweden, Ragnar defeated a king Sorle and installed his son Bjorn as the king. He defeated a rebellion from another son Ubbe, and the two were later reconciled when Ivar was granted his Danish kingdom.

Ragnar's other son Hwitserk (Halfdan) became king of the Hellespontines, the historic name of a major waterway, the modern-day Dardanelles, in northern Turkey between Europe and Asia, but was later deceived and executed by a Daxo, who was then spared death and reinstalled as a tributary king by Ragnar. These conquests probably relate to the foundation of the Rus kingdom by Rurik in the latter-ninth century, often associated with the Rorik who ruled in Frisia.

One of the early Rus kings, Askold, who reigned with Dir (Saxo's account gives Daxo a brother and father called Dia) possessed the Old Norse name Haskuldr, which may have become confused with Hvitserk.[10]

With Ivar governing in England, the text by Saxo makes Siward (Sigurd) a king of the Danes after a historical civil war between royals in 854. Sigurd's reign should be placed after the next ruler Horik II because he was first mentioned in the contemporary *Annals of Fulda* as a co-ruler alongside Halfdan in 873.

Many of Ragnar's numerous supposed conquests in western Britain and Scandinavia were unlikely to have been covered by contemporary Anglo-Saxon, Frankish and Irish chronicles. However, Saxo's narrative is far-fetched and cannot be treated as historical record. It is a sprawling tale of genuine Viking Age conflicts, some of which did involve Ragnar or his sons, conflated with Old Norse legends, the deeds of previous semi-legendary characters and turned into an epic story of an all-conquering Danish king and his sons.

If he had survived the Paris aftermath, an ageing Ragnar possibly ruling in Zealand may well have grown jealous of his son's fame and embarked on an ill-advised final expedition before he was captured and killed by Aella of Northumbria, but there's a complete blank in sources from northern Britain at the time. Saxo places Aella in Ireland but his 'Hibernos' (Irishmen) is probably a misreading of 'Humbros', which means 'Northumbrians'.[11] To provide motive seemingly, Saxo claims that Ragnar had killed Hama, the father of Aella, a name shared by a warrior deity in Anglo-Saxon and Norse mythology.

Thirteenth-century chronicler Roger of Wendover wrote that a King Raedwulf of Northumbria died in 844 after he 'fought a battle with the pagans at Aluthelia (which is unidentified) in which himself and general Alfred fell with the greatest part of his forces'. Scholar Andrew Breeze in *British Battles 493–937* believes Aluthelia includes the Old English plural *thelu*, meaning 'planks', and mirrors Auckland's Celtic name of Alclit. He plausibly suggests it means 'plank bridge of Bishop Auckland', situated on the Roman road known as Dere Street.[12] The discovery of old Northumbrian stycas, small copper alloy coins, do include some bearing Raedwulf but revised dating suggests he died around 858, just seven years before the Great Heathen Army arrived. Raedwulf was succeeded by an Ethelred who ruled for four years until 862 and then Osberht before Aella usurped the throne.[13]

While Aella was described as a 'tyrant, not of royal birth' by Asser, a later text from the heartland of Northumbria called the *History of St Cuthbert* said that Aella was the brother of Osberht, but their parentage and links to Raedwulf are unknown.

Even if Ragnar died at Aella's hands, which is not impossible, it is highly unlikely he did so in a pit of venomous snakes because Britain had no such creatures to bring about such a gruesome ending.[14] The tale of Ragnar being killed off by poisonous snakes is clearly ripped from the story of Gunnar in Germanic and Old Norse mythology, which is based on a historical king of Burgundy in modern France in the fifth century being murdered by the notorious Atilla the Hun. In the *Prose Edda*, Gunnar is thrown into a snake pit after being captured by Atli:

> *'Gunnarr he caused to be cast into a den of serpents, but a harp was brought secretly to Gunnarr and he struck it with his toes, his hands being bound, he played the harp so that all the serpents fell asleep, saving only one adder, which glided over him and gnawed into the cartilage of his breast-bone so far that her head sank within the wound, and she clove to his liver till he died.'*[15]

Gunnar and Hogni, who are brothers and Burgundian warriors in heroic Germanic legend, had Sigurd the Dragon Slayer killed and his grief-stricken wife Brunhild, the sister of Atli, took her own life, but before her death, she prophesied retribution for his murders, which Atli and the snakes delivered.

This element of 'Ragnar's Saga' that features Aslaug, whose parents are Brunhild and Sigurd, was an updated version of this earlier myth, with the main protagonists in both slaying serpents, while Ragnar perishes at the hands of snakes as does Gunnar.

Most snake-like beasts in Old Norse sagas were called *ormr*, which translates as 'worm' or 'snake', and the word may have come to represent all limbless creatures. Moments before his death, Ragnar says 'I never expected that worms would kill me'. This implies Ragnar was reflecting on the irony because he killed snakes at the start of the saga or how the soil with worms awaits the dead, according to the academic Kornelia Lasota.[16]

Snakes feature prominently in Old Norse tales from the monstrous Jörmungandr, which can wrap around the entire human realm of Midgard and still bite its tail. The dangerous dragon Nidhogg, which dwells under the root of the world tree Yggdrasill, gnaws on people going to hell for crimes such as murder, adultery or oath breaking. When Sigurd mortally wounds the dragon Fáfnir, it is revealed that the dying monster possesses an extraordinary amount of knowledge about the cosmos. While clearly feared in Old Norse cultures, snakes were seen as an inseparable part of the universe, crucial to human existence.

In perhaps the most infamous part of the tradition, Aella suffered a brutal 'blood eagle' death at the hands of Ragnar's sons. His body would have been slashed open with his ribcage smashed apart and his lung pulled out and sprayed across his torso in a macabre representation of an eagle. Different versions emerged with 'Ragnar's Saga' claiming Ivar directed the horrific ritual, while Saxo wrote that Bjorn and Sigurd ordered the ritual killing and afterwards salted the 'mangled wounds'.

This gory death must have stemmed from a misunderstanding of a poem by Sigvat Þórðarson, also known as Sigvat the Skald, who composed the 'Knútsdrápa' ('Drápa of Knút') in honour of the Danish and English king Cnut the Great in the eleventh century. In the poem, he wrote '*Ok Ellu bak,/at, lét, hinn's sat,/Ívarr, ara,/ Iórvík, skorit.*', which has been translated as: 'And Ella's back, at had the one who dwelt, Ivarr with eagle, York cut.'[17]

After the stanza was published in 1038, the belief that Ivar had personally carved the 'blood eagle' into Aella began to enjoy widespread circulation. However, the 'ara' for eagle signifies a killing and represents how they are carrion beasts, a pale bird with red claws that is slashing on the back of the fallen Aella, according to the academic Roberta Frank.[18] Skaldic verses from the Viking Age regularly speak of warriors falling under the talons of eagles, which stalk battlefields to feast on the dead, along with wolves and ravens.

Snorri Sturluson's version of 'Ynglingatal' describes the body of Swedish king Ottar the Brave being 'torn' by the 'eagle's claw', while Torf-Einarr in his saga ponders over whose 'lot it will be to stand under the eagle's claws'. As eagles were used in multiple kennings to signify death, the stanza is in effect representing how

Aella is dramatically reduced to prey for an eagle, gripped by its claws, after Ivar's great victory. A misinterpretation of the kenning saw the myth of a blood-eagle rite gain notoriety. The contemporary *Anglo-Saxon Chronicle* makes no mention of the barbaric act.

So, what really happened at York? The Great Heathen Army departed along the River Humber towards York in 866, which was then the main city of the southern part of the Northumbrian kingdom known as Deira. The kingdom extended to the Firth of Lothian, with its northern part known as Bernicia covering the area up to the firth above the River Tees.

Northmen deliberately targeted the important religious festival of All Saints Day on 1 November 866 when the city was full of people and wealth. Vikings probably arrived by stealth along the River Ouse and slaughtered the inhabitants who were completely unprepared. King Aella fled the city but later reconciled with his brother Osberht, and they gathered their forces, which included eight earls according to Symeon of Durham, for an assault on York, which was the great former Roman city of Eboracum.[19]

Outer Roman walls, which have stood the test of time and included the stunning 30ft-multangular tower, enclosed a rectangular space of around fifty acres on both sides of the River Ouse. The fortress had been designed with a grid of streets and buildings and four timber gate openings in the wall, which were entrances to the main roads leading to and from the city.[20]

Given Aella and Osberht waited four months until they marched on the city having gathered troops and supplies it is likely the Northmen had prepared various earthworks, reinforced the weakened old Roman defences and devised a cunning strategy for the inevitable fightback because there are numerous references to their surprise attacks and fake retreats.[21]

Individuals within Northumbria may have been conspiring against them as well because the twelfth-century chronicler Geoffrey Gaimar claimed the wife of a local named Beorn the Butescarl had been raped by Osberht and he was helping the Northmen.[22] When recounting the Battle of York, the *Fragmentary Annals of Ireland* also blames the defeat on the 'deceit and treachery of a young man of his own (Aella's) household'.[23]

Vikings appeared to flee as the army of Aella and Osberht approached, and according to Asser, the 'Christians, perceiving their flight and the terror they were in, determined to follow them within the very ramparts of the town, and to demolish the wall'.[24] As part of a ruse, the Vikings probably left an opening in a section of the Roman wall for the Northumbrians to smash down and rush through. Once inside, the tables turned decisively. Hiding behind woodworks, Vikings sprung out on the wave of Northumbrians who were now entrapped inside the Roman fortress.

'When the Christians had broken down the wall, as they proposed, and a great part of them had entered the city at the same time as the pagans, the latter, urged by distress and

Bootham Bar in York, where the army of Ivar and Ubbe lay in wait for the Northumbrians, was one of the four main entrances to the Roman fortress.

necessity, made a fierce assault upon them,' wrote Symeon of Durham in his *Historia Regum* (*History of Kings*), who places the battle on 21 March on the Friday before Palm Sunday.[25] While the Vikings often sought to avoid large-scale pitched battles, the chaotic and bloody street fighting that unfolded suited them down to the ground.

Swords, axes and spears were the favoured weapon of choice for Viking warriors based on grave finds in Scandinavia.[26] When launching into a battle, a Viking would either be clutching a round wooden shield, with a diameter of about 60cm and an iron boss, in the same hand as their spears or strapped to their backs so they could use both hands.[27] Depending on their favoured weaponry, a scabbard case for the sword and a small knife known as a *saexe* were suspended from their waist belt. Swords were mainly wielded by nobles and kings, who were typically adorned in chain mail suits, and favoured doubled-edged, pattern-welded swords were imported from the Rhineland, with the hilt, or handle, plated with tin, copper, silver and gold. These prized weapons were typically around a metre long, with the blade measuring 70–90cm and the hilt covering 12–18cms.[28] Vikings typically wore round top helmets hammered from one sheet of metal, which could feature a naval or ear guard. Some were clad in an upper-body armour known in Old Norse as *spangabrynja,* which were oblong iron plates laced together with straps. Perhaps their most feared weapon was the axe, which was either narrow, broad-bladed or

Artist's impression of the fearsome weaponry and armour of Viking warriors who clashed with the forces of King Aella. (Laurent Cusolito)

bearded in shape.[29] Most Vikings would have been armed with a spear with a winged blade that was designed in such a way it could easily be pulled out after wounding the enemy. Ivar's and Ubbe's forces brutally cut down the trapped Northumbrians, who were used to ordered shield-walls and packed formations.

Recalling the slaughter, Asser told of how the Vikings:

> *'impelled by grief and necessity, made a fierce sally upon them, slew them, routed them, and cut them down, both within and without the walls. In that battle almost all the Northumbrian troops and both the kings [Aella and Osberht] were slain; the remainder, who escaped, made peace with the heathen.'*[30]

The deaths of both kings was a fatal blow for Northumbria, and the Vikings immediately inherited the established system of government and tribute. A puppet ruler Ecgberht beholden to the Vikings was installed as ruler beyond the River Tyne. Just over 300 years earlier, the Anglian kingdom of Bernicia, which later formed one half of Northumbria with Deira, first captured the fort on the site of the spectacular coastal fortress of Bamburgh Castle and set about wrestling power away from Brittonic rivals. One early-seventh-century king, Ethelfrith, had 'conquered more territories of the Britons', either making them tributary or driving them out, than any other Anglo-Saxon ruler at the time, recalled the famous eighth-century monk and scholar Bede.

While Northumbria was eclipsed by Mercia from the eighth century, the Viking capture of the kingdom must have sent shockwaves through the land.

A kingdom that survived on and off warfare and plotting against Wessex, Mercia, the Picts and the Strathclyde Britons for 350-plus years had now fallen. Not since Ethelfrith had the balance of power been so dramatically upended in the north.

Icelandic scholars writing centuries later recognised this had been a spectacular feat for the sons of Ragnar, and one of the greatest triumphs of the Viking Age. Unsurprisingly, they sought to link their patron kings to these glories through sometimes dubious lineages.

Archaeological traces of this turbulent ninth-century period in York have been scarce, suggesting it was abandoned. One rushed grave of a man aged 36–45, who was dumped unceremoniously in a pit in the late-ninth century, may have been a victim of the Great Heathen Army.

The famous Viking trading settlement of Jorvik (meaning 'wild boar bay'), derived from the Anglo-Saxon name of Eoforwic for the city, did not emerge for at least another 25 years because the house and building plots of its centre at Coppergate were not laid out until after 900.[31]

Vikings overwintered in Nottingham during 867/68, where a force of Mercians and Wessex had headed to face them but eventually made peace without a confrontation. The Great Heathen Army was likely based on and off around Aldwark, around 12 miles north-west of York, which stems from the Old English *ald* (old) and *weorc* (fort), where a remarkable collection of more than 7,000 items has been discovered. These include more than 290 weights, fifteen fragments of the Middle Eastern coins known as a dirham, ninety Northumbrian stycas and more than seventy silver items including hacksilver and ingots. Ideally placed next to the navigable River Ure, the site threw up evidence of craftworking and metalworking, covering an area of roughly 30 hectares.[32] Life within the Viking winter camps, focused on a massive site at Torksey, will be featured in Chapter Thirteen.

The contrast between Aella and another victim of the Great Heathen Army, King Edmund of East Anglia, could not have been greater. Resulting from Aella's behaviour and demise, the death of 'nearly all the English people could thus be blamed on the king (Aella)', claimed the *History of St Cuthbert*.[33] Symeon of Durham wrote that Osberht and Aella had 'paid the penalty' for taking away six churches, including Tynemouth, Crayke and Billingham, from St Cuthbert and his followers.[34]

A selection of the gold and silver ingots found at the Aldwark Viking camp near York. (Julian Richards/Gary Johnson)

By the early-eleventh century reign of king Cnut, the death of Aella was clearly hugely popular among the Danish nobility, evidenced by its mention in the famous poem honouring Cnut, because they championed the victory to justify their imperium over the English.

Traditions about Aella's horrific punishment developed after a simple misinterpretation of a kenning in a stanza honouring King Cnut. Such a brutal death fitted with the depiction of Vikings as blood-thirsty pagans, and it provided a dishonourably fitting end for the unpopular Aella, face down on the battlefield being picked apart by wild beasts instead of receiving the lavish sendoff reserved for such figures.[35]

A fable relating to the earlier Norse mythological figure Sigurd Dragon Slayer, perhaps stemming from confusion because the father of the potential real-life Ragnar shared the same name in the *Ragnarsdrapa*, added the second key element of the tale. Skalds told of how Ragnar was killed in a snake pit, the same fate that befell Gunnar who killed Sigurd Dragon Slayer, before his sons sought vengeance with a 'blood eagle'. The legend then became set in stone. Ragnar Lothbrok's death had been emphatically avenged.

Chapter 8

HOUSE OF MUNSÖ

Thus he [Odin] established by law that all dead men should be burned, and their belongings laid with them upon the pile. Thus, said he, everyone will come to Valhalla with the riches he had with him upon the pile…It was their faith that the higher the smoke arose in the air, the higher he would be raised whose pile it was; and the richer he would be, the more property that was consumed with him.

Ynglinga saga, Snorri Sturluson, 1225[1]

Dwarfed by these mysterious royal mounds at Old Uppsala, the people walking alongside appear as miniature figures from a distance. Measuring up to 29–32ft (5–10m) high, these gigantic barrows retain their prestige and mystique. The scale was designed to illustrate the superiority of those buried underneath. They were the giants, gods and goddesses among men and women, and they demanded a final resting place big enough to accommodate them.

Many believed the mounds housed from west to east – Thor, Odin and Freyr or descendants of Freyr namely Aun, Egils and Adils, the Ynglinga kings who had divine power from this ancestry. According to Skaldic poems, every new king who ascended had ritual intercourse with a mythical woman who represented the land they protected, modelled on Freyr's marriage with the giantess Gerd. If the union bore fruit, the animals multiplied, the field produced a great harvest and the fishermen prospered.[2] As the god of agriculture, Freyr had the greatest impact on people's lives with power over the rain, the golden grain, the sun and fertility.[3]

Old Uppsala's centre of power emerged in a land grab by a warrior elite after the devastating Volcanic Winter and Justinian Plague. The royal mounds were created around 600 alongside a large wooden palace and two monumental rows of posts, with a large industrious settlement, housing up to fifty farmsteads, supplying the monarchy with their every need. These posts may have marked off a ritual horse-racing arena, where the fastest animals were sacrificed and the area of the 'Thing of all Swedes'; the all-powerful governing assembly.[4]

The king's realm had no fixed boundaries but was based on alliances with local chieftains, often confirmed with gifts such as gold rings, and the overlord kings

Old Uppsala's famous historical site with its three gigantic barrows in the background.

were expected to be the most generous of all. The Viking Age warrior culture has its roots at Old Uppsala.

Famously, Adam of Bremen spoke of a pagan temple at Old Uppsala and sacrifices to Thor in the case of plague and famine, to Odin when war broke out and to Freyr if marriages are celebrated. Every nine years, a great feast would be held in which they offered 'nine heads' of males:

> *'The bodies they hang in the sacred grove that adjoins the temple. Now that grove is so sacred in the eyes of the heathen that each and every tree in it is believed to be divine because of the death or purification of the victims. Even dogs and horses hang there with men and a Christian told me that he had seen seventy-two bodies suspended promiscuously.'*[5]

While the grove's location has not been identified, sacrifices were regularly made to bridge the gap between the living and the dead. Animal bones discovered there include goose, mallard, peregrine falcon, carp, bream, grey sparrow, wolves, marten, Eurasian eagle-owl, salmon, wild boar, squirrel, red fox, reindeer, dogs, cats, pike and herring. Everyone was cremated and buried with items for the afterlife, including food, household utensils, weapons, ornaments and pets as companions.[6]

More than 3,000 burial mounds were formed at Old Uppsala but only a fraction including the royal mounds survive today. Epic funerals could have lasted for days and almost certainly involved a long ritual procession where the animals were sacrificed. A log building burial chamber, with a floor space of 5m by 10m, was built on the clay floor. Ritually, the body was laid on the chamber with the grave goods, and then the pyre was lit and would burn spectacularly. Remains were collected several days later and placed in an urn, which was put into a hole dug into the ground. An oval cairn with large stones was created over the hole with a diameter of around 15m (49ft) and then finally a massive mound was formed above the cairn.[7]

Around 60 miles away, there was another monumental barrow formed after a similar process, which according to legend housed the real-life Bjorn Ironside. After the notorious Mediterranean raid, Bjorn's fate remains a mystery. William of Jumièges believed Bjorn suffered a shipwreck around 861/62 in which he lost several ships and had 'great difficulty' being received in port in England. Bjorn then went to Frisia, which is closely associated with his brother Ubbe and the Great Heathen Army, where he died at an unknown date.[8]

A shipwreck was attested by the early-14th century historian Ibn Idhari, from the Maghreb region of North Africa, who was drawing on earlier texts. He told of how Bjorn's Viking fleet 'lost more than forty' of its sixty-two ships in a storm before they fought against the Emir Mohammed's fleet on the coast of Sidona, a city in modern-day Lebanon, where they lost two more ships 'laden with great riches'.[9]

Writing around a similar time as Idhari, al-Nuwayri, an Egyptian Muslim historian, told of the same battle with the emir in which they lost four ships, two of which were torched and the other two fell into the hands of the caliphate. Vikings began to fight 'furiously', and a 'great multitude' of Muslims were killed according to al-Nuwayri.[10]

The accounts give weight to Bjorn Ironside's fate, who is never referenced again in Frankish or Anglo-Saxon sources from the time. However, William of Jumièges is the sole source of Bjorn's death, and Old Norse sagas tell a different story. The 'Tale of Ragnar's Sons' has Bjorn joining his brothers Ivar, Hvitserk (Halfdan) and Sigurd in killing Aella and avenging his father. Afterwards, Bjorn returned home and took the kingdom of Uppsala and all Sweden and their dependencies.

Saxo Grammaticus told of how Bjorn had led the forces and slew the Swedish king Sorle, who had usurped the throne after the previous king Herodd (Thora's father) and 'robbed' Ragnar's sons of their inheritance. For his valour, which had earned the infamous Ironside moniker, Ragnar 'presented Bion (Bjorn) with the lordship of Sweden for his conspicuous bravery and service'.[11]

Later after the death of Ragnar, the same source tells of how Bjorn (Biorn in texts) and Sigurd (Siward in texts), led the invasion of Northumbria and were responsible for the infamous 'blood eagle' murder.

'Siward and Biorn came up with a fleet of 400 ships, and with open challenge declared war against the king [Aella]. This they did at the

*appointed time; and when they had captured him, they ordered the
figure of an eagle to be cut in his back, rejoicing to crush their most
ruthless foe by marking him with the cruellest of birds. Not satisfied
with imprinting a wound on him, they salted the mangled flesh. Thus
Aella was done to death.'*[12]

Bjorn, along with Sigurd, returned to his kingdom after slaying Aella and is only
mentioned once more. Saxo's depiction of Bjorn seems inspired by an earlier Bjorn
associated with a legendary Danish king Fridleif, who was also famed for his fighting
skills. Notably, Saxo's Danish king Fridleif had a brother called Halfdan and a character
of the same name is also a son of Ragnar from his first union with Lagertha.[13] This
storytelling method is repeated with Ubbe, whose indestructibility on the battlefield
mirrors that of 'Ubbe the Frisian', mentioned earlier by Saxo, who fought in the Battle
of Brávellir and was only defeated after being struck with 144 arrows.

While Saxo's narrative can be dismissed to a large degree, it does include
numerous historical events. Most likely drawing from brief references, Saxo
fleshed out the stories of Ragnar and his sons by repeating the deeds of previous
characters and motifs such as beasts guarding the properties of maidens.

Undoubtedly, however, the real-life Bjorn Ragnarsson gained widespread
notoriety after raiding further into unchartered lands than any fellow Norse fleet
before. Their raid became 'the most famous tale in the Norse tongue' proclaimed
the 'Tale of Ragnar's Sons'.[14]

The earlier 'Ragnar's Saga' boasted they became so famous that 'there was not
a child, no matter how little, who didn't know their names'.[15] For the people of
modern-day Italy, Morocco and Spain that encountered Bjorn's fleet, whose loved
ones were slain or carted off to a lifetime of slavery, they were no doubt simply
known for the horrors they inflicted.

By the late-twelfth century, a king Harald Kesja of Denmark, according to the
Knýtlinga saga, had named his son Bjorn Ironside in honour of the real-life warrior,
which showed the tale was well known in royal circles and considered heroic.[16]

The *Hervarar saga* (the saga of Hervör and Heidrek), a thirteenth-century
Icelandic text about the legendary sword Tyrfingr, claimed that after King Ragnar's
death Bjorn 'inherited Sweden' and had been the ancestor of future kings. This saga
claims the sons of Bjorn were Eirik (Erik) and Refil, who were a warlord and sea-
king respectively. Refil's son Eirik (Erik) inherited the kingdom and was a 'great
warrior and very mighty king'. Eirik's sons were Onund of Uppsala and Björn, who
ruled after Eirik and divided the kingdom between themselves.[17]

According to the saga: 'King Björn built the place called Barrow, and he was
called Björn of the Barrow, Bragi the skald dwelt with him.'[18] This is a reference to
the massive Nordic Bronze Age tumulus, known as King Björn's Mound, dated to
1,000 BC near Uppsala, which is 22ft (7m) high and measures 147ft (45m) wide.

As discussed in Chapter Two, Bragi Boddason had composed the *Ragnarsdrápa* (*Ragnar's Poem*) at some point in the ninth century, which could be a contemporary reference to the historical Ragnar Lothbrok. After angering King Bjorn, Bragi had written the poem, which was a pictorial representation of various myths and saga tales found on a shield that had been presented to him by Ragnar. According to the *Skáldatal* (catalogue of poets) by Snorri Sturluson, Bragi had also been a court poet for Eysteinn Beli, who was killed by Ragnar's sons and known as King Eysteinn, as well as skald for Ragnar and Bjorn.[19]

Given the numerous references to Bragi, he is considered historical, but the Swedish dynasty of Bjorn Ironside is generally disregarded by scholars, and the first recognised king of Sweden is Eric the Victorious, who reigned around 970 and was another supposed ancestor of Bjorn Ironside.

The tale could have stemmed from the *Vita Anskarri*, which was composed by Saint Rimbert. When Anskar first arrived at Birka in 829, a king Bjorn had allowed him to preach the Christian religion in his kingdom, which was centred around the Lake Mälaren valley and possibly extended to Uppsala. When St Anskar left, Bjorn had given him letters for the Emperor Louis the Pious 'in characters fashioned after the Swedish custom', believed to be the ancient runes alphabet. It is an intriguing detail highlighting how some Scandinavian kings were communicating at diplomatic level with Frankish counterparts using runes and opens the possibility of undiscovered runic texts that document royal affairs.

Around a decade later, Rimbert mentions there was a King Anund, possibly the Onund from the *Hervarar saga*, who had been expelled from the kingdom and was living among the Danes. This Anund launched an invasion with the Danes, but he accepted 100 pounds of silver from Birka residents to prevent the attack.[20] Afterwards, around the year 851, the same text refers to a king Olof who had succeeded Anund and was ruling over Birka. The text also refers to an earlier king called Eric, the predecessor and possible father of the Bjorn who welcomed Anskar. The compiler of the *Hervarar saga* may have drawn early kings from Rimbert's account before the historical Bjorn Ironside's known timeframe between 856–62 and used them as his descendants.

One academic, Birger Nerman, claimed the *Hervarar saga* list of kings were all real people, derived from Rimbert in the case of Eric's sons Bjorn (who Anskar met in 829) and Anund, and Bjorn's son Olof. In his suggested pedigree, Nerman also adds another Eric before Olof and a Bjorn after him in the same timeframe as Bjorn Ironside – but Nerman doesn't make a connection. According to Nerman, this new dynasty appears to have been founded by a Bjorn around the late-eighth century and relocated from Uppsala to the Birka region. Later rulers were buried on Adelsö at the Hovgården site, where three large barrows are named 'Kungshögar' (king's mound).[21]

Bjorn's supposed role as the founder of the House of Munsö emerged with a legend that the kings of Uppsala in the ninth century transferred their stronghold from Uppsala to the island of Munsö in the Lake Mälaren.[22] This is based on how Rimbert described the kings as ruling near Birka, which is also located within the great lake, and the massive burial site on the island of Munsö contains more than forty barrows – the biggest and most prominent of which is known as Björn Järnsidas Hög (Bjorn Ironside's mound).

The island of Helgö, just 9 miles from Munsö, became a centre of trade and crafts between the fifth and ninth centuries, with workshops for goldsmiths, bronze founding and bead-making, backed by the Uppsala dynasty. Finds have included a famous sixth-century Buddha statuette from North India.[23] During the eight century, there was a royal manor at Adelsö, an island in the middle of Lake Mälaren opposite Munsö, most likely housing a king of the Ynglinga dynasty from Uppsala.[24] Birka on Björkö island off the southern edge of Adelsö was founded around 750 and the proximity to Munsö is striking.

Many antiquarians who became fascinated with the Anglo-Saxons and Vikings took to associating historical landmarks with figures from the age, often near where they lived, with little actual evidence to back it up. One eighteenth-century Swedish antiquarian, Johan Peringskiöld, who extensively studied ancient monuments and runes, associated the biggest mound on Munsö with Bjorn Ironside.

When walking towards the mound from the west via a mud track next to a few small farm properties, the barrow is a sight to behold at the top of a steep bank. Sitting on the crest on a very steep bank, overlooking Lake Mälaren, the barrow takes pride of the place within the burial park on Munsö, which contains some 45 burial mounds measuring between 5m (16ft) and 20m (65ft) in diameter, and around 150 ancient remains and 104 round stone settings.[25] As you edge up the slope through a woodland that falls steeply towards the lake, the scale of the barrow is unmistakable and it dominates the landscape, measuring 20m (65ft) in diameter and standing at 5m (16ft) high. Whoever was buried in the mound, was high ranking in society and clearly a king or chieftain.

Although far smaller than the Old Uppsala mounds, it is the barrow's unique position which stands out. While the view is now largely shielded by trees and some are sprouting from the barrow itself, as the woods are almost certainly much younger, it was a spectacular monument from the lake more than 1,000 years ago. It does have parallels to the Sutton Hoo royal burial site in England, where the aim was patently for the traffic along the River Deben to marvel at the centrepiece mound from afar, long before the current woods were present. This focal-point mound at Sutton Hoo was believed to be occupied by the seventh-century king Raedwald from the Wuffingas dynasty, which feature in *Beowulf* and likely hailed from Sweden.

Fragments of a mysterious runestone can be found on top of the supposed Bjorn Ironside mound. Part of the message on the broken-up runes reads '[r]kutr þaiʀ ... ... atu 'ok| |ku[þ].' It is said to include mention of the 'spirit' and 'the Gods'.[26]

This huge mound on the island of Munsö is known as Björn Järnsidas Hög (Bjorn Ironside's mound).

According to Nordic people, runestones emerged several hundred years before the Viking Age and were the gods' creation. In mythology, the runes derive from Odin with the *Hávamál*, which is part of the *Poetic Edda*, telling of how Odin sacrificed himself on the world tree and hung for nine nights and nine days without any food or drink and is rewarded with the gifts of runes.[27]

The runes were actually a derivation of the ancient language systems of the Mediterranean, particularly Latin. Their creators changed the letters and made new ones adapted to the phonology of their language. Around 800, a runic alphabet of sixteen characters, known as the Younger Futhark, developed from a previous system, which had twenty-four.

Runes were often inscribed in stone and used as heartfelt monuments to the dead and used to state ownership. They were also found in jewellery and on objects in which the creator has carved their name to show who owns the item. During the eleventh century, as Christianity spread through Scandinavia, some 2,800 inscriptions were known, which often featured prayers and crosses.[28] One of these runestones was the one that now sits on top of the Bjorn Ironside mound dated to the same period, after Bjorn's time, and was moved to its current position from another spot nearby.

In 1846, a Swiss archaeologist Frédéric Troyon investigated twelve barrows on Munsö, including the central mound linked to Bjorn Ironside, and described how two urns had been found in the graves but were not preserved.[29] His investigation found the dead people and animals were burned on a pyre at a different location, as with Old Uppsala, because there were no obvious signs of the fire's impact on the ground surface. Scattered remains of a horse, cat, sheep, cow, dog and chicken were uncovered. Dogs would have accompanied their master to the grave for the afterlife, but Troyon believed the cat's presence was unusual. Commenting on Bjorn's supposed mound, Troyon's report said:

> *'Between the stones and the sand in the lower layer was a thick layer of charcoal and ash in which I found only traces of iron and a few bronze fragments but no trace of any urn. Among the animal bones were a tooth and femur of a sheep, ribs and a femur of a cow.'*[30]

Traces of iron would suggest that the occupant had been buried with weapons. Husby farm owner Charles Wallöf had told Troyon that 'long swords, urns and spears' had been found in the mounds, which must have included the biggest one associated with Bjorn. Troyon noted that as the layer of remains was high in the barrow, they dug down further without finding anything else but sand. With regards to the timeframe, Troyon believed that they should be placed between the seventh and eighth centuries, long before Bjorn Ironside:

> *'Judging by the character of the objects found, they seem to go back to the last period of paganism in Sweden, I would say before any Christian elements had yet penetrated these regions. It might even be possible that they are somewhat older if one takes into account the coarseness of the pottery, the shortcomings in the pottery art and the simplicity of the jewellery, when comparing these objects with others from a somewhat later period, such as those found together with foreign coins.'*[31]

Notably, traders heading to and from Birka, which emerged from 750, would have travelled along the opposite side of Munsö via Lake Mälaren and bypassed the barrow. When Troyon applied for the permit to excavate, he was informed the supposed Bjorn Ironside mound had been damaged and previously excavated. He concentrated on specific damaged mounds.

Another eighteenth-century Stockholm-based antiquarian Dr Anders Blad claimed previously that a ninth-century Slavonian coin was removed from the tumulus linked to Bjorn Ironside.[32] Blad pointed to how Estonian and Slavic traders were visiting Birka, and he noted the coins were given to the Varangians, the elite military unit of the Byzantine empire from the late-tenth century that was made up primarily of Scandinavian mercenaries. Slavonian grivna coins were long and thin silver bars, also known as ingots, used as currency in Kievan Rus. Blad also revealed

Bjorn's legendary burial mound is the largest and most prominent of more than forty other barrows, situated at the top of a ridge overlooking the lake.

that a cameo, typically a raised carved relief image on a shell or hardstone, from the Boeotia region of ancient Greece was discovered in the supposed Bjorn Ironside barrow. It consisted of a 'fiery yellow' steatite rock, which Blad suggested had been cut in the ninth century or slightly before. This lavish silver cameo depicted Cupid with a quiver container as he treads on a Catharus (sea shell) with what Blad presumed was the mountains of Helicon and Cithaeron either side, which feature in Greek mythology and are sacred to Bacchus, the Greek god of fertility, wine and theatre. A rich cameo found in the western royal mound at Uppsala suggested the occupant had considerable wealth.

Nerman also referenced the finds but argued their existence was 'extremely doubtful' and the association with Bjorn Ironside stemmed from 'literary speculation'. He claimed the mound on Munsö was possibly once called 'Björnshögen', meaning Bjorn's mound, as far back as 1741 but sceptically linked it to an earlier Bjorn who he believed founded the Birka-based dynasty around 800.[33]

Expectations are tempered when approaching the barrow on Munsö because the information board nearby states despite Peringskiöld's claims 'there is no real evidence that Bjorn lived or that he was buried here'.

While the Bjorn Ironside of the Ragnar Lothbrok legend was based on a real-life person documented in Frankish sources between 856 and 858, who had led an infamous expedition to the Mediterranean, the association with the mound on

Munsö is far less secure in comparison. Given the occupant must have been a king or chieftain, it is certainly interesting that Blad believed the cameo and coins could date to the ninth century when Bjorn lived. Unfortunately, there is no mention in his report whether the cameo or coin were preserved, and these finds are not mentioned in a catalogue of items from Blad that is held by the Swedish Historical Museum.[34,35]

Despite the understandable scepticism surrounding the House of Munsö, one understated point is Halfdan and Sigurd were actual kings in the Danish realm as stated in the 'Tale of Ragnar's Sons', which is mentioned in the same breath as Bjorn ruling Swedish territories. After the capture of York, Bjorn may have returned home and simply lived out his remaining days ruling around Birka. The list of early Swedish kings after Olof in the 850s up until Eric Victorious more than a century later is a source of mystery.

A core part of the Ragnar Lothbrok tradition is his marriage to a Swedish princess, although Thora is from Gautland, and his sons capturing a Swedish kingdom. Perhaps Bjorn's mother was in fact a Swedish princess, which would explain the tradition, but it is not something that can be proven. While Bjorn's name was absent from the contemporary Anglo-Saxon texts, no Great Heathen Army leader was named before the Battle of Ashdown in 871.

Bjorn may have also died a few years before the Great Heathen Army arrived or later in Frisia as William of Jumièges claimed. He would have become a Viking celebrity overnight following the Mediterranean expedition but died soon afterwards, mirroring his father's fate after Paris. Later saga writers, who often wanted to connect whichever Scandinavian royal dynasty to Ragnar Lothbrok, then constructed epic conquests based on those of previous mythical warriors and other Old Norse legends because there were few actual sources about the real-life people, despite their prestige.

In 863, a year or so after Bjorn Ironside returned from the Mediterranean, Danes sailed up the Rhine in January towards Cologne and sacked Dorestad in Frisia, according to the *Annals of St Bertin*. The Northmen took refuge on an island near Xanten, a town in modern Germany next to the Rhine, where they were attacked by Lothair II who ruled in Middle Francia. Eventually, the Danes departed in April on the advice of Rorik, the Viking ruler of large parts of Frisia. Perhaps Bjorn met his demise at this point, although it is strange that his death was not recorded by any Frankish annals, particularly as he was a leader known to chroniclers, and they normally recorded the slayings of prominent Vikings.[36]

William of Jumièges may have known Bjorn headed to Frisia but nothing beyond that and assumed he died there, mirroring how Ethelward placed Ivar's death four years too early after he disappeared from Anglo-Saxon sources.

Many legends grew around the potential mound of Bjorn Ironside, such as that it was so large it could be viewed from the other side of the lake. Supposedly, the

Fans of the *Vikings* TV series have left tributes on top of the barrow next to the runestone, including a photo of Bjorn's epic stand against the Rus army.

dead would come to pay their respect at night, and their revelry could be heard for miles around. Offerings continue to be left next to the runestone, including on my visit a fake sword and sheep heads, beer cans and even wooden combs. A framed photo showing the epic scene from the *Viking* series when a mortally wounded Bjorn faces down his brothers Ivar and Hvitserk (Halfdan) and the Rus army alone has been left there. The legendary figure of Bjorn Ironside in fiction and reality was the epitome of a Viking warrior – ambitious, fearless, adventurous and almost indestructible.

Chapter 9

THE MARTYR AND THE WOLF

Thus, while the words of prayer were still on his lips, the executioner, sword in hand, deprived the king of life, striking off his head with a single blow. And so, on the 20th November, as an offering to God of sweetest savour, Eadmund [Edmund], after he had been tried in the fire of suffering, rose with the palm of victory and the crown of righteousness, to enter as king and martyr the assembly of the court of heaven.

Abbo of Fleury, 985–87[1]

Metal detectors stumbled upon a spectacular find in 1994 highlighting the Viking presence in East Anglia when a tiny 4cm Thor pendant hammer was unearthed in South Lopham in Norfolk, around 11 miles from Thetford.

With stamped triangle shapes, each with three pellets, the decorated gold alloy pendant shares the same design with silver versions found at Sibton in Suffolk, Swithland in Leicestershire and in the Cuerdale and Goldsborough Hoards.[2] These pendants were worn as amulets by Vikings to invoke Thor's protection and were a tell-tale sign of connections and beliefs as much as crucifixes, inspired by the Christian population wearing cross pendants.[3]

One academic study identified forty-five cases of Thor hammers of which most are associated with the Great Heathen Army and suggest worship of Thor was widespread.[4] In the ninth century, the cult of Thor became so powerful that supporters were burning down statues to Odin at Uppsala.[5] A massive concentration lay in East Anglia, a metal-detecting hotspot, where eleven have been discovered; ten of those in Norfolk and the silver one from Sibton in Suffolk. Four are made of lead, which was a cheaper material, but most are silver, mirroring the colour of any freshly cast hammer, and they often feature geometrical punch-stamp patterns. The most spectacular was a pendant from Great Witchingham, which had been inlaid with a gold filigree wire.[6]

While Odin was all powerful in Norse mythology, his son Thor was the most respected and worshipped. Lightning represents the swift bolt of his famed hammer Mjolnir, and the thunderous sound of storms are sparked by his chariot as it roared across the sky pulled by his two goats, Tanngnjóstr (teeth-grinder) and Tanngrisnir

Thor hammer pendants such as this one found at South Lopham became a signature of the Great Heathen Army. (Norfolk Museums Service)

(teeth-barer). Matching Jupiter and Hercules, Thor is armed with a destructive thunderbolt but while terrible in might only evil beings had to fear his wrath. For Thor was the 'Son of Earth', the most human of all gods, racing across the world to battle giants and sea monsters for humankind, displaying unrivalled power and unflinching bravery.

Thor was a companion to the sailor and fisherman, who prayed that he would ensure a trip free from perilous storms. In Thor's fishing adventure the 'Lay of Hymir', he kills the biggest oxen to use as bait, snares two gigantic whales and then has a brutal struggle with Jörmungandr, who was also known as the fearsome Midgard Serpent.[7]

As Thor desperately tried to hoist the beast from the waves, his companion, the giant Hymir, became fearful as water rushed up and onto the boat and cut the line. Eventually, the oceanic beast escaped his clutches and disappeared below. Crestfallen by the failure, Thor struck Hymir in anger who plunged overboard. This shows Thor could be human after all, which is one reason why he was so revered. Jörmungandr and Thor were fated to kill each other at Ragnarök.

Mythological creatures and gods adorn Viking jewellery and weaponry as a badge of honour in the face of a Christian population. Pagan deities were important to their belief system and offered strength as they embarked on foreign conquest.

One striking Viking metalwork design discovered in East Anglia features a warrior mounted on a horse being greeted by a female presenting the man with a drinking cup or horn. Beneath the horse is a chequered item, which probably represents a gaming board.

Similar examples have sprung up in the Peterborough area, in Bylaugh in Norfolk and at Lake Tisso in Denmark. These are metal mounts for objects and celebrate the Valkyrie, Odin's handmaidens who choose the slain for Valhalla. 'Borre' style Scandinavian artwork, usually featuring gripping beasts, appears on a silver-gilt pendant discovered in Little Snoring in Norfolk and a lavish gold lozenge brooch from a field in Attleborough in Norfolk, which has four outward facing beasts.[8]

The Viking presence in East Anglia can be traced back to the Great Heathen Army. After overwintering in 867/68 in Nottingham, the Vikings returned to York for a year and were likely based around Aldwark before targeting East Anglia where they had arrived three years earlier.

Abbo of Fleury told of how Ivar landed by stealth with a massive fleet in East Anglia catching the residents unaware while Ubbe was based in York after they had devastated Northumbria. While Edmund had supplied the Vikings with horses when they landed four years earlier, he was no longer prepared to make a deal after the Northmen demolished Medehamstede (Peterborough) and killed the abbot and monk, where the ninth-century Hedda stone commemorates them.[9]

A Valkyrie mount discovered in Bylaugh, Norfolk, honouring the mythological figures who took slain warriors to Vahalla. (Norfolk Museums Service)

In the autumn of 869, Edmund confronted Ivar's army at, most likely, Thetford but was defeated and fled to his royal villa, which was called Haegelisdun, a combination of a personal name *Haegel* and *dun*, which means 'hill'. He was pursued by the victorious Ivar, who demanded he share his wealth and agree to reign under him. The king refused to give up unless Ivar converted to Christianity and was instead shackled in chains, mocked and 'tortured with terrible lashes' while tied to a tree in a neighbourhood. When he cried out to Christ with a broken voice, it 'roused the fury of his enemies' claims Abbo of Fleury.[10] They used the stricken king as target practice and fired so many arrows that he 'actually bristled with them, like a prickly hedgehog or a thistle fretted with spines, resembling in his agony the illustrious martyr Sebastian'. When it became clear Edmund would not submit, Ivar ordered his executioner to chop off his head.

According to Abbo of Fleury, who wrote his account while based at Ramsey Abbey in Cambridge between 985 and 988, Edmund's head was dumped in a woodland and a council agreed to send a search party equipped with horns and pikes to scour the undergrowth. Then the tale clearly falls into the realms of fantasy as Abbo of Fleury claims the severed head had alerted the search party to his whereabouts. The head shouted in the native tongue: 'Here! Here! Here! In Latin the same meaning would be rendered by Hic! Hic! Hic! And the head never ceased to repeat this exclamation, till all were drawn to it.'[11]

A medieval manuscript illustration of Edmund's torture and martyrdom at the hands of Ivar and Ubbe. (Morgan Library, New York/WikiCommons)

When they discovered Edmund's head, it was being protected by a 'monstrous wolf', laying outstretched on the ground and protecting Edmund's head from further harm. Onlookers were astonished by the wolf, which was never seen again. Wolves were still roaming Britain, but this could have alluded to the kingdom's founding dynasty the Wuffingas (kin of the wolf), who featured in *Beowulf*.[12]

In 1848, there was a fascinating discovery at St Edmunds Abbey, in Bury St Edmunds, then known as Beodricsworth, when they found the remains of twenty wolves and one large dog close to the old Norman gate tower. Theories on the bizarre discovery range from a payment by a hunter who owed the abbey, a pet cemetery or the wolves were guarding the dead, including St Edmund whose body had been moved there.[13]

The martyrdom's location became a place of pilgrimage with a wooden shrine erected in Edmund's memory. In 1978, the archaeologist Stanley West pointed out that an 1843 tithe map of Bradfield St Clare, a village just 6 miles from Bury St Edmunds, featured a Hellesden Ley, which may have evolved from Haegelisdun. He also highlighted how a road leading to the village was called Kinghall Street, and there was a local place named Sutton Hall.[14]

An eleventh-century account from Archdeacon Herman claimed that Edmund had been buried in a little village called 'suthtune', which was the Old English word for 'Sutton'. The area where Edmund's head was possibly uncovered is the modern-day Bradfield Nature Reserve, which must be the 'neighbouring forest' next to Haegelisdun that Abbo of Fleury mentioned. Notably, it sits next to a Monks Park Wood, a former medieval deer park owned by St Edmunds Abbey.

Some scholars dismiss the account as essentially another Passion of Christ because the title Passion of St Edmund was intended to evoke sympathy for Edmund and put him on par with previous martyrs, such as the third-century St Sebastian, who also happened to be struck with numerous arrows.[15]

There are clear religious overtones because the bravery and faith of Edmund is contrasted with the barbarity of the pagans, and both Ivar and Ubbe, who were described as men of 'equal depravity', are physical embodiments of Jeremiah's warning about a 'disaster from the north'.

Ivar's forces are accused of brutally killing young and old males in the streets, married couples on their doorstep and even babies, which were snatched from their mothers. The 'tyrant' Ivar due to his 'sheer love of cruelty' had given 'orders for the massacre of the innocent'. Harrowing similar descriptions of bodies piled up in the street feature in other religious texts, such as Gildas' polemic verse telling of destruction by Saxon confederates in the fifth century, but the Vikings were capable of such atrocities.

Abbo of Fleury claimed he learned of the story from Dunstan, Archbishop of Canterbury, who knew a very 'decrepit old man' at King Athelstan's court, who was the grandson of Alfred the Great. Standing before the king, most likely at his stronghold in Winchester, this old man had 'sworn on oath' that he was Edmund's arms bearer. The text that had been sent for approval to Archbishop Dunstan, who himself was aged around his mid-seventies, states the day of Edmund's death – 20 November 869 – which fits with the *Anglo-Saxon Chronicle*'s record.[16]

Within twenty-five years of Edmund's death, memorial pennies featuring the inscription 'SCE EADMVND REX' ('O St Edmund the King!') began appearing in circulation from 895. More than 200 examples are known, which were produced by around 70 different moneyers and concentrated across East Anglia and the Midlands.[17] The cult of Edmund had become so powerful, presumably because of his brutal death, that the Vikings adopted the king they killed on their coinage. This early rise of the Edmund cult suggests a basis of fact underlays the martyrdom tale.[18]

Given the Great Heathen Army installed puppet rulers in conquered kingdoms as it continued campaigning, Edmund's refusal to submit may well have infuriated Ivar and Ubbe, who had him executed and beheaded. It was not unusual for the heads of enemies to be taken as trophies after battles. Germanic and British Iron Age tribes believed the heads could provide power and wisdom.[19]

While the exact nature of Edmund's death is unclear, the signs of the subsequent Viking settlement are unmistakable in East Anglia, with the incredible number of Scandinavian place names. Eight hundred names (centres of administration) have been identified alone in Norfolk.[20] More than twenty place names end in 'by', from the Old Norse *byr* for settlement, of which most are on the Isle of Flegg, which encompasses Great Yarmouth. Other Viking names include Lowestoft from the Old Norse *toft*, meaning 'homestead settlement', along with eyke (the place where the oak tree grows) from the Old Norse for oak tree (*eik*) and Lound from the Old Scandinavian word *lundr*, relating to a 'small wood or grove'.[21]

Vikings must have set up camp in Thetford at either the Red Castle or the old Iron Age fort at Thetford Castle, which later became a huge Norman motte and bailey castle. They may have taken over Ipswich and used it as a port, with

Thetford Castle, which became a huge Norman motte and bailey fortress, may have been used as a camp by Vikings.

suggestions there was a Viking assembly 'thing' mound, where they resolved disputes, in Christchurch Park.[22] Along with areas around Norwich and Thetford, there have been a cluster of finds within 5km of both banks of the River Waveney near a major Roman road from London to Colchester, such as five silver ingots, an inset weight and a silver penny of Charles the Bald. The village of Congham has also proved an unlikely hotspot for Viking artefacts with a silver Thor's hammer, two disc brooches, four St Edmund pennies, a silver ingot and several lead weights among the discoveries.[23]

The earliest settlers in East Anglia may have included Ubbe or his followers. His name is found in Ubbeston, a parish within Suffolk on a Roman road, which is thought to mean 'Ubba's settlement or farmstead', and was recorded in the *Domesday Book* as 'Ubbestun'.[24] An Ugg Mere can be found close to Ramsey in Cambridgeshire, which was mentioned by Abbo of Fleury's student Bryhtferth, and may have also been named after Ubbe because the earliest examples include 'Ubbemere', 'Hubbamare' and 'Ubbamare'.[25,26] Bryhtferth describes how the father of the uncle of Oswald, a former archbishop of York he was commemorating, had been 'one of the Danes in the ship army of Ubbe and Ivarr'. The 'mere' is related to either a watercourse or lake in the marshy Fenland region.

These place names lend support to claims from the twelfth century-chronicler Henry of Huntingdon that Ubbe, who he said possessed 'extraordinary courage', was awarded East Anglia after Edmund's death.[27] Another chronicler Geoffrey Gaimar, who avoids the more questionable aspects of Abbo of Fleury's account, claimed Ubbe was present at the martyrdom as well.[28]

Ivar's chief role in torturing Edmund may have given rise to his famous epithet of the *beinlauss* (boneless). This tale clearly influenced Adam of Bremen, writing about 90 years after Abbo of Fleury, who described Inguar (Ivar) as the 'most cruel' Viking leader of them all who 'everywhere tortured Christians to death'.[29]

The later 'Ragnar's Saga' says Ivar was left boneless because his father refused to wait three nights before having sex with Aslaug, then called Kraka, which means 'cow' when in hiding, despite her warnings: 'For three nights, we two, we shall sleep separately ere, we sacrifice to the wholly gods. This delay will do no damage to my child, you're brash to beget one whose bones will be lacking.' As his mother feared, Ivar was born 'boneless, as if there was gristle where his bones should be'.[30] In the saga, Aslaug was the daughter of Sigurd Dragon Slayer and Brunhild, but after their deaths, she ended up living as a farmhand with peasants Áke and Grima, who killed her foster father Heimir.

One theory suggested Ivar suffered from brittle bone disease although there is no contemporary reference. The earliest reference to Ivar being boneless appears to come from the Roskilde Chronicle in Zealand composed around 1137–38, which confuses the fact that the name 'Ywar' (Ivar), which developed from the older

Norse form 'Yngvarr', was the same person as Ivar and that he and Ubbi (Ubbe) were brothers:

> *'In this time, Ywar [Ivar] son of Lothpardi [Lodbrok], the cruellest king of the Northmen, who was said to lack bones, whose brothers Ingvar [Ivar] and Vibbi [Ubbi] and Byron [Bjron] and Vlf [Ulf] ruled the northern people summoned his troops as well as the king of the Danes in aid in destroying the realm of the Franks.'*[31]

Around a decade later, the 'Hattalykill', an Old Norse poem possibly composed on the Orkney Islands that mentions Sigurd, Hvitserk and Bjorn as well, recounts Ivar's slaying of King Elle (Aella) and refers to him as 'boneless'. This shows that the story of Lodbrok's multiple sons leading the army into England was popular and part of heroic folklore in Scandinavia by the twelfth century, long before the sagas and Saxo's text emerged.[32]

In the *Vikings* TV series, when Ivar is born severely disabled, Ragnar leaves him out in the forest before his mother Aslaug saves him. Later, Ivar does the same to his deformed child, but this time the baby is not rescued.

Infanticide was part of Old Norse culture, as it has been throughout history, when an unwanted child would be allowed to live for a few hours and then left out in nature for someone else to have or to die. The phrase *bera ut* meaning 'carry out' is often used in sources when a child is not wanted.

Sagas tell of how infanticide often resulted from the parents suffering from extreme poverty or the child having defects or disabilities, which would hinder their ability to work and provide in future. Resources were often scarce, summers were short and children of all wealth suffered from malnourishment in particularly bleak and prolonged winters. Remain of babies have been found in springs and wetlands across Scandinavia, which could be linked to a ritual belief of these places as gateways to another world.[33]

Evidence for infanticide is scarce, but analysis of Icelandic and Norwegian laws suggests the practice was entrenched in Norse culture, according to the academic Johanna Katrin Fridriksdottr, author of *Valkyrie*: 'After the conversion in Norway, laws were repeatedly passed against infanticide, suggesting however much lawmakers regarded it as a pagan and despicable custom, it was an uphill struggle to get people to change their ways.'[34]

Infant mortality rate in Scandinavia at the time could range from thirty to sixty per cent and many children died within a year of birth. Historians estimate that women in Norway during the Viking Age had children on average every 30 months and 'scores' died from giving birth or with complications, according to Fridriksdottr.[35] The emotional bond between mother and child was every bit as strong in Norse stories, with the *Grettis saga* using the phrase *'best er barni modir'* (a mother is best to a child). They fed their children, taught them social skills and trained them in household tasks.[36]

Leading Vikings with disabilities were found at two famous Viking Age archaeological sites. The head of the Salme ship expedition in the eighth century had suffered from fused vertebrae, while the elderly woman buried in the Osberg ship burial had arthritis and two fused neck vertebrae. Pagan gods such as Odin who was missing an eye and Tyr who lost a hand after fighting the wolf Fenir show disabilities featured in the mythology.[37]

Many Vikings were disabled from battle wounds but continued to raid and fight on battlefields. Having a disability could be clearly accepted and common in wider society. However, it is strange there are no references in earlier sources or by Abbo of Fleury, who claimed to have first-hand testimony. Sources are notoriously brief, often just a sentence or two, but in Abbo's more detailed story it surely would have been mentioned.

Another theory regarding the Boneless epitaph highlights how *beinlaus* was used by fishermen as a term for the 'wind' so the title Ivar Beinlauss could imply that he was a skilful navigator.[38]

Some suggest the 'boneless' epitaph is a result of sexual impotence or the opposite and a compliment of Ivar's sexual prowess. The 'Tale of Ragnar's Sons' tells of how Ivar had no children because he had no 'love or lust in him'.[39] This

The ruins of St Edmunds Abbey, where the former king was believed to have been buried underneath the modern-day tennis courts.

can be easily dismissed given the historical Ivar had sons who ruled in Dublin, Sichfrith and Sihtric, and possibly Guthred who ruled Northumbria.

The obvious answer would seem the most logical because the 'boneless' title is believed to result from a simple misreading of the Latin adjective *exosus* meaning 'cruel' with *exos*, which equals 'boneless'.[40] As Adam of Bremen described Ivar as 'cruel', there was a simple misunderstanding, which gave birth to the 'boneless' epitaph in later Old Norse sagas.

While the historical Ivar was most probably not disabled as depicted in the *Vikings* TV series, the snarling and wild portrayal by Alex Høgh Andersen in the TV series was befitting because Ivar achieved infamy through his actions in East Anglia.

For Edmund, his cult would rapidly rise with the new shrine at St Edmunds Abbey, which quickly began attracting rich votive offerings. Many miraculous feats were attributed to St Edmund, including famously the murder of the Danish king Sweyn Forkbeard in 1014. The abbey grew into a thriving monastic community and magnificent stone complex before it was dissolved in 1539 and gradually demolished.

During a warm spell on a visit in early spring, the abbey memorial park was filled with families, and people of ages, spread out amongst the spectacular ruins. Edmund's remains are believed to lay under the tennis court on the site of a former monk's burial ground at the back of the park. Whatever the nature of his death, it seemed fitting that an Anglo-Saxon king, who stood up to the Vikings, now rests in such a place that remains so treasured in the region he sought to protect.

Ivar was far from finished. He set his sights on Britain's most impregnable fortress.

Chapter 10

THE FALL OF ALT CLUT

Clyde's wide bed ten thousand torrents fill, his rage the murmuring mountain streams augment: redoubled rage in rocks so closely pent: then shattered woods, with ragged roots uptorn, and herds and harvests down the waves are borne.

The Clyde, John Wilson, 18th century[1]

Having scaled the more than 500 steps of Dumbarton Castle, the glorious expanse of the River Clyde was the prize at the top of the white tower crag, which is the highest point of the site. At 74m (240ft) high, it offers a spectacular 360-degree view, including to the south-east across the Clyde towards Glasgow and west to the edge of the Highlands.[2]

Surrounded by water, this dramatic landmark appears completely inhabitable with its steep and rugged slopes known as crags. Jagged disc-shaped rocks penetrate through the front of the white tower crag, as a striking purple heather in contrast to the rugged facing terrain blankets the eastern side. These steps head through the cleft of the two volcanic plugs under the old guard house and then via a very narrow and steep path built into the landmark to the white tower crag, where you can study the opposite gigantic 'Beak', which once housed a powerful post-Roman fortress.

In 870, the inhabitants made the same climb to see the terrifying sight of a Viking fleet with dragon-prowed longboats, huge square sails and painted shields placed over the side as they neared the enemy for intimidation, filled with warriors known for pillaging and bloodshed. A monk may have gathered the flock for a prayer, begging the lord to save them in the darkest hour, as those who listened intently glanced every now and then at the approaching horde, who were banging their shields to stoke up the fear. Children and weaker inhabitants were huddled into the fortress on the Beak, which was surrounded by a rampart. Clyde Rock had the distinction of being Britain's oldest occupied fortress, but it was about to face its most terrifying foes yet – Ivar the Boneless and Olaf the White.

Often known as Clyde Rock, the landmark is a spectacular twin-peaked volcanic plug, which is essentially the core of a long-extinct volcano that erupted 300 million years ago. These plugs are formed when magma hardens and gets trapped inside an

In 870, terrified inhabitants of Dumbarton Castle looked out on the River Clyde to see the massive fleet of Ivar the Boneless and Olaf the White approaching.

active volcano's vent and then cools with the hot ash creating an igneous rock that moulds into a cylindrical pillar which can extend to hundreds of feet high.[3]

Its people themselves proudly called themselves *Cumbri*, i.e. 'countrymen' or 'compatriots', related to the modern Welsh *Cymry*. Their language mirrored Old Welsh and along with modern Welsh, Cornish, Breton and Pictish belong to the ancient Brittonic tongue.[4]

This remarkable setting was once the stronghold of Strathclyde, the modern Anglicised version of Strat Clut or Strad Clud, which appeared in earlier sources. Its core territory was the 'strath' meaning 'lower valley' of the River Clyde, which runs for 110 miles from the Firth of Clyde, through the modern city of Glasgow, to the Lowther Hills in South Lanarkshire.[5]

At its largest extent, in the tenth century, Strathclyde extended from Clach nam Breatann (the rock of the Britons), a large stone that marked the boundary with the Alt Clut-Strathclyde, Pictish and Dál Riata kingdoms on the slopes of Glen Falloch in Stirling, all the way to Eamont Bridge over the river of the same name in Penrith, Cumbria.[6]

Originally, the kingdom's stronghold was likely the walled Carman Iron Age hillfort, which overlooks Dumbarton Castle from a height of 230m (754ft) just 6 miles away, but the rulers favoured a location nearer to the river to import luxury goods with their growing prestige.[7] Strathclyde rulers relocated to the current Dumbarton Castle, situated in a prime position at the junction of the rivers Clyde and Leven, which was known in Welsh as Alt Clut, meaning the 'rock of the Clyde' or 'Clyde Rock', and the name for the kingdom as whole.

While the western summit of the White Tower Crag was too steep for occupation and was most probably the lookout spot during the early medieval period, the eastern summit has a flat, level top of 30m (98ft) by 20m (65ft), which was more than suitable for settlement. Excavations at Dumbarton Castle by Leslie and Elizabeth A Alcock in 1972–73 found the 'more or less' level terraces along the cleft on the route up to the Beak would have been suited for further occupation alongside extensive flat areas next to the Leven and Clyde.

Their report compared Alt Clut to similar well-networked and defensible rocky hill forts, such as Dinas Emrys in Gwynedd, north-west Wales, and Dunadd in Argyll and Bute, the capital of the Dál Riata. They believed the rich post-Roman rulers occupied a citadel on the Beak's summit, but traces of the actual building were not found:

> *'Over a period of several centuries they (Alt Clut rulers) imported wine from the Mediterranean, and probably from Gaul as well, and drank it from glass cups and beakers of Germanic origin. In the vicinity, bronze was probably being worked to create high class jewellery. In the context of the early historic references to Clyde Rock, this household must have been a royal one.'*[8]

Traders were possibly drawn to Alt Clut by the sale of white fur, such as the 'winter coat of mountain hares' used in coats and hats and the 'fur of the newly born pups of grey seal' that was also used for clothing, along with the 'feathers of over-wintering

The incredible site of Dumbarton Castle was formed from a long extinct volcano and became one of the most formidable fortresses in Britain. (Russell Davies)

geese' and 'the down of eiders', a luxury for the wealthy, who stuffed it in their pillows and duvets because it was extremely lightweight.[9]

Archaeological investigations found trade dropped off from the eighth century, but Clyde Rock was still a 'strongly fortified civitas', according to Northumbrian scholar Bede writing in 729. Strathclyde faced the powerful Picts to the north, the Gaelic kingdom of the Dál Riata in western Scotland and north-east Ireland, and the Northumbrians who ruled from the River Trent to Edinburgh.

This pressure was evidenced when Alt Clut king Dyfnwal submitted at the stronghold on 1 August 765 to the Picts and Northumbrians led by the kings Onuist and Eadberht, according to the 12th-century Northumbrian chronicle called the *Historia Regum* (*History of Kings*).

Returning Northumbrian troops were massacred, by Picts or Cumbrian Britons, after stopping at a place called Ovania, a Latinised form of 'Govan' in modern Glasgow where a royal site and church of great spiritual significance was based since the sixth century, which was connected to Clyde Rock's rulers.[10]

Northumbrians were ambushed at Niwanbirig (meaning new fort or settlement), which would be Caer Newydd in Cumbric/Welsh and possibly identified as Carnwath, around 30 miles from Glasgow, according to scholar Tim Clarkson.[11] He said it has an earlier form of 'Carnewyth' that preserves the Welsh pronunciation of *-ydd*.

The Clyde-based kingdom would soon face an even more fearsome enemy. Viking presence on the islands around Scotland, particularly Shetland and Orkney, began to increase from the early 800s. As the century wore on, it appears they had bases in the Hebrides, the Isle of Man and the Isle of the Clyde, later known as the Kingdom of the Isles, which extended to within 10 miles of Dumbarton Castle.

Dublin-based Vikings led by Olaf eventually turned their sights on modern Scotland. Olaf and Auisle headed to Fortriu in 866 and 'plundered the entire Pictish country and took away hostages', recorded the *Annals of Ulster*.

At the same time, the Irish began brutally wiping out Olaf's followers as his former ally Áed Finnilaith, the High King from the Northern Uí Néill, destroyed the longphorts in Lough Foyle and then beheaded 100 followers, stole their flocks and herds and torched Olaf's fort at Clondalkin (Cluain Dolcáin) near Dublin, according to the *Annals of Ulster*. In the following year, the same source reports that Auisle was 'killed by his kinsmen in guile and parricide'.[12]

The eleventh-century *Fragmentary Annals of Ireland* claimed in a possibly imagined tale that Olaf murdered his brother in a fit of rage after he declared an interest in his wife, believed to be the daughter of Cináed mac Ailpin, king of the Picts and Dál Riata, or Cinaed mac Conaing, ruler of Brega.[13,14]

The following year, in 868, Áed continued his campaign with attacks in Dublin and Brega and slew Olaf's son Carlus. In response, Olaf plundered and burned down Omagh in his territory and killed or enslaved 1,000 people who had amassed for the St Patrick's Festival. The violence from both sides was truly unimaginable.

Ivar and Olaf reunited in 870 for their most ambitious raid yet as they targeted the fortress of Alt Clut. The rulers of the fortress still held considerable sway as they had destroyed the stronghold at Dunblane, an ecclesiastical centre in southern Pictland, just over twenty years before the Siege of Dumbarton. Arthgal ap Dyfnwal ruled the Alt Clut at the time of the siege, which was unprecedented in terms of Viking warfare, being a drastic change of tactics from the hit-and-run attacks on poorly defended estates or coastal monasteries.

Dublin Vikings clearly wanted to destroy the power of the northern Britons and plunder its vast riches and enslave its people. They may have even sought to use Clyde Rock as a ship base for future raiding.[15] The Firth of Clyde was also a gateway to not just trade with Ireland and mainland Europe, but it also gave access to lowlands

Noble warriors such as Ivar and Olaf would have been clad in chainmail as they attacked Alt Clut. (Laurent Cusolito)

between the Campsie and Kilpatrick Fells and the Southern Highlands and joined the Loch Lomond waterway via the Leven, which is a little over 6 miles away.[16]

It was indicative of Ivar's ambition and lust for glory that after conquering the long-standing Anglo-Saxon kingdoms of Northumbria and East Anglia, he desired to do the impossible and capture one of the most powerful strongholds in northern Britain. Ringed by crags and surrounded by water, Dumbarton was 'exceptionally difficult to assault' and 'formidable' because of the towering rock steps that supported its level eastern summit, said the Alcocks.[17] Traces of a timber, stone and rubble rampart on the Beak were uncovered which was created as early as the sixth century and possibly reinforced in the seventh century. Intriguingly, the timber used left open the possibility it was thrown up close to the actual siege.

Although the rampart itself was not a significant earthwork (about 2m (6ft) in both height and width), it was positioned on a rising slope above vertical crags on the Beak. This was deliberately placed in a commanding position overlooking the strip of land that connected Clyde Rock to the mainland, visible from the current approach to the castle entrance past the Dumbarton FC ground. Despite the steepness and crags, it was one of the easier approaches to the Beak.[18]

When the attack began at Dumbarton, it quickly turned into a waiting game. Vikings would have been channelled through the narrow and steep cleft, which separates the two peaks, at the mercy of lighter javelins, arrows and other missiles. High-born warriors, such as Ivar, Olaf and their chieftains, were armed with a sword that could range from around 90cm long, based on finds at Hedeby, with a large pommel to make it easier to manage and decorated with silver and sometimes

The forces of Ivar and Olaf would have been channelled through a narrow gap at the mercy of enemy forces, who occupied the beak (to the right).

had curved hilts. Many would have been clutching the terrifying long-handed, broad-blade battle axes that gave the Vikings such a fearsome reputation. Leaders were typically adorned in chain mail, which could absorb some cutting and slicing blows, but it was an expensive luxury, and concentrated blows would drive the metal rings into the body.[19]

Vikings were forced to try to pick off individual Alt Clut defenders with arrows, which are well attested during the period. A complete Viking Age bow, a longbow made of yew, also discovered at Hedeby, had a draw weight of up to 104lb and a range of up to 180m. Most arrowheads were leaf-shaped and suitable for hunting and against an unarmoured, rank and file foe, but the 'Bodkin type' favoured by Vikings during combat were a menacing squared metal spike that could penetrate mail armour.[20]

Given the existing well is located at the back of the cleft next to the old French Prison, the Alt Clut rulers must have held the higher ground, and Ivar's army were restricted to taking pot shots at their enemy on the higher ground or trying unexpected raids. The four months it took before the Alt Clut capitulated suggests there was a considerable force, strong enough to withstand the mighty Dublin Vikings. When the end came, it was due to the well drying up. The *Fragmentary Annals of Ireland* records:

> *'In this year [870] the Norwegian kings besieged Srath Cluada in Britain, camping against them for four months; finally, having subdued the people inside by hunger and thirst – the well that they had inside having dried up in a remarkable way – they attacked them. First they took all the goods that were inside. A great host was taken out into captivity.'*[21]

The *Annals of Ulster* also confirms the length of the siege stating 'Amlaíb [Olaf] and Ímar [Ivar], two kings of the Norsemen, laid siege to the fortress and at the end of four months they destroyed and plundered it.'[22]

Evidence of the Viking attack was discovered by the Alcocks, who found that the timber and stone ramparts on the eastern summit were destroyed by fire. Investigations showed timber beams, which were 'burning strongly', had been in contact with the rock where its front face had rested. Charcoal and verified stone in the deeper layers suggested the timber beams had been fastened with carpentry joints and treenails.[23]

Destroying the rampart was a departing act from the Vikings, who frequently burned the dwellings of wood, thatch and clay found in Frankish villages, perhaps in fear that the rock may be later reoccupied. Part of the reason Vikings often burned down buildings was to ward off potential revengeful spirits.[24] Vikings may have captured the lower level of Clyde Rock and the well, and the burning of the

Excavations in the 1970s by the Alcocks at Dumbarton discovered this pommel bar from a Viking sword. (© The Hunterian, University of Glasgow)

rampart was part of a fully pronged assault on the fortress on the Beak after its inhabitants retreated inside.

The Alcocks also discovered a pommel bar from a Viking sword of Petersen Class I (after Jan Petersen who classified different Viking Age swords) and a lead weight, ornamented in characteristic Viking fashion, with a fragment of jewellery, in this case a segment from an Irish glass bangle. This could link to the Dublin stronghold of Ivar and Olaf, but the Alcocks cautioned the weight could be a product of later trading.[25]

Alt Clut's fall was also devastating for the hinterland communities under their rule and beyond. The *Annals of Ulster* records in 871: 'Amlaíb [Olaf] and Ímar [Ivar] returned to Áth Cliath from Alba with two hundred ships, bringing with them in captivity to Ireland a great prey of Angles and Britons and Picts.'[26] Among the captured was the Alt Clut king Arthgal and his family.

Alt Clut's rulers survived this traumatic period and relocated further downstream to Govan, at a fording point of the Clyde near its confluence with the River Kelvin. This was near an early Christian cemetery from the fifth century, an ancient church and a massive prehistoric mound known as 'Doomster Hill', which based on an eighteenth-century record was 5.1m (17ft) high and 54.8m (180ft) in diameter.[27]

Similar steeped mounds have been found at Tynwald Hill on the Isle of Man and the Thingmote at Dublin, which both include the Old Norse word *thing*, meaning an assembly place, where freemen could air grievances and the decisions were binding. The name 'Doomster' relates to the open-air courts that dispensed justice. Govan's name, from when people spoke a Brittonic dialect close to Old Welsh, is derived from '*go/gwo*' meaning 'small' and 'ban' meaning hill.

The spectacular landmark of Doomster Hill also served as a venue for ceremonial gatherings and religious rites and was connected via a walkway to the modern Old Govan Church.[28]

As the kingdom relocated, its name changed to 'Strathclyde' and there were no further references to 'Alt Clut'. The *Annals of Ulster* reports in 872 that 'Arthgal, king of the Strathclyde Britons, was killed at the instigation of Constantine I, son of Cináed.'[29] The next Strathclyde king, Rhun was married to Constantine I's daughter, and Constantine I may have had Arthgal killed by the Dublin Vikings while he was held captive.

After the sack of Alt Clut, increasing Viking presence can be seen in the famous collection of tenth-century carved stones at Govan's Church. This includes forty-seven stunning sculptured stones ornamented with Celtic designs, originally housed in the churchyard, of which the majority are burial monuments and four are upright crosses, all sharing similar designs and styles. The centrepiece is a remarkable sarcophagus carved from a single block of stone and elaborately decorated with deer-hunting scenes, a favourite pastime of nobles. The church itself is dedicated to a St Constantine, which many believe to be Constantine I.

This collection also features five stunning Viking hogbacks, which are massive sandstone blocks, with intrinsically designed roof ridges and shingles, believed to represent the classic Scandinavian long houses. As the hogbacks were found at three ecclesiastical sites in Scotland at Govan, Luss and Dalserf, which each have a saint dedication, it implies they were an offering by a new Scandinavian community, which brought the tradition from the Danelaw region, in recognition of local religion and customs.[30]

Emerging Scandinavian impact on the Clyde region was also evidenced by the ninth-century Viking warrior burial mound on the banks of Loch Lomond. The site featured a large mound known as 'Boiden' covered by a stone cairn, which included a Viking sword that had been purposefully bent, along with a shield boss and spear that showed damage.[31]

One of the five remarkable hogbacks at Goven church, which were believed to represent Viking longhouses.

There was no body discovered, but it may have been cremated, or the body dissolved as the destruction of weapons, including the bending of blades, was common in such Scandinavian rituals.[32]

At nearby Midross, now Carrick Golf Course around 9 miles from Dumbarton Castle, they uncovered a cemetery containing fifteen burials that have been radiocarbon dated to the late-ninth and tenth centuries, of which six included grave goods. Two of the six with grave goods featured multiple finds such as a whetstone, a slotted tool, a knife blade, an iron fitting or rod, and an Anglo-Saxon coin fragment attached to the iron fitting or rod. The whetstone was made of Eidsborg schist from the Telemark region of Norway, providing a direct link with Scandinavia. One of the six graves was believed to be a female because it included several decorative items such as a shale arm-ring and finger-ring, a copper-alloy bracelet and a blue glass bead. Another burial included a child-sized ring and pierced Anglo-Saxon coin. This cemetery provided a strong hint of Scandinavian settlers, including women and children, being laid to rest alongside an existing community using local rites, given the nine unfurnished graves.[33]

A discovery at Port Glasgow in 1700 of a 'great number' of Anglo-Saxon coins and two penannular arm-rings, one of which featured a design of three twisted rods and a global pendular mirrored in hoards at Burray and Sandwick in Orkney, was further proof of the Vikings in Clyde.

The most eye-catching discovery, which best represents the changes taking afoot as Celtic and Norse cultures merged, was the incredible Hunterston Brooch, a large silver design of Irish style with gold Anglo-Saxon-style filigree and amber settings. While produced around 700 at the Dál Riata stronghold of Dunadd, around 200 years later someone had inscribed 'Melbrigda owns [this] brooch' into the back. This is a distinctly Brittonic/Irish name, but the inscriber used Scandinavian runes.[34]

Dumbarton Castle's fascinating history certainly didn't end with the siege although there is no mention of a stronghold there until the Scottish King Alexander II made a reference to a 'new castle' in 1222, amid strained relations with the Norwegian kingdom on its doorstep in Argyll and the Hebrides. Two tenth-century recumbent cross slabs found behind the governor's house are possibly from a St Patrick chapel.

This site became a famed royal castle, regularly featuring at key points in Scottish history. William Wallace was taken there before being transferred to London for execution, with the Wallace Tower and guard house (formerly Wallace Prison) a reminder.[35] His ally Robert the Bruce had a large manor in Cardross parish near the castle in Renton, and his internal organs were taken to the old medieval churchyard of Cardross in the Levengrove Park behind Clyde Rock. Dumbarton Castle's militarised nature developed after the Jacobite Rising in the early-18th century, with four batteries around the site that boasted artillery,

The stunning Hunterston Brooch, which featured Scandinavian runes but had been produced around 700 – some 200 years earlier. (© National Museums Scotland)

including the cast-iron muzzle-loading cannons on the Duke of Argyll Battery on the Beak. On the same peak, a massive power magazine was built that housed 150 barrels of gunpowder and a crane bastion that hoisted up munitions and stores from 200ft below.[36]

When touring this historic site, the sombre image of thousands of captives being led to the Viking ships was hard to shake off. Slavery was endemic globally at the time, but it does not make it any less sobering. Two hundred ships filled with captives, stolen from their homes around the Clyde and its hinterland, were now bound for the Dublin slave market.

One of the main purposes of the longphorts in Ireland, such as Dublin, was the redistribution of wealth from raiding, so the Vikings who had plundered Alt Clut would later be trading from the harbour market stalls.[37]

The reference to 'Picts' and 'Anglo-Saxons' and that the ships returned a year later suggested they captured large numbers of people from Southern Pictland and Lothian, which had been under Northumbrian lordship. Increasing pressure from Áed and other Irish rulers may have led Olaf and Ivar to begin the large-scale capture of slaves to fuel the Dublin market and cement their status as the most powerful among Vikings and Irish kings. Frankish annals recorded 26 Viking attacks in which slaves were taken between 834 and 896, of which 15 took place between 873 and 896, showing the demand increased significantly in the final quarter of the ninth century.[38]

Unfortunate, captives were bound and bundled onto the longships and merchant vessels on the Clyde. Excavations in Dublin have found large chains that would be tied around the necks of slaves to keep them from escaping, such as one found near Strokestown in County Roscommon by a crannog.[39]

Some of those captured were traded in Scandinavia, where owning a slave was a sign of prestige, to work on farms to carry out demanding indoor and outdoor tasks and others might have been used to barter for rich goods in eastern Europe. Through markets such as Kaupang and Birka, many were sold to the Abbasid Caliphate in the Middle East at places such as Baghdad, via the Volga River trade route, where there was a huge demand for slaves, or to the Byzantine empire at Constantinople via the Dnieper River.[40]

Iceland was being settled intensely, and men were needed to clear the land, manage domestic animals and haul timber and turf, while women were needed for domestic duties.[41] Research by Oxford University and deCODE genetics suggests up to 62 per cent of the female population and around 19 per cent of males of the earliest settlers in Iceland had ancestry from the British Isles, specifically Scotland and Ireland.[42] Indications suggest that women and children were preferred for slavery, and that men were taken if they had specific skills – presumably over fears they would be more difficult to manage.[43] The early raids in Ireland do suggest a preference for female slaves, who were often kept as concubines. Repeated references to Irish slaves in Icelandic sagas suggest large numbers were taken.[44]

One notorious Viking called Rodulf, suggested as the historical Ubbe, when under siege from the Franks in 873 threatened to 'kill all the men and lead their women and children and all their property into captivity'.[45] Mercantile relations were already set up by the late-ninth century in Ireland evidenced by the flow of Arabic silver from Scandinavia via Dublin chieftains and blacksmiths. Captured Irish or British women and children, along with skilled craftsmen, were thought to be a form of payment.[46]

This bleak trade, which had been the big driver for the first Viking ports in Ireland, was now a wide-reaching global operation that showed no signs of abating. And neither was the Great Heathen Army showing any signs of slowing down. The campaign was about to enter its most turbulent year yet.

Chapter 11

THE RAVEN'S FORT

The berserks were roaring, for this was their battle, the wolf-coated warriors howling, And the irons clattering
'Hrafnsmál', Þorbjörn Hornklofi, ninth century (translation taken from an English edition of Snorri Sturluson's *Heimskringla* by Erling Monsen with A. H. Smith)[1]

Odin had two ravens Hugin and Munin, which mean 'thought' and 'memory', who fly across the world seeking news and bring the knowledge of all things back to their master. As far as they travel, the ravens always return for the spectacular feast every evening at the halls of Valhalla. Perched on the shoulders of Odin, the 'raven god', they whisper tidings into his ear. Dated to around 900, the silver cast figurine of Odin from Lejre, shows ravens standing next to the god appearing to whisper.[2] 'Huginn and Muninn hover each day, the wide earth over,' according to the *Prose Edda*, compiled by Snorri Sturluson in the thirteenth century. 'I fear for Huginn lest he fare not back, yet I watch more for Muninn.'[3]

Once the ravens informed Odin of Suttung's mead, known as the 'mead of poetry', which was stolen and fiercely guarded by the dwarves Fjalar and Galar before they gave it to the giant Suttung to save their lives after killing his brother. Stirred by the tale, Odin set out to capture the mead that could turn anyone into a skald capable of reciting fabulous stories of monsters, gods and heroes.[4]

Suttung entrusted the mead with his giantess maiden daughter Gunnlod, but Odin found where the mead was hidden behind a rock that was bored through, and he turned into a serpent to crawl through the hole. Then Odin slept with Gunnlod for three nights and persuaded her to let him drink the mead from three draughts. After becoming an eagle, Odin managed to escape the giant's wrath and, on his return, spat out the mead into vats and selflessly shared it with the Aesir and poets. Family vengeance is a persistent theme throughout Norse sagas and the hallmarks of Odin, such as his cunning, penchant for violence and ability to shape shift.[5] Odin is again portrayed as generous, one of the most essential qualities a Viking lord could possess, which is evidenced in Valhalla because he always gives his food board to his wolves Geri and Freki.[6]

Viking life often meant death was nearby, and the raven was a morbid reminder overhead. Ravens were repeatedly linked with battlefields as poets spoke chillingly of how the scavengers, along with wolves and eagles, stalked the aftermath and feasted on the corpses. These creatures were given such kennings as the 'seeker of the slain' and the 'spears-clash cuckoo'. Harald Hardrada, the last great Viking king and a poet, told of how the prince had made a 'Christmas meal for Gudena's ravens', while Egil Skallagrimsson who fought alongside King Athelstan recounted their presence at the Battle of Brunanburh and how the earl Hring 'held a weapon-moot, the ravens did not starve.'[7]

As carrion beasts, they have been deeply connected with humans for thousands of years, with Native American and Iron Age Scandinavian art and masks, including at Sutton Hoo, depicting the birds as the face of humans, representing the inner nature of humanity.[8]

Drawing on the association of ravens with war and death, one place name in an ancient charter could finally reveal the location of the Battle of Ashdown in 871. After taking over leadership of the army, Halfdan, whose name means 'Half Dane', rose to prominence, as the *Anglo-Saxon Chronicle* refers to a 'Halfdene' (Halfdan) who along with Bagsecg was one of two 'heathen kings' at the Battle of Ashdown, which was the first time this contemporary source had ever named any leaders.

Ivar had headed to join up with Olaf and besieged Alt Clut, while Ubbe may have accompanied him or headed to Ireland, where he is linked to the slaying of southern Brega king Máel Sechnaill around the same time. While Halfdan's movements in the historical record are unknown beforehand, he would prove just as warlike and ruthless as his brothers.

Sometimes called 'Halfdan of the wide embrace', he had been the archetypal Viking Age ruler, always on the move, seeking plunder, glory and vengeance. He led the army into possibly seven of eight battles in a year against Wessex as he ruthlessly sought to wipe out the most powerful Anglo-Saxon kingdom and continued warring until the bitter end as many comrades began finally settling down. Known as Hvitserk or Hwitserk in the sagas, which means 'white shirt', he was the third son of Aslaug and Ragnar after Ivar and Bjorn. While the name Halfdan never appears in the sagas, the fact both Halfdan and Hivitserk were leaders of the Great Heathen Army and ruled in Danish realms in contemporary texts and Old Norse tradition does strongly suggest they were the same person. For some unknown reason, he was known as Hvitserk rather than Halfdan, which was a popular name among Scandinavian nobles.

Although not explicitly stated, the texts suggest that Halfdan headed with his brothers on the legendary Mediterranean raid headed by his brother Bjorn. Upon hearing the news of his father's death at the hands of King Aella in a snake pit, Halfdan gripped and squeezed a board game piece so hard that 'blood spurted out of every nail' and then co-led the invasion of Britain to avenge his father's slaying.[9]

Northumbrian sources from the eleventh century onwards are unforgiving of Halfdan, giving him a suspiciously humiliating exit. One states that Halfdan had led the massive Viking army from its arrival. The early twelfth-century *Historia Regum* (*History of Kings*), which Symeon of Durham edited, records that in 866 'a great fleet of pagans' from the land of the Danes was under the command of 'king Haldane' (Halfdan) alongside Hinguar (Ivar) and Hubba (Ubbe).[10]

According to the *History of Kings*, Halfdan was a '*rex*' which means 'king' in Latin and his brothers Ivar and Ubbe are simply '*ducibus*', which equates to the role of chieftains and leaders. Symeon of Durham's *History of the Church of Durham* named Halfdene (Halfdan) first among the army leaders ahead of Hinguar (Ivar) and Hubba (Ubbe). *The History of Saint Cuthbert* twice makes a distinction between Ubbe as a '*dux*' compared to Halfdan being a 'king' of the Danes.

Notably, Halfdan was described as the 'scourge of the English people' and the co-leader of the Great Heathen Army alongside Ubbe, duke of the Frisians, according to the eleventh-century *About the Miracles and Translations of Saint Cuthbert*. There is clearly a distinction of Halfdan as a king while his brothers are not given the same authority, which suggest the Northumbrian chroniclers had better knowledge of the army's leadership.[11]

This language could reflect Halfdan having authority over a more established Danish realm, which is backed up by the *Annals of Fulda* description in 873 of a Danish king 'Halbden', the brother of a king 'Siegfried', who was clearly the historical archetype for Sigurd Snake in the Eye.[12]

Halfdan must have made a name for himself raiding, but there are no associated references before 871. Based on the sagas and Ireland's *Fragmentary Annals*, Halfdan would have joined Bjorn on the Mediterranean raid before he ruled the Jutland Danish realm, while Ivar launched the Great Heathen Army invasion and then joined the army in Anglo-Saxon England a few years later.

The year 871 proved the most turbulent year of warfare in Britain since the Roman invasion in the first century. Vikings set up a winter camp in 870 at Reading, on the south bank of the Thames in Berkshire, which was a gateway into Wessex heartland. They built a large rampart on the right side of the royal vill, the administrative centre of a royal estate, on a wedge-shaped ridge overlooking the rivers Kennet and the Thames near the modern-day Reading Abbey. Just north of the railway station, this is still remembered by Vastern Road as 'Vastern' meant 'stronghold' in Old English.

A fascinating discovery of a Viking sword alongside a man and a horse was made just 100 yards from the station's engine sheds (originally near platform 10) when workmen were digging a ballast pit in the early-nineteenth century.[13] Featuring a characteristic 'gripping beast' Scandinavian type of the period, with copper-alloy guards at each end of the hand grip, the sword, which has now been lost, had bent into the ribs of a complete horse skeleton next to the man.

Further potential evidence of the Viking encampment in Reading emerged through a late-ninth-century silver penny coin hoard at St Mary's Church, which was found in the coffin of a man in 1830. Eleven coins, consistent with a date of 870–71, were found among the hoard, which included seven from Mercian king Burgred and one from Edmund of East Anglia, along with Wessex mints with two from Ethelbert and one from Ethelred.

In 1966 at Sonning, close to the Thames in Reading, they found two adult men who were buried with a sword, a ringed pin (matching ones from the Viking cremation site at Heath Wood), an iron knife, six arrowheads and an iron strip with rivets. In addition, a sword, battle axes and spear heads have been uncovered at the mouth of the River Kennet.[14]

The grave unearthed in the modern-day station could have been a Viking chieftain killed in a skirmish with a local militia, which gave Wessex a much-needed ray of hope. Asser told of how Ethelwulf, the ealdorman of Berkshire, confronted two Viking earls who were raiding with their men at Englefield (the field of the Angles), and after a hard-fought battle, one of the earls was killed and a 'greater part of his army destroyed'.[15]

This victory would prove a false dawn. Brothers Ethelred and Alfred tried to storm the Viking encampment in Reading, but the enemy 'rushing like wolves out of every gate' defeated the Wessex army and exacted revenge by slaying Ethelwulf. In a desperate escape, the brothers headed to a river crossing at nearby Twyford, which the Vikings did not know about. Sensing their opportunity, the Vikings led by Halfdan soon followed in hot pursuit and most likely headed to Goring, around 10 miles away, where they could link up with the Ridgeway, believed to be England's oldest trackway.

At this stage, the chronicle and Asser downplay a perilous situation for the Wessex royal brothers. If they had been both killed or banished, the kingdom would have collapsed in the same manner as Northumbria, and a puppet ruler beholden to the Vikings installed in their place. Britain would have been robbed of one its most famous kings before his reign had begun.

Asser's glowing biography cemented Alfred's legacy, but he was groomed for greatness at an early age despite being the youngest of five brothers. He was in Rome meeting Pope Leo as a four-year-old and then returned three years later when his father Ethelwulf went on pilgrimage in 856. In the view of Asser, a monk from Dyfed in Wales who lived closely alongside Alfred at court, he 'surpassed all his brothers both in wisdom and in all good habits'.[16] As a result, Alfred was more 'greatly loved' than his brothers by his parents and everybody in fact. It wasn't until the thirteenth century that the moniker 'great' was attached to Alfred by the historian Matthew Paris, but it became a permanent association with the publication of *The Life of Alfred the Great* in 1709 by John Spelman.[17]

While illiterate as a child until aged twelve, Alfred began studiously learning Saxon poems and desired to boost literacy and champion the Old English language among all freeborn. He contributed to this goal by personally translating, or arranging the translation of, a series of seven Latin texts, which would prove one of his many enduring legacies. Old English was used in administration documents and charters from the seventh century, but great works of literature were almost exclusively written in Latin or Greek.

One of the seven works was Bede's eighth-century *Ecclesiastical History of the English People* as Alfred strived to promote a sense of nationhood and shared identity among the Anglo-Saxon kingdoms. To this end, Alfred's monks later compiled the *Anglo-Saxon Chronicle* after he was inspired by the Frankish annals. Alfred believed that Old English was the 'language we could all understand' but ultimately wanted to revive the use of Latin literacy, according to Marc Morris, author of *The Anglo-Saxons*.[18]

Once Alfred's mother challenged her sons to a reading contest in which the one who read every volume of a Saxon poem book would get to keep it. Alfred duly 'learned it by heart' and went back to his mother and recited the whole book. At all times, he also kept a prayer book close to hand and lamented how there were 'no good teachers' in the kingdom. As a marker of his character, Alfred gave away half of his income to found religious houses, which cared for the sick and poor.[19]

Throughout his life, Alfred himself was 'harassed day and night by many unknown diseases', which scholars believe was Crohn's disease, which caused an inflammation of the intestines. The Viking threat must have haunted the royal pretender, and at different points, Asser compares the violent attacks of his illness with the heathen violence.[20]

As the Viking threat intensified, there was an increasing burden on the landowning class to contribute to defences that Mercian kings Offa and Ethelbald had instigated. Wessex kings were able to demand an unusually large number of resources from their subjects in the form of manual labour, money and military service, which churches and landowners begrudgingly accepted.[21] One development was a select *fyrd*, drawn from every five hides of land, who were well equipped and soon became ambitious warriors. A general *fyrd* of all freemen in a shire could also be summoned in emergencies, but they did not have to serve for more than a half a day's march without pay.[22]

After their defeat at Reading, Asser's account recalls: 'Roused by this grief and shame, the Christians, after four days, with all their forces and much spirit advanced to battle against the aforesaid army (the Vikings), at a place called Ashdown, which in Latin signifies "Ash's Hill".'[23]

As Halfdan's army made their way down the Ridgeway, they may have stopped at the spectacular 360ft long chalk horse figure carved around the late Bronze Age, which gives the region its popular name – the Vale of the White Horse. The massive

Iron Age hillfort above the white horse offers the perfect spot to look for enemies at 275m (902ft) above sea level. Clearly, this small corner of England was a place of deep spiritual, religious and regional importance to ancient Britons for thousands of years, as evidenced by the nearby Neolithic chambered long barrow, known as Wayland Smithy.

Downlands and dramatic hilltops dominate the rural landscape, many formed from erosion, around the nearby village of Ashbury, and this area has long been considered the most persuasive choice for the battle's location.[24] The area itself is called Asshedoune (Ashdown) in a charter issued by King Ethelwulf, the father of Alfred and Aethelred, when he granted twenty hides to his minister Dudda in 840.[25] The charter was headed 'Asheburi' (Ashbury), which suggests it was a manor within an area known as Ashdown and other grants suggest the two names were interchangeable.[26]

Around 3 miles east outside the village, the National Trust owned Ashdown House is where the original charter begins and ends. The name Ashbury is thought to mean 'fort by the Ash tree', with the 'bury' related to the common Old English word *burh*, which was associated with a small enclosure with a V-shaped ditch and rampart, which Victorian antiquarians later named Alfred's Fort next to Ashdown House.

Fascinating research by a local historian Peter Knott supports the case for Ashbury after he found that in 1519 there was a record drawn up of the arable

The region of the Uffington White Horse next to the Ridgeway was the scene of a famous battle between Alfred and the Great Heathen Army. (Hedley Thorne)

land of Ashbury manor that made repeated references to 'the Wayte', which once covered most of the downlands between the Ridgeway and Icknield Way, east of the modern-day Ashbury village, in scrubs, bushes and trees.

Significantly, the Wayte, now arable and pastureland, is thought to mean 'the lookout place' or 'the ambush'. According to Knott, the name related to where Alfred's army waited to pounce, and they chose a wooded section to surprise the Great Heathen Army as they headed along the trackway. It would have made perfect sense in the chaotic war with the Great Heathen Army, because the Anglo-Saxons were repeating the tactics from the success at Englefield rather than the disaster at Reading. Knott noted.[27]

> *'Once the decision had been taken to use the Wayte as an ambush site, everything was subordinated to the element of surprise and to catching the Vikings in a poor formation. And the decision to set an ambush was a logical result of Ethelwulf's success against a moving column at Englefield and Ethelred's failure in his set piece confrontation at Reading.'*[28]

However, the plan backfired because Alfred was forced to either confront or avoid the Vikings without his full army, as Ethelred spent a 'long time in prayer', according to Asser. He recalls how the Vikings formed two divisions, arranging two shield-walls of similar size, which were split between the two kings – Halfdan and Bagsecg – and the earls on the other.

Viking shield-walls were a formidable sight as they often featured more than five deep ranks of men, with the better armoured and armed warriors at the front to meet the enemy head on. It is debated how closely packed the shield-wall could be because there was a great degree of hand-to-hand combat involved and room was needed for violent twisting, dodging and jumping back movements. A ninth-century tapestry in Osberg in Demark shows a shield-wall with partially overlapping shields. Experts believe that shields were interlocked at first to receive the impact of the initial charge before the formation loosened up.[29]

Mysterious figures known as *volur* meaning 'staff bearers' may have joined the Viking army, blessing their weapons, summoning dark spirits and calling for help from the all-father Odin, the god of war, in a ritual before battle commenced. Chanting from the monks accompanying Alfred's forces may have proved equally disturbing for the pagan warriors.[30]

In response to the Vikings forming shield-walls, Alfred divided his forces into two shield-walls and 'marched up swiftly with his men to the battlefield'. Glowingly, Asser boasts that Alfred rushed into battle like a 'wild boar, (and) courageously led the Christian troops against the hostile army'. After finally finishing his prayers and entering the fray, Ethelred's entry into the conflict proved

Reenactors line up in a shield-wall, a favoured battle tactic, which often featured five ranks of heavily armoured warriors. (Jennifer Robinson, Regia Anglorum)

a key turning point, but the Vikings still held the advantage, according to Asser, who added the 'heathen had seized the higher ground, and the Christian array was advancing up-hill. '[31]

When walking north-east along the Ridgeway, in the direction of Wayland's Smithy, there are pockets of small woodland, such as a strip between Odstone and Kingstone Coombes that extends to the Ridgeway where Alfred's army may have hidden until they were spotted.

Alfred could simply not wait for his brother and allow the Vikings to escape and compose themselves – it was now or never. The Vikings retreated and sought an advantage, which may have been the higher ground at Tower Hill to the east of the Ridgeway, where memorably Asser records how the bulk of the fighting had occurred around a lone thorn tree. While the thorn tree has obviously long since vanished, there is a tantalising and morbid clue.

In a 947 land charter of a grant of 20 hides from King Eadred to an Eadric, a mysterious boundary point along the route called 'Rammesburi', which means 'raven's fort', could have great significance as the second to last point before the boundary returns back to its original spot near Ashdown House according to Knott. This is a reference to the carrion creature that is synonymous with the aftermath of warfare in Old Norse and Old English texts, and it could prove pivotal in identifying the location of the battle. The actual 'raven's fort' suggested by the academic Margaret

Gelling was Weathercock Hill next to Ashdown Estate, where it's claimed ravens still habitat.[32] As you head from Ashdown Estate, you are confronted with this very steep hill, which is notably situated above Kingstone Down and the area includes a Kingstone Coombes, Kingston Lisle and a Kingston Warren. The famous Alfred's Blowing Stone just over a mile east of the White Horse hill is where legends say the king blew into the stone to summon his troops.

Knott believes the 'the pursuit and slaughter would have been south and east of the Wayte, which is the natural direction of flight, which fits with the belief that the Rammesburi was in the south-east part of the parish'.[33] The actual 'Rammesburi' is after a place called Horeston Ford, which is harder to identify because there is no obvious nearby ford.

The preceding 'wide gate', before the Horeston Ford, which is referenced in the 947 Ashbury charter, also features in another charter dated eight years later in a grant of eight hides from King Eadwig to Alefheah that covered the Compton Beauchamp parish next to Ashbury, which states 'to the wide gate east of Wayland's Smithy (Yelandes Smiððan).[34] This 'wide gate' was potentially related to an Iron Age or Romano-British settlement with an associated trackway running north-west to south-east and linked to the boundaries, which has been discovered just north of Tower Hill and near an area called Knighton Down.[35]

Horeston Ford is somewhat more of a puzzle. One local writer Nicola Cornick suggested Odstone found in various local place names is sometimes referred to as

The forces of Alfred and Ethelred most likely hid next to the Ridgeway to ambush the incoming Viking army.

'Ordeston', which shares obvious similarities.[36] Gelling believed the 'Horeston Ford' must have been a boundary stone, a view shared by some local walkers and historians who considered it formed part of a burial. In one case, a Horestone in Lower Swell, Gloucestershire, is derived from the elements *hār* and *stān*, meaning 'boundary stone'.[37]

I turned to the Oxford County Council's Historic Environment Records (HERs), which provides a wealth of information about landmarks, such as trackways, barrows and other monuments. Scouring the record provided a clue to the location of this famous battle between the Vikings and Wessex. The boundary stone in question appears to have been placed on the Woolstone parish boundary, just north of the Lambourne one, and next to a former Bronze Age barrow. This mound is no longer visible on the ground but estimated to have been 20m (65ft) in diameter and could still be seen in aerial photography in the late 1960s.[38]

Barrows were frequently used on land boundaries to mark the extent of territory. The presence of a barrow and large boundary stone on an open plain would naturally have been a significant feature when it came to mapping the land. The most likely 'Horeston Ford' candidate is roughly around a half mile from Weathercock Hill, which seems to be a rough distance between boundary points in Anglo-Saxon charters based on a previous Roman system, supporting its association with the 'raven's fort'.[39]

After the battle swung decisively in Alfred's favour, this must be where Halfdan's tired and fleeing warriors were cut down and slaughtered. Such a scenario would fit with a flight from the main area of warfare around Tower Hill. Many of the fleeing Vikings, exhausted and battered from fierce fighting, were seemingly cut down on the large open expanse between Tower Hill and Weathercock Hill.

Describing their casualties, Asser said they lost one of their two kings – Bagsecg and five ealdormen Sidroc the Elder, Sidroc the Younger, Obsern, Fraena and Harald, along with 'many thousands of their men were either slain at this spot or lay scattered far and wide over the whole field of Ashdown'.[40] Sidroc the Elder was possibly a big scalp as he is thought to be the same feared Viking leader who terrorised Francia in the 850s and was once joined by Bjorn Ironside's fleet. Halfdan himself may have suffered a personal loss because the Norman chronicler Geffrey Gaimar described Earl Harald as his nephew.[41]

The resulting horrific sight of the bodies strewn across the battlefield and these downlands led to the dark association with the raven's fort in a brutal age. One where the prospect of death for many young men was always so close that such creatures were revered.

Ragnar's famous final words 'laughing shall I die' represented a fearlessness when it came to death in Viking warrior culture, as they confronted mortality head on. Valkyries may have helped as they were clearly part of propaganda to convince countless people that the bravest and best warriors would be taken care of in Valhalla.[42] And the chief Viking god was always accompanied by his trusted ravens.

Weathercock Hill was once known as the 'raven's fort', a morbid recall of the slaughter of the Great Heathen Army after its defeat at the Battle of Ashdown.

A god whom the Anglo-Saxons called Woden and honoured by naming landmarks and days of the week (Wednesday) after, while kings claimed him as their ancestor.

Anglo-Saxons pursued the Vikings all the way through the night and the following day until they reached their stronghold in Reading 'slaying all they could reach, until it became dark', Asser wrote. A 30-mile hasty retreat to Reading by a Viking army being chased by Wessex forces could fit with the timescale, as historian Thomas Williams noted.[43]

In the chaotic years since the Great Heathen Army had arrived, Ashdown was overwhelmingly the biggest defeat of the Vikings so far. With the seemingly heroic part Alfred played, it was only natural for Asser to have dedicated so much attention to what proved a largely inconsequential victory, apart from galvanising a battered populace. Vikings were soon back in ascendancy and bolstered by a massive influx of new recruits. Within weeks they turned their attention again on the south-west as Wessex still teetered on the brink.

Chapter 12

WARRIOR BISHOP

Men of prayer, men of war, men of work. Without these (a king)
cannot perform any of the tasks entrusted in him
Boethius' *Consolation of Philosophy* translated
by Alfred the Great, ninth century

Crowds outside a small stone-built Saxon minster church were devastated as the defeated Wessex army returned from the Battle of Merantun with their fallen warrior bishop. Blood was visible on his sleeveless protective mail shirt, a mesh of hundreds of interlocking steel rings, while a Christian cross necklace hung from his neck and his trusted pattern-welded Frankish sword with a walnut-shaped pommel was carried alongside.[1]

Memorably depicted in the *Vikings* TV series by the Irish actor Jonathan Rhys Meyers, the character of Bishop Heahmund was based on a real-life Bishop of Sherborne killed during the Battle of Merantun and later buried in Keynsham between Bristol and Bath.

Claims thousands of Vikings had been killed at Ashdown were clearly an exaggeration because just over two weeks later Alfred and Ethelred were defeated at a royal estate known as Old Basing, east of modern Basingstoke on 22 January 871. After Halfdan's army was victorious at Basing, the situation for Wessex grew even bleaker as Asser remarked 'another heathen army came from beyond the sea and joined them' to reinforce their numbers, dubbed the 'Great Summer Army' (*micel sumorlida*) in the *Anglo-Saxon Chronicle*.[2] Two months later, the armies met again on 22 March 871 at the Battle of Merantun, where Bishop Heahmund was slain.

Tenth-century chronicler Ethelward, a descendant of Alfred's brother Ethelred, told of how Wessex fought against an 'army of barbarians on a wide front' at 'Merantun' and 'a multitude was killed on either side'. According to Ethelward: 'The barbarians won the blessing of victory. Then fell Bishop Heahmund, killed by the sword, and his body lies buried at Keynsham. Many fell in the same battle, and [many were] put to flight.'[3]

During the years 854 and 867, Bishop Heahmund witnessed several charters on behalf of Wessex's kings, according to Keynsham-based historian

Andy Williams, whose research is shining a light on this enigmatic figure. Williams said:

> *'The threat from the Great Heathen Army was so great that they wanted the church to stand up to these Vikings as well and what better role model than this warrior bishop, who is not only a man of God but is there defending the Christian faith and the king.'*[4]

Williams has reviewed the charters for Heahmund tracing an earlier career within the royal court of Wessex. Bishop Heahmund regularly signed charters that concerned grants of land to religious institutions, earls or nobles. He is either described as an *episcopus*, which means a bishop in a Christian church who governs a diocese, or a *presbiter*, derived from the Greek word *presbyteros* meaning elder and signifies an officer or minister in the Christian church.

One 863 charter where Heahmund is named involved the grant of nine *sulungs* (an old Kentish term for ploughlands) from King Ethelbert to a minister called Athelred in Mersham, Kent, in exchange for 400 mancuses (equivalent to 30 silver pence) in gold.[5]

In 867, Bishop Heahmund was consecrated as the Bishop of Sherborne and continued overseeing land charters such as a grant in the same year of fifteen hides from King Ethelred to St Paul's Monastery in Essex.[6]

Anglo-Saxon religious life was severely impacted by the repeated Viking raids on monasteries and churches in the ninth century, but Alfred the Great believed the church's decline was apparent long beforehand. By the ninth century, there was a clear shift in religious monastic life within monasteries. These were increasingly seen as economic assets and staffed by monks who acted more as clerks and abandoned strict religious disciplines, as can be seen at Coldingham monastery, which was severely damaged by a fire in the late-ninth century. Twelfth-century chronicler Symeon of Durham blamed 'lax' monks for their 'feasting, drinking, conversation and other improprieties' instead of dedication to prayer and study.[7] Book production between 835 to 885 ceased almost entirely with just three manuscripts written.[8]

With the Viking threat, Alfred may have been driven to extreme lengths and have taken land from the church or its resources to aid military campaigns, as a letter from Pope John VIII to the Archbishop of Canterbury accuses the king and others of 'wronging the house of the lord'.[9]

In 742, at the Concilium Germanicum, the first major church synod in eastern Francia, Emperor Carloman with the Anglo-Saxon missionary St Boniface established a requirement for military chaplains. At first, Frankish bishops were praying from higher ground during battle and providing contingents of troops.[10]

These became known as the *casati* ('the housed ones') and were under the bishop's direct command, and he provided them with land or accommodation along with money and equipment for warfare.[11]

This church militarisation could be seen in Wessex, which was greatly influenced by the West Franks, where Bishop Heahmund's predecessor, Ealhstan, was another warrior bishop, who fought against the Vikings in 848 with Somerset forces, which ended in a 'great slaughter' of the Northmen.[12] Williams believes that Eahlstan had been a mentor to Bishop Heahmund, which may have extended to the art of warfare. Many Anglo-Saxon nobles were expected to be skilled warriors, as well as being dedicated Christians and learned to hunt from an early age, but instances of warrior bishops are rare.

Bishop Heahmund had possibly hailed from a powerful family in Kent as the *mund* element is an Old English word for 'guardian', shared by a Kentish king Ealhmund, a late-eighth century ruler who was Alfred's great-grandfather.

Professor James Clark from Exeter University, who is overseeing the research by Andy Williams, said Heahmund was a 'loyal' government servant doing the king's business, but is unlikely to have had a following or family ties in Wessex.

> *'Heahmund is something of an outsider who has just risen in royal government service and the bishopric of Sherborne is the reward. He doesn't fit any template for a bishop and that might suit his royal master, but it doesn't sit easily with the churchmen around him.'*[13]

A puzzling question is why Bishop Heahmund was buried in Keynsham and not the church of Sherborne, the centre of his diocese, but his warrior status most likely sat uneasily with the Christian congregation. The same was true with other religious warriors in Francia, where Hincmar, the Archbishop of Reims who authored the *Annals of St Bertin* from 861 until his death in 882, objected to bishops taking up arms even though he himself had fought on battlefields.[14] Most religious churchmen thought the act of spilling blood by the clergy should only be done by military orders, such as through the Knights Templar or Teutonic Knights.[15]

Prof Clark said: 'At the time of his death, the monks of Sherborne were already promoting the saintly reputation of their first bishop, Aldhelm, who died in 709 and whose career as a monk and scholar was more in keeping with their priorities than the unconventional churchman, Heahmund.'[16]

Heahmund's final resting place probably became a shrine with his newfound martyrdom status, and devoted Christians flocked to pay their respect and offer up thanks with gifts. Given the bishop is remembered in Ethelward's chronicle, which was out of living memory, Clark believed that 'people were still beating a path to this place' which they would only do for a place of significance: 'Burying a man who has died battling the pagans, not close to Wessex's heartland but on the frontier where the pagan threat is most real makes a lot of political capital because you have this churchman who is in effect a martyr for the faith.'

Merantun proved a massive blow for Wessex because a few weeks later Ethelward notes King Ethelred died and was buried at Wimborne Minster in Dorset. Before his death, Ethelred, who was probably wounded at Merantun, had agreed to pass the throne to his brother Alfred, a now experienced military commander, rather than his own sons, Ethelhelm and Ethelwold, who were still young children.

Wimborne is 14 miles away from Martin, which has compelling claims as the location of the battle. It had been recorded as 'Mertone' in 946 in a grant from King Edmund, then ruler of a now unified England, to his queen Ethelflaed in a large land grant of 100 hides at Damerham, Martin and Pentridge in Dorset.[17] This richly historical area centred around the chalk grasslands of Martin Down nature reserve, includes the old Ackling Dyke Roman road and the Bokerley Dyke, a three-mile-long earthwork, which still marks part of the Dorset and Hampshire boundary and remains remarkably well preserved. Martin Down, which matches Ethelward's description of a 'wide front', is home to more than a dozen burial mounds, including bowl-shaped barrows, such as a cluster of three north of Bokerley Dyke that are still detectable, possibly hastily created for slain Vikings.[18]

Williams believes the similarly named Marden in Wiltshire, around 6 miles south-east of Devizes and recorded in the *Domesday Book* as 'Mersedene', has stronger claims and shares the same landscape as Martin.[19] He highlighted how

This barrow at Martin Down is one of a cluster of three and is possibly linked to the Battle of Merantun, where Bishop Heahmund fell.

Marden is closer to Keynsham – 33 miles compared to 54 for Martin – and easier to reach via the River Avon, which was significant when factoring in possible decomposition. A few miles away also lies the ancient Ridgeway trackway and Wansdyke, a huge ditch extending across the south-west in three sections.

Bishop Heahmund was buried on the possible site of an old Anglo-Saxon minster church, where the later Keynsham Abbey was built around 1166. During excavations in the 1960s to create the modern-day bypass and in the 1870s by Loftus Brock, the abbey had thrown up Anglo-Saxon artefacts. A skull was discovered some four feet under the foundations of the south transept, a walkway across the main body of the building, potentially dated to the Anglo-Saxon period from the excavations in the 1960s. Medical evidence showed signs of trauma and indicated a violent death. An Anglo-Saxon grave slab was found in the south aisle, which connects to the transept. In the chapter house, there was evidence of Anglo-Saxon stone carvings and slab-sided burials from a similar era orientated to suggest they were Christian because they faced the sun from the east where the Lord would rise.[20]

Williams is convinced the final resting place of Heahmund had been in the ruins of Keynsham Abbey, now a modern-day memorial park, as 'people who suffered a violent death' were also buried there. He found that the person who suffered

The ruins of Keynsham Abbey, which was believed to have been the site of an old Saxon minister, where Bishop Heahmund was laid to rest. (Rob Callaway)

a major head wound had survived the injury, and he may well be Heahmund.[21] As a warrior bishop, such battle scars may be unsurprising. Williams has gained funding for a plaque for Heahmund in Keynsham 'to better remember and celebrate Bishop Heahmund, who he was, why he died and who he died fighting alongside, because over time, he has been forgotten and deserves to be better recognised and celebrated.'[22] His research is ongoing, and he stressed his viewpoints may change, including on the location of Merantun as he also suggests Marten in Wiltshire.

After Bishop Heahmund's death, the situation remained grave for Alfred and Wessex. His forces clashed again with the Vikings at Wilton, which Wiltshire is named after, but they were defeated after a Viking retreat 'took advantage of their pursuers' rashness'. Asser said the Christians only had 'a small number of men' left after eight battles against the Vikings and 'countless skirmishes.[23] Afterwards Wessex made peace with the Vikings on the condition they would depart the kingdom, which they did.

Vikings led by Ivar, Ubbe and Halfdan had repeatedly outwitted and defeated the Anglo-Saxon kingdoms including Wessex, launching campaigns during the winter months, which were normally avoided because of the difficulties of marching armies on wet or frozen trackways, and they often caught the Anglo-Saxons off guard before and during battles. The Great Heathen Army must have won six of the eight battles during 871 – two of which are unknown – referred to by Asser, including Reading, Old Basing, Merantun and Wilton.

Academic Simon Keynes said the *Anglo-Saxon Chronicle*, which was composed by Alfred's monks, often draws positives from the continuous defeats in 871. At Reading, Merantun and Wilton, the descriptions talk of how a 'great slaughter was made on both sides' or the 'West Saxons were victorious far into the day' but in each case conclude the Danes held or took possession of the battlefield.[24] Keynes said it was akin to 'the Danes may have won but didn't the English do well?'

The chronicle also describes how Alfred made peace with the Vikings in 871, 876 and 877 as if he had 'pacified the enemies on advantageous terms', according to Keynes. In reality, the peace deal would have involved a payment of tribute and supplies to the Vikings, an exchange of hostages and a reciprocal swearing of oaths and agreements.

Clearly the chronicle was putting a positive spin on the repeated Viking victories in battles and negotiations, but there was solace because the warfare of 871 had taken its toll on the Great Heathen Army. Wilton would prove the last major conflict between Wessex and the Vikings for the next six years.

Chapter 13

WINTER CAMP

When winter follows summer, the long ships take a rest after the journey. Ale wearies the host of men, the hall is again filled and the full cup swings empty after the gift of gold.

Háttatal, Snorri Sturluson, 13th century[1]

Excavations for a new boiler house in the Houses of Parliament revealed an ancient sword deep in the foundations. Surrounded by marshland, Thorney Island was a former gravel island of between twelve to fifteen hectares through which two channels of the former River Tyburn passed and entered the Thames. Uncovered in 1948, the sword ended up at 35ft below in a layer of clay underneath the current Victoria Tower Gardens, and in the same south-east corner, they found two horse skulls and limb-bones. The pattern welded weapon was made after iron and steel layers were rolled, twisted, ground down and then welded together. While the pommel and upper guard was missing and it was broken in two when excavated, the sword was around 74.6cm in length and 4cm in width, and it is still on display in the English Heritage-run Jewel Tower across from the Houses of Parliament, where kings stored their wealth.[2]

Lundenwic (meaning 'London trading town', as *wic* is associated with markets and settlement) around Covent Garden in central London had been a booming trade market of some 150 acres, but Viking raids caused havoc from the ninth century. Since its days as a Roman fortress to the modern metropolis, there have been few eras when London has not been central to the politics, power and fortunes of the island. Amid the increasing threat of Viking raids, the war with the Great Heathen Army was one of those rare moments when the influence of the city dwindled as Lundenwic fell into terminal decline for several decades, but it remained significant enough for Halfdan and his army to set up camp in the winter of 871. This sword uncovered in the Houses of Parliament might just be a remnant of their overwintering.

As far as the Vikings travelled across Britain and Ireland, it is fascinating to realise that they could have made camp on Thorney Island in 871, where modern politicians debate and shape the laws of the land. A small but iconic corner of Britain and the capital city that is so synonymous with the island's past and present. The

The ancient sword discovered deep in the foundations of the Houses of Parliament could be linked to the Viking camp of 871/72. It is now on display in the Jewel Tower. (Paul Harper/English Heritage)

Viking encampment was ideally situated near a major church and the Lundenwic market area and they either stayed on Thorney Island or holed up further along the north side of the river in the old Roman walled fortress, which at its peak covered 330 acres and a vast area – the modern City of London district, between Temple and Tower Bridge.

Other camps could have accommodated the different contingents of the army. Described as an 'innumerable summer army' by Athelward, the reinforcements that had arrived earlier in the year and joined forces with the Vikings camped at Reading were probably led by Guthrum, who was the later nemesis of Alfred. Guthrum could be related to the similarly named Gudrum, who fought a devastating civil war against his uncle Horik I, which supposedly wiped out the royals, except for the next ruler Horik II.[3] Army leaders such as Halfdan and Guthrum were pacing alongside the River Thames and plotting their next steps.

A report into the Westminster Palace sword by Gerald Dunning and Vera Evison noted how the sword has similarities with the one found alongside the skeleton of a man and a horse in Reading station, which featured the gripping beast creatures common on Viking Age jewellery and weapons. This person buried in Westminster

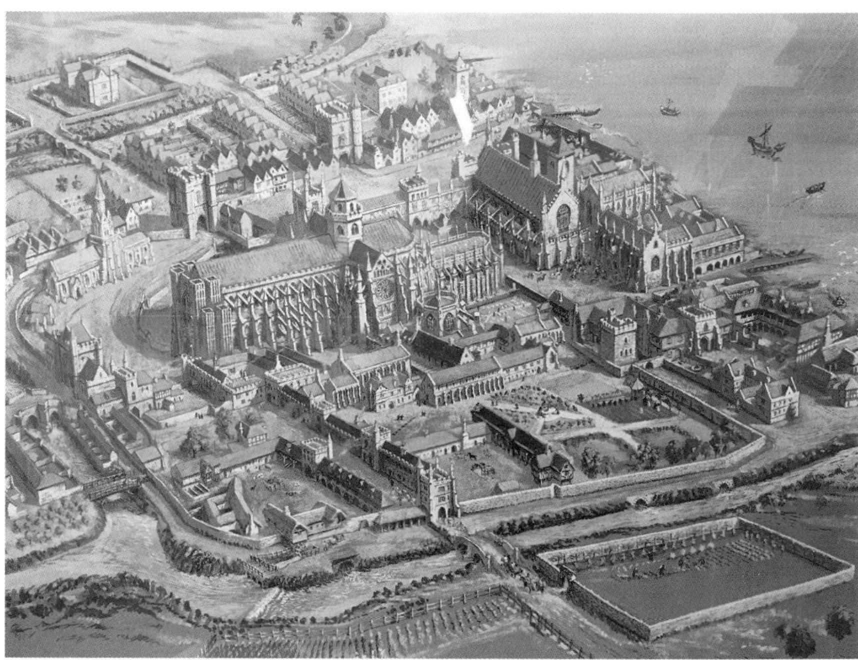

A chalk drawing of the iconic Palace of Westminster and Thorney Island from the sixteenth century when it was still a gravel island. (*The Abbey of St Peter and Palace of Westminster about the Year 1537*, pastels on paper by Percy Drake Brookshaw after a 1936 engraving by A. E. Henderson, reproduced by permission, Woodmansterne)

may have been a leading Northman laid to rest alongside his horse after being killed in the final battle of 871 at Wilton.[4]

The handle belonged to a series that was common across north-western Europe during the eighth century. It was possibly made in Rhineland within the Frankish kingdom, and based on other similar finds, the production centre has been narrowed down to Dendermonde in Belgium and Mannheim in Germany. The leaf-shaped scroll design that features in panels on the hilt guard may have been inspired by Anglo-Saxon art styles, such as the bronze Tassilo chalice, gilded with silver and gold, dated to 777, which featured intricately designed animals and foliage. Another similar high-quality sword found in Fetter Lane in the Farringdon area of London, around 2 miles away, featured gold-leaf scrolls in a black setting that includes a serpent monster as the focal point.[5]

Pattern-welded Frankish swords became the weapon of choice for Viking nobles, which often featured a heavy pommel to counterbalance the weight of the blade.[6] The report into the sword's discovery by Gerald Dunning and Vera Evison said the Britons found out the hard way about the blades after the Great Heathen Army arrived: 'The English were (unlikely to be) in possession of swords of a fighting quality equal to those wielded by the Vikings at the time of invasions. The virtues of heavier guards and pommels are presumed to have been learnt by the natives after bitter experience.'[7]

A hoard of coins was uncovered under Westminster Bridge in approximately 1895, which included one of the Mercian king Burgred dated to roughly 871, but the hoard was sold before it could be documented. Two other swords found in 1840 and 1897 near the same bridge were dated to the late-ninth or early-tenth century.[8] Westminster Abbey was founded in the late-tenth century, but it is believed to have replaced or situated near an existing church.

In 1862, a large haul of more than 250 Anglo-Saxon coins, ingots and hacksilver, known as the Croydon Hoard, was found near Colliers Water Lane in Thornton Heath during the laying of a railway line, seemingly left by a Viking who decided to hide his loot. Many coins have fallen into private hands, but the hoard is believed to have included ninety-six kings associated with Mercian rulers, twenty-four connected to East Anglian kings and fifty-six from Wessex that were made up of twenty-five issued by Ethelred I (866–71) and thirty-one of Alfred.[9] Mercians made peace with the Vikings in the winters of 871 and 872, which would have inevitably involved giving a large tribute and supplies to keep the army at bay.

One fascinating imitation coin, based on two Alfred designs, has been linked to Halfdan and the 871 overwintering, which features the Old English spelling of his name 'Healfdene'. One of these coin types, issued by Alfred and Ceowulf II together, was known as the 'Two Emperors' because it featured two seated rulers. The other type was known as the 'London Monogram' because it depicts 'LYNDONIA' (London) on one side and features a stylised portrait of Alfred.

Historic coin expert Gareth Williams said the 'London Monogram' type, which was also found in the early-tenth century Cuerdale Hoard, was issued between 879–80 after Halfdan was known to be active in Britain and must have been associated with a later Halfdan. This was possibly the 'Healfden' killed alongside a Hingwaer (Ivar) and Eowils (Auisle), the latter is the same name of an Irish ally of the historical Ivar the Boneless, at the Battle of Tettenhall in 911, or another one who ruled during the late 880s or 890s.[10] The obvious similarity with the names suggests these were descendants, grandchildren, of the original Ivar, Halfdan and Auisle.[11]

In 872, the Vikings returned to quell a rebellion in Northumbria, where its puppet ruler Ecgberht and the Archbishop Wulfhere were driven out by locals for collaborating with the Northmen. In the same year, they fixed their winter quarters at Torksey in Mercia.

A massive investigation led by archaeologists Dawn Hadley and Julian Richards with English Heritage sparked by metal detector finds at Torksey has provided a fascinating insight into the Great Heathen Army. Measuring around 55 hectares (136 acres), equivalent to 75 football pitches, and bigger than the four contemporary Scandinavian trading sites – Birka at 6 hectares; Kaupang at 5.4, Ribe at 12 and Hedeby at 24 – this winter camp was enormous. By now, the army was numbering many thousands, with a population of up to 5,000 people. Located on a prominent buff around 5–10m (16–32ft) in height, the camp was effectively an island bordered by the River Trent to the west and surrounded by marshes and wetland, close to a Roman Road and the Humber estuary.[12]

Investigations showed Torksey was a hive of trade and activity – in effect a temporary Viking town. A large civilian population accompanied the army, including carpenters and blacksmiths who were in demand with their mobile forges, which could repair damaged or captured weapons. With heat and steam rising from their gorge, the blacksmith would be forging new rivets for the ships and happily sharpen a knife or sword.[13]

A burial discovered in the Aust-Adger county of south-east Norway of a Great Heathen Army member, underneath a mound of roughly 20m (62ft) in diameter, found they were laid to rest with two lead weights inset with Northumbrian stycas featuring Eanred, who was an early-ninth-century ruler of the kingdom. They were also buried with a sword, an axe, iron anvil, pliers, an ingot mould and a soapstone with a hole in it, which would have been used in the forge to direct the current of air from bellows on the fire. This individual was remembered as a warrior, silversmith and a trader – highlighting the skillset common among the Great Heathen Army.[14]

Silversmiths could be found further along, armed with hammers, tongs and a set of lead weights, who could craft impressive objects, such as arm rings and necklaces. Trees were being cut down for replacement planks for the longships and other vessels, while tar was extracted from birch, which was a vital component for coating the ships and sails to make them water and wind resistant. A hoard of iron woodworking tools, including four axe heads, an axe hammer and a two-edged blade along with iron bark-stripper show the preparation of felled trees for the new longship planks.[15]

Food was their Achilles heel as one tonne per 500 men along with animal fodder was needed every day. Sheep, cows and pigs stolen from surrounding farmlands or handed over as tribute were kept in one designated part of the camp.[16,17] Another area featured ovens for heating the grain, which was essential for porridge, bread and perhaps most importantly wine. Hooks and several pieces of chain were likely from a cauldron of stew or soup above a campfire. Different sections housed brotherhood gangs of Vikings sleeping in wooden-framed tents lined with furs and blankets.[18]

Most of the Vikings spent their nights huddled around a fire, gambling, exchanging war stories and arguing about board games. More than 300 tiny lead gaming pieces have been discovered which were cut out of a lead sheet and pressed into a conical shape. Viking nobles loved board games such as *hnefatafl*, which means 'fist table' and was played on a chequered board (*tafl*) of thirteen by thirteen or eleven by eleven squares. Darker pieces had to defend the *hnefi* (fist) and the lighter pieces would surround and attack it. The *Hervarar saga* speaks of how the dark pieces guard their 'defenceless king' but the fair go 'forth and attack'. Based on a reference to 'eight (and) horns', an eight-sided dice may have determined how many moves a player could make. These games honed the tactics and strategy skills needed for battlefields when relying on might alone was never enough.[19]

And they were also linked to fate as shown in 'Völuspá' when Norse gods are playing in a meadow and three supernatural women arrive and warn of Ragnarök:

Artist's impression of the massive Viking winter camp at Torksey, which was the size of 75 football pitches. (Compost Creative)

'They played chequers in the meadow, for them there was no want of gold, until there came three Ogres' daughters of reputable strength from giant realms.'[20]

As the alcohol flowed, tempers flared as well. Fragmented human remains were found in two areas of higher ground on the camp, belonging to possibly two males aged 18–25 and 18–35. A skull fragment from one showed two separate blows from a sharp implement, which suggested a violent death.[21]

Children and women were part of the winter camp based on the discovery of textile working. The spindle whorls, needles, needle cases, linen smoothers and shears found are consistently associated with female graves. The large number of Anglo-Saxon dress accessories and jewellery, which include 136 copper-alloy strap ends and hooked tags for fastening leggings, are thought to relate to hostages captured by the Vikings after their military victories and raids to keep as concubines or trade. Slaves at Torksey were traded regularly in exchange for gold and silver.[22] They may have also been used for labour and sexual services.[23]

Evidence emerged of major economies running alongside, with bullion playing a significant role.[24] Before it fully adopted a monetary economy, the Vikings used bullion when the weight and size of the metal determined its value. This bullion was often in the form of ingots, a solid shape of silver, copper-alloy and more rarely gold, which had been melted down and then moulded into a shape. The copper-alloy ones may have also been used in metalworking.

The concentration of gold at Torksey was unique compared to other Viking winter encampments and suggested it was being melted down from church treasures and other loot. Gold, silver and copper alloy were being used in bullion and monetary form. This was a result of trade with the local communities, and the distribution of precious metals by leaders who sought to maintain their status.[25]

Torksey finds included thirty-seven pieces of hacked up silver and jewellery fragments and nine pieces of cut up gold. Numerous fragmented or whole blocks of ingots, the metal bars used in bullion transactions, were picked up including forty-three that were made of silver, seven using gold and seventeen with copper alloy. More than 200 Northumbrian copper-alloy styca small coins have been found despite them not circulating widely outside the kingdom. Eighty-three coins featured the king Ethelred II who possibly ruled between 841–49 and 858–62 and eight belonged to the shadowy Raedwulf mentioned in Chapter 7.

A total of 147 dirhams, the largest concentration on any site in Britain or Ireland, were found dropped on the campsite.[26] These coins had been cut into smaller fractions for bullion rather than for monetary value and had clearly exchanged hands among army members. Dirhams were regarded as a more trusted piece of silver content compared to Frankish and Anglo-Saxon coins, which were frequently debased, meaning the level of pure silver in the coin was reduced to increase the number they could produce.[27]

An assortment of the multitude of finds from the Torksey winter camp, including ingots, weights, coins and a Thor hammer. (© The Fitzwilliam Museum, University of Cambridge)

Remarkably, it is believed the dirhams at Torksey from the Middle East, originating in possibly Iraq, Iran or Uzbekistan, had travelled via the vast trading routes to Scandinavia through Birka and Kaupang and onto Torksey. This journey of 1,900 miles may have taken just five years.[28]

And the Vikings were soon on the move again. At one of their next sites, perhaps the most spectacular archaeological discovery connected to the legend of Ragnar Lothbrok and his sons was uncovered.

Chapter 14

KING OF THE NORSE

The wind is sharp tonight he throws up the white mane on the sea;
I have no worries that the wild warriors from Lothlind shall lay their
course over a calm sea.

Found in the margins of a copy of *Institutiones Grammaticae*,
Priscian, possibly ninth century[1]

A 'nine foot long' giant was uncovered in a mysterious burial mound outside St Wystan's Church in Repton in the late-seventeenth century, surrounded by 100 bodies with 'their feet pointing towards the skeleton'. Labourer Thomas Walker, who made the discovery in 1686, sounded almost fantastical as he described a massive stone coffin and gigantic occupant in an underground structure.[2]

For another 200 years, the discovery remained a mystery until the archaeologists Martin and his wife Birthe Kjølbye-Biddle began investigating. They uncovered a sunken two-roomed stone building west of the church that dated from the late-seventh to early-eighth century, which had probably been a mortuary chapel. This building had been cut down to serve as the chamber of a burial mound in the Vicarage Gardens, with the bones of at least 264 people stacked against the walls in one of the chapel's two rooms around a central figure in a sarcophagus. Covered with flat stones resting on wooden planks, the chamber had been sealed by a low stone cairn, surrounded by an earth mound.[3]

Sadly, the central burial had not survived, or the sarcophagus, and it was claimed the head had been given to the then master of Repton School. Among the bone fragments, excavations found an iron axe, a double-edged sword, two fighting knives (known as *saexes*), precious metalwork and five silver pennies dated to 872–74.[4] Four children, aged between 6 and 17, who were found on a corner of the mound with a sheep's jaw at their feet may have been ritually sacrificed.[5]

Studies showed that 80 per cent of those buried were mostly male aged 18 to 45 and a 'massively robust' non-local population, according to Martin Biddle, which matched burial sites in Scandinavia, while the females were possibly Anglo-Saxon and may have been enslaved during the Great Heathen Army campaign. Investigations revealed a D-shaped ditch, a feature of Viking Age settlements including Hedeby and Birka, which used the church as a gateway. The straight line

The mysterious mound, possibly the final resting place of Ivar the Boneless, was created above a sunken two-roomed former building – believed to be a mortuary chapel. (Martin Biddle)

at the back ran along the banks of the Old Trent Water, an abandoned channel of the River Trent.[6]

Radiocarbon dating had been skewed by an issue known as the 'maritime effect', which suggested the Repton mass burial dead were buried long before the Viking arrived, but this was resolved because carbon in fish from the ocean is much older than in land-based food, and the Viking crews naturally ate a lot of seafood.[7]

The Biddles concluded the dead were from the Great Heathen Army. This was supported by the contemporary *Anglo-Saxon Chronicle*, which told how the Vikings had overwintered in Repton between 873–74 and kicked out the Mercian king Burgred. He was replaced by an 'unwise king's thane' called Ceolwulf II, a puppet king for the Vikings, who were now pulling the strings of rulers in East Anglia and Northumbria as well.

Given the obvious shrine-like importance of the burial, this must have been a leader of the Viking army and the prime candidate for the central burial at Repton was immediately suspected to be Ivar the Boneless who, after raiding across Ireland with Olaf's son Eysteinn in 872, had died the following year. The *Annals of Ulster* reported in 873: 'Ímar [Ivar], king of the Norsemen of all Ireland and Britain, ended his life.'[8]

This was the first time a Viking leader had been given pre-eminence over all the groups in Britain and Ireland, and his potential grave became a shrine, which was evidenced by later burials to the east of the mound that featured gold-embroidered and silver garments of Viking type.

In a report, Professor Martin Biddle said: 'whether or not this mound was the burial place of Ivar *beinlausi* (Boneless) who died in 873, whose brother Healfdene (Halfdan) was one of the four leaders of the Viking Army at Repton in 873–74, it is clear that this mound and the area of Viking interest shown by burials around the church had become in some manner a place of memory, a *mindesmærke* (memorial), for the people of Scandinavian origin now settled in the Repton area'.[9]

In the penultimate ever *Vikings* TV episode, Ivar wonders whether the people who discover his bones will know he was the 'most famous Viking of them all' and this may have been that real-life moment. Whether Ivar was the actual army leader has been debated, but as one scholar pointed out, the chroniclers only tended to name Viking rulers when the Anglo-Saxons won battles, and Ivar had never lost.[10]

Conquests of Mercia, Northumberland and East Anglia must have generated enormous wealth that was shared among the army, and the epic burial was their tribute in return. As shown by the possible war dead alongside, there had been a heavy cost.

St Wystan's Church from above, one of the most famous Viking Age archaeological sites. The mass grave was discovered in the garden to the right of the main church building. (Martin Biddle)

Although Ivar became synonymous with cruelty through texts by later religious figures, this is contrasted by how the Scandinavian people clearly viewed him as a hero for conquering new lands to settle, and as descent from Ivar became crucial to future kings of the 'dark foreigners' in Dublin and York, it shows his acclaim.

St Wystan's Church was named after a murdered ninth-century Mercian prince, who shunned the kingship for religious life. His bones were placed in the remarkable crypt underneath the church, which soon became a place of pilgrimage. When visiting Repton on a gloomy winter day, I had a nervy experience of creeping down the narrow stone steps down to the crypt, which was also in near darkness. A sense of intrigue at this hallowed place, surely shared by the hordes of pilgrims who made the same journey, gripped me as I edged down the steps. For somewhere at the centre of such a dark yet fascinating chapter in British history, it was a fitting mood.

The tiny crypt, about 16ft square and 10ft high with nine square bays, features four central columns and arched windows to the north, east and south. Bones of the Mercian kings Ethelbald and Wiglaf, along with Wystan, were placed in caskets and put in one of the four recesses in the wall. Monks were given advance warning of the Viking arrival and managed to remove Wystan's remains and the wealth in time. The church was severely damaged by fire, but the Vikings left the crypt alone.[11]

As I stood near the spot where Ivar was likely buried and which became filled with the bones of hundreds of fellow Vikings, the church's looming spire was inescapable in the adjacent churchyard, and it remains intriguing that such devoted pagans, in such a divisive, religious age, chose the site. Many who had no doubt taken part savoured the violence of raiding religious sites and wore Thor hammer pendants as a blunt rejection of the Christian faith. They were now hedging their bets with the afterlife and trying to appease the Christian god. With Vikings now being buried at a place that held such deep resonance for the Mercians, it was also a clear statement of power over surrounding communities.

Ivar's ally Olaf the White, who co-ruled in Dublin, was killed at a similar time when collecting tribute in Pictland by the kingdom's ruler Constantine I. Based on the Pictish Chronicle, this occurred three years after a raid in Armagh in 869, which coincided with St Patrick's Festival. A harrowing brief note in the *Annals of Ulster* claims Olaf's forces killed or enslaved a 'thousand' people and a 'great rapine' was committed.[12]

Olaf's final years are confused because he left Ireland to help his father, Gofraid, back in Norway in 872 based on the *Fragmentary Annals*. However, it refuses to say anymore because it has 'little relevance' and the Irish who they are most concerned about 'suffer many evils from themselves.'[13]

One puzzling aspect is that the *Fragmentary Annals* claim Ivar and Olaf were brothers and the sons of a Gofraid and grandsons of a Ragnall, but it is likely the term was a metaphor that meant 'brothers in arms'.[14] They are never linked as brothers in contemporary sources or later sagas.

The vicarage gardens, next to the church in Repton, where the mass burial was discovered.

Curiously, Ivar's death is not mentioned in the *Fragmentary Annals*, but it does record in 873 that Gofraid, king of Lochlann, died in the same year from a 'sudden hideous disease, thus it pleased God'. These two deaths were most likely mixed up after Ivar was called a 'king of the Norsemen', and notably 'Ragnar's Saga' says Ivar 'died of a sickness'.[15] While the association of Ivar and Gofraid as father and son is unlikely, names among Ivar's dynasty suggest someone of this name played an important role in founding the port of Dublin because they could include six kings with this name, along with five Ragnalls (Rognvald but linked to Ragnar), nine Amlaibs (Olaf), four Sichfriths (associated with Sigfrid-Sigurd) seven Imars (Ivar) and two Albanns (Halfdan).[16] The names Godfred-Gofraid, Sigurd and Olaf were, however, very popular with Viking Age nobles. Gofraid's identity is tied to his apparent kingdom of 'Lochlind', which was also known as 'Laithlind' in Old Irish and later became 'Lochlann' (thought to mean 'land of lochs') and was associated with Norway from the eleventh century.[17]

Olaf has been identified with a legendary figure named Olaf Gudrodsson, also known as Olaf Geirstad-Alf, from Old Norse sagas such as 'Ynglingatal', who was associated with a powerful dynasty that emerged at Uppsala called the Ynglinga but which relocated to Vestfold, south-east Norway, where the Kaupang market was located. According to Snorri Sturluson, who quotes the saga, this Olaf ruled a large area of 'Vestmari', believed to be area west of the North Sea that could imply Dublin.[18]

The father of this Olaf from the Old Norse sagas was known as Gudrod, often called Gudrod the Hunter, which is the same as Gofraid in Old Irish. In the ninth century, Norway was a collection of petty kingdoms often at war with each other, and its name Norvegr, traditionally meaning 'north way', was indicative of it being a trade route rather than a nation.[19]

Halfdan the Black, Olaf's half-brother in the sagas, is the father of Norway's founder Harald Finehair, who united the various realms. The date of his famous victory at Hafrsfjord, which gave birth to modern Norway and has been pinpointed to a site near Stavanger in the south-west, is traditionally given as 872, which is a year after Olaf left Ireland to help his father fight the Norwegians, although it could have occurred up to thirty years later.

While there are conflicting issues with the various genealogies for Harald Finehair, and his dubious sixty-plus year timeframe, it seems plausible a father and son called Olaf and Gofraid from a powerful dynasty in Norway were closely connected to the Dublin kingdom.

Lochlann's power base is often placed at Avaldsnes on Karmø on a sheltered route northwards between islands off the south-west coast of Norway, which had the richest concentration of insular metal finds from the period and became the seat of Norway's royal family for the next 500 years. Avaldsnes was perfectly placed between the coast and the mainland for controlling trade and the transport of iron, antlers and hides to farms.[20]

The mysterious kingdom known in Old Irish as Laithlind, which was ruled by Gofraid, is the same as the later word *leiðlind*, deriving from Old Norse *leið* that is found in other Germanic languages and usually means 'road' or 'journey'. Norway's meaning could relate to the word *nór* ('narrow'), the scholar Arne Kruse claims. Laithlind-Lochlann became Norway in later Irish texts, and the word 'narrow way' would be apt for the route between the islands along the south-west coast.

While the Vikings were using St Wystan's Church in Repton, another group of the Great Heathen Army were cremating their dead a few miles away at Heath Wood, where 59 barrows containing animal remains and grave goods, such as weaponry and dress accessories, have been found. The Viking camp at the time was likely at nearby Foremark, less than a mile away, which stems from the Scandinavian *forn* ('old') and *verk* ('fortification').

There have been further revelations from the Repton site.[21] An almost perfect Viking archetype, tall, aged 35–45 and with possible blonde hair, blue eyes and hailing from southern Scandinavia, most likely Denmark, was also discovered at Repton, buried with a Scandinavian type of sword and a Thor hammer pendant around his neck, which was the hallmark of a warrior. Grave goods included two knives, a bone from a jackdaw, perhaps symbolic of Odin's ravens Hugin and Munin, glass beads either side of the pendant, along with evidence of a wooden

In 1686, hundreds of bones were found surrounding a figure described as a 'giant' in a massive stone coffin underneath the mound. (Martin Biddle)

box. A boar's tusk was carefully placed near his pelvis. Horrific injuries included a blow to the head and eye socket, with scars indicating he was wearing a helmet. Cuts to his vertebrae were consistent with his internal organs being removed. By far the most severe injury was a massive cut into his left thigh from an axe, which sliced downwards through the hip joint and thigh bone. The man identified had clearly been castrated, and the boar's tusk was used to replace what was missing as his followers worried a penis would be needed in Valhalla.

Another younger man, who died aged 17 to 20, later buried alongside with a single knife also suffered a violent death. Radiocarbon dating found they were related and most probably father and son.[22]

Dr Cat Jarman, who co-led the later investigations at Repton, believed they were Olaf and his son Eysteinn, who was slain in 875, because it was a 'father-and-son of the right age, dating to precisely the right time', as the graves were dated to 873–86, although given the context the earlier end of the scale is more likely.[23]

This theory is supported by Olaf's graphic death as Constantine I's forces exacted revenge in brutal fashion after his raiding in Pictland, and it explains the removal of his internal organs to slow down decomposition, which was common when bodies were being transported long distances as in this case from Scotland to Repton.

Ivar and Olaf had been the most powerful and ruthless Vikings of the ninth century in Britain and Ireland, but their reign of plunder and chaos was over. Descendants of Ivar, known as the Ui *Ímair* dynasty, would rule in Dublin until the mid-eleventh century as it grew into a prosperous commercial market town with more than 4,500 inhabitants and developed a distinctive Scandinavian-Irish culture known as 'Hiberno-Norse'.

Ivar's descendants also held power in the 'Kingdom of the Isles', covering the Hebrides, Isle of Man and the islands of Clyde, for most of the period between the early-tenth and late-thirteenth century, before it was taken over by Scotland.

The assumption of Ivar and Olaf being buried at Repton has been open to question as the 'Geristad' part of Olaf's name in Old Norse sagas has obvious parallels with the famous Gosktad or Gjekstad ship burials, but the burial has been dated to around 900, nearly twenty years after Olaf died.[24]

Ivar's final resting place is also mired in uncertainty because the sagas claim the famed Viking was buried in a huge mound near the sea, which was so important that William the Conqueror had to destroy it before he could even think about capturing England.

Chapter 15

IVAR'S HOWE

The greatest of corpse-fires coiled to the sky, roared before the mounds. There were melting heads, and bursting wounds, as the blood sprang out, from weapon-bitten bodies. Blazing fire, most insatiable of spirits, swallowed the remains of the victims of both nations. Their valour was no more.

Beowulf, author unkown, sixth century[1]

Few places in Britain and Ireland show the impact of the Viking settlement as much as Cleveland in North Yorkshire with its abundance of Scandinavian place names. This area began to be settled intensely by the Vikings from 876 and throughout the tenth century. Northmen left a permanent mark on the region, which developed a distinctive Anglo-Scandinavian culture reflected in languages, artefacts, fashions, sculpture and the naming of local locations.

Many places end in 'by', which derives from Old Norse *byr* meaning 'farmstead', 'village' or 'settlement'. Kirkby-in-Cleveland means 'farmstead or village with a church' and Mickleby equates to 'large farmstead or village'. Some relate to ethnicity such as the three Inglebys, i.e. 'village of the English', whilst Danby and Normanby may mean 'village of the Danes' and 'village of the Norwegians-Northmen' respectively.[2]

Others feature personal names such as Swainby for 'Svein's farm' or Faceby that equates to 'Feit's homestead or farm', indicating prominent early settlers. The coastal village of Boulby derives from the Old Norse personal name 'Bolli' and means 'Bolli's farm'. Cleveland originates from the Old Norse word *kliflond*, meaning 'cliff-land', which is a more than apt description.

Historically, Cleveland roughly covers from the lower Tees Valley in the north to the edge of the North Yorkshire Moors in the south and includes Middlesbrough. The River Tees, which runs through the city, often marked the boundary between the old Northumberland kingdoms of Bernicia, which had its seat of power at Bamburgh, and Deira, which was controlled from York. This same river often forms the northern boundary of the later Danelaw region, where the laws of Vikings held sway, although the whole of Northumbria that extended to the Firth of Forth was controlled by the Great Heathen Army from 867, but it installed a puppet king Ecgberht to rule beyond the Tyne. When the Vikings finally decided to settle from around 876, they particularly favoured the Cleveland district.

In the study 'Vikings in Cleveland', scholars found Scandinavian place names clustered around bays, along the Tees and lower slopes of hills. They founded or took over farms and settlements and relied on an economy that included mixed agriculture, hunting and fishing, combined with trading and craft work. Some settlers may have returned to Viking ways or embarked on mercenary work. Farmers on the slopes of the hills used higher land and low-lying wetter ground for grazing animals, while the land on gentle slopes in between hills was used for crops. Vikings who settled on the coast in places such as Runswick Bay could rely on fishing and trade as well as farming. For trading, they could turn to natural supplies of jet, particularly at Whitby, which was used for necklaces or sculptures, or turn to the hills for building stone and iron from places such as Roseberry Topping.[3]

Scandinavians avoided the flatter plains because they preferred to be seen, but large hills, including Freebrough Hill, and prehistoric burial mounds were an important part of their culture and often the meeting places known as *things*. Colonist farmers, traders and craftsmen would often meet to resolve issues at these gatherings, which were run by a local lord and held at longhouses situated on impressive hill tops or near major barrows.

Upsall ('high hall' in Old Norse) on Eston Moor, and Stanghow ('pole mound' in Old Norse), which is located on a high ridge of land north of the Cleveland Hills with extensive views, could be examples of such local meeting places, where settlers integrated with locals. Standing at 320m (1050ft) tall and featuring a jagged cliff with a distinctive cone-shaped summit, Roseberry Topping was a sacred place to the Vikings, originally called Othenseberg in 1119, which honoured Odin because the Danish spelling was *Othen*.[4]

Names such as þing-haug meaning 'assembly mound' (the 'þ' denotes a 'th' sound) are found across the British Isles in Shetland, Orkney, Tinwald (Dumfriesshire), Dingwall (Ross Shire), Thingwall (the Wirral), Lancashire and Tynwald Hill (Isle of Man). At the latter, the Manx parliament is still called and meets on the hill on 5 July every year for 'Tynwald Day'.[5]

Evidence suggests local lords were largely independent of York and created the remarkable monuments known as 'hogbacks', which were often found in churches or churchyards, such as at Govan in Glasgow, to display their power and connect to locally important places. Hogbacks were long carved stone monuments that often resembled the Viking long houses and featured beasts from Norse mythology or creatures biting the roof edges. Interestingly, the hogbacks emerged in Viking controlled areas of England because there are no equivalents found in Scandinavia.[6]

These were Scandinavians carving new identities, using their own art and building styles, distinct from the North Yorkshire communities in which they were now settling and from their homeland.[7] There is a remarkable cluster of hogbacks in and around the Cleveland region at Lythe, Sockburn, Ingleby, Arncliffe, Crathorne and Brompton.

The impact can also be evidenced by the influence of Old Norse on the English language. The Vikings and the Anglo-Saxons, whose languages were both Germanic and shared similar cultures, were mutually intelligible to some degree on a basic level based on the way in which place names and other vocabulary was hybridised.[8] Around 150 Old Norse loanwords have been adopted into modern English, and it is fascinating how many are everyday words. The examples below show contemporary English words and the original Old Norse.[9]

anger	*angra*
bag	*baggi*
earl	*jarl*
egg	*egg*
food	*fæða*
husband	*hūsbōndi*
knife	*knífr*
law	*lagu*
long	*langa*
leg	*leggr*
market	*markaðr*
mistake	*mistaka*
outlaw	*utlagi*
race	*rás*
same	*sami*
steak	*steik*
shilling	*skilling*
take	*taka*
window	*vindauga*
wrong	*rangr*[10]

While a distinct genetic presence from the Danish-led Great Heathen Army is absent from a large DNA genetics map of Britain, these key loanwords demonstrate the impact of the Viking Age.[11] The bulk of the settlement in Danelaw and the Western Isles occurred in the tenth century, after Ragnar's sons had died, but it was the invasion they headed, supposedly to avenge their father's death, which kick-started the process.

One Old Norse placename popular across Britain is 'howe' from *haugr*, which means 'burial mound' and can occasionally refer to a 'hill'. At some point during the Viking Age, there was according to legend a place on the coast in North Yorkshire known as Ivar's Howe where Ivar the Boneless was supposedly laid to rest. So, was there any substance to the fascinating claim? According to the thirteenth-century 'Ragnar's Saga':

'Ívar ruled over England until his dying day, when he became deathly sick. And when he lay with that killing-illness, he said that he should be moved to that place which was most exposed to raiding, and he said that he expected that any who would land there would not gain victory. And when he breathed his last, it was done as he had said, and he was then laid in a how.'[12]

The story relates that when Harald Hardrada landed in England he arrived at the place of Ivar's Howe and later died on the expedition at the Battle of Stamford Bridge, but when the 'Vilhjálm Bastard' (William the Conqueror) landed he 'broke open Ívar's how(e) and saw Ívar unrotten. Then he had a great fire made and had Ívar burned in the fire, and after that he battled across the land and had victory.' As Ivar's mound remained so did the Anglo-Scandinavian hold on England and through destroying Ivar's bones, the connection was lost forever.[13]

Ivar's Howe is referenced in the thirteenth-century Icelandic saga *Hemings Þattr*, which is quoted in part in the *Hrokkinskinna*, *Flateyjarbók* and *Hauksbók* sagas. This saga appears largely based on Icelandic kings' sagas, including principally *Morkinskinna* and Snorri Sturluson's *Heimskringla*.[14] The *Hemings Þattr* tells of when King Harald Hardrada lands in North Yorkshire before the Battle of Hastings as he launches his own bid for control of the English kingdom with Tostig Godwinson, brother of the King Harold of England. Often called the last Viking king, Harald was killed in the brutal Battle of Stamford Bridge against Harold Godwinson, which was so devastating that only 24 of the 300 ships they arrived in were needed for survivors.

When they landed in Cleveland, Harald and Tostig supposedly had a remarkable conversation about a feature of the landscape in the distance. Harald asked Tostig:

'"What is the name of the mound which is along the land to the north?" Tostig replied "Not every hillock is given a name." The king said: "But this one has a name, and you're going to tell me what it is." Tostig said: "That's the burial-mound of Ivar the Boneless." The king replied: "Few who have landed in England near this mound have been victorious." Tostig responded dismissively: "It's just superstition to believe such things now."'[15]

This tale of Ivar's mound may have simply been a 'guardian burial' of a legendary figure. These burials are found in medieval literature and had the power to halt invasions, such as one connected to the fifth-century ruler Vortimer, which could prevent the Saxons from conquering the land. Vortimer's mound shares clear parallels with Ivar's Howe as on their deathbed both ordered their men to bury them on the shore to protect against other invaders. Vortigern, the unpopular father of Vortimer, digs up his son's body so the Saxons can re-enter Britain. Most burials were 'fictional or legendary' with little evidence to suggest they were real, found the academic Lily Hawker-Yates.[16]

Notably, the early-fourteenth-century 'Tale of Ragnar's Sons' also mentions that Ivar was laid to rest in a mound but simply says 'he died of old age in England and was buried there in a howe'.[17]

The story that William the Conqueror broke open Ivar's mound and burned his body would not fit with the well-documented narrative of his landing at Pevensey in Sussex with a huge invasion force of around 7,000 soldiers. A few weeks later, William defeated Harold Godwinson at Hastings, but there is no mention of him visiting or attacking the north beforehand, and surely, Harold's army would have been quickly redirected to meet him after the victory at Stamford Bridge near York. The tale can be dismissed as folklore, even though William did soon turn his attention on the region in the infamous 'Harrying of the North', which brutally quashed a rebellion.

While sagas often contain a mix of legend and mythology, in various cases, they have appeared to be accurate. The famous eighth-century ship burial at Salme on the Estonian island of Saaremaa, the first known Viking expedition, was apparently referenced in sagas. Excavations discovered more than forty Vikings, including four brothers, were laid to rest alongside six dogs and two hawks. The *Ynglinga* saga, compiled by Snorri Sturluson in the thirteenth century, refers to how a Swedish king Ingvar (Ivar) was defeated and killed in Estonia by a large army and placed in a mound on Sýsla, which is likely an abbreviation of the Old Norse name for the island of Saaremaa, where the ship's burial was uncovered.[18]

In another instance, a disturbing burial was uncovered at Gerdrup in modern Denmark of a man and a woman, aged 35–40 and 40 respectively, lying side by side on their back. Based on his skeleton and twisted cervical vertebrae, the man had died from hanging, which according to old Scandinavian laws could be a penalty for murder, treason and offences of a sexual nature, including seduction, abduction or adultery. Two large boulders were placed on the woman's chest and right leg. Later DNA analysis has revealed the pair were in fact mother and son. The burial mirrors a passage in the *Eyrbyggja saga*, which tells of how a woman named Katla is stoned to death for performing malevolent magic and her son Oddr is hanged after cutting off a woman's arm.[19]

The setting on the North Yorkshire clifftops would mirror a Viking burial at Ballateare on the west coast of the Isle of Man, dated to the late-ninth and early-tenth century. The man, who was aged between 18 to 30, was buried with a deliberately damaged sword, axe and three spears, along with a woman of a similar age who had suffered a sword blow to the back of her head. She may have been ritually sacrificed with animals that included a horse and a dog. Notably, the spear at the foot of the grave may indicate someone who had conducted valiant deeds, such as great military victories, based on iconography that shows Odin pointing a spear downwards.[20]

If the legend is true, then the landing spot of Harald Hardrada could have been the village of Staithes, derived from an Old English word *staep* and a Norse one *stod*, which means 'landing place' and associated with 'harbour'.[21] One of the most iconic cliffs on Britain's east coast to the north would have been in Harald's line of sight after coming ashore. At 200m (660ft), Boulby Cliffs are the tallest on the east coast with breathtaking views.

Old Boulby seems to have been thinly occupied in the *Domesday Book*, but one of the two tenants in chiefs for the area described as one plough land, equivalent to the size of a football pitch, was William the Conqueror. To put this into context, however, William was the tenant in chief of 2,331 properties, including many other small plots in North Yorkshire, after the *Domesday Book* had been compiled following the comprehensive seizure of land, which left just 5 per cent in the hands of Anglo-Saxon lords.[22]

Ordnance Survey maps dated to the early-20th century suggest Old Boulby was set back from the cliffs near an ancient site known as Three Cross Well, with it making sense that a settlement would be near an existing water supply. Woods just a few miles west from the Boulby Cliffs are called Sigurd Wood, a name shared by Ivar's grandfather, brother and son, but there's nothing to suggest a connection.

Boulby Cliffs' incredible setting sparks the imagination of a possible connection with Ivar's Howe. The location is so inspiring it has been linked to *Beowulf*, the epic Old English poem of a Germanic hero set in pagan Scandinavia in the sixth century, which was possibly composed in Northumbria at ecclesiastical centres such as Lindisfarne or Whitby just 11 miles from Boulby. After dying from injuries sustained in the final battle with a dragon, Beowulf is buried in a huge mound overlooking the sea. Writer Henry Morley suggested in 1873 that Germanic settlers were so captivated by Boulby it became the inspiration for Beowulf's burial site:

> *'High sea-cliffs, worn into holes or nickerhouses many with glens rocky and wooded running up into great moors, are not characters of the coast of Sealand (Zeeland in Denmark), opposite Sweden, but they are special characters of that corner of Yorkshire in which the tale of Beowulf seems to have been told as it now comes to us in first English verse.'*[23]

Swedish archaeologist Bo Gräslund has, however, argued persuasively that golden rings mentioned in *Beowulf*, given as gifts and tokens of loyalty, were not found at Anglo-Saxon sites before the seventh century and were clearly from the Vendel period in Sweden and that the Wuffingas, who founded East Anglia, brought the famous poem with them.[24]

Exhilarating views along the Cleveland Way, which at times skirts immediately next to the edge, were apparent when visiting Boulby. Often known as the 'dinosaur coast', the Lower Jurassic rocks of the eroded cliff shelves that meet the sea are layered with miles upon miles of sloping vegetated landscape of farmland, acid heath, heather and shrubs, and isolated red-roofed farm and residential buildings. It is one of the most spectacular coastlines in Britain. At one time, Boulby featured at least eleven large barrows, often more than 18m (59ft) in diameter and at heights of 1.5m (5ft) to 3m (12ft), on the fields within a mile of the sea cliffs.[25]

Documented by the Redcar & Cleveland Historic Environment Records (HERs), these former barrows, burials and cists, which are coffin-like stone boxes where remains were placed, are dotted next to the Cleveland Way walking route between the Yorkshire towns Staithes and Skinningrove. This area was excavated by William Hornsby and JD Laverick in the early-twentieth century. With their position on the cliff in relation to the harbour at Staithes. three of the former mounds are notable.[26]

The nearest mound to the harbour, east of a quarry, is now described as a 'low swell in a field' with a diameter of 11m (36ft) and 0.3m (1ft) high, and it contained an inverted collared urn with cremated material. Another burial situated around an area called Rockcliffe Beacon is in a prominent position at the highest point and nearest the cliff edge. This sub-circular barrow, which is still 1.7m (5.5ft) high and 20m (65ft) in diameter and made of stone and earth, is still visible as a low-lying mound just off the main Cleveland Way path near to where it runs unnervingly close to the drop. At its full height, with some barrows as high as 12ft or more, it

Spectacular view from Boulby cliffs, which once featured around eleven barrows – it was later claimed Ivar the Boneless was buried in a huge tumulus in the same Cleveland region.

would have made for a very significant feature from a distance for ships passing on the coast.

Hornsby and Laverick uncovered a cist burial, consisting of stone slabs set into the old ground surface beneath the mound, which would originally have surrounded cremations. Two cremations were found as well as mysterious cup-marked stones linked to the central burial. The barrow, later used for a beacon, could be part of a complex of eight mounds laid out deliberately in the shape of Ursa Major, the largest star constellation in the northern hemisphere.[27]

Another possible barrow was marked on Ordnance Survey maps from the early-20th century just north-east of Boulby Barn Cottages and nearer the cliff edge. It has now been destroyed and is only visible as a stone scatter.

Despite the excavations, there was no mention of any Viking finds, and they were dated to the Bronze Age. With the presence of so many barrows, it would also seem confusing how Tostig knew which one related to Ivar.

The obvious location would have been Whitby, which was raided during the Great Heathen Army campaign and featured a famous monastery attached to the Northumbrian kingdom. Its name was later recorded as Hwitebi and Witebi, from the Old Norse *hvítr* ('white') and *býr* ('village'). However, the unknown author with their evident local knowledge would have presumably mentioned Whitby because he also describes Harald Hardrada stopping at Scardaborg (Scarborough) before he supposedly saw Ivar's Howe and then after the initial Battle of Fulford returning to his fleet on the coast and sailing south down to Rafnseyrr (Ravenscar).

The supposed mound must have been between Cleveland and Ravenscar, and there is another prominent coastal burial mound further down the North Yorkshire coast. A few miles from Runswick Bay to the north there was once a massive, long barrow – an elongated stone walled monument to the dead, which featured an earth mound on top with an entrance and chambers that were once numerous across Britain.

Now only visible as a cropmark from aerial photographs, Lingrow How measures a staggering 42m (137ft) in length and has a width of 10m (32ft). According to records held by Historic England, the barrow was disturbed by ploughing in 1883 when human remains were discovered, but thirty years later, it had been destroyed by further ploughing. One academic, Frank Elgee, described Lingrow How as an oval stone-walled enclosure, 29m (96ft) in diameter and surrounded by an oval outer ditch. He claimed it included 'three hut-pits' lying within.[28]

When visiting, however, it seems unlikely that the long barrow was connected to Ivar and had been the one described by Harald and Tostig in the *Hemings Þattr* because Lingrow Howe sits above the rocky Port Mulgrave, where no respectable Viking fleet would have landed. As Harald and Tostig approached along the coast, the view of Lingrow Howe from afar may have appeared as a strange and unusual feature, which grabbed their attention, but they certainly wouldn't have been able to see it from the top of Runswick Bay after scaling the extremely steep hill because the mound was situated behind a noticeable ridge.

In early 2026, there was widespread media coverage after archaeologist Steve Dickinson claimed Ivar was buried in a ship underneath a huge mound, measuring 60m (197ft) in diameter and 6m (20ft) high, near the sea in west Cumbria, based on references to 'Coningeshou', meaning 'King's Mound', in Icelandic sagas. However, Ivar's Howe was clearly placed on the opposite coast in the *Hemings Þattr*, and there are no contemporary references to Ivar or the Great Heathen Army in the west Cumbria region. Viking settlement in the north-west is traditionally connected to after their expulsion from Dublin in 902 – thirty years after Ivar died. The tenth-century hogback discovered in Gosforth, west Cumbria, supports this conclusion.[29]

The compelling evidence would suggest Ivar was laid to rest at Repton, where the mass burial site dates to around the year of his death in 873. Whoever was the occupant of the massive mound, which became a shrine for the Scandinavian community, must have been the ruler of the army. The likelihood the warrior buried next to the church was Ivar's ally Olaf the White strengthens the case that Ivar was almost certainly buried in the shrine mound.

There was once a massive long barrow known as Lingrow Howe on the ploughed field just beyond the gap in the cliffs.

Perhaps the author of the *Hemings Þattr,* probably writing around several decades after 'Ragnar's Saga', wanted to shoehorn in a reference to Ivar the Boneless when recounting the story of Harald Hardrada's failed invasion. Given his local knowledge, he knew the coastal shelf in Cleveland contained various barrows and mounds including at Boulby and near Runswick Bay. Drawing on 'guardian burials' in medieval texts and 'Ragnar's Saga', he placed the leader of the Great Heathen Army on the Viking-dominated coastline to defend against future invaders. Interestingly, a Norman poem by Guy of Amiens called *Carmen de Hastingae Proeli*o (*Song of the Battle of Hastings*) talks of how Harold Godwinson was buried on a nearby sea cliff so 'he may be guardian over the sea and shore'.[30]

Alternatively, Scandinavian settlers may have sought to explain these large mounds on the coastal cliffs and concocted a story that one must belong to perhaps the most notorious Viking of them all – Ivar the Boneless. As legends grew about Ivar's tyranny and cruelty, the association with one of these mounds, either Lingrow Howe or Rockcliffe Beacon, may have flourished as well. Such prominent coastal barrows may have guided the Vikings who arrived on the final step of their journeys.

If one thing was certain, Ivar Ragnarsson had secured notoriety, and he surely craved to be the subject of such legends. Only his father Ragnar Lothbrok eclipsed his fame among the extensive rollcall of Viking warriors. While Ragnar sits on the cusp of history after Paris, with his fate unknown, the impact of Ivar and his descendants was indisputable as they continued to hold power for most of the next 80 and 180 years in York and Dublin respectively.

The massive cultural legacy, evidenced in language and in place names in North Yorkshire alone, began when Ivar and Ubbe destroyed the Northumbrian forces. References to the historical Ivar are frustratingly brief to paint a picture of his character, but in leadership terms, he clearly commanded enormous respect as the head of such a coalition of Northmen and completely subdued most of what became England in a fraction of the time it took the Romans. With shock and awe tactics, Ivar ripped up the rule book of set piece, shield-wall warfare that the armies of the day were so accustomed to.

Sagas immortalised Ivar with the gruesome 'blood eagle' rite and cemented his formidable reputation. Even in death, there was no other Viking more intimidating to guard the coastline against invaders. His brother Halfdan Ragnarsson was determined to follow in his wake.

Chapter 16

THE MADNESS OF HALFDAN

*I heard that the brave, who injured the lair of the snake [gold],
fastened. The prince often made of blood, gladdened, sated. Hvítserkr
[Halfdan] went to battle, always he was a man. halted the flight. The
leader, as with the shield.*

'Hattalykill', author unknown, twelfth century[1]

Merchants from Russia, Germany, France and Scandinavia once travelled to a tiny island located in Strangford Lough, called Dunnyneill Island, just off the Northern Ireland coast where they traded furs, seal skins, slaves and famed Irish wolfhounds for wine and luxury pottery during the sixth and seventh centuries.[2]

Measuring just 100m (328ft) long and 13m (42ft) high, the trade emporium next to Killyleagh was controlled by the Dál Fiatach, which often ruled the Ulaid kingdom in north-east Ireland. Rulers travelling from their nearby stronghold at Downpatrick hosted foreign merchants and they dined on fine boar meat as they exchanged exotic goods, which were sold on in their kingdom. This island is possibly named after a semi-legendary Irish king 'Niall of the Nine

Killyleagh was an area of thriving trade in the sixth century centred around the tiny Dunnyneill island in the background to the right. (eOceanic.com Roam Free)

Hostages', a supposed ancestor of the Uí Néill dynasty (descendants of Niall) that dominated medieval Ireland.

Traces of luxury Mediterranean glass vessels for drinking wine have been found, along with a circular enclosure with a bank and ditch, known as a 'rath', evidenced by how the 'dun' indicates a fort. Significant numbers of shards of imported E ware pottery, a wheel-thrown version found in jars, jugs, beakers and bowls, from north-west and western France have also been uncovered.[3] Trade ended on Dunnyneill Island after the seventh century, which was linked to a change in mercantile routes and the rising power of monastic settlements, but several hundred years later, the vast Strangford Lough, the largest inlet in the British Isles, faced new foreign arrivals, one of whom was Halfdan Ragnarsson.

Halfdan Ragnarsson emerged as a feared character in a long cast of infamous Vikings, including his brothers Ubbe and Ivar, terrorising Britain and Ireland. And Halfdan was determined to remain a warrior until his last breath. In a crucial moment of the Great Heathen Army campaign in 876, according to the *Anglo-Saxon Chronicle*, Halfdan 'divided up the land of Northumbria; and they (the Vikings) were ploughing and providing for themselves'. A decade after their arrival, the Great Heathen Army members finally settled, which must have been a massive incentive to have taken part. Surely Halfdan could have done the same after subduing three Anglo-Saxon kingdoms, but the lure of more rich plunder and another famous victory proved overwhelming.

Based on historical records and later sagas, Halfdan also held Scandinavian regions. According to the 'Tale of Ragnar's Sons', after the death of his father, Hvitserk (Halfdan) had been awarded Wendland, part of the south Baltic coast and modern Germany, but occupied by Slavic people known as the Wends during the Viking Age, and Jutland, the mainland peninsula of modern Denmark.[4] Curiously, Halfdan's name never features in the Old Norse sagas where he is known as Hvitserk (white shirt). The later 'Tale of Ragnar's Sons' seems to confirm this identification by placing Hvitserk as ruling in Jutland, which is supported by a contemporary source.

In 873, the *Annals of Fulda* tells of how a 'Sigifrid', a 'king of the Danes' and the historical prototype for Sigurd Snake in the Eye, sent envoys to the villa of Biesenstätt close to Worms (modern Germany) in East Francia, who met with King Louis the German, seeking to make peace with the Saxons so merchants 'could come and go in peace' and bring 'merchandise to buy and sell'.[5] Later that year, a 'Halbden', described as 'Siegfried's' brother and associated with Halfdan, again sent messengers to Louis to meet in Metz making the same request, which was for the king to 'ratify a perpetual peace' between the Danes and Saxons on the River Eider. The territory ruled by Sigurd and Halfdan must have included Jutland, which bordered the Saxons, and it seems that Halfdan left England to resolve the border issues before returning the next year:

> *'These same messengers [envoys of Halfdan and Sigurd] also offered the king a sword with a golden hilt as a gift, and pleaded with him that he should deign to treat their lords, the aforementioned kings, as if they were his sons, while they for their part would venerate him as a father all the days of their life. They also swore on their weapons, according to the custom of that people, that henceforth no one from their lords' kingdom would disturb the king's kingdom, nor inflict damage on anyone in it. The king accepted all these promises gracefully and promised he would do what was asked.'*[6]

The brothers may have sought the alliance to protect themselves from the powerful Viking Rorik, an ally of Louis and nephew of Harald Klak, who controlled large parts of Frisia and had made an unsuccessful attempt to capture Hedeby in 855 but may have done so two years later when he was awarded a part of the kingdom between the sea and the River Eider.[7] It was short-lived as Rorik presumably returned to Dorestad after a Viking raid in the same year.[8]

Notably, Halfdan is not mentioned in Anglo-Saxon sources in 873 when Ivar's death is recorded. With the pre-eminence of Ivar as king of all the Norsemen in Ireland and Britain on his death, Jutland had plausibly been claimed by the 'dark foreigners', shortly before the Great Heathen Army arrived in 865. The previous king Horik II was last referenced a year earlier. This takeover could explain how they recruited such a huge military force and waves of reinforcements. Ragnar's Paris raid and the notorious Mediterranean expedition may have fuelled the rise of the brothers as Great Heathen Army leaders.

Such an invasion would have been impossible under Horik I, who ruled between 827 and 854 and was anxious to 'check piracy and unauthorised adventure' to appease Frankish kings, according to academic Frank Stenton. A new arm of the royal family, as Ragnar was most likely Horik I's first cousin once removed, was now in charge and the same rules no longer applied. Vikings could not be held back from lucrative expeditions, and the dark foreigners could draw on greater territorial resources at their disposal to rally other Northmen to their cause with the offer of plunder and rich farmland in return.[9]

Halfdan left a lasting impression in Northumberland, where he was treated with scorn by later sources. Following York's capture in 867, the Vikings were de facto rulers of the Northumbria territory, which extended to the Firth of Forth, but they only took direct control of the southern part Deira, roughly matching modern Yorkshire, while two puppet kings, Ecgberht until 873 and Ricsige for three years afterwards, ruled the northern part of Bernicia beyond the River Tyne as essentially tax collectors for their Northmen overlords.

After Repton, Halfdan launched raids in Northumbria including beyond the Tyne, which had so far escaped the army's wrath. The Benedictine monk Symeon of Durham, in his *Historia Dunelmensis Ecclesiae* (*History of the Church of Durham*) compiled sometime between 1104 and 1115, told of how Bishop Eardulf of Lindisfarne and Abbot Eadred fled from Lindisfarne with the remains of St Cuthbert, an influential late-seventh-century bishop, to escape the 'cruel barbarians':

> *'A fearful storm swept over that place [Lindisfarne], and indeed of the whole province of the Northumbrians, for it was cruelly ravaged far and wide by the army of the Danes, under the guidance of Halfdene [Halfdan]. Everywhere did he burn down the monasteries among the churches, he slew the servants and the handmaidens of God, after having exposed them to many indignities; and, in one word, fire and sword were carried from the eastern sea to the western.'*[10]

Desperately, Bishop Eardulf and Abbot Eadred fled to Ireland from the River Derwent with the holy remains as their fellow monks watched from the shore as 'miserable and imprisoned sheep, consigned to the teeth of ravening wolves'.[11] Before they could reach Ireland, a violent storm that sparked 'three astounding waves' capsized the boat of Bishop Eardulf and Abbot Eadred, and they returned begging forgiveness for their 'foolish enterprise' from St Cuthbert.

Symeon of Durham was clearly influenced by Gildas describing fifth-century British rulers recruiting Saxon confederates as 'inviting wolves into the sheepfold', who then spread 'devastation from sea to sea', so his text should be treated with a pinch of salt. Vikings may well have committed various acts of violence and destruction but also presumably wanted to keep the native population on side.

The Great Heathen Army split into two factions in 875, with one main contingent, headed by the kings Guthrum, Anwind and Oskytel, setting off for Cambridge. Another group, led by Halfdan, entered the River Tyne and landed at Tynemouth with 'a considerable fleet', where Halfdan planned to winter before 'pillaging the whole of the district' above the Tyne.

Viking presence had been scarce beyond the Humber Estuary, but a fascinating discovery at East Thirston in the River Coquet valley has plugged a gap in the archaeological record and provided evidence of where Halfdan was based. Situated roughly 53m (173ft) above sea level with steep falls on three sides, there was easy access to the river, where longships and merchant vessels could be laid up and repaired and used for a quick getaway to the North Sea if they came under siege. Mirroring other Great Heathen Army camps, this was a prominent riverside

Archaeologists at East Thirston next to the River Coquet, which shares clear parallels with the other Great Heathen Army camps. (Jane Harrison)

position that took advantage of natural features near the Devil's Causeway trackway between Hadrian's Wall and Berwick-upon-Tweed, which connected to the Roman road of 'Dere Street' that extended to the Firth of Forth. Finds at East Thirston suggested the Roman army used the same site on its forays into the north with a possible market function.[12]

Viking Age metal detecting finds at East Thirston have been numerous, and the 'rich assemblage' matches other Great Heathen Army camps, according to a report. Metal detectors uncovered between twelve to fourteen lead gaming pieces, which were used by the army members in their downtime to play board games such as mill or *hnefatafl*, as discussed in Chapter Thirteen, where they gambled away their loot.

Investigations have found several copper-alloy items related to Anglo-Saxon dress, including three dress pins and seven strap ends, which all had a split end secured by two rivets, a terminal with an animal head and a Trewhiddle-style decoration (named after the Trewhiddle hoard discovered in Cornwall of Anglo-Saxon items that often had animal designs).

Strap ends may have been brought to East Thirston from northern England with the army because they were also widespread at Torksey, possibly worn by Anglo-Saxon slaves captured and held hostage, or were instances of the Viking copying local dress styles. They could have been used to fasten straps on purses or bags where the Vikings held their newly acquired wealth. Four stycas, copper alloy coins of ninth-century Northumbria kings, have also been recorded at East Thirston.

From this base, Halfdan set off and 'ravaged the Picts and the people of Strathclyde' according to Asser. The Pictish Chronicle reports a battle between

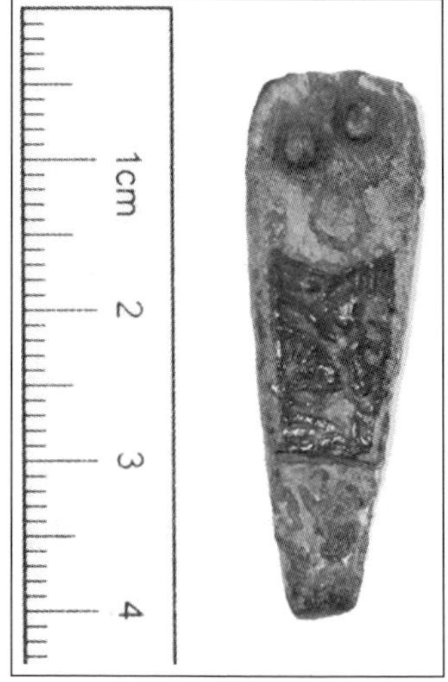

Above left: One of the copper-alloy strap ends discovered at the East Thirston camp linked to the Great Heathen Army campaign. (Portable Antiquities Scheme/CC BY 4.0)

Above right: This fascinating Alfred the Great coin found at Burghead fort had been double pierced and was possibly worn on a necklace or bracelet. (Northern Picts, University of Aberdeen)

Halfdan's forces at Dollar in Clackmannanshire before another one at Atholl, which was a Pictish kingdom centred around the River Tay, where the Picts were slain.

Notably, the Latin term Scotti, from Scotia, which had originally meant Ireland, was first used to describe the Picts and evidence of the kingdom's increasing Gallicisation. According to an *Annals of Ulster* entry in 875, the 'Picts encountered the *Dub Gaill* (dark foreigners) in battle, and a great slaughter of the Picts resulted'.[13]

Constantine's I death was placed at the 'black cave' in the *Chronicle of Melrose*, from an abbey of the same name, but its location has been the subject of much debate. A sign at one potential site at Balcomie near Crail in Fife drawing from the *Scotichronicon,* a fifteenth-century text from the historian Walter Bower, claims the Danes were offered peace and provisions by the Picts if they ceased raids but they refused which sparked the warfare.

Pictish forces fled before the battle, and Constantine I was left 'deserted, surrounded and killed by the enemy', claims the *Scotichronicon*. Halfdan's forces advanced deep into Pictland as two fascinating pierced coins of Alfred the Great were discovered at the former Burghead fort near Moray, which may have been worn on a necklace and bracelet, perhaps displayed as a badge of honour.

Meaning 'land of the painted ones', Pictland was undergoing a massive transformation because by the early-tenth century it became known as the 'kingdom of Alba (derived from the Latin for Britain 'Albion' from Ancient Greek)'. Terms such as the Gaelic *Goidill* (Gaels), *Albanaig* or *fir Alban* (men of Alba), as well as *Scotti*, were now used for inhabitants of Pictland.[14]

The *Prophecy of Berchan*, dated to the eleventh century, described how Dál Riata king Kenneth MacAlpin, the father of Constantine I, destroyed the race of the Picts, branding them the 'stupid savages of the east'. This supposed ethnic destruction draws obvious parallels with the Anglo-Saxon conquest because both may have resulted from longer-term cultural processes as well as conflict.

Archaeologist Dr Gordon Noble, in *Picts, the Scourge of Rome Rulers of The North*, points to a movement of Gaelic speakers eastwards from as early as the fifth and sixth centuries, and the increasing influence of the Gaelic church, evidenced by dedications to early Irish saints at various churches in Pictland. Some 25 ogham stones, which feature inscriptions using an early Irish alphabet, have also been found in Pictland.[15]

Ogham has also been found on spectacular Pictish symbol stones, including a rare, rounded cross-slab at Old Kilmadock, which includes *nimi*t or *nemet* – a term derived from the Gaelic *nemeton* meaning 'sanctuary, shrine or sacred place'.[16] This was found next to a medieval church, the most western discovery in Scotland so far, which sprung up shortly after the Battle of Dun Nechtain in 685 when the Picts

The Pictish stone at Old Kilmadock featuring Ogham was a sign of the increasing Gaelicisation of the kingdom as early as the late-seventh century. (Murray Cook)

obliterated the Northumbrian army. The discovery highlights the influence of Gaelic speakers in the Pictish heartland around 150 years before Kenneth MacAlpin's reign. Noble believed the kingdom's new name of Alba, i.e. Britain, better represented a kingdom, which now included Britons, Picts, Gaels and Scandinavians.[17]

Constantine I's death had not been in vain because later Viking settlement in Scotland was restricted to Orkney, Shetland and the far northern and western fringes, which began to be intensely settled from the tenth century. Although dated to 900, shortly after Halfdan's time and possibly linked to raids by Ivar's descendants, the Galloway Viking hoard, a remarkable collection of more than 100 gold and silver objects including arm rings, brooches, rings and a pectoral cross, was uncovered in Dumfries and Galloway in 2014.

Unity between the various Scandinavian factions collapsed as Halfdan was waging war on Pictland. In 875, it was recorded in the *Annals of Ulster*: 'Oistín (Eysteinn) son of Amlaíb (Olaf the White), king of the Norsemen, was deceitfully killed by Albann (Halfdan).'[18] The lack of a location suggests the killing took place outside Ireland, and as it is placed after the conflict with the Picts, implies Eysteinn had helped Halfdan avenge his father's brutal death at the hands of Constantine I before he was double-crossed. Eysteinn, who was aged between 17 to 20, was likely buried next to his father at Repton with next to no grave goods, indicating Halfdan's forces gave him a respectful but not elaborate burial.

According to Symeon of Durham, the fortunes of Halfdan took an embarrassing turn for the worst as he was driven from the Viking camp after falling victim to a hideous and odorous disease:

> *'God's justice determined that the wicked king Halfdene should at last suffer the punishment which he had caused by his cruelty towards the church of the saint and other holy places. He was attacked at the same time by mental insanity and the severest bodily suffering; the intolerable stench exhaling from which made him an object of abomination towards the whole army. Thus despised and rejected by all persons, he fled away in three ships from the Tyne, and shortly afterwards he and all his followers perished.'[19]*

This expands on the *History of St Cuthbert*, which also told of Halfdan's madness and foul smell that led to his banishment, which they believed was divine retribution for his reign of terror: 'Soon the wrath of God and of the holy confessor fell upon him, for he began to rave and to reek so badly that his whole army drove him from its midst and he was chased far across the sea and was never seen again.'[20]

The divine intervention has obvious similarities with Ragnar's dramatic fate after Paris. Given Halfdan's madness and foul-smelling episode is absent beyond Northumbrian sources, it is likely entirely fictitious and an obvious desire to show

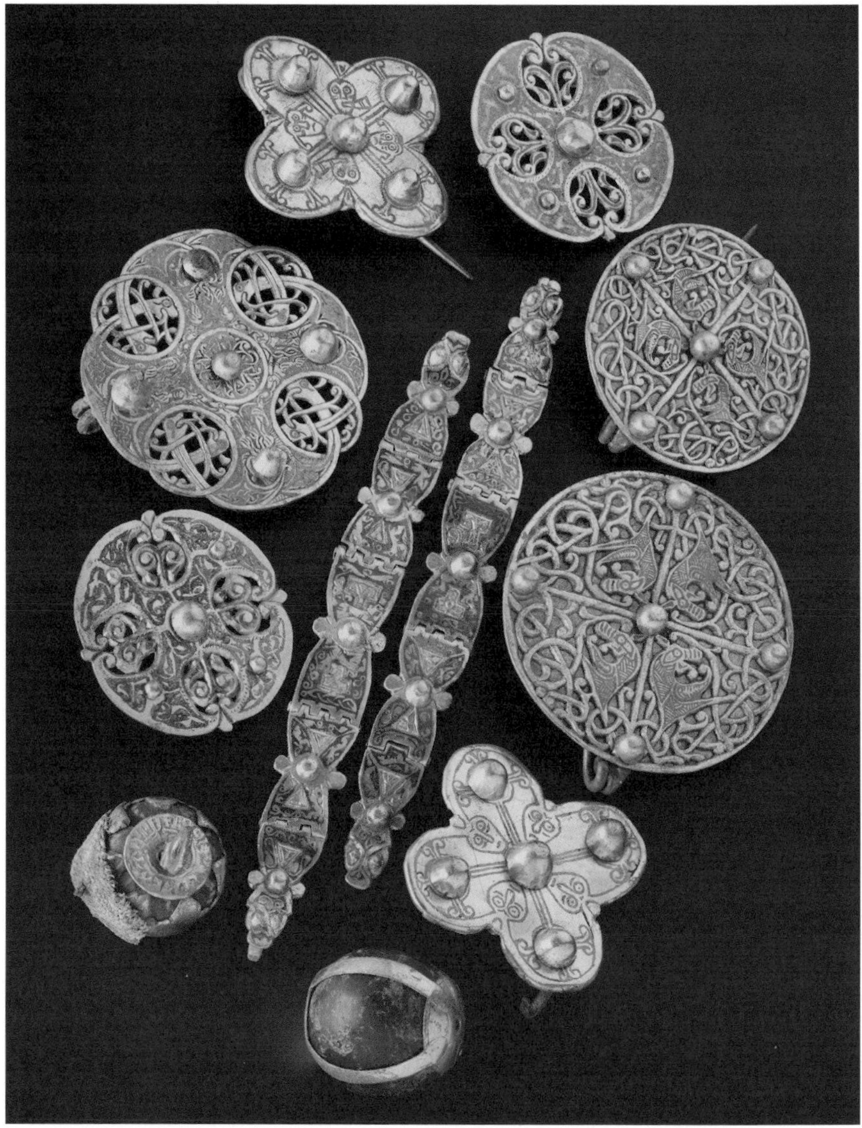

Some of the remarkable brooches in the Galloway Hoard, which may have been linked to raids around 900 by Ivar's grandsons. (© National Museums Scotland)

such torment that Halfdan had inflicted on the region was rightfully punished. As Halfdan had just shared out the land in Northumbria among fellow Vikings, he presumably retained their support despite killing Eysteinn. If the Vikings under Halfdan had committed half of the atrocities they were accused of against religious institutions, it is unsurprising Symeon of Durham writing several hundred years later sought to ensure the story ended with abject humiliation and divine punishment for their tormentor. To the Great Heathen Army and Scandinavian people, he was surely revered for leading the conquest of new lands, but unfortunately, their voices from the time are silent.

Rather than enjoying the spoils from dividing up Northumbria, Halfdan pressed his claims on the Dublin kingdom, which culminated in a clash at Strangford Lough. His opponent Barid, the king of the fair foreigners, was called a son of Ivar in the twelfth century *Chronicon Scotorum* (*Chronicle of Scots*), but the connection is never made in the *Fragmentary Annals* or also the *Annals of Ulster*, which names Ivar's descendants for fifty years afterwards. When Barid was killed in Dublin four years later, he was branded a 'great despot of the Northmen' in the same annals, which shows he was well known. Moreover, when a son of Barid called Eloir was killed in 891 and his unnamed grandson via another son Uathmarán was raiding in 921, they are associated with Barid and not Ivar as was customary.[21]

Barid appears to be the 'Baret' raiding Fleury in 865 when the Great Heathen Army campaign began, and as Ivar was first mentioned in a contemporary source in 857, it seems unlikely, they were father and son.[22] Two years after the Fleury raid, Barid is described as an earl of Lochlann in the *Fragmentary Annals*, which is the mysterious kingdom ruled by Gofraid the father of Ivar's ally Olaf the White. This detail suggests that Barid was a powerful Viking from this kingdom allied with Ivar and Olaf, and that he may have assumed power over the various Northmen in Ireland after Ivar's death or co-ruled alongside Olaf's son Eysteinn because presumably the sons of Ivar were not old enough to rule. Another possible relation of Barid with same name, as they often reoccur in dynasties, was killed in a naval battle with Ivar's grandson off the Isle of Man coast in 914.[23]

The *Cogadh Gaedhel re Gallaibh* twice refers to Halfdan as a 'son of Ragnall', which possibly references Ragnar as outlined in Chapter Four.[24] The story then later became confused as Ragnar was conflated with another similarly named Old Norse legendary figure called Rognvald of More. The Irish text told of how a 'son of Ragnall' and his followers had been invited to a great banquet at Áth Cliath (Dublin) by Áed Finnilaith, the High King of Ireland, where there was a 'great slaughter'. Afterwards, Halfdan may well have suspected Barid's involvement as he had fostered a son of the High King.

Pinpointing their subsequent battle and a potential Viking ship camp within Strangford Lough, which covers 150km² and includes more than seventy different islands has been a source of intrigue. The name Strangford itself derives from the Old Norse *Strangfyorthe* meaning 'place of the strong currents' but was known before in Old Irish as Loch Cuan, i.e. 'loch of the havens'.[25]

Dunnyneill Island could provide a clue to this chapter of Halfdan's tumultuous reign. Across from the island lies Holm Bay, derived from the Old Norse word *Holmr*, meaning 'small island or inlet', which has been designated in Northern Ireland's Historic Environment Records (HERs) as an 'archaeologically sensitive area' because of the potential Viking association.[26] Just north of Holm Bay, a nine-foot stone-lined grave containing the burial of a man in his late teens to early twenties without any grave goods was uncovered by a farmer when ploughing in 1979. This field is known locally as a burial site with various bones dug up there. The grave dates to between 500 to 900 and suggests a possible lost church or monastic site as similar cist burials have been found near Saul and at St John's Point Church in Downpatrick within County Down as well.[27]

Excavations on Dunnyneill Island have also highlighted a long, sub-rectangular structure, which included a slab-lined feature, suggesting a potential building was occupied between the eighth and tenth centuries based on radiocarbon dating of animal bones. However, the investigations were unable to confirm Viking activity and conclude whether the occupants, who were involved in a wide range of craft activities including metalworking and the assaying of silver, were native Irish or Vikings.[28]

Dunnyneill Island's position just 2 miles from the lough's entrance and its previous history as a thriving trade market, where it could be easily located by foreign merchants, make it a prime contender for the battle region. Located just a few miles from Dunnyneill Island, the town of Killyleagh would later house a grand Anglo-Norman castle showing the significance of this small corner of Strangford Lough.

The lough was part of the Ulaid kingdom territory in north-eastern Ireland, roughly equivalent to modern-day Down and Antrim, which was dominated by the Dál Fiatach rulers. The Dál nAraide were the other key Ulaid faction, while the Dál Riata may have been another subgroup, which migrated to Scotland where it controlled the western seaboard around Argyll and Bute from the sixth century.

The tiny Dunnyneill Island, with the mouth of the lough in the background, was likely the setting for a Viking death duel between Halfdan and Barid. (eOceanic.com Roam Free)

With the presence of rich monastic sites at Downpatrick, Nendrum (next to Strangford Lough) and Bangor, the Ulaid kingdom suffered from repeated Viking raids throughout the ninth century.[29] Around a decade before Halfdan's battle in 866, Áed Finnilaith of the Northern Uí Néill had destroyed Viking longphorts in the north, taking away their 'heads, flocks and herds'.[30]

By 877, the Vikings must have reestablished a foothold and were likely based or operating around Holm Bay. Despite his now expansive territory in Britain and Scandinavia, Halfdan was looking to press his overlordship over Viking groups in Ireland. From his arrival in 871 when he fought eight battles against Wessex in a single year, his story is one of continued warfare. Vikings could be many things from traders to farmers to craftsmen but the prospect of great riches, fame and a place in Valhalla ensured that for many conflicts and raiding were their favoured pursuits. Few embraced and pursued this lifestyle with as much vigour and success as Halfdan Ragnarsson. At Strangford Lough, his luck finally ran out.

The *Annals of Ulster* reported a 'skirmish at Loch Cuan (Strangford Lough) between the fair heathens and the dark heathens, in which Albann (Halfdan), king of the dark heathens, fell'.[31] The use of 'skirmish' suggests a meeting between Halfdan and Barid descended into violence or a fight to the death between the two kings, which erupted in a larger confrontation after Barid killed Halfdan.

Interestingly, a 'hólmganga', which is referenced in Icelandic sagas, was a death duel between Vikings and a legally recognised way of resolving disputes. Hólmgangas may have occurred on a small island (as *holmr* in Old Norse means 'small island', it could translate as 'go to a small island'), and so it is fascinating that the tiny Dunnyneil Island sits next to Holm Bay.[32] Trials by combat took place in an area roped off using a large cloak, which resembled a modern boxing ring, within a week of the challenge, normally to resolve debts, lost honour or avenge deaths. Many brutal duels resulted in the death of one combatant, and this settled the dispute, with the deceased's family not able to legally seek revenge.

One famous Viking called Weland was killed by a Northman who accused him of 'bad faith' and challenged him to a duel in front of Charles the Bald some fourteen years before the Strangford Lough confrontation.[33]

Given the jostling for leadership in Ireland after Ivar's death, Eysteinn's killing and the Dublin ambush, it seems plausible that Barid and Halfdan sought to resolve their conflict with a trial by combat. From an early age, Viking nobles such as Halfdan and Barid had been learning to fight, developing into lethal killing machines, and the sagas indicate the hólmgangas typically involved members of the aristocracy, who had the training and weaponry for such duels.[34]

The victorious Barid had avenged Eysteinn's death but was left seriously injured as the *Cogadh Gaedhel re Gallaibh* reported 'Ragnall's son and many men fell' and Barid was left wounded. One manuscript described how Barid was 'left lame ever after' from his injuries and the dark foreigners were driven from Ireland.[35]

The burial site of Halfdan remains a mystery, but he was most likely brought back to a Viking-controlled region in northern Britain or Ireland. Perhaps some fallen Vikings were hastily buried on the foreshore near Holm Bay.

After seven long years in exile, St Cuthbert's remains were taken to the safety of Crec (Crake) monastery, while Bishop Eardulf served until his death in 899. Symeon of Durham claimed St Cuthbert instructed Abbot Eadred to find a young Viking called Guthred, the son of a Hardacnut who was sold to a widow, so he could be raised from a 'slave' to the kingship.

The academic Clare Downham suggests more plausibly that Guthred was another son of Ivar, but the connection was missed because he never reigned in Ireland where annals documented Ivar's descendants, many of whom shared this name.[36] Adam of Bremen refers to Guthred (whom he calls Gudrod) having two sons, Reginald and Sigeric, the same names as Ivar's grandsons Ragnall and Sihtric, who were also kings at York in 918 and from 921.[37] According to Adam of Bremen, Guthred had another son called Aulaf (Olaf), which was a recurring name among Ivar's descendants. Guthred ruled Northumbria from 883 and had a far more amicable relationship with the St Cuthbert community than his uncle Halfdan, granting land and gifts to the saint's followers. He may have been baptised as well.[38] Halfdan's descendants may have included a king of this name killed in the Battle of Tettenhall around 910 or 911, while Sichfrith (Sigurd), who ruled Northumbria after Guthred, could have been his son.[39]

Across the sea, after Halfdan's death, the war was far from over and about to enter a climax with Alfred the Great facing a perilous situation trapped in marshland. Just as his predicament could seemingly not get any worse, Ubbe Ragnarsson returned.

Chapter 17

UBBE AND CYNUIT

*I must step out on the moors again and walk the meandering lanes
past the churchyards and the farmyards, out to the Roebuck's domains
where a ribbon of river, in distance a-glitter, dances away to the sea,
and the peat bogs and the granite tors still whisper intrigues to me.*

Nick Wale, Dartmoor, 2019

Mysterious stone monuments, hundreds of granite tors breaking through the surface, ritual sites and archaeological remains dating back to the Neolithic have ensured Dartmoor has been the subject of legendary tales. One such myth called the Legends of the Abbot Way tells of how between the abbeys of Buckfast and Tavistock, there was a wide stretch of bleak moorland with treacherous bog, high tors and fast flowing streams, but along this route, there was a track skirting and winding around the hazardous elements.[1]

When Walter, the abbot of Tavistock, set off to resolve a quarrel with the abbey in Plymstock (a suburb of modern Plymouth), four monks who resented his wealth and authority exploited his absence, feasting and drinking to their hearts' content. When intoxicated, the notorious monk Milbrosa, stole silver communion vessels from the altar and sold them to wandering gipsies. When he sobered up, his crime dawned on him, and so the monks devised a plan to ambush a rich old Jewish resident. Discovering his packs were filled with gold, they killed the Jewish man and his horse and discarded them in a nearby bog and used the wealth to buy back the silver communion vessels from the gipsies.

The next morning when a thick blanket of snow blanketed the moorland, they rejoiced believing their evil deeds would be undetected. Later, a messenger arrived and spoke of a miracle at Buckfast Abbey and asked the four monks to visit and find out more, and they duly obliged as they expected more feasting After the messenger set off ahead, the monks on their horses were caught in a gloomy fog. Suddenly, the moon shone through the clouds and to their horror they were facing their crime scene. Out of nowhere, the skeleton of the old Jewish man emerged, staring dead ahead and with arms outstretched. Horrified by the ghastly sight, the monks rode forward on their horses but became trapped in a deep bog. They were never seen again.

The rugged landscape of Dartmoor is associated with various legends and myths.

Abbot Walter learned of their crimes and ordered granite crosses to be placed along the dangerous track between Buckfast and Tavistock marking the path between the monasteries. He also instructed the monks to stop at each cross and pray for the four souls who perished. Since the eighteenth century, the path has been known as the Abbott's Way. This tale points to the vastness of Dartmoor's massive terrain, which covers 368 square miles, serving as a reminder to follow the right path in life and on the expansive moors because of the hidden hazards that await.[2]

One of my favourite main routes in Devon, my home county, is just past the tiny village of Mary Tavy where the A386 becomes a Dartmoor highway, with sweeping views of the rugged and lush terrains on either side, a land of remoteness and tranquillity with small groups of ponies and sheep grazing, and tors bursting through the ground. At Brat Tor, which is 454m (1489ft) above sea level and features the Widgery Cross, the tallest cross on the moors, the splendour of Dartmoor is apparent in every direction with its rolling hills, pierced by small streams and scattered stone formations.

Dartmoor is, however, just a small part of the much bigger rural Devon landscape, which is famed for its seaside villages, beaches and spectacular scenery. Devon's remote setting was not the kind of place you'd expect to stage a battle in 878, thirteen years after the Great Heathen Army had arrived, which would decide the fate of what became England. But that's exactly what happened.

The Battle of Cynuit, which pitted Ubbe Ragnarsson against that Devon *fyrd* at such a crucial moment, has long fascinated me. The site has always been the subject of fierce debate, with numerous places staking a claim. When writing this book, I was determined to uncover the real story behind this famous battle.

Wessex set its sights on the south-west in the seventh century, but its efforts to conquer the region were a bloody and protracted affair. The kingdom of Dumnonia, which was centred around modern Devon and Cornwall, along with parts of Somerset, was frequently labelled 'west wealhs', which meant 'west foreigners' because the inhabitants spoke the old Brittonic language.[3] Devonshire, which was first mentioned in 823, stems from *Defna* (people of Dumnonia) and the Old English *scir* (district).

In 710, Geraint, the last king of Dumnonia fought King Ine of Wessex and was never heard of again. Thirteen years later, the Britons won three victories over Wessex, which may have controlled eastern and northern Devon, given the late-seventh-century English monk Saint Boniface was born in Crediton, north-west of Exeter, and attended a monastery in Exeter, on a site next to the modern-day Exeter Cathedral, where the abbot bore the Old English name of Wulfhard.[4]

As early as 729, signs of West Saxon control were evidenced when King Aethelheard was able to grant ten hides to Glastonbury Abbey in the Torrington river valley in North Devon.[5] The same king granted another twenty hides to Forthere, the Bishop of Sherborne, in Crediton near Exeter.[6]

Lands given by the king to his thegns and churches were often the most desirable alongside river valleys such as Crediton, but the existing Brittonic name for the river was retained in the earliest recorded name of 'Cridi'. This suggests there were enough Old English speakers to impact the documented changing place names, but the local Brittonic population was not driven off and carried on living in isolated farmsteads paying rent to new Wessex-backed lords.[7] In North Devon, the West Down inscribed stone to a named eighth-century British leader 'Gwerngen' showed that the culturally Brittonic population also still had considerable influence.[8]

In the early-ninth century King Egbert, Alfred's grandfather, seems to have kick-started the final conquest when he 'ravaged the West Wealhs (Wales)', and Cornwall became a rump state within Dumnonia, with sub-kings under Wessex's overall authority. The same king clashed with the Cornish who had allied with the Vikings in 838. Cornwall's last recorded king Donyarth drowned in 876 according to the Annales Cambriae, but in Irish annals, this type of death was punishment for collaborating with the Vikings.[9] His death could also have been a consequence of the king failing to back defensive work or providing men to Alfred for military service as the Vikings would overwinter in Exeter in 876/77.

At the time of the Battle of Cynuit, the slow but sure takeover of royal estates, taxes and trade in Devon was well underway, but now it would face a much more menacing threat than their new Wessex overlords. Ubbe had gathered a fleet of 23 ships and landed on the North Devon coast as Wessex stood on the brink of collapse. Alfred the Great was holding out on the Isle of Athelney, a tiny island in Somerset surrounded by marshland, with a small band of loyal followers and one or two priests. Folklore famously claims it was at this point Alfred was scolded for burning cakes.

Guthrum had driven Alfred into the marshes after taking over a royal vill at Chippenham in late 877. His force could unite with Ubbe's warriors from the coast in a pincer movement and trap Alfred at his most vulnerable. Alternatively, Guthrum may have asked Ubbe to raid Devon and prevent the region's ealdorman Odda and his select *fyrd* from helping the stricken king. Devon had to rise to the challenge in a real test of their allegiance to Alfred the Great and the kingdom. England's fate was decided by what happened next.

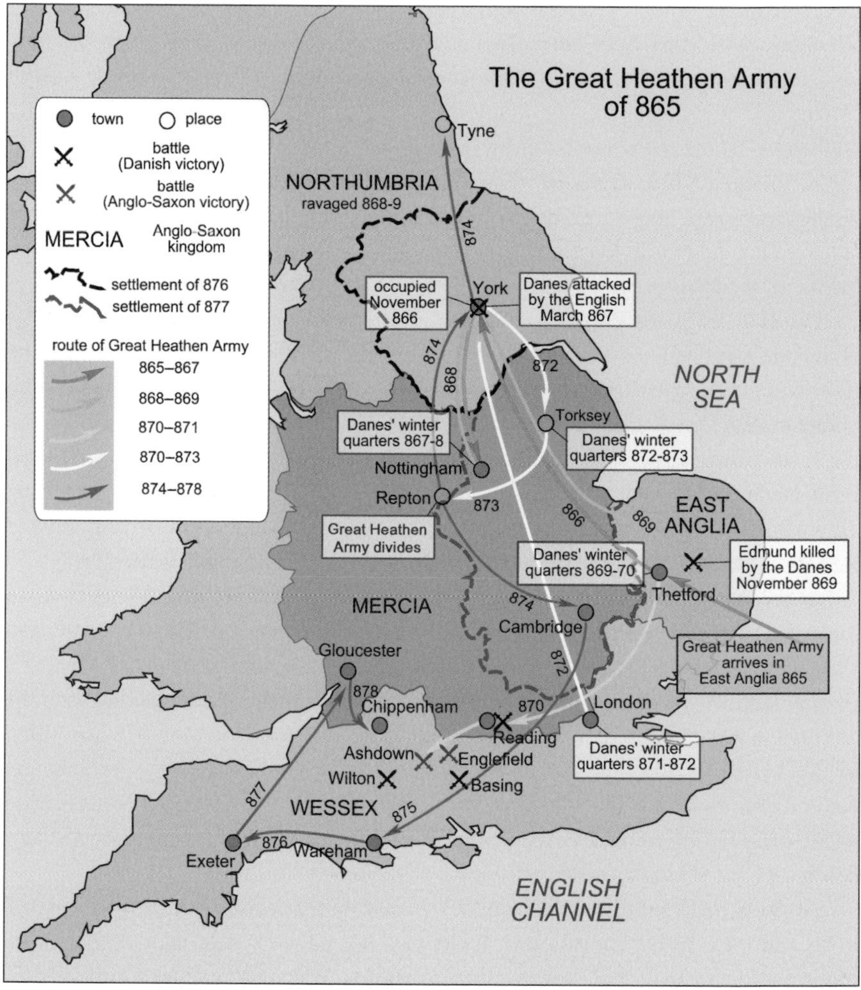

Battles, movements and the camps of the Great Heathen Army from their arrival in 865 to the warfare in 878. (Hel-Hamma/CC BY-SA 3.0)

Given he is not associated with the legendary figure in the Old Norse tales, Ubbe is the most contentious of Ragnar's five sons but is linked to Ragnar by the Danish historian Saxo Grammaticus.[10] This source claims Ubbe was the son of Ragnar and a daughter of a king called Osbern, who resented that his father had relations with a woman of low birth and joined him on a campaign against the Hellespontines and then later led a revolt against his father by attacking Zealand at the instigation of his grandfather Osbern.

In the resulting battle, Ubbe 'felled so many of the enemy's line' that their corpses became a bulwark, but he was 'overwhelmed by the thickening masses', captured and placed in chains.[11] Sometime later in Saxo's history, Ubbe reconciled with Ragnar and was 'embraced with a father's love and restored to ancient favour' when Ivar was handed his Danish kingdom.

One academic, Stephen Lewis, believes the 'Ubbe' was a prominent Viking leader called Rodulf and not a son of the legendary Scandinavian king.[12] As outlined in Chapter Five, Ubbe is described as a 'duke of the Frisians' and leaders of the Great Heathen Army are called the Scaldingi, which many scholars believe is a reference to the River Scheldt in Frisia, which is Scald in Old English.[13] Vikings controlled the region since 841, when Walcheren was granted to the deposed Danish king Harald Klak or his nephew Harald the Younger, the father of Rodulf.[14,15] A decade later, his nephew Rorik, the uncle of Rodulf, invaded the once thriving trading port, and when the East Frankish forces could not remove him, they handed it over on the proviso he would collect taxes and stop other Viking raids.[16]

In 864, the *Annals of St Bertin* reported Middle Francian king Lothar II raised 'four denari' from every manse (church house) and handed the cash plus masses of flour, livestock, wine and cider to the 'Northman Rodulf, son of Harald, and his men' for their services.[17] The payment was referred to as a *locarium*, which described mercenary payments, and Frankish kings often employed Vikings as mercenaries to fight their dynastic wars.[18] This is, however, the only time that Rodulf is mentioned in Frankish annals during the 860s.

Later, in 872, the *Annals of St Bertin* describe how Rodulf and Rorik met with Charles the Bald, but while his uncle was given a 'gracious reception' for his loyalty, the same was not afforded to his nephew. He was 'dismissed empty-handed because he had been plotting acts of treachery and pitching his demands too high'.[19] Notably, Rodulf is also among the five Vikings including Ivar described by Adam of Bremen as being the most powerful Northmen of the age.

Intriguingly, Lewis notes Rodulf was not active in Francia between 865 and 871 from when the Great Heathen Army arrived and up until Edmund's martyrdom. The *Annals of Xanten* records how Rodulf had wasted many regions 'over the sea', along with those in the Frankish realm, which Lewis believes is a strong hint that he had also been raiding in Britain and Ireland.[20]

Lewis points to how a Viking leader called Rodlaibh, an Irish form of the Old Norse name Hróðólfr/Hróðúlfr (Rodulf), is reported in Irish sources as being active in and around Waterford and on the Rivers Barrow and Nore from 860 and 862. Based on the *Annals of the Four Masters*, in the year 862, his base was 'torn apart' by a Cennétig, son of Gáethíne, lord of Laigis. Two years later, the Rodulf of Frisia, who he believes to be the same individual, first appears in Frankish sources.[21]

Rodulf's name is an early Frankish version of the Old Norse name Hróðólfr/Hróðúlfr and does not instantly appear to share similarities with Ubbe, which stems from the Old Norse name of Ubbi. However, Lewis believes that Hróðúlfr could be shortened to 'Ulfr' and pointed to how 'Ubbi' can be an associated pet name as Alfred or Wilfred is shortened to Alf, Wilf or Fred. In the eleventh century, a son of Danish king Sven Estridsen known as Úlfr was 'Ulf who was called Ubbi' in the *Knýtlinga saga*.[22]

Lewis argues this is significant as the *Annals of Ulster* records how in 870 that 'Máel Sechnaill son of Niall, one of the two kings of southern Brega, was treacherously killed by Ulf the dark foreigner'.[23] Both Ubbe and Rodulf are absent from records in both Frankish and Anglo-Saxon sources in this particular year.

It is strange, however, that the two names given in the Irish annals, Rodlaibh and Ulf, vary so dramatically, and this Ulf could equally have been the Ubbe from legend as the dark foreigners are continually linked with Ivar's dynasty. Lewis highlights how it is unusual that chroniclers refer to a 'brother of Ivar and Halfdan' and didn't know his name, but this was mirrored in the *Royal Frankish Annals*, which referred to 'sons of Godofrid', without mentioning specific names, for nearly twenty years after their father's death.[24]

The biggest issue regarding Rodulf's identification as Ubbe is that he was killed in 873 five years before the Battle of Cynuit. According to the *Annals of Fulda*, Rodulf who often raided Charles' kingdom with 'pillage and arson' besieged Oostergo in the modern Netherlands, demanding tribute from inhabitants and warning after killing all the men he would take the women and children into captivity.

Militia led by the Frisian count Albdag confronted Rodulf, who was killed instantly along with 800 men in a devastating loss. The rest of his army took refuge in a building – believed to be the church of Dokkum – before being allowed to leave with 'great shame and loss'.[25] The Annals of Xanten bluntly records 'even though he (Rodulf) had been baptised, he ended his dog's life with a fitting death.'[26]

Ubbe is named as the Viking leader at Cynuit and a 'brother of Ingvar (Ivar) and Healfdene (Halfdan)' by Anglo-Norman historian Geoffrey Gaimar between 1136 and 1140, who appears to have had access to an older northern version of the chronicle.[27] This is supported by how the *Annals of St Neots*, dated to a similar time as Gaimar, tells of how three sisters of Ubbe and Ivar, the 'daughters of Lothbrok', weave a raven flag to take into the battle, which was captured.

The *Annals of Lindisfarne* also claimed that Ubbe, Halfdan and Ivar landed at Sheppey in 855, which although questionable and thought to be confused from the later accounts of the Viking arrival and capture of York around a decade later, highlights the connection between these figures.

The 'Tale of Ragnar's Sons' mentions how Ivar had two sons Husto (believed to be a corrupted form of Ubbe) and Yngvar (a duplicate of Ivar) torture St Edmund, which seems simple misreading of the text from Abbo of Fleury.[28]

Based on the Anglo-Norman poem *La Vie Seint Edmund le Rey* by Denis Piramus, who was a Benedictine monk of Bury St Edmunds Abbey in the twelfth century, a 'Lothebroc' had three sons. Yngar (Ivar) who was fierce and wily, Hubbe (Ubbe) who was a sorcerer and Baerin (Bjorn) who tortured and maimed his victims, with all three being outlaws and living with their father in a corner of Denmark.[29] This is notable for being one of the few English sources to mention 'Lothbrok', and the tradition of his famous sons was clearly known in some parts of England before later accounts from the sagas and Saxo Grammaticus.

This theme of Ubbe being a sorcerer featured in a work by Geoffrey of Wells, who wrote the *De Infantia Sancti Edmundi* (*About the Childhood of St Edmund*) between 1148 and 1156. Geoffrey was possibly based in a religious house in Norfolk within the same region as Denis Piramus and describes how Lothbrok was a 'wealthy and infamous man, deceitful and shameful' whose names sounded something like 'loathsome brook'. He also had three sons namely 'Inguar (Ivar), Hubba (Ubbe) and Bern (Bjorn)', and they all relied on the supernatural powers of Ubbe.

> *'They did not rely so much on their arms as on the demonic arts of Hubba (Ubbe) who was instructed in sorcery and trickery. Truly, he was completely a servant of antiquity and a master of those learned arts yielding to him. And he had grown in such freedom from danger by this art that he would say to his comrades when a hostile army was approaching "lift me up high, so that I might look over the army," which if he succeeded in casting a look around, came to perish in the part he directed his attention to, having superior power over it with certain magic songs.'*[30]

Geoffrey must have been influenced by the Annals of St Neot's sorcery aspect and notably connected Ivar, Ubbe and Bjorn as sons who had all been linked to Lothbrok by this stage. The same tale of one of Ragnar's sons being lifted above comrades before an enemy force appears in 'Ragnar's Saga', although it is Ivar who is hoisted up high, before being launched into a magical cow. As discussed in Chapter Three, with the Ibn Fadlan account of a ship cremation burial where a slave is held up before her death, this may be a symbolic act opening a connection with the supernatural and afterlife. While the tales related to Ivar and Ubbe are clearly invented, they do appear to reference an act associated with cremation ceremonies and a perceived link to the supernatural.

The Danish *Chronicon Roskildense* (*Chronicle of Roskilde*), likely composed around 1137–38 by a canon of Roskilde Cathedral again links Ivar with Ubbi and Lothbrok: 'In this time, Ywar (Ivar), son of Lothpardus (Lothbrok), the cruellest king of the Northmen, who was said to lack bones, whose brothers Inguar (Ivar) and Ubbi (Ubbe) and Byorn and Ulf ruled the northern people.'[31]

As neither Bjorn or Sigurd are associated with the Great Heathen Army campaign, and Ivar and Halfdan were dead, Ubbe must have led the invading army against Odda, ealdorman of Devon and his thegns.

While Ubbe is absent from contemporary and later sources in the previous eight years, there were no large-scale battles between the Anglo-Saxons and the Vikings during this timeframe either. Ubbe was probably the 'Ulf dark foreigner' who treacherously killed the southern Brega king Máel Sechnaill in 870 and then joined up with Ivar when he was attacking Alt Clut. According to Henry of Huntingdon, Ubbe was awarded East Anglia, which seems a distinct possibility with two place names linked to him. He may have accompanied Halfdan when he launched raids into Pictland and Northumberland in 875 before his death at Strangford Lough two years later.

According to Asser's text, the brother of Halfdan and Ivar arrived after overwintering at Dyfed in South Wales, where he had committed 'many massacres of the Christians', which gains credence as Asser himself hailed from St David's in Dyfed.[32] Rhodri Mawyr, the king of Gwynedd, was driven from Wales to Ireland in 877 by the 'dark foreigners' attached to Ivar's dynasty, according to the *Annals of Ulster*.[33] Ubbe had possibly been based in South Wales while preparing to reclaim territory in Ireland after Halfdan's death at Strangford Lough but was called to assist Guthrum and drive out Alfred.

While Ubbe's fleet must have arrived on the south-west coast around the time of spring tide in mid-March when conditions were favourable in the Bristol Channel, the location of where they fought against the Devon force has been a source of mystery.

It is suggested the Battle of Cynuit did not happen in Devon. Cannington Camp in Somerset, a Bronze and Iron Age fort situated on an 80m (360ft) hill west of the River Parrett estuary, has often been associated with the battle. Thirty-three years earlier in the same area, the Vikings had been defeated with 'great slaughter' by a force commanded by the Bishop of Sherborne Ealhstan, the predecessor of Heahmund, and the earls Eanwulf and Osric, who led the *fyrds* of Somersetshire and Dorsetshire respectively.[34]

Vikings supposedly returned to Combwich at the mouth of the River Parrett, a mile from the hillfort, before the Battle of Cynuit according to some theories.

William Clifford, Bishop of Clifton, whose family owned Cannington Court situated less than a mile from Cannington Camp, promoted the association in the mid-nineteenth century, but it is thrown into question by how all the ancient sources place Cynuit firmly in Devon, including Asser who claims to have visited the site in person. Although Cannington is some 36 miles away from the current border between Devon and Somerset, Clifford argued that the River Parrett was the boundary during the late-ninth century.[35]

Cannington is certainly a commanding old hillfort overlooking the nearby estuary. It features a single rampart and outer ditch, which would have been a formidable stronghold, and it was also a royal estate that were chief targets for Vikings.

Despite Clifford's claims that Cannington matches Asser's description, it was quickly apparent on visiting that the entrance from the east, which was the weakest part according to Alfred's biographer, is steeper and more exposed compared to the gentle slopes on the western side. Moreover, the fort sits on a natural limestone rock that soaks up water, but Asser said there was no water adjoining the battle site.

Two excavations in the early-20th century have revealed numerous finds from the Neolithic to Roman period, but no Viking or Anglo-Saxon artefacts, hinting at a major conflict.[36] Perhaps the most obvious factor in ruling out Cannington is the fact it was only 15 miles from where Alfred was hiding in the marshes. When a large select *fyrd* of thegns and their followers, which must have numbered around

The imposing Cannington Camp, a former Iron Age hillfort in Somerset, has been associated with the Battle of Cynuit but contemporary sources placed the battle in Devon.

1,000 strong, was able to gather locally, it seems highly unlikely that Alfred would have faced such a predicament.

The region commonly associated with Cynuit is North Devon, and the link stretches back to the 16th century, when the historian William Camden in his famous survey of the island called *Britannia,* placed the battle near Chulmleigh in North Devon but then switched it to the confluence of the River Taw and Torridge in a later edition published in 1607.

A contemporary antiquarian Tristram Ridson, who was known for a large survey of Devon, then put forward that the battle occurred at Hennaborough (Henni Castle) near Northam, a mile or so from Bideford, which is now known as Kenwith Castle.[37] This theory gained further prominence when the antiquarian Robert Studley Vidal supported the claim in a nineteenth-century paper.[38]

As it happened, Vidal conveniently lived within a mile of Kenwith Castle. He believed the setting, which featured a small or natural mound, matched the description of Asser because it 'exactly corresponded' to his description of being vulnerable from the east and that another site a few hundred metres to the east known as Godborough Castle showed signs of short lived and abandoned siege work, where the Danes may have gathered. In addition, he believed the 'Henni' element may have been 'Kenni', hence the current Kenwith Castle as a modern-day variant of 'Cynuit'.

Antiquarian Inkerman Rogers wrote another paper published by the Devonshire Association in 1948 claiming that Kenwith Castle was an old Iron Age fort occupied during the Anglo-Saxon period and that he discovered traces of a ditch that covered a circuit of 250m (820ft) and a loose stone wall 2m (6ft) high and 100m (328ft) long close by, which formed a 'herring bone structure' that was 'characteristic of Saxon architecture'.[39] As Vidal noted, Rogers pointed to the Godborough Castle site, around 350 yards to the east of the supposed fort, which is recorded in Devon's HER as a prehistoric rather than medieval cross-ridge dyke (ditch) with a bank to the east and a ditch to the west up to two or three feet deep.

Rogers claimed it featured a 385-yard long trench, which followed the contours of the hill running north and south, with a single heaped bank and ditch that showed signs of being 'hurried and incomplete', presumably because the Vikings abandoned the fortification afterwards. He noted that the enemy raiding did not require large-scale construction. Rogers was certain that Kenwith Castle was the site of Cynuit 'in all probability' and that 'in all likelihood there was no water supply near Kenwith Castle a thousand years ago', which would tie with Asser's text. Historic England records dismissed the association because the site is a 'natural hill' resembling a motte, which was terraced and enhanced for decorative purposes in the eighteenth century, when the grand site, which now houses a nursing home, was built.[40] The HER believes the siege work was mutilated by quarrying hence the unfinished look.

This corner of North Devon's association with Cynuit remains remarkably persistent with Bonehill viewing point a few miles away in Northam supposedly where Vikings were buried. On the road to Appledore, the 'Bloody Corner', where according to local tradition workmen found human bones, has also been linked to Cynuit's bloody aftermath.

I spoke to a local history tour guide who told of how two local fishermen were completely terrified by the ghosts of dead Vikings and dropped their lines and rushed home one night. Historian and writer Nick Arnold, best known for the children's book series *Horrible Science*, who has investigated the Battle of Cynuit extensively, has a different but convincing theory altogether. He lives in Appledore, where he founded its popular book festival to save the village library, and argues the Kenwith Castle and Bloody Corner associations were simply dreamed up by local antiquarians.

Countisbury Castle in North Devon, also known as Wind Hill, is one of the most spectacular old Iron Age fort settings of any in Devon and it is consistently associated with the battle. Positioned on a dramatic cliff ridge overlooking the Bristol Channel, the fort lies in an area peppered with steep coombs and perilous cliffs as the rugged terrain of Exmoor meets the ocean. Nearby Lynmouth, situated just over a mile away, is a picturesque seaside village at the bottom of a 700ft (210m) gorge below the neighbouring Lynton at the top. Thousands of holidaymakers' flock to the quaint villages each year which are connected by a unique cliff railway.

Having lived in Ilfracombe in North Devon for a spell when working as a journalist for a local newspaper, I was immediately dubious that a large fleet of Vikings, in the case of Ubbe's 23 ships, would have chosen Lynmouth to land because this was the opposite of the sheltered harbours that they preferred for safety and ease of access. Besides from the natural dangers of submerged rocks, there is no shelter for such ships at Lynmouth, and the beaches are filled with stones and boulders.[41] As one local historian Lois Lamplugh observed, the Vikings would have seen the area as a 'massive wall of cliffs' and then have been forced to locate the narrow inlet of Lynmouth and beach their ships in the equally narrow rocky space before setting out to climb some 1,000 feet up a most likely wooded slope.[42] Given the Vikings always preferred when the odds were stacked in their favour, it seemed they would be, quite literally, giving themselves a mountain to climb.

The link with Countisbury stems from the possibility it could be linked to the Old Welsh 'Cynuit'. Place name expert Professor Andrew Breeze showed how the word 'Countisbury' would equate to the Old English *Cunet*, which became the Latin *Cynuit* and the Welsh *Cynwyd*, and the site would have been known as the 'fort of Cynwyd'.[43] It is thought Breeze is correct in associating Cynuit with this personal name 'Cynwyd', who must have been the current or original holder of the fort. The name appears popular among the Britons and was shared by a Strathclyde warrior son of Coroticus, who was denounced by St Patrick, along with another Scottish chieftain and a Welsh saint.

The 'bury' element of Countisbury stems from the Old English word *burh*, which signified a fort. Curiously, however, the settlement of Countisbury in the *Domesday Book*, almost 200 years after the battle, was referred to as 'Contesberie', which shows the fort was associated from an early stage, and Asser refers to the similarly named Congresbury as Cungresbyri.[44] This also includes a Brittonic personal name and the Old English word for 'fort'. It is odd Asser uses a Latinised version of the fort's Brittonic name rather than the hybrid formula he used for Congresbury.

It grew in popularity as the location when one nineteenth-century historian Charles Plummer visited along with many other Victorians as Lynton and Lynmouth emerged as a popular holiday destination. This connection has stood the test of time, and it remains the commonly chosen site for this famed battle.

Together with Nick Arnold, I headed to Countisbury following the scenic 4.2 mile toll road through idyllic woodlands, along a bendy small lane, which runs alongside cliff edges through Porlock Estate in Somerset. Mouth-watering glimpses of Porlock Bay can be viewed along the route, which has the steepest gradient of any A-road in Britain and the setting for rally car races.[45] I wisely travelled at a much slower pace along the zigzag lanes, admiring the bedazzling scenery, while making sure not to plummet 700ft below.

The spectacular setting of Countisbury Castle near to Lynton and Lynmouth is repeatedly said to be the battle location.

If Countisbury was truly the place where Ubbe and the Devons locked horns, then surely Porlock Bay would have been much better suited for the landing. And it would not have been the only occasion a fleet of Northmen would turn up there. Vikings would have faced the extremely difficult challenge of scaling Porlock Hill and then trekking another 9 miles further along the coast before they began to besiege the fortress from the east, which was the fort's most vulnerable side as described by Asser.

Porlock was also around 10 or 12 miles from the Somerset marshes where Alfred the Great was hiding out. Why would the Vikings head to Devon instead of attacking their greatest foe at his most vulnerable and destroying the last remaining Anglo-Saxon kingdom standing? Surely, there would have been either some coordination with Guthrum's forces in the south-west in a pincer movement to trap Alfred or some knowledge of the king's bleak predicament.

After reaching Countisbury via the A39, which heads directly past the old fort, I was struck by the incredible landscape with the dramatic ridge, steep combs and vertical cliffs. North Devon's splendour makes it one of most stunning parts of the county. Today, aside from a scattering of properties in Countisbury, there lies a church and the homely Blue Ball Inn, which doubles as a hotel, and little else in the way of property.

Countisbury loomed large in the background with its huge ramparts, which would have covered this mighty cliff fort on the east and west sides, clearly still distinguishable from the east. Earthworks of the old fort extend for a staggering 400m alongside a huge slope from the north-west to a steep sided cliff on the south-east. Situated on a huge ridge, half a mile wide, the fort is sandwiched between a cliff with an 800m drop on the south side and the same distance down a valley to the River Lyn on the north. According to records from 1841, on the eastern side, it featured a rampart that measured 29ft (8.8m) from the bottom of the ditch, while the ditch itself was 4–5ft deep. On the south side, the rampart stands at a height of 42ft (13m) on the south side and no lower than 8ft (2.5m) elsewhere.[46]

This would have been a very difficult fortress to penetrate because if the Vikings had landed at Lynmouth, thegns of Devon would have been wise to bunker down in such a location engulfed by a massive rampart and with its natural defences. It would have been near impossible to conquer. The issue is the Vikings would first have been faced with marching another 1.5 miles along the East Lyn River towards the south side of the fort and then along a narrow valley up a very steep combe to reach Countisbury's eastern side.

At this stage, they would have been sitting ducks to the hundreds of Anglo-Saxons watching from 700ft in the fort above, and it seems highly improbable that they would have allowed the Viking army to traverse this dangerous route unmolested.

It is, however, strange that Odda's army would have been at Countisbury in the first place, which was so far away from the main Exeter town and vulnerable to

Vikings travelling along the Fosse Way. Neither would this isolated nor sparsely situated stretch of coastline offer many opportunities for plunder for Ubbe.

Moreover, Asser clearly describes how the fort had no adjoining water supply, but OS maps dating from 1904 and 1888 do show a spring within the area of the fort on the west side near a quarry, which would not coincide with the account written just 15 years later. But the elephant in the room is at no stage does Asser mention the sea, which seems completely bizarre to have missed out. Nick Arnold said simply that Asser doesn't mention the sea because 'this wasn't the place'.

Countisbury was not where this famous battle had occurred, but Nick Arnold had his own compelling theory, which can explain this seismic chapter in the Great Heathen Army war – as the king was trapped in Somerset marshes. It tells the real story of what unfolded when Ubbe came to Devon.

Chapter 18

DAWN OF ENGLAND

Odin: What a dream, I dreamt I woke up at dawn to tidy Valhalla for the fallen ones. I woke the einherjar, made them get up, to cover the benches and wash the cups, made the Valkyries bring wine, as a prince was coming. I'm expecting some renowned heroes from the human world, my heart is glad.

King Erik Bloodaxe is expected in Valhalla,
anonymous, tenth century[1]

Vikings led by Guthrum had already made their presence felt in Devon after they overwintered within the old Roman walls of Exeter in 876–77. Alfred the Great had made peace with the Northmen when they were based at Wareham in Dorset in the previous year and exchanged 'hostages and solemn oaths', but they soon broke their promise and escaped in the dead of night. A massive fleet of 120 Vikings ships, most likely Guthrum's forces, were lost at the time in a storm off Swanage on the Dorset coast.

Later, as they were being pursued again by Alfred's forces, the Great Heathen Army reached the secure fortress of Exeter and possibly camped within the modern-day castle site. After the winter and an agreed truce, the trapped Viking cavalry left and headed to Gloucester before ransacking Wessex, driving 'many of the people over sea' while the rest were 'rode down'.

In desperation, as the Vikings moved to Chippenham, Alfred the Great 'sought the woods and fastnesses of the moors' to escape the army and held out on the Island of Athelney, according to the *Anglo-Saxon Chronicle*.[2] The situation was dire for Alfred and his kingdom just as things got worse when Ubbe arrived on the North Devon coast.

The tiny village of Bishop's Tawton in the River Taw valley once held Devon's most valuable and populous land.[3] It is widely believed to have been a royal estate and the first see (seat) of the Bishop of Exeter around the time of the Great Heathen Army, before it was transferred to Crediton in the early-tenth century.[4]

Royal estates, which were awarded to lords and religious institutions by the king, who extracted food and goods rent from various family farms, were rich pickings for the Vikings looking for supplies and wealth. This region of the south-west featured a swathe of royal estates close to the Taw and Torridge river valleys, which included Hartland (and Yarnscombe within a detached portion) and Stratton in North Cornwall, which were mentioned in Alfred's will and known as Buckland.[5] Great Torrington, Little Torrington and Newton St Petroc may have also been royal estates.[6]

Nick Arnold believes Ubbe's force was drawn to North Devon by the cluster of estates and set up a temporary camp opposite the most lucrative one, Bishop's Tawton, which most likely had a farm filled with livestock. With its higher and more defensible ground, the Tawstock side would have been favoured. Sites such as Deer Park and Tawstock Park matched the trend for Viking encampments, such as at Torksey and Repton, because it was in a prominent position overlooking a major river and near a place of wealth. However, their stay in Devon would prove to be short lived.

Nick Arnold's favoured location for the Battle of Cynuit lies at a site called Castle Hill in Beaford near Great Torrington – not to be confused with a Norman and later medieval castle of the same name around 5 miles away. When I first visited Castle Hill, just off the A3124 road to Exeter, an Indian summer brought warm sunshine in late-September 2023. Remarkably, the site houses a former garden centre called Kenwith Nursery, which shares the same name as the Kenwith Castle care home in Bideford, where the former nursery owners, who have just sold the property, had lived previously and another possible location for the Battle of Cynuit. The owners said it was a truly 'remarkable coincidence'.

Situated deep in the sparsely populated Devon countryside, it was immediately obvious when visiting why this Iron Age fort was the perfect place for a fortress. Castle Hill is perched on a promontory, a high head of land or headland, almost surrounded by the River Torridge. At the time, the area was almost certainly marshland between the existing track and the current A3124 road, providing another obstacle for the invaders. A ford in the River Torridge is located east of the trackway, but on visiting at the same time of year as the Battle of Cynuit in mid to late March, it would indicate the ford was impassable.

With huge slopes on three sides and a position offering panoramic views so the enemy could be spotted for miles in the distance, Castle Hill was a commanding place for the *fyrd* to converge and prepare, and it was not as isolated as it would appear. An ancient trackway that leads to Exeter from North Devon is thought to have passed directly past Castle Hill. A map of the county from 1765 shows the road turning north at Woolleigh to cross the Woolleigh Brook, with the place name 'Harepath' in Beaford indicating a highway of military importance to either Exeter or Okehampton and Dartmoor.[7]

This road appears to follow the Mariner's Way, a legendary 66-mile path across Dartmoor between Bideford in the north of Devon and Dartmouth in the south, which sailors used to travel between ports.[8] On this path lies North Tawton, where an old Roman Road could be followed to Exeter, known as 'Margary 492' after a system of classification of such roads by Ivan Margary. Research by the University of Exeter has uncovered an extensive network of previously uncovered Roman roads in Devon, stretching for more than 100km between forts, including one at North Tawton but the only one west of Exeter diverts south-west towards Okehampton.[9]

However, the Devon and Cornwall Historic Environment Records (HERs) have identified a potential Roman Road between Crediton and Burrington Moor, only 4 miles from Castle Hill, evidenced by the 'deep valley being crossed by a series of zigzags' and suggested the road continued to Bideford in North Devon.[10] It does seem almost certain that a very old and established trackway, most likely used by traders and farmers to drive cattle to Dartmoor in the summer, ran very close to Castle Hill.

Such trackways were favoured not just by local *fyrds* but also by the invading Vikings. Medieval battles in England were consistently located near such major routes, and often fords, as they were easily identifiable and accessible locations in rural areas. It seems highly improbable the armies of Odda or Ubbe were traipsing randomly across the rugged Dartmoor and Devon landscape. Moreover, the famous Hartland Abbey-owned land at Warham, which is west of the site, and the Exeter Road may have been linked to a road from the abbey.[11]

Ubbe must have got wind that Devon's thegns were assembling in the fort, and his surprise arrival explains why the fort was unprepared. Asser described how the Vikings had decided against attacking the fort because of its unique natural defences and instead decided to wait for the Devon men to surrender through famine. He notably mentions the only weak spot of the fortress was its eastern side:

> *'The heathen, seeing that the fortress was unprepared and altogether unfortified, except that it merely had fortifications in our manner, determined not to assault it, because that place is rendered secure by its position on all sides except the eastern, as I myself have seen, but began to besiege it, thinking that those men would soon surrender from famine, thirst, and the blockade, since there is no water close to the fortress.'*[12]

Geoffrey Gaimar mentions how the battle was fought in 'Penwood' (*bois de Pene*), which is derived from the Brythonic word *penn* meaning 'headland', suggesting together with Asser's description that the fort was on a headland with woods only accessible from the east. This matches Castle Hill and lessens the case for Countisbury, which probably never had woods to the east.[13]

Although Gaimar's account mistakenly attributes the victory to Alfred personally, which may have reflected the fact the select *fyrd* were ultimately fighting for the Wessex king, his account includes fascinating details not mentioned by Asser or Ethelward. Evidently, Gaimar had access to an original lost version of the *Anglo-Saxon Chronicle* or Asser as he uses Old English words such as *hlāw* meaning 'mound' or 'tumulus', and *hræfn* meaning 'raven', along with the Old English name of Deveneschire for the county.[14]

In his research, Nick Arnold had analysed Iron Age and Roman forts across Devon and Dartmoor using Historic Environment Records and Ordnance Survey maps and concluded: 'This study demonstrated that Castle Hill is the only location in Devon that fits the description of a headland fort with comparatively weak defences, secure from all directions except the east.'[15]

Its unique landscape means there are steep slopes on all three sides, which any attacking force would have to face before reaching both inner and outer ramparts. Woods to the north-east also lie within the headland and are accessible through a narrow ridge. Nearby Woolleigh, which means 'wolves' clearing', indicates the wood was located to the east of the fort in medieval times.[16]

Heritage England records have confirmed traces of the fort at Castle Hill with a ditch of 1.5m on the south-east side, where the ditch has been terraced and filled to form a trackway.[17] Since Nick Arnold's research was released and his championing of Castle Hill as the site for the Battle of Cynuit, the fort has now been designated a scheduled monument, and it is a criminal offence to cause damage to the site.

Records state the bank and ditch on the south-west side have been reduced by ploughing to a 'faint scarp', which is 0.8m high, and on the northern side, there is evidence of an inner and outer bank, which are 1.6m and 2.6m respectively.

Castle Hill fort matched the descriptions by Asser and Gaimar of a headland next to woods, with its eastern side vulnerable to attack.

Ramparts would likely have been constructed as 'box ramparts', which were common throughout northern Europe in the Iron Age and typically built using wooden stakes knocked into place to create boxes filled with earth and stone, which explains their narrow width. Outlines of the former ramparts can be seen in various places and most visibly directly in front of the fort, where an existing hedge follows its former course. The soil is filled with numerous stones, which explains why the fortifications have stood the test of time.

According to Asser, the fort was 'completely undefended' (*omnino immunitam*) except for 'walls raised in our fashion' (*moenia nostro more erecta*). In this instance, Nick Arnold believes that Asser is referencing a story from Bede and originally Gildas, who described how the British built the Antonine Wall with turves to form a bank of earth because they didn't know how to build in the Roman method using stone.[18] The only entrance to the fort would have been through a narrow ledge in the woods with a steep drop on one side. Enemies would have been channelled along a path in a huddle and left at the mercy of spears. Ubbe and his comrades were wise in avoiding such a scenario. They were particularly astute because despite the obvious protection offered by Castle Hill, they knew the Devon thegns and their followers were effectively doomed. 'Ubbe never had any intention of attacking the fort,' said Nick Arnold. 'Why risk his death and hundreds of men when he knew that waiting out the situation would deliver the same result?'[19]

Asser mentions how there was no water close to the fortress. According to Arnold, however, the original translation sees Asser use a very particular Latin word that states there was no water 'adjoining the fort' (*arci contigua*). Although *contigua* is often translated as 'near', its literal meaning is 'connected to' or 'adjoining'.[20] Water can be found close to Castle Hill in the form of a small stream fed by a seep spring situated at the bottom of a steep bank around 150m south-west from the edge of the fort. There was absolutely no way the Devon army could have brought enough water for around 1,000 men up the steep bank while surrounded by Ubbe's warriors. Moreover, the presence of a supply just outside the fort but cruelly out of reach for the Devon *fyrd* again adds weight to the case for Castle Hill over Countisbury, where a spring water supply can be found around 500m west of the rampart and within the defences of the actual fort.

Alfred gave Asser the monastery of Exeter, which included responsibility for the shrine of St Nectan at the king's estate in Hartland in North Devon. If Asser visited the holy monument in person, he would have almost certainly followed the previously mentioned old road to Exeter past Castle Hill with a local guide, who may have recalled the battle.[21]

Its significance must have fascinated Asser and the fact of how perilous the situation must have been for the Devon *fyrd*. This was a waiting game, and Ubbe had every reason to be confident. England's last remaining kingdom, Wessex, was on the verge of oblivion, with Alfred the Great hiding in the Somerset marshes with just a handful of followers. Vikings controlled most of eastern and northern England as well as large parts of the Wessex kingdom.

Ubbe surely knew that another army led by Guthrum was fast approaching the south-west, and Alfred's days were numbered. There was simply no need to risk life and limb. This was the son of Ragnar, who together with his brother Ivar and Halfdan had led the Vikings to their greatest triumph to date. By now, Ubbe must have been feared, respected and revered in equal measure.

Ubbe had other reasons for caution because he had ambitions to claim control of the Dublin trade port in Ireland, which had been lost after the death of Halfdan at Strangford Lough. His next destination after the Devon men surrendered, and Alfred was flushed out of the marshes, was most likely across the Bristol Channel in the direction of Dublin to take back the Irish trading port and avenge his brother's death. Devon's select *fyrd* had other ideas. At dawn, after possibly a few nights of siege, they broke out from their fortress while the Vikings were sleeping and everything changed in a heartbeat.

Described by Asser as the 'king's thegns' (*ministri regis),* this select *fyrd* would have been drawn from every five hides of land across Devon. It would have been largely made up of thegns, who acted as royal bodyguards, alongside members of the upper peasantry, who were all well-equipped and trained for warfare.[22] The shire's ealdorman Odda had responsibility for administration and justice as well as calling up the select *fyrd* and leading the men to war. Fire beacons may have been lit at high points in Devon when the Vikings arrived to alert other freemen to join up with the select *fyrd*. Northmen are believed to have often copied this tactic to confuse their enemies. Militia would have been primed for warfare as news of the repeated Viking victories and territorial gains filtered back across the country. Tales of their cruelty had spread across Britain – perhaps including the brutal murder of Edmund – which would have only fuelled their readiness.

When Ubbe's forces began pillaging in North Devon and the beacons were ignited, the men of the select *fyrd* headed to the impressive natural fortress of Castle Hill, which conveniently could be found easily enough by following the old Exeter Road trackway. They knew the lord of the fort, possibly the Cynwyd whom the fort is named after or an ancestor, who most likely paid rent to Glastonbury Abbey. The abbey was awarded five hides 'next to the River Torrington', which included Castle Hill in Beaford, by Alfred's grandfather Egbert in 802.

Odda's select *fyrd*, which was the bulk of the force, may have gathered first or were in part stationed in Exeter to prevent further Viking incursions after they held the city in the previous year.

The *fyrd* holed up in Castle Hill had a simple choice between surrendering the fort to the Viking horde amassed outside, facing the prospect of being in desperate thirst or launching an attack on their foes. They chose to fight. Under the cover

Odda's *fyrd* faced being starved out with the Vikings camped behind the woodland.

of near darkness, the army broke out from the fortress at dawn and attacked the sleeping Vikings who were completely defences. Describing the devastating offensive, Asser records:

> *'But the result did not fall out as they expected; for the Christians, before they began at all to suffer from such want, being inspired by heaven, and judging it much better to gain either victory or death, sallied out suddenly upon the heathen at daybreak, and from the first cut them down in great numbers, slaying also their king [Ubbe], so that few escaped to their ships.'*[23]

When the attack came at Castle Hill, the Vikings had little time to respond. Devon's select *fyrd* probably only needed between thirty to forty seconds to charge through the small woodland from the fort to the Viking camp – roughly 200m – behind the woods.

The heathens may have been worse for wear after celebrating the night before, as thefts of wine from local estates and reports of rowdy behaviour are commonly associated with their camps. Vikings were even paid off with wine in 866 when Charles the Bald gave tribute to Northmen, causing havoc on the banks of the Seine with 4,000lbs of silver raised from all free Franks and wine as well.[24] This would have been the hangover from hell. Most if not all the Vikings would have not been wearing chainmail armour, or had time to form a shield-wall, and they were awoken by hordes of the screaming enemy with spears, charging towards them.

This was a scene of slaughter after the Anglo-Saxons charged out at dawn and ambushed the sleeping Vikings.

Many would have been fatally or severely wounded with the initial blow into their chest and upper body, particularly those closest to the woods. Given battle deaths were held in such regard by the Vikings with the reward of entering Valhalla, it is likely that Ubbe's men would have fought back. 'But they were fighting at a massive disadvantage, they didn't really stand a chance,' says Nick Arnold.[25] Eventually, many of the Vikings would have fled the battlefield in the direction of the modern A3124 and then north towards the Taw-Torridge estuary where their ships were holed up. Both were around 12 miles away, and they were no doubt pursued by the furious *fyrd* and exposed to attacks from other villagers.

Ultimately, the precise death toll recounted by Gaimar and the *Anglo-Saxon Chronicle* was staggering, suggesting few made it back to the vessels. The chronicle describes how Ubbe was slain along with 'eight hundred men with him and forty of his army' and the same figure is provided by Gaimar. He remarks: 'There was great slaughter of men, Eight hundred and forty died there, So what? They were criminals and oath-breakers.'[26]

This figure gains further credence because it implies that each of the 23 ships had thirty-six crewmen ($840 \div 23 = 36$), which is the exact same number in the Gokstad Ship, uncovered in Denmark in the nineteenth century, and reflected the type used during the Great Heathen Army war. While it may be exaggerated, Asser wrote that the true number was even higher, and that 1,200 Vikings were killed, including the brother of Ivar and Halfdan: 'He [Ubbe] met with a miserable death, being slain, while committing his misdeeds, by the king's thanes, before the fortress of Cynuit.'[27]

Amid a chaotic scene in which the Devon *fyrd* brutally cut down the Vikings, who stood and fought without armour, the distinction of 'forty men' in the *Anglo-Saxon Chronicle* suggests a forty-strong bodyguard attached to Ubbe who defended him to the last breath. Ubbe and his elite contingent of warriors still had double-edged swords and huge axes, and they bravely contested an ultimately futile battle against hundreds of Anglo-Saxons.

In his account, Ethelward reports that following fighting 'inside and outside' the fort (*intus et foras*), 'the Danes held the field of victory' (*uictoriæ obtinent locum etiam Dani*), which suggests the course of the battle was not clear cut. Nick Arnold believes the Devon select *fyrd* holed inside the fort wanted to escape the blockade and charged out and through the Viking camp, killing as many as possible, and pursuing others who fled back towards the River Taw.

The aftermath would have no doubt been horrific, with the battlefield full of dead and severely injured combatants. Amid the carnage, it appears a raven flag, a war banner and symbol of Odin that was flown by many chieftains during the Viking Age, was captured by the Devon *fyrd*. Its capture is mentioned by several versions of the *Anglo-Saxon Chronicle* and Gaimar, who recalls 'taken was the war flag of Ubba, called the Raven.'[28] This raven banner had even greater importance.

The *Annals of St Neots*, which was written at Bury St Edmunds Abbey at some point between 1120 and 1140, tells of how the Anglo-Saxons captured a raven flag made by the daughters of Lothbrok and sisters of Ivar and Ubbe, which could foresee the outcomes of battles – acting as an oracle.[29] According to this source, the banner was found in the Viking ships. The association of ravens with death and war meant banners featuring the birds held deep rooted and powerful significance among the Vikings and were an ominous threat to its enemies.

Sigurd the Stout, the earl of Orkney, was famously given a raven banner to carry into battle weaved by his mother, which was cleverly embroidered in the shape of a raven so that when the 'banner fluttered in the breeze it seemed as if the raven spread its wings'. According to the *Orkneyinga saga*, his mother warned him it will bring 'victory to the one it is carried before but death to the one who carries it'. In the resulting battle, Sigurd lost three standard bearers but emerged victorious. The same was true at the Battle of Clontarf in 1014 when Sigurd lost several standard bearers before his men refused to carry it, and he was forced to rip off the staff and carry it in his pocket, and he was soon killed afterwards.[30]

At the Battle of Cynuit, the omens may have been bad. Along with a 'great deal of spoils' the banner called 'raven' was captured according to the *Annals of St Neots*.[31]

> *'It is said that three sisters of Hingwar and Hubba [Ivar and Ubbe], i.e., the daughters of Loðbrok, had woven that banner and*

gotten it ready during one single midday's time. Further it is said that if they were going to win a battle in which they followed that signum [standard], there was to be seen, in the centre of the signum [standard], a raven, gaily flapping its wings. But if they were going to be defeated, the raven dropped motionless. And this always proved true.'[32]

Notably, it was claimed that Ubbe was buried on the battlefield in Devon. Gaimar believed that the Vikings found Ubbe's body and laid him to rest where he fell under a huge barrow called 'Ubbelawe' which translates as 'Ubbe's Mound'. He wrote: 'Over him the Danes built a great mound, when they found him. They called it Ubba's Mound (Ubbelawe). The burial mound is in Devonshire.'[33]

Ubbelawe's location has been a source of fascination for local history enthusiasts and academics for the past 200 years, and some theories have placed it on the banks of the River Torridge in Appledore. Nineteenth-century academic Thomas Wright noted in his translation of Gaimar that he was informed there was 'formerly a mound on the barrows or sand beach at Appledore, which was called Hubbaston, Ubbaston, and Whibblestan, but swept away by the tides.'[34] The Whibblestone, as it became known, was next to a quarry and almost certainly a spoil heap. There is even a commemorative 6ft granite stone, which stands as a memorial to local Viking incursions including 877 and later ones in 893 and 1069 at the end of Appledore next to the River Torridge.[35]

Other theories suggested by Leslie Grinsell, a twentieth-century archaeologist, put forward that there was a barrow at Clovelly Dykes, one of Devon's largest hill forts, which would fit Gaimar's description 'admirably', where he believed the battle was fought. He also identified another similar huge barrow as the potential Ubbe mound at the nearby Gallantry Bower, overlooking Bideford Bay, which would have made for a spectacular setting. Grinsell points out how there is no known barrow within the confines of Countisbury fort.[36]

Local Charles Chappell claimed Ubbe had been buried at the 'Bloody Corner' near Northam, where he erected a stone tablet in 1890 with a declaration.[37] A sign reads:

> *'Stop Stranger Stop,*
> *Near this spot lies buried*
> *King Hubba the Dane,*
> *who was slayed in a bloody retreat,*
> *by King Alfred the Great.'*

Notably, the date ascribed to the battle, 892, is wrong. Nick Arnold believes this Bloody Corner site may be based on an actual old tradition, circulating around at

A stone tablet placed on this spot near Northam in the late-nineteenth century claimed Ubbe had been buried here.

least 100 years before Chappell, but it relates to a later battle between the Normans and the sons of Harald Godwinson in 1069 in the same area of Northam near the River Torridge, which he has been investigating.

The much-debated actual site of Ubbelawe may have lay in plain sight because there is what appears to be a large barrow near Castle Hill. The siting of a mound supports the scenario of a last stand in which Ubbe and his loyal companions were slain just outside the woods. A Viking leader was expected to be at the front in battle driving the charge, and they were highly respected for not fleeing as the Norwegian king Magnus Barefoot remarked 'one should have kings for honour, not for long life'.[38] The leader had to be the foremost warrior and display great skills and physical prowess in battle.

This site also fits with Gaimar's claim they buried him on the spot. The feature, which has been preserved from being placed on a land boundary, could just be the final resting place of Ubbe. Ovoid in shape and situated on a rocky outcrop, it measures between 12m wide and 22m long, and roughly 1.4m and 2.5m in height. A geophysical survey found the mound is situated on a rocky outcrop and has been filled with stony material, possibly quarried from an area to the east.[39]

While the western side of the mound appears to have been reduced by a stone wall, the rest remains intact. It is not typical of a Bronze Age burial mound and appears too large to be a quarry spoil heap or field boundary, according to Grinsell.[40] He has speculated that the feature, which is shapeless and covered with trees, must be a 'barrow or castle mound'.[41]

Devon and Dartmoor's Historic Environment Records cast doubt on the feature being a burial mound after a site visit: 'The feature lies on the south side of a small e-w (east-west) ridge is not a good barrow situation. It lacks the strength of a castle mound and probably represents a spoil heap. This is a very large mound and its siting on quite a steep slope makes it unlikely to be a barrow.'[42] Nick Arnold argues that it is strange how they dumped a big heap on a rocky outcrop on higher ground when it would have been much easier on lower ground.

Given the compelling case for associating Castle Hill with the Battle of Cynuit, the mound would appear to be a very strong candidate for Ubbelawe, however it was more customary for the Vikings to remove their dead from the battlefield. Perhaps the Vikings were not allowed to remove their king but had permission to give Ubbe a dignified cremation burial, or they were simply in a hurry to leave after the calamitous defeat and hastily constructed the barrow over his ashes, which could have been completed within a day, as a mark of respect.

The chronicle explicitly states the number of dead, which was unique during the Great Heathen Army conflict, and suggests that the Anglo-Saxons were in complete control of the surrounding area. At this point, they had been weathering the storm of the Vikings for more than a decade, and the severity of the losses clearly suggests there would be no quarter.

There is a fascinating alternative to the final resting place of Ubbe on the picturesque tiny island of Lundy, which is around 3 miles long and just 10 miles from the coast of North Devon. The island's name itself is thought to mean 'puffin's island', derived from the Old Norse word *lundi*. Vikings are believed to have used the island, which features in the *Orkneyinga saga*, as a base from the late-eighth century. Human remains were uncovered in 1856 in two massive granite stone cist burials during the extension of a farm in an area called Bull's Paradise. Mirroring Repton, this was also labelled a 'giant's grave and a large stone cist burial surrounded by other skeletons' when discovered originally in the seventeenth century.[43] The case for Lundy remains far more speculative than Castle Hill because further investigations have failed to shed new evidence.

Having visited Castle Hill several times and becoming convinced this is where the Battle of Cynuit transpired, it would be the logical conclusion for Ubbelawe given Gaimar clearly had access to much older *Anglo-Saxon Chronicle* texts. This huge mound is completely out of place in the landscape, and it was recorded as a tumulus in old Ordnance Survey maps.

Nick Arnold also uncovered a fascinating link between Gaimar and the Castle Hill site. At the time of the *Domesday Book*, the tenant in chief of Woolliegh, which includes Castle Hill, was Baldwin FitzGilbert, while the lord of Castle Hill was a Colwin,

The large mound near Castle Hill, which may be the final resting place of Ubbe Ragnarsson.

who had served as a royal reeve to Godwine's daughter Queen Edith. Intriguingly, Gaimar's patron was Constance FitzGilbert who held Alton in Hampshire, and this same manor was held by Queen Edith in 1066 when Colwin was managing her estates in Devon.[44] Could Gaimar have gained the information from books held by Queen Edith, who had an avid interest in history, or from Danish people in Lincolnshire where his patron's family were based? A further investigation into the mound near Castle Hill with the various landowners' approval would be fascinating.

Much like his brothers, Ubbe had shunned the easy life. He could have settled in the lands won through bloodshed in Ireland or in East Anglia and spent the rest of his days living off the spoils. The lure of Viking life, the elusive ultimate high from violence and the prospect of immortality from a glorious death, proved too strong.

As his forces were cut down, the realisation that he was going to fall bravely on the battlefield may have offered some solace. He would await the Valkyrie to swoop down and carry him smiling to the hall of Odin. Roars from the air river Thund, which surrounds Vahalla, would ring out as another warrior is brought to the hall of the slain. Most of the other dead, unlike the Chosen Warriors, were either heading to Folkvang with Freya or the place known as Hel.

A magnificent building of spear rafters, shields lining the roof and mail shirts drooped over the benches awaited those destined for Valhalla.[45] There, waiting for Ubbe would be the monstrous boar Saerimnir. Every night, the hundreds of fallen warriors would feast on the boar's meat, which is boiled in the Eldhrimnir, the fire-smoked cauldron by Andhrimnir, the sooty-faced chef. Magically, every morning, the animal would reappear to be devoured again. This would be washed down by the finest mead from the goat Heidrun, served by the beautiful Valkyries. Heidrun sat at the top of Valhalla and ate leaves from the tree of Laerad, a branch of Yggadrasil, the world tree that Odin had hung from.[46] This was the ultimate warrior paradise where the slain could eat, drink and spend every day fighting and training in the courtyard as they prepare for Ragnarok, the end of days, before the worlds are reborn. Ubbe may have ushered a similar defiance to his father's immortal final words 'laughing shall I die'.[47]

Ubbe's death and the loss of more than 800 men was a devastating blow to the Vikings as they stood on the brink of defeating Wessex. The course of the war changed dramatically. 'If the Vikings had won, King Alfred would have been dead in weeks,' said Nick Arnold. 'There would have been no fight-back and England would have become a patchwork of Danish states. Our language, culture and history would be drastically different.'[48]

Arnold believes a later tale in the eleventh-century *Miracles of St Cuthbert* about Alfred having a vision of the saint around this time may relate to him learning news of the Battle of Cynuit victory. He suggests Cynuit fell on or around 20 March, which is St Cuthbert's Day and after the spring tides, so Vikings could access the River Taw. After the battle, Alfred may have prayed to the saint on 20 March 878, which was the anniversary of St Cuthbert's death, and most likely credited the famous religious figure, who died in 687, for the triumph.

Alfred emerged from the marshes of Somerset and headed to a place referred to as Egbert's Stone at Selwood Forest in Frome and met the neighbouring *fyrds* of Somerset, Wiltshire and Hampshire. The forests once marked a frontier between Wessex and its Dummonian rivals, and a border between Somerset and Dorset dating as far back as the sixth century, but now the regions were united by a common enemy. Witnessing their king alive after such 'tribulation', the militia were consumed with 'immeasurable joy', Asser recalls.

After camping the night, Alfred led the *fyrds* to one final battle with the remaining Viking forces under Guthrum at Edington in Wiltshire. With a close shield-wall, Alfred defeated the heathens with 'great slaughter' and 'pursued them flying to their stronghold'.[49] Whereas before Alfred may have sought terms, this time he slew all the men and captured all the cattle and horses he could find outside the fortress before pitching his camp directly outside the Viking base. After two weeks, the 'heathens terrified by hunger, cold, fear and last of all despair, begged for peace'.[50] The same ruthlessness that saw the Devon select *fyrd* decimate Ubbe's army was repeated.

Guthrum became the first Viking king to be baptised in Britain in a remarkable feat for Alfred after they famously held twelve days of negotiations. Notably, the treaty they later agreed includes the term *'ealles Angelcynnes Witan'*, meaning it was 'approved by all counsellors of the English race'.[51]

Alfred's vision for a united Anglo-Saxon realm in which all the kingdoms shared a common ethnicity, which had its origins during the powerful reigns of Offa a century earlier and his grandfather Egbert, was nearing reality. Vikings remained in control of a huge area spreading from the outskirts of London to East Anglia through the Midlands and up to northern England. It ran from the River Lea in the east of the modern capital to Bedford, then up the Ouse to Watling Street. This became known as 'Danelaw', where the rules of the Vikings held sway. Descendants of Alfred would gradually claw the lost lands back over the next 70 years, but the settlement had a permanent and lasting impact on the culture and make-up of Britain.

The Vikings began to settle in the northern portion of Mercia, which became known as the 'Five Boroughs', namely Nottingham, Leicester, Derby, Lincoln and Stamford, where language and legal customs in a code of Ethelred the Unready, more than 100 years later, showed it was a Danish state, and it retained a distinctive Scandinavian identity that mirrored Yorkshire. As late as the thirteenth century, peasant landowners were still giving personal Danish nicknames to their children.[52] Some Vikings returned to Scandinavia evidenced by thirty-three lead weights, which may have been brought home by Great Heathen Army members and kept as campaign badges.[53]

Alfred's legacy was further enshrined as he ordered a complex set of burghs, including four in Devon, which could be readily defended in Viking raids and meant no village was more than 30km from these fortified places. These strongholds listed in the *Burghal Hidage* included temporary forts with an enclosing embankment and ditch, former Roman buildings and in some cases new towns. Each 'hide' of land, which was the equivalent of land for one peasant family, would have to provide a man for the defence and they would be charged with defending just over a metre of wall in times of danger.[54] Many burghs became the sites of temporary and permanent markets, the heartbeats of towns and villages.

While Alfred's feats in inspiring a renaissance of Old English, learning and education, and the arts were legendary, the networks of burghs to revitalise urban life was his crowning achievement. Not only had Alfred staved off the conquest of England but ensured future generations would be better prepared for the Northmen. Alfred's son Ethelstan would realise his dream when he became the first king of the English who exercised authority over the whole of modern England in 937 after the famous victory at Brunanburh over a combined Scottish, Welsh, Irish and Viking force. Northmen were led by Olaf Guthfrithson, a great-grandson of Ivar.

After Edington, there were no further large-scale battles with the Vikings for another fifteen years, as they changed course and settled in the hard-won lands in Yorkshire, the Midlands and East Anglia. Others headed back to the land that had brought so much joy since Ragnar first turned up outside Paris in 845. A new leader emerged, purported to be the last of Ragnar's five famous sons. And he may have embarked on the most spectacular raid of the Viking Age so far.

Chapter 19

SIEGE OF PARIS

I see in no young swain, except Sigurd alone, bridles [snakes] laid in the bright stones of the brow's borderland [eyes], the daring beasts' day-disminisher [hunter] is discerned by this mark, the dark forests' ring [serpent] flashes from the fences of his eyelids [eyes].

The Sagas of Ragnar Lothbrok and his Sons,
author unknown, 13th century[1]

'One asked in amazement, where had the river vanished?' recalled Abbo Cernuus of the Abbey of St-Germain-des-Prés, describing the arrival of the largest Viking fleet on the Seine in November 885. 'It could not be seen as though, hidden, by a veil of fir oak.' The sheer scale was a terrifying sight for the city's inhabitants, reportedly five times bigger than Ragnar's fleet in 845.[2]

Abbo Cernuus (which means 'crooked') claimed 700 'high-prowed' ships and 'many smaller ones', appeared along with an 'enormous multitude of smaller vessels'.[3] Barques were small sailing ships and merchant vessels with three or more masts. The fleet extended for 'more than two leagues' down river – a league was a mile and a half in ancient Rome. With around 300 to 400 ships and a crew ranging from 5,000 to 8,000 strong, this was the biggest Viking force to date in Francia.

At the helm was a Danish king called Siegfried (often confused with Sigurd in Old Norse texts), believed to be the prototype for Sigurd Snake in the Eye.[4] Forty years after his legendary father carried out the lucrative attack on the powerful Frankish city, Sigurd Ragnarsson is thought to have returned with hundreds of ships all packed with warriors' intent on plunder.[5] Depicted so spectacularly in the *Vikings* TV series, this siege would prove every inch as chaotic.

Soon, Siegfried made his intentions clear to Gozlin, the Bishop of Paris, who had authority to defend the settlement from Odo, count of Paris, and Hugh the abbot. Interestingly, the potential Sigurd was labelled a 'king in only his name', but one who 'commanded many warriors', which could mean he was a sea-king without large territory.[6]

This enormous Viking fleet was desperate to reach the rich regions of Marne and Burgundy beyond the city, but the garrisoned stone bridge of the Grand Pont, with two stone towers and fortified gates at either end, and the wooden Little Pont, which also had towers and gates, blocked their path.[7]

These two bridges on either side were connected to the Île de la Cité, the small island in the middle of the River Seine. Frankish forces had retreated there for a last stand at the formidable fortress with Roman walls that encircled half of its outline – varying in height from 12ft to 25ft because of the uneven surface and constructed as close to the water as possible.[8] While the TV series shows the Viking crews trying to scale the massive fortress walls, destroying the Grand Pont was the focus as it covered a bigger width of the Seine for the massive fleet.

Due to the water and marsh edges, only half of the island was enclosed, covering an area of roughly 8 hectares, 490m long and 180m wide. Inside this area, the royal palace was in the western section, with the former Baptistery of Jean Le Rond on its northern side, which survived until the 18th century before being demolished.[9] The cathedral of Saint-Étienne was next to the current Notre Dame Cathedral, which replaced it in the twelfth century.

Initially, the Vikings were prepared to avoid bloodshed and offered the Franks a compromise if they could travel upriver. In a plea, Siegfried said:

> *'O Gozlin, show mercy to yourself and the flock given you. That you may not come to ruin, grant our plea, we ask you. Give us your consent that we might go our way, well beyond this city. Nothing in it shall we then touch but shall preserve.'*[10]

A modern-day view of the Grand Pont in Paris, which was the scene of chaotic warfare between the Vikings and the Franks.

Abbo's account was written around four years later in 890 and finished in 896 after Odo had become the king in 888, and he had Siegfried describing Odo as the 'noblest of all counts' and 'future king'. It fell on deaf ears as Gozlin made clear in response:

> *'The realm must not suffer by the destruction of this city, but rather this city must save the realm and preserve the peace. Now if by chance these walls are entrusted to you as they are to us and you were asked to do all that you have asked of us, would you deem it right and agree.'*[11]

Thousands of Vikings hellbent on rewards were not about to turn around as Siegfried made this abundantly apparent with a chilling threat:

> *'By my honour, rather my head were lopped off by a sword and thrown to the dogs. However if you do not agree to my requests, we shall have our siege engines at daybreak hurl poisoned darts at you. With sunset you shall know hunger's curse. It shall go on for years.'*[12]

Portrayed by the actor David Lindström in the *Vikings*, Sigurd suffered a shocking early exit but appears to have become the most powerful Viking leader, along with a Godafrid, in the decade after the Great Heathen Army campaign was halted in Britain. In the sagas, Sigurd's mother is Ragnar's second wife Aslaug, and he is so named because of a 'mark in his eye like a serpent around the pupil', linked to astigmatism, a curvature of the eye that can cause blurred vision. Based on the saga, Sigurd is the youngest son and was three when his brothers overthrew Eysteinn. When Sigurd is born, in the earlier saga version, Ragnar says: 'The child shall be called Sigurd, he'll hold court in battles, much like his own mother's mighty father shall he be. Of all Odin's kindred, he'll be accounted best. Showing a snake in the eye, he'll be the slayer of many.'[13]

Scholar Rory McTurk suggested the Old Norse name Sigurðr ormr-i-auga meaning 'snake-in-eye' alludes to a 'narrow opening' (*vindauga*) and references how Odin in the form of a serpent (*ormr*) crawled through a narrow opening (*aura*) to seduce the giantess maiden named Gunnlod and steal her father Suttung's magic mead.[14]

According to Saxo Grammaticus, who refers to Sigurd as Siward, he was severely injured in a battle against the Skanians and remedies failed until an old man of 'enormous size' arrived:

> *'The old man suddenly, by the help of his hand, touched and banished the livid spot, and suddenly scarred the wound over. At last he poured dust on*

*his eyes and departed. Spots suddenly arose, and the dust, to the amaze of
the beholders, seemed to become wonderfully like little snakes.'*[15]

It was prophesied that Sigurd would be 'cruel in future' and another older woman was shocked by the vision of snakes in his eyes: 'She was seized with an extraordinary horror of the young man and suddenly fell and swooned away. Hence it happened that Siward got the widespread name of Snake-Eye.'

According to the 'Tale of Ragnar's Sons', Sigurd joined his brothers on every raiding journey, including in the Mediterranean, and gripped a knife so intensely after hearing of Ragnar's death it ended up 'sticking to the bone'. While the Paris siege is absent from the saga, it notes Sigurd harried widely in Francia.[16]

In 865, there was a first possible reference to Sigurd when the Aquitanians in south-west France fought with Vikings under a 'chief Sigfrid' and slew 400 and the rest returned to their ships, reported the *Annals of St Bertin*.[17]

While Sigurd may have joined the Great Heathen Army over the channel, there is no mention of him in Anglo-Saxon or Irish texts. After avenging his father, the 'Tale of Ragnar's Sons' claims Sigurd returned to Scandinavia and was rewarded with Zealand, the neighbouring Swedish county Skåne, and Viken and Agder in what is now south-eastern and southern Norway respectively.[18]

As discussed previously, Sigurd and Halfdan, as kings of the Danes, were negotiating with Louis the German in 873 to make peace with the Saxons so merchants could travel freely, and their realm must have included Jutland.[19]

Sigurd and Ivar were named as sons of Ragnar Lothbrok when his name in full was mentioned for the first time in the *Íslendingabók* (*The Book of the Icelanders*) written by the medieval scholar Ari Thorgilsson between 1120 and 1133. In his own genealogy, he includes a *Sigurdar Ragnasson Lodbroka*.[20]

Sven Aggesen claimed that Sigwarth (Sigurd), who he called a son of Regner Lothbrogh (Ragnar Lothbrok), had killed and usurped a king before marrying his daughter, but this twelfth-century Danish account fails to mention well-documented previous kings. Whether the usurped king was Horik II, who ruled only a small portion of Jutland and disappeared from sources after 864, remains a mystery.[21] When he began ruling in 854, he was described as a 'small boy' in the *Annals of Fulda*.[22]

In some sagas, Sigurd is either a grandfather or great-grandfather of Harald Finehair, the founder of Norway, via his descendant Ragnhild, but Harald's questionable timeframe and inclusion in various conflicting genealogies cast doubt on the claims. The connection seems an obvious attempt to tie the Norwegian rulers, which was exerting control over Iceland when the texts emerged, with the Ragnar Lothbrok dynasty.

A possibly contemporary Skaldic poem 'Hrafnsmál' mentions Ragnhild as a Danish bride of Harald Finehair, but a person of the same name is Harald's mother in the 'Tale of Ragnar Sons'. The story of Halfdan the Black, Harald's father, rescuing Ragnhild from a berserker and then marrying her clearly appears to be a fictionalised saga tale.

Academic Niels Lund suggested the same Danish king in 873 and the prototype for Sigurd Snake in Eye had returned to Viking ways after losing his royal status and was leading the raiding in Francia, which is supported by how Abbo Cernuus called him a 'king in only his name'.[23]

Sigurd Ragnarsson must have still had a large base with a hinterland population, equipping his fleet with new ships, supplies and manpower, and the trappings of monarchy also did not stop many Viking Age kings from raiding.

While there are numerous references in Frankish annals to a king or prominent Viking called Siegfried, Sigifrid or Sigfrid in the 880s, the deeds of Sigurd should be treated with some caution because Ivar's son Sichfrith in Old Irish (Sigfred in Old Norse) shared the same name and likely became a Great Heathen Army leader in Francia. However, nothing is recorded about Sichfrith Ivarsson in any texts other than a brief note of his death.

A menacing new fleet of Vikings arrived at Fulham in autumn 878, which grew into an 'great army of pagans' according to Asser but later crossed the channel and resumed raids in Francia, presumably after Guthrum persuaded them to honour the agreement with Alfred.[24]

The original core of this group must have been the remaining dark foreigners who left Ireland after Halfdan's death, and it was then bolstered by recruits from Guthrum's forces and possibly from Scandinavia.

Sigurd may have abandoned or left his kingship in other hands to reclaim the dark foreigners' interests and avenge the deaths of Halfdan and Ubbe, but no leaders of the Fulham-based Vikings are named, presumably because their stay was brief. This departure also coincided with instability among the Frankish leadership after the deaths of Charles the Bald and Louis the German in the previous three years, which the Vikings surely sought to exploit.

The continental army of Vikings first overwintered in Ghent on the River Scheldt and soon began targeting the rich agricultural regions around rivers in modern Germany.[25] According to the contemporary Regino of Prüm chronicle, Vikings led by two kings, Sigifrid and Godafrid, later set up camp at Asselt with a large force of cavalry and burned down cities, including Liege and Cologne, various monasteries, including Linden, and even the palace of Aachen, where the Frankish emperor Charlemagne once resided, was reduced to ashes.[26] Poorly armed farmers who confronted the Northmen were 'butchered like dumb animals' in one grim confrontation, according to Regino.[27]

With a massive force, Charles the Fat, the king of East Francia after the death of his brother Louis the Younger, planned to storm the camp at Asselt, but his 'courage failed him' and he came to terms according to the *Annals of St Bertin*.[28]

Described as a sea-king, Godafrid was awarded Frisian territory held by Rorik, who was possibly a relation, as well as being baptised.

Sigifrid and his accomplice Gorm (Wurm in Middle German) were given several thousand pounds of gold and silver, which Charles the Fat had taken from the treasury of St Stephen's Cathedral in Metz (the resting place of other saints), and given permission to continue 'ravaging' his cousin's kingdom, specifically West Francia then known as Neustria in northern France, which included Paris and Orléans.[29] It showed how Frankish rulers were often at war with each other as the Northmen loaded up their ships with their bounty and hundreds of captives and departed.

As Gorm is the Danish version of the Anglo-Saxon name Guthrum, this must have been the same person who led the Great Heathen Army. Guthrum, whose name means 'battle-snake', was suspiciously largely quiet in East Anglia until his death in either 890 or 892, but he must have had spells raiding in Francia and joined the Fulham fleet. Given Sigfrid was described as a 'king' while Guthrum was a 'prince' in a Bavarian continuation of the *Annals of Fulda*, this must be the real-life Sigurd Ragnarsson, who clearly ruled in the main Danish realm of Jutland, which was the most important kingdom in the eyes of the Franks.[30] He became a figurehead for the army, negotiating with Frankish kings on their behalf.

Sigurd's grandson was also called Gorm in the 'Tale of Ragnar's Sons', which claims a Gorm 'looked after all the land of the sons of Ragnar while they were away raiding'. Gorm had also been a foster father to Sigurd's son Harthacnut or Cnut, the saga claimed.[31]

Academic Jan de Vries also believed the Sigurd of 873 and 882 at Asselt was the same individual and he joined the Great Heathen Army after losing his Danish kingship. It is possible, however, that Sigurd remained a king in a portion of the Danish realm and was simply coming and going from Scandinavia but took an active role in leading the Great Heathen Army after his brothers Ubbe and Halfdan were slain.[32]

Branding the decision to pay off the Vikings 'shameful', the *Annals of Fulda* said Charles had used hidden church treasures and handed over 2,412 pounds of the purest gold and silver and ruled anyone who attacked the Northmen should be blinded or strangled to death: 'The army was greatly saddened at this and regretted that such a prince had come to rule over them, one who favoured the enemy and had snatched victory over the enemy away from them and they returned to their homes greatly shamed.'[33]

The Mainz version of the *Annals of Fulda* from the 840s to 882 was overseen by Archbishop Liutbert, who was hostile to Charles the Fat, but a Bavarian continuation of the same annals from 882 blamed sickness caused by rotting corpses for the siege being called off.

While the core army remained in Francia, over the next two years, Viking brotherhoods splintered off and raided in Ireland and Britain. An unnamed son of

Ivar was recorded burning down Waterford in 883. The following year, Alfred's Wessex drove out Vikings from Rochester in Kent and fought naval battles against Northmen on the River Stour in East Anglia.[34]

After the siege of Asselt, it seems that Sigurd negotiated another deal with the Franks two years later, which he agreed with various princes of the Viking Great Heathen Army at Amiens. The *Annals of St Vaast* tells of how this Dane, called Sigefredus and Siegfried, was loyal to the king and a Christian, who was also related to the former Danish king Horik I or his successor Horik II.[35] The wording *qui nepos fuerat* includes *nepos*, which grew to become 'nephews' but could also mean a 'grandson', 'cousin', 'foster son' or 'close relation'.[36]

This relationship is unknown, but traditions claim Sigurd had married a king's daughter, supposedly either Horik II or King Aella the slayer of Ragnar. The baptism remark could stem from an earlier error in the Bavarian *Annals of Fulda*, which described how the potential Sigurd was baptised at Asselt when it seemed to mean Godafrid. Many Vikings converted for rewards when negotiating with the Franks and then quickly reverted to paganism again.

The ulterior motives of the figure who could be Sigurd seem abundantly clear because he negotiated an exchange of hostages and a massive tribute payment of 12,000 pounds of silver and gold, with the Vikings promising to leave the kingdom alone for twelve years in return. This was an extraordinary amount of tribute and the largest in the ninth century paid by the Franks, suggesting the potential Sigurd was aligned with the Viking group and negotiated a favourable deal. And still the tribute failed to satisfy their insatiable greed. Afterwards, Viking simply crossed the River Scheldt in the northern part of the realm and resumed their plundering after the death of West Francia ruler Carolman II voided the deal in their eyes. The Great Heathen Army told the Franks they would have to pay the same amount again to get them to leave. Charles the Fat took the throne in West Francia and united the realm for the final time.

Around this period, Vikings suffered a crushing defeat in Frisia by an army led by Saint Rimbert, Archbishop of Hamburg-Bremen, who prayed before the battle and inspired the victory near Norden in modern Lower Saxony, Germany. After the defeat, Adam of Bremen said that in revenge Godafrid and Sigefrid, who does appear to be the historical Sigurd Snake in the Eye because he links the figure to Halfdan, invaded Gaul by way of the Scheldt, Meuse and Rhine rivers and 'slaughtered Christians in woeful carnage'.[37]

After ignoring Danish raids, Godafrid was killed in 885 by nobles led by Henry of Franconia, the count of the Saxons, when reportedly making further excessive demands and plotting a conspiracy with his brother-in-law Hugh of Alsace, the illegitimate son of Lothair II, to overthrow Charles the Fat.

Academic Joachim Peters believed the Middle German poem 'Nibelungenlied', dated to around 1200, in which a Germanic prince Siegfried comes to Worms and is later murdered after being betrayed by his brother-in-law Gunther was inspired by Godafrid's demise.[38]

The murder of Godafrid and loss of his Frisian territory, where Vikings had dominated for nearly fifty years, must have sparked the massive fully pronged assault on Paris.

When the Vikings arrived in Paris in the winter of 885, the Grand Pont was the main battleground for a truly turbulent year. When visiting the former Grand Pont, now the modern Notre-Dame bridge in the heart of Paris, the contrast is stark. Now, this is a tranquil place in the heart of one of the world's most famous cities. Crowds sit and relax along the grass verge with a small, paved spot, including workers eating their lunch or just tourists catching a breather from all the sightseeing, taking in spectacular views. Cyclists and joggers both stream past the boulevard along with dog walkers, adding to the serenity as Paris rumbles on above. The bridge is one of eight, four on either bank, to the mainland from the Île de la Cité, the stunning focal-point island best viewed looking towards its western grass-fronted side on the Pont Neuf. This whole stretch of the city with its grandiose architecture and hive of activity exerts a gravitational pull. Hordes of tourists and visitors head along the Seine on the left southern bank past the markets, while others sit on the former Petit Pont to the right bank sampling the famed crepes and admiring the frequent cruise boats.

As the potential Sigurd set his sights on Paris and beyond with the largest raid so far of the Viking Age, the Grand Pont stood in his way. What followed was intense warfare, bloodshed and heroism as the Vikings repeatedly attacked the Grant Pont and the Franks showed unflinching bravery in defending their city and realm. In a remarkable near contemporary account of the raid, unrivalled in the Viking Age, this legendary siege was documented by Abbo Cernuus of the Abbey of St-Germain in his Latin poem *De bellis Parisiacæ urbis (The Wars of the City of Paris)*. Multiple Franks are singled out for heroics in what reads like a newspaper report. This account has been translated in full in the book – *The Viking Attacks on Paris* – with extensive commentary by Nirmal Dass, which was published by Peeters.

The chronicler Regino of Prüm claimed 30,000 Vikings were besieging Paris, which although clearly an exaggeration shows the scale of the Northman army.[39] The main Viking leader 'Siegfried' who headed the huge initial force must have been either the historical Sigurd Ragnarsson or his nephew Sichfrith Ivarsson.

Another famous Viking, Rollo, was supposedly present in Paris alongside Ragnar's heirs. And he may not have gone unnoticed as in the Old Norse tales he was called Hrólf the Walker because he 'was so big that no horse could carry him', although such sagas often described their subjects as either bigger or more beautiful than anyone else.[40] While depicted as Ragnar's brother in the *Vikings* series and played by Clive Standen, Rollo has never been named his relation in any texts. He became a legendary Viking Age figure having been awarded Normandy (meaning 'land of the Northmen') in France in 911, and his descendant Duke William would famously conquer England.

Rollo's biography written in the early eleventh century, the *Historia Normannorum*, by the cleric Dudo of Saint-Quentin, claimed he was a Dacian (Denmark) duke, banished after his father and brother Gurim were killed. He aligned with a king, Alstem in Angles (England), and was often associated with Guthrum whose baptismal name was Athelstan.[41] Dudo's claim that Rollo attacked Rouen in 876 was recorded in the *Annals of St Bertin*, which refers to 100 Viking ships in the Seine in that year.[42] He has Rollo besieging Paris and then leaving to help Guthrum.

Rollo's origin and timeframe are, however, widely debated as the first known reference to him is in a charter of 918 – more than 30 years after the siege. Scholar Stephen Lewis believes Dudo took historical Viking raids from Frankish annals in the 880s and made Rollo the 'main protagonist'.[43] His slain brother Gurim may have been based on Danish royal Gudrom killed in the civil war of 854. While Rollo's presence is doubtful, the resulting chaos at Paris is indisputable.

Soon after Siegfried's threat to starve the inhabitants, he launched into action. The next day at midday, on 26 November 885, Siegfried's army launched arrows at the Frankish troops and stones at the Grand Châtelet, a large stone tower that anchored the Grant Pont on the northern, right bank of the Seine. People grew fearful as the bridge swayed, but many rushed to defend the tower, which had not yet been completed, from the relentless onslaught.

Abbo Cernuus singles out Count Odo, his brother Robert I, Count Ragenar and the 'stalwart abbot' Ebolus, the bishop's nephew, for leading the resistance. One young warrior, Frederick, was killed by a sword, but Bishop Gozlin, who was wounded by an arrow, survived thanks to 'God's own medicine'.[44] Relentless Vikings were forced to fall back to their camps, taking 'many of their lifeless' crew.

Vikings had set up their main base at the Saint-Germain l'Auxerrois, across from the modern Louvre, named after the Bishop Germanus of Auxerre, a leading west-Roman clergyman who famously visited Britain in the 5th century to tackle a Christian theological position called Pelagianism. If you visit the Roman Catholic church today, situated on the right or north bank of the Seine facing the Louvre Museum, among the spectacular stained-glass windows that adorn this historic building, there is an image of St Germanus taking pride of place close to a scene from the Bible at the very back. Remarkably, more than 1,000 years later, these famous religious figures and buildings remain so prominent and referenced at every turn.

Alongside the initial camp, a secondary camp was later created at the abbey of St-Germain-des-Prés on the opposite bank of the Seine. Typically, the camps would be surrounded by defensive earthworks that were formed through excavating a ditch and elevating a bank inside that was topped by a wooden palisade.[45] Abbo Cernuus notes how the Northmen were fashioning stakes, gathering stones and earth to build the makeshift fortifications.

Beaten back but not defeated, Siegfried launched a renewed assault on the Grand Pont after the Franks had built a wooden tier around the Grand Chatelet tower across the stone bastion, which was 'half as high as before'. The unfinished tower was missing another level but was still several metres high and possible for the Vikings to scale with ladders.[46]

The second attack was even more ferocious, recalls Abbo Cernuus. 'Arrows flew here, there through the air, blood gushed and flowed. Darts, stones and javelins were hurled by ballistae and slingshots. Nothing was seen between heaven and earth but these projectiles.'[47] Abbo Cernuus' account reveals the tower 'groaned' from the arsenal of weapons, and 'the city quakes, its people terrified', as battle horns rang out and defenders in their droves rushed to protect the 'trembling tower'.[48]

Harrowing scenes in a *Vikings* TV episode shows how a combination of oil, wax and pitch (a resin made from petroleum and coal tar) was heated on a furnace to create a lethal hot liquid that was poured on the Vikings trying to scale the walls. Franks used the brutal method on the Northmen as they were trying to dig tunnels to undermine the foundations of the tower. Directed by Odo and described vividly by Abbo Cernuus, the scene would have been unimaginable, as the boiling liquid 'burned the hair of the Danes and made their skulls split open'.[49] Many were killed while the others plunged into the river in desperation. Mockingly, the Frankish troops shouted, 'right badly scorched you are' and advised them to run to the Seine to 'allay your pain and restore your flowing manes'.[50]

Despite the horrific weapon, the Vikings battled fiercely, repeatedly hurling rocks, but their groans could be heard as the arrows struck their target in return. Reinforcements arrived from Vikings on horseback, who returned from pillaging to bolster the ranks of Siegfried's army, but they too suffered the same fate.

Finally, after giving up the second attack, Vikings returned to their camps, where instead of a hero's welcome, according to Abbo Cernuus, they were greeted with scorn by their women, who remarked was 'it all for nothing I gave you Ceres (grain), Bacchus (wine) and boar meat'.[51] Showing little sympathy, they branded their retreating husbands and sons seeking a second meal as 'gluttonous' and warned the others returning would face the same frosty welcome.[52]

Humbled, the Vikings headed back for another attack on the tower, again targeting the foundations to bring it down, but after a breach opened on one side, a huge wheel was launched from above that killed six men.

The Franks added an extra level on the tower so it could no longer be scaled and continually repaired damaged sections with wooden planks overnight. They constructed a moat around the fortification to make attacks even harder.[53]

Count Odo defends Paris against the Northmen in this painting by Jean-Victor Schnetz in 1837. (WikiCommons)

The Vikings changed tact and set fire to the gate of the tower creating, a 'dreadful pyre' that engulfed the entire fortification so it 'vanished completely in a great gloom'.[54] Two standard bearers, however, rushed out from the city and climbed the tower. While holding the standards, tinted golden with saffron, they frightened off the Danes, who were then struck down by a barrage of 100 quick arrows, says Abbo Cernuus triumphantly, who draws on the mythical Greek legend about the god of fire Hephaestus from the island of Lemos.

Water soaked the remaining flames and extinguished not only the blaze but the will of the Scandinavians, who finally gave up. Three hundred Vikings were killed but the Frankish losses were comparatively light in comparison, it is claimed. Battered Viking contingents retreated to their camps to recover from the intense warfare, which occurred just before December 885.

There was a brief lull as Vikings on horseback began pillaging the surrounding villages and killing everyone in their path, young and old, Abbo Cernuus claims. He mourns a 'wealthy land, stripped of teeming wealth' as a 'savage company lays waste with bloody wounds'.[55] As the Danes ransacked their way through the countryside, locals fled and offered little resistance without a royal army to call on. Neither did the defenders in Paris attempt to meet the Vikings in open field, and they had abandoned either side of the Île de la Cité.

With winter fast approaching, Siegfried's army targeted grain stores where the harvest was stockpiled. The crew of one longship required around 24kg to 27kg of unmilled wheat per day, or the equivalent in dried or smoked meat and fish, showing the scale of the supplies needed.[56]

Cattle, pigs and sheep from farms were driven to Paris, and Abbo Cernuus recalls there was so much livestock outside the Viking camp, presumably at St-Germain-des-Prés but not specified, the sacred hall resembled a stable. Given the squalid conditions, countless bulls, young sows and sheep died from disease, infested with worms. There was a horrible stench from the corpses, and the diseased animals were dumped into the Seine rather than taken to the cookhouses. The church 'belonged to the cows' and 'none could be slaughtered for food', Abbo Cernuus recalled.[57]

At this point, Siegfried's men began constructing three massive battering rams using 'unknown monsters, with sixteen wheels'.[58] Each of the battering rams were shielded by a roof made from rawhide, with men hiding underneath who would drive the huge structures into the tower's gates. Two workers were taken out by arrows from the Franks when creating the battering rams, which were tipped with forged iron plates.[59] In response the Northmen erected 1,000 tents, held up by poles, to protect the others from further missiles.

Returning to their assault on the Grand Châtelet, the Vikings hurled 1,000 pots of molten lead and managed to knock down the turrets, the mini towers on the main fortification, by catapults. Church bells rang out, and the city's forces led by the inspirational Odo held firm and defended the tower. Siegfried's men formed three corps, with one heading for the tower and two others, aboard painted ships, heading for the bridge.

Describing the ferocity, Abbo Cernuus recalls the ground below was completely hidden by painted shields, neither was anything visible from the tower to the sky apart from the mass of arrows, which resembled a 'swarm of bees'.[60] No man, according to Abbo Cernuus, had ever seen so many foot soldiers with swords gathered in one place. The 'bridge wept' over the countless warriors who were killed and washed away. 'No path to the city was left unstained by the blood of men,' mourned Abbo Cernuus.[61]

He told of how 1,000 stood shoulder to shoulder in battle, while the same number gathered in smaller groups to overwhelm the tower, but the Frankish guardians unleashed a constant barrage of arrows. The garrison kept torches burning at night to prevent the Northmen from approaching in the cloak of darkness, while the Vikings erected tents near the tower made from forest wood and hides of the slaughtered oxen, which they pierced holes in to fire the occasional arrow overnight.

The following morning, Siegfried's men began filling in the ditches that surrounded the tower with hay from meadows, scrub and vines, along with the corpses of cows, young and old, and even captives were killed and thrown into the trenches. This horrific sight moved Gozlin to make a desperate plea to the Virgin Mary for retribution. To divert the Franks, the Northmen began attacking the base beneath a 'tortoise' style shield-wall known as a *testudo*, where shields are held above and at the side. The tower somehow survived the onslaught.

Fierce fighting renewed at the end of January 886, when over three days, one of the siege's most dramatic moments occurred. Franks began using mangonels, a medieval siege weapon, which launched massive stones at the Vikings below.

In response, Siegfried's army set fire to three ships in the Seine, which had been filled with branches and leaves, and using a rope from land, guided them towards the Grand Pont from east to west.

Terrified Franks held their breath as the flaming vessels slowly edged closer. Desperate Frankish inhabitants cried out so much that the 'walls resound St-Germain on every tower', but the Vikings ridiculed the Parisiens and with 'mocking laughs' banged their shields.

St Germain, according to Abbo Cernuus, heard the cries and saved the city. The engulfed vessels crashed into a heap of stones underneath the tower as support and gave the Franks time to douse the fire and prevent catastrophe. They even kept the ships as plunder. A demoralised Siegfried finally gave in and called off the siege.[62]

Abbo Cernuus said above all men Siegfried was 'most prone to gouge out the tower's eyes, that is it gates'.[63] Viking leaders had to be at the front as their honour demanded. This was ingrained as the Roman historian Tacitus said how it was embarrassing for Germanic leaders to not be the best among the entire army at fighting.[64] Charged with being on the frontline in brutal combat, it is a small wonder how Ragnar's sons survived long into adulthood. Such kings must have been training constantly for these encounters from an early age and developed into highly skilled and lethal warriors.

The day of the victory – 2 February 886 – fell on the Feast of the Purification of the Blessed Mother of Christ. Soon after, the Vikings decided to begin raiding the eastern regions, the 'only portion of poor France' not ravaged.[65] Robert the Quiver, the Count of Troyes, was slain during the pillaging after cutting down two raiders, but his death was quickly avenged by his nephew Adalhelm, who confronted and slaughtered the Vikings with a local militia.

Around this time, while encamped on the meadow outside St-Germain-des-Prés, one Viking broke into the main church and with a 'cudgel' (short stick) dared to break all the glass in the windows. As he returned to the meadow, a 'seething madness' gripped him, which drained all his strength and led to his death. Another Viking climbed up the spire of the church but tumbled and fell below, shattering the bones in his body. A third Norseman was struck down when trying to reach the sepulcher (a small room or monument) to the saint, and a fourth was killed from a great height. Finally, a fifth Viking pried open Germannus' tomb, but the very first stone removed hit him hard and the 'deadly blow impelled his soul'.[66]

Abbo Cernuus also claimed the saint miraculously cured a noble whose flesh had withered and was dying from an unknown disease after appearing in his dreams, and he woke completely healed. During a bleak moment, it was claimed St Germain appeared during the midst of battle and drove the Danes back.

For chroniclers such as Abbo Cernuus, the war was a simple battle between the good of the Christians and the supposed evils of the heathens. The conflict was spiritual as well as physical because Vikings were seen as both the embodiment of sin in Frankish society and their violence was the punishment. The power of the saints such as Germain, however, was unparalleled, and faith in their divinity must never waiver. Such invented tales of divine intervention from Germain, miracles and accidental deaths of the pagans, which were attributed as acts of gods and saints, served to reinforce this belief.[67]

The faith of the Franks would soon be questioned in the darkest hour of the siege. Pulled apart by 'floods that raged with swollen wrath', the banks of the Seine burst and the mid-section of the smaller wooden Petit Pont bridge on the left side of the river collapsed. 'The city trembles, trumpet blare and walls are wet with tears, all the country groans and waters roar.'[68]

Re-energised Danes filled their ships with weapons and shields and crossed the Seine and surrounded the Petit Châtelet and 'together stones and darts fly densely through the air' as the Northmen sensed a breakthrough. 'Earth shakes while our

The smaller Petit Pont on the left bank of the Seine would eventually collapse amid a massive flood and the Vikings seized the opportunity.

side mourns but their side cheers instead,' Abbo Cernuus said ruefully, who stated twelve brave Franks remained to hold off the Vikings.[69]

Sensing blood, the Vikings set ablaze a wagon piled with dried hay and pushed it against the tower, and despite the best efforts of the dozen Frankish defenders, it engulfed and destroyed the building. Vikings had sworn not to harm the twelve men but then slaughtered them. They were heralded as martyrs by Abbo Cernuus, who said the Danes sent their 'souls to heaven as red blood flowed'.[70] One of the twelve Eriveus, however, was spared as the Vikings noticed his noble demeanour and sought to ransom him. Having seen his comrades killed, Eriveus furiously urged the Vikings to chop off his head and swore they would 'get nothing for their greed'. He was killed the following day.

Remarkably, the names of the Paris defenders – Hermanfried, Eriveus, Herland, Odoacer, Herric, Arnold, Gosbert, Uvido, Soli, Hardrad, Einhard and Gozwin – are honoured to this day with a marble plaque near the Crypte Archéologique dc l'Île de la Cité.

After their deaths, the *Annals of St Vaast* told of how the 'cry of the multitude went up to heaven, and the bishop from the wall of the city, together with all who were in the city, wept exceedingly, because they could not help their own, and because he could do nothing else, he commended them to Christ.'[71]

After the Petit Pont collapsed, the twelve defenders made a heroic last stand against the Vikings – depicted by the French school in the early-twentieth century. (Stefano Bianchetti/ Bridgeman Images)

Chapter 20

WARRIOR OF THE VALKYRIES

The rough storm has robbed me of my best riches. It's cruel to recall the loss of that kinsman, the safeguard, the shield of the house has sailed out in death's darkness to a dearer place.

Egil's Saga, possibly Snorri Sturluson,
thirteenth century[1]

With the tower finally destroyed, the Vikings portaged their ships and then floated the vessels just past the Île Saint-Louis, a smaller island in the Seine further down. Most Vikings headed for the Loire Valley to plunder the region but faced fierce resistance at Chartres and Les Mans. After returning to Paris, Siegfried began negotiations with Odo away from the tower, but Danes rushed out to try and kill the count of Paris. Odo struck several down while armed with a shield and spear before his warriors rushed out to save him.

Vikings had taken over the Abbey of St-Germain-de-Prés as a secondary encampment and made ramparts, hemming in the saint like a 'thief in prison'.[2] Siegfried negotiated a 60lb tribute of silver to be paid directly by the church and promised to depart for good. This was less than one-hundredth of the amount awarded to Ragnar in 845 and suggested the potential Sigurd believed the siege was doomed to failure or had gained enough plunder from raiding between Troyes and Le Mans.

Abbo Cernuus claims Siegfried wanted to depart 'for his own land' and follow the river home where the '(English) channel seizes the white tail of the Seine'. Many of Siegfried's men refused to leave, and he responded mockingly by urging them to 'swarm the strong walls of the city' and 'besiege the ramparts' and to 'charge forward' as their shoulders were weighed down by bows and quivers full of arrows, while others carried stones and javelins. 'I will do what I can as I watch you fight fiercely,' he said, unhelpfully.[3]

As the Vikings had failed to defeat the Frankish resistance after more than five months, this possibly imagined and certainly biased speech may have captured the mindset of Siegfried, who had previously been described as the most aggressive in leading the attacks. After Siegfried's address, which highlighted his overall command, the Vikings launched another doomed assault.

When the attack failed, Siegfried was described by Abbo Cernuus as laughing and ironically cheering at their attempts to storm the fortress. 'Come brave warriors, charge the ramparts, overrun the city. Take measures of the houses you wish to live in afterwards.'[4] The remark suggested the Vikings were planning far more than just plundering the city and sought to live there, but they first had to destroy the Frankish resistance, which never seemed likely to happen.

Turning to his remaining followers, Siegfried said 'let's go, the time has come when it will please us best to no longer be here' and finally abandoned the siege. Not long afterwards Gozlin, the Bishop of Paris, died from illness on 16 April and was poignantly heralded by Abbo Cernuus as 'our lasting tower, our shield, our double sharpened sword'.[5] He was replaced by Askericus, who served until his death four years later.

The siege of Paris had become a stalemate as the Vikings repeatedly failed to overwhelm the fortress, while the Franks were unable to completely remove the Northmen. Three hundred Danes stormed the island, but a handful of Franks including twins Segebert and Segevert, who were slain, held them off. Odo and three battalions bravely stormed through the horde of Vikings to reach the city gates.

A king of the Vikings called Sinric, one of only two named by Abbo Cernuus, was killed alongside fifty men when their boat capsized in the River Seine. Apparently, Sinric had warned he would rather camp on the riverbed than leave and so the 'Lord let him keep his word', boasted Abbo Cernuus.[6]

Notably, Ivar's son Sihtric shared the same name, a variation of the Old Norse one 'Sigtrygg', but he was killed in 896. Abbo Cernuus may well have invented humiliating deaths for Vikings as other medieval monks have done.

The Franks suffered a huge blow in August 886 when their key military commander, Duke Henry of Saxony, was killed in a trap near a camp of Northmen in Quierzy, close to the River Oise. Over the previous twenty years, Duke Henry had served various Frankish kings and consistently led armies against the Vikings, particularly in East Francia. He had killed their king Godafrid in 885 and reclaimed the region of Frisia for the Franks in the process. Vikings had dug pits one feet across and three feet deep and covered them with reeds and other refuse around their encampment in Quierzy. When Henry led attacks on the camp, his horse tripped over the concealed pit and the Northmen rushed out and killed him before he could escape.[7]

A few months later, a 'Sigifrid' came with a 'great host of Northmen' to help other Vikings in what was likely Paris but not explicitly stated and caused 'great fear among the Christians', based on the *Annals of Fulda*.[8] As a result, Charles the Fat, who finally arrived in the city in late October, was left terrified and allowed the Vikings to raid the rebellious Burgundy region and promised a 7,00lb tribute, quoted by Abbo Cernuus, if they left by March the following year.[9]

Charles the Fat's decision to agree to pay off the Vikings in a humiliating peace infuriated Parisiens and those in the surrounding regions, who had endured misery from the Norse horde for nearly a year before their emperor finally arrived. Instead of confronting the Northmen, he allowed them to continue raiding and slaughtering rebelling citizens.[10] This sealed the fate of an all-powerful Carolingian dynasty, and the former vast empire of Charlemagne, as the Frankish realm splintered into five kingdoms.

In November 887, Charles' nephew Arnulf had seized East Francia (most of modern Germany) for himself, which had forced Charles to retire before his death three months later. Arnulf also claimed the kingdom of Lortharingia, which included the Netherlands, Belgium, Luxembourg and Germany west of the Rhine. Berengar I was crowned king of Italy and Louis the Blind became the ruler of Provence. Odo was elected the king of West Francia, which largely corresponds with modern-day France, for his heroism. This was a hugely important development in France's history, as it became known from the late-tenth century. While the Carolingians enjoyed a brief revival, a grandson of Odo's brother Robert, called Hugh Capet, formed a long-lasting dynasty.

According to the *Annals of St Vaast*, after the emperor granted them permission to plunder beyond Paris, a group of Vikings led by a 'Siegfried' burned down the great monastery of St Medard in Soissons in northern France, along with a royal palace and another monastery, and they enslaved and killed inhabitants. Siegfried was hunting down Charles the Fat, who fled the monastery beforehand, which suggests he was a different figure than the Northman king of the same name paid off by the emperor at Asselt four years earlier.

Another group of Northmen then left the Seine to raid Sens in the Burgundy region of east-central France. Siegfried returned to the Seine at the end of spring 887 'acting as usual' and in autumn of that year, according to the *Annals of St Vaast*, he headed to Frisia, where he was slain and afterwards the group returned to Paris to collect the tribute.[11]

The similarly named Viking leader killed in Frisia must have been Ivar's son Sichfrith in Old Irish (Sigfred in Old Norse), the nephew of Sigurd, whose death is recorded at roughly the same time in the *Annals of Ulster*, and the lack of a location provided implies he died outside of Ireland.[12]

Variants of Sigurd, Godfred, Harald and Olaf were popular among Viking royals, and it would not be unusual for two related kings to share the same names. Sichfrith headed the Dublin-based 'dark foreigners' in the 880s and was eventually succeeded by his other sibling, Sihtric. With Guthred, the Northumbrian king from 883 at York, another suspected son of Ivar, Sichfrith must have been ruling in Dublin as the second-eldest son. He is a shadowy figure because he is only mentioned once in the *Annals of Ulster*, when he was deceitfully killed by a kinsman in 888, or by his brother according to the *Chronicon Scotorum*.[13,14]

His death cannot be tied to a known battle in Frisia, which suggests an internal conflict among the Vikings as stated. Given his near absence from Irish sources, Sichfrith was seemingly active with the army in Francia and headed a large brotherhood at the Paris siege.

By nature, the Viking brotherhoods, and their various kings that made up the army were coming, going and returning as they pleased. However, Abbo Cernuus' detailed contemporary account, which features Siegfried prominently, never mentions him again or has him returning to the Seine or Paris after he was given tribute.

It is strange that Abbo Cernuus gave Siegfried such a dramatic departure if he had simply returned to the Seine with a huge army later in the year, which led to the emperor promising the 700lb tribute (only Abbo mentions the exact amount) and again the next summer. In the following summer, the Vikings reoccupied the fields outside the abbey of St-Germain-des-Prés, where Abbo Cernuus was based.

At the start, this suggests that Sigurd Ragnarsson headed the siege of Paris but gave up halfway amid the determined defence. By then, Sigurd had raided beyond the city, which was the original goal, after destroying the Petit Pont bridge and saw the continued attempts to storm the walled island fortress as pointless. He may have joined two Viking groups overwintering at the royal vill called Chézy on the River Marne or in Yvonne for the next two winters or returned to Scandinavia. For Sigurd Ragnarsson, all roads appear to have ended in Leuven.

Just outside the railway station, Leuven's striking peace memorial stands as a permanent reminder of a very dark episode in its history. German forces began brutally pillaging and looting in the city during World War I. However, Leuven's origins can be traced to the relentless raids on Francia by an offshoot of the Great Heathen Army during the 880s. Raymond Kenis, chair of the Leuven history group, believes 'without Vikings there would be no Leuven in the first place'.[15]

Pride of place in the city is the beguiling town hall, a late-Gothic-style fifteenth-century building filled with intrinsically carved biblical scenes of figures from local history, which draws comparisons with the town hall in the spectacular Grand Place (Grote Markt) in central Brussels built around a similar time.

Nearby, the Oude Markt was possibly at the centre of the Viking camp and later battleground and has been researched by the local history group for the past twenty-five years. Vikings first camped in Leuven in the winter of 884 after the massive tribute payment of 12,000lbs of gold and silver when they were based in Amiens but soon returned after Emperor Carloman II died. Regino tells of how after leaving the Somme, they 'pitched their camp at a place called Louvain (Leuven) on the edge of the same realm' and 'wearied both kingdoms' with raiding.[16]

Leuven was situated at the border of the historic counties of Brabant and Hesbaye and near the boundary between eastern and western Francia. Two years before the army returned to Leuven in 891, the Vikings were driven out by the Bretons after they had camped at Saint-Lô and then overwintered next to the River Waal in Nijmegen in modern-day Netherlands.

Pursued by King Odo, this army was roaming through Brabant before crossing the River Scheldt and finally settling in Leuven, as another group led by Bjorn's veteran Mediterranean ally Hastein headed to Amiens.[17] A main Roman road, known as the Via Belgica, which ran from Cologne in Germany to the port city of Boulougne-sur-Mer in the north coast of France passed directly through Leuven.[18]

Featuring a D-shaped enclosure with a ditch and earth, the wooden camp in Leuven would have been reinforced with a wooden palisade wall with a breastwork at the top. The northernmost reach of the camp is thought to have been the intersection of the modern-day Karel van Lotharingenstraat and the Vaartstraat, with the southern end located near the Hogenheuvel College on the present-day Naamsestraat. The eastern side is believed to have extended to Herbert Hooverplein, and one side of the camp was defended by a rampart.[19] Due to the jagged and bendy course of the River Dyle, another existing channel may have been created by the Vikings to make it easier to defend. This layout had striking parallels to Repton, which used the Old Trent Water for its D-shaped enclosure. Repton's moat was up to 4m deep and 4m wide and the earth wall up to 6m high.[20]

Local historians in Leuven believe the makeshift Viking camp was later replaced by the city's medieval walls, which is supported by how the layout of the Belgian cities of Antwerp and Ghent, around 30 and 50 miles away respectively, apparently follow the outline of Viking ring forts.[21] Leuven's Romanesque city walls measured some 2,700m in length and enclosed an area of 60 hectares.[22] Archaeological finds are scarce, but there is some fascinating potential place-name evidence showing the traces of the Vikings in Leuven around the modern Oude Markt.

A place name known as the Wolvenpoort, which translates as Wolf's Gate, has also been associated with the Viking camp by the Leuven history group, as has the existing Noormannenstraat (Northmen Street).[23] Drinkwaterstraat is believed to be derived from 'rinc-water', meaning wall or ring around water, while Wierinckstraat in 1370 was Wie-rinc, or 'weering' (in Dutch), derived from 'Wy', which implies a circular defending hill or wall linked to a sanctuary. Notably, buildings and routes in the heart of the city centre follow an inner circle at this point just before the River Dyle. The 'wie' element suggests a pagan shrine or sanctuary within the camp as in Old Dutch *wī* referred to temple, while *wih* meant 'idol' in Old English and in Old Norse *vé* applied to 'temple'.[24] Originally, the element possibly meant a sacred place. Waaistraat in Leuven, said to be derived from 'Wij', has also been linked to the sanctuary. A nearby place once called Ocialistraete may stem from the Old Norse word Oski, according to the Leuven history group, as another name for Odin.[25]

Lisa Van Ransbeeck, the city archaeologist in Leuven, said a 'lack of deep excavations', as most only reach the twelfth and thirteenth centuries, could explain the scarcity of finds related to the Viking camp.[26]

Six mysterious wooden posts were found during excavations at Barbarahof but were thought to be part of a later-twelfth century moat. One of the archaeologists involved, Wouter De Maeyer, said 'no traces or finds' were linked to the Vikings.[27] A mysterious skull fished out of the River Dyle in Leuven in 2016 and a vase found along the same riverbed have been potentially linked to the Vikings but require further analysis according to the Leuven history group.

Leuven's mysterious Viking shrine could have resembled one witnessed by the Arab traveller Ibn Fadlan. In his remarkable first-hand account, dated to 922 (just over thirty years after the Leuven camp), Ibn Fadlan describes how the Rus on the Volga River would frequently make offerings to the gods near a figure with a man's face surrounded by little figures, with timber stakes behind these objects.

When trying to sell their 'sable skins' and 'young slave girls' to merchants, Ibn Fadlan said they leave a gift at the post, so they get a merchant who 'buys everything' and 'doesn't argue over the price'. If he has difficulty, the Rus trader will return with further gifts and even start rewarding the little idols. After a successful sale, they would remark 'my Lord has satisfied my needs, and it is fitting that I should reward him for it.' As a thanks, the Rus would hang the heads of slaughtered sheep and cows on the wooden stakes and when they were gone the next morning, after dogs ate the gifts, they believed their Lord was pleased.[28]

Leuven is situated between two very different landscapes because a mile north of the modern-day city, the River Dyle enters the Flemish Valley, commonly known as the Lowlands. After its confluence with the River Demer near the village of Werchter, around 7 miles away, the River Dyle flows in a westerly direction towards the River Scheldt, which is frequently linked to Viking raiding. In the opposite direction after Leuven, the river enters a hillier landscape with a significant rise in altitude and forms a 1km-wide flood plain, which would have been impossible for the Viking fleet.[29]

The Dyle between the River Demer to Leuven becomes as narrow as 12m (39ft) wide – a Viking longship could be 5m to 6m wide – with several twists and turns as well as sharp bends. However, the Northmen could have brought supplies and manpower in their smaller vessels known as *ask,* which were oar-powered transport vessels with a mast that could accommodate a crew of between 30 to 35 men and featured about 30 oars.[30] Abbo Cernuus referred to a 'multitude of small vessels' at the start of the Paris siege.[31]

Under their new king Arnulf, the East Franks were determined to get revenge on the Vikings after a humiliating defeat at the Battle of Geule on 26 June 891. Here, they unexpectedly encountered Viking scouts but were quickly overwhelmed when the enemy cavalry turned up and a 'multitude' of nobles were killed. Regino of Prüm wrote: 'As the fighting got worse, the army of the Christians (the shame

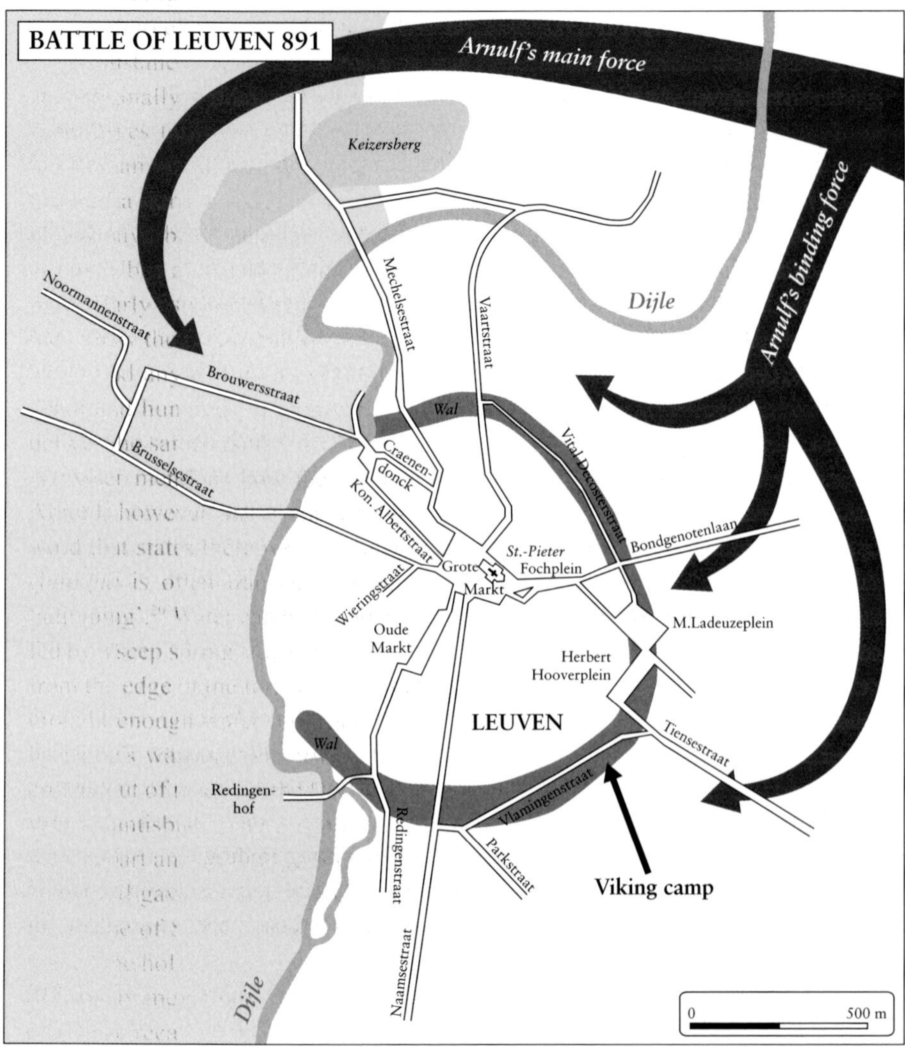

Arnulf's main force attacked in a fording point over the river while three waves attacked the front of the Viking camp. (Luc De Vos/Paul Harper – original plan of the battlefield from Luc De Vos (1995), *Veldslagen in de Lage Landen,* Davidsfonds)

of it!) committed a sin and retreated.'[32] The stage was set for a confrontation at Leuven.

Unexpectedly, King Arnulf and his massive army arrived on the other side of the Dyle, which caught the Vikings by surprise. Academic Herman Vander Linden placed the battle in late September before the autumn when Arnulf was near the River Meuse on 9 October and was then in Nijmegen on 1 November, where he granted a charter.[33]

Drawing on research by military historian Professor Luc De Vos, Leuven's historians believe they know Arnulf's movements. After first crossing the Dyle from the east, Arnulf was able to arrive without warning by heading around the back of a hillside, which later became the Keizersberg Castle. Arnulf's force may have numbered as many as 10,000 men in comparison to the roughly 3,000 Vikings camped in Leuven.[34]

A substantial part of the Eastern Frankish contingent would have been a warrior elite who preferred fighting on horses rather than foot, equipped with a 80cm-long double-edged sword, which often bore the inscription 'Ulfberht', and clothed in chainmail armour, a helmet that resembled a slanted bowl attached to a neck guard and armed with a wooden shield that could fend off blows and be used as a weapon with its metal boss.[35]

Despite their overwhelming numbers, a bank of the river on one side with the marsh behind it, meant there was 'no room for the cavalry to attack'. At this point, the *Annals of Fulda* have Arnulf delivering a rousing speech to rally his forces, who were reluctant to disembark from their horses and confront the Vikings. Arnulf urged his men to think of 'revenging the blood of your pious relatives'.[36] In response to the rallying cry, the Vikings reacted furiously with war cries and waved their banners:

> *'The shouts of the Christians rose to heaven and the pagans after their fashion shouted no less, terrible battle-standards moved through the camps. Swords were drawn on both sides and armies clashed like iron on stone. The Danes were there, the most powerful people among the Northmen, who had never heard to be captured or conquered in any fortification.'*[37]

Many fearsome Danes, which must have included Sigurd, were veteran members, or their descendants, of the Great Heathen Army that Sigurd's brothers Ivar, Ubbe and Halfdan first spearheaded. The *Anglo-Saxon Chronicle*, which had been tracing its movements since it left Fulham in 879, records the army moving eastward and the subsequent battle.

The army was clearly planning to bed down for winter and launch renewed raids in the spring, but their reign of chaos in Francia was coming to an end. Vikings were clearly doomed as they were outnumbered by more than three to one.

Research suggests Arnulf's forces embarked at a fording point where the camp was only protected by the Dyle, located between the current Brouwersstraat and Mechelsestraat. Three columns of Frankish troops attacked the ramparts on the opposite side. Describing a 'fierce battle', the *Annals of Fulda* told of how the Vikings were defeated and then when trying to flee found that the river that had provided protection was now a death-trap:

> *'The Northmen sought safety in flight and found that the river, which they had thought of as a wall to their rear, was now their death. For with the Christians bringing death from the other side, they were forced to throw themselves into the river and grasping at each other in heaps by hand, neck and limbs, they sank in hundreds and thousands so that their corpses blocked the riverbed and it seemed to run dry. In that battle two of their kings were killed, that is Sigifrid [Sigurd] and Godafrid, and sixteen royal standards were carried off and sent to Bavaria as a witness.'*[38]

As a leader's honour demanded, Sigurd was likely one of the first cut down by the overwhelming number of Franks. Abbo Cernuus' account of the Paris siege has Sigurd at the front directing troops and being the most determined to tear down the

Hundreds of Vikings may have drowned in a gruesome scene when trying to flee the Battle of Leuven.

tower. As the Franks brutally wiped out the Viking contingent, Sigurd would have fallen knowing in his mind that his place in Valhalla was secured with a warrior death.

Once a king in the Danish realm, Sigurd had returned to Viking ways as the figurehead of Viking brotherhoods terrorising the Frankish realm during the 880s and amassing unimaginable wealth through plunder. He shared the same unrelenting thirst for battle and glory as his brothers Ivar, Halfdan and Ubbe before him. This story was always going to end one way.

Vander Linden suggests the rulers 'Sigifrid' and 'Godafrid' slain at Leuven were mistakenly taken from the siege of Asselt in 882, which featured the same names, but it seems highly unlikely the contemporary chroniclers invented this detail, and Godafrid's murder in 885 by Frankish nobles was extensively recorded in contemporary annals.[39]

When referring to the 'utter destruction', Adam of Bremen gives the wildly exaggerated figure that 'although hundred thousand pagans were killed, scarcely a Christian was found to have fallen.' This is clearly a simple error of translation as the *Annals of Fulda* stated 'hundreds and thousands' drowned in the river. The number of dead is repeated in the 'Tale of Ragnar's Sons', which claims this was where Sigurd perished: 'Anulf fought with the brothers and a hundred thousand Danes and Norwegians fell there. Sigurd Snake in the Eye fell there and another king fell there whose name was Gudrod.'[40]

The 'Tale of Ragnar's Sons' improves on the earlier saga to a degree and makes the Gudrod who died a member of the Dagling dynasty from Ringervike, Norway. It also says his brother Helge the Kleen survived and later married Sigurd's daughter, also called Aslaug, and ruled the kingdom while their son Sigurd Hart, who grew into a famous warrior, was growing up. The claim gains some credence because Adam of Bremen refers to a Danish king Helge who 'ruled Norway' and was 'beloved for his justice and sanctity' in the late-ninth century.[41] A later king called Chnuba, whose father Olaf from Sweden had overthrown Helge, is attested on two runestones as 'Gnupa' near Schleswig. His son 'Sigtrygg', who Adam of Bremen mentions ruled afterwards, is also mentioned on the runestones.

Ragnar Lothbrok and his sons were seen as great empire builders and linked to Norwegian, Swedish and Danish dynasties with dubious lineages as they sought to show their right to conquer Scandinavian territories was in their blood. The conquest of England became a defining moment of the Viking Age, and future Scandinavian kings and chieftains claimed them as ancestors with genealogies that are often chronologically impossible.

Claims that Ragnar via Sigurd had been a famed ancestor of Danish kings are more plausible but not universally accepted. Sigurd's son Harthacnute (or

Cnut in other sources), who according to legend was via his union with Blaeja, daughter of Ella or a daughter of Horik II, could be the ruler in Northumberland who featured on some 3,000 silver coins in the Silverdale hoard as 'CNVT REX' (King Cnut) that are dated between 900–5.[42] One single coin with the same design also features a ruler called 'Airdeconout', an Anglicised version of Harthacnute.

In turn, Harthacnute/Cnut may have been the father of Gorm the Old, seen as the founder of the Danish dynasty, who ruled from the 930s. Adam of Bremen mentions 'Hardecnudth Vurm' as ruling around this time, which as 'vurm' is the Old German word for 'Gorm', suggests this meant 'Gorm son of Harthacnute'. When discussing various tyrants ruling a decade or so earlier, he refers to a 'Hardegon, son of Svein from Northmannia', possibly Normandy, but the original Latin spelling 'Hardegon', compared with 'Hardecnudth Wrm' suggests a different ruler.[43]

Notably, the Jomsviking saga speaks of Gorm's sons conquering Northumbria and 'claiming it as their inheritance from the sons of Ragnar Lothbrok and other ancestors'.[44]

The *Heimskringla* (*The World's Orb*), compiled by Snorri Sturluson in the thirteenth century, features Harald Bluetooth, son of Gorm the Old, who reacts angrily when asked to divide up Denmark in Olaf's Saga: 'King Harald became very angry at that claim, he said no one demanded that of his father Gormr, nor of his father Horda Knut or Sigurdr ormr-i-auga or Ragnarr Lodbrok that he should make himself half-king over Denmark.'[45]

Leuven was positioned as the final defeat of Vikings, who would return to a renewed campaign of raiding in modern-day England from 893, led by the now veteran Hastein, but it was a devastating famine that spread through the countryside after a mass crop failure that led to the Vikings crossing back over the channel. The *Annals of St Vaast* claims defeated Northmen later established a base in Leuven for the winter, and surely, they would have cremated their dead with burial goods. One day, there is the fascinating possibility a major Viking archaeological site will be discovered in Leuven. 'With its location along the Dijle and rich medieval history, Leuven offers a fascinating field of research into the impact of the Vikings,' said the Leuven history group.[46] 'It is a story that, although partly shrouded in mystery, continues to inspire and intrigue.'

Leuven was the culmination of more than a decade of relentless Viking raids and warfare from the same Great Heathen Army in Francia that had terrorised Britain for some thirteen years beforehand. Mirroring Ubbe's fate at Cynuit, the Vikings under Sigurd had been caught off guard, overwhelmed and dealt with ruthlessly. As expected, it was the final gory chapter in the real story of Ragnar's sons. Their feats were infamous from Bjorn's notorious Mediterranean expedition, the capture of three Anglo-Saxon kingdoms by Ivar, Halfdan and Ubba and the sustained campaign in Francia under Sigurd. This had been just as epic as the TV adaptation and sagas.

Equally, the destruction, misery and grief caused in their unrelenting quest for wealth and fame is impossible to fathom. In a brutal age, kingdoms in the realms they targeted in Francia, Britain and Ireland were constantly engaged in warfare, non-Christians were persecuted on an industrial scale and so many were enslaved with unimaginable conditions.

Violence, conquest and slavery in the Viking Age reflected the world they existed in. Descriptions of atrocities including rape, torture and mass murder committed by the Vikings who terrorised western Europe are horrific in any era, but they should be balanced by how most of our knowledge comes from their enemies, with often clear religious overtones.

Powered by their ship technology, the Vikings prospered and expanded beyond all imagination – encapsulating the gods who accompanied them, Vikings had a lasting and dramatic influence on the western world with their trade, culture, fashions, mythology and sagas. York and Dublin alone developed into two of the most prosperous trading settlements in western Europe. What began as just a few ships of traders had an unmistakable impact from the Irish coast to the middle east. Ragnar and sons personified this bloody and epic era of history, which continues to enthral the modern world. Violent equivalents of modern thrill seekers, no glorious victory, rich plunder or captured kingdom ever seemed to satisfy their burning desires until they finally reached Valhalla. In their pursuit of legacy, of their feats being sung by future skalds and told through timeless sagas, they were victorious because there is no other Viking more famous than Ragnar Lothbrok with Ivar the Boneless following closely behind. No Viking warrior family could match their fame.

Fittingly, in the 'Tale of Ragnar's Sons', it was left to Aslaug to commemorate Sigurd, when undoubtedly, it was their real-life mother who fed, raised and equipped them. As Ragnar continued his Viking ways, she looked after the children until they reached the age when they could embark on similar voyages.

When he returned to the Danish realm with his forces after Leuven, Helge the Kleen brought back the banner, sword and shield of Sigurd and returned it to his mother. Even as she mourned her son, she spoke of vengeance unclaimed as she sought as ever to uphold the family honour. Her words suggest that Sigurd had been given a warrior send-off and cremated after falling at Leuven. Surely, she hoped, the flames had been burning high to signify the wealth that awaited him in Valhalla. With sadness, Aslaug spoke a verse to commemorate her son, having outlived all her children. She said her final goodbye to the last of Ragnar's five famous sons:

'The seekers after the slain [ravens],
sit on the fortress-neck [walls],
a shame that the swart raven leaves Sigurd's namesake unavenged,
let the body's blithe enjoyers [flame],
blaze on the wood chips around him,
all too soon,
Odin let the alf [warrior] of the Valkyries die.'[47]

Sigurd, the last surviving of Ragnar's famous sons, may have been given a similar ship burial after his death at Leuven. (Vahalla Viking Festival/Paul Harper)

ACKNOWLEDGEMENTS

I have been extremely fortunate to have been allowed to use numerous pictures for free or for a minimal fee. Many of these images are fantastic drone views, ancient artefacts or historic archaeological investigations, which bring to life the Ragnar Lothbrok legend perhaps more effectively than any words could hope to achieve.

Moreover, I would also like to thank the experts who have taken time to respond to random queries, which have pointed me in the right direction.

I would like to express my immense gratitude to Michael Harpur from eOceanic, photographers Hedley Thorne and Russell Davies (please see their incredible images of ancient sites and Scottish landscapes respectively on social media), scholars and archaeologists such as Martin Biddle, Tim Pestell, Jane Kershaw, Graham Nisbet, Gordon Noble, Julian Richards, Gareth Williams, Murray Cook, Phillip MacDonald and Charlotte Hedenstierna-Jonson, as well as the National Museum of Ireland and Swedish Historical Museum.

I'm particularly grateful to historian Nick Arnold for allowing me to feature his excellent research on the Battle of Cynuit, and to the current and previous landowners around Castle Hill, including Clinton Devon Estate. Thanks to Andy Williams for letting me use his impressive study of Bishop Heahmund, and James Clark for his additional guidance. The Leuven History Group has been enormously helpful and accommodating – so a massive thanks to them.

In the book, I have often drawn on translations such as the *Sagas of Ragnar Lothbrok* (by Ben Waggoner), the *Annals of St Bertin* (by Jane Nelson) and *Annals of Fulda* (by Timothy Reuter) and *The Bella parisiacae urbis of Abbo of Saint-Germain-des-Prés* (by Nirmal Dass), which are all highly recommended. *Vikings in the West: The Legend of Ragnarr Lothbrok and His Sons* by Elizabeth Rowe has been a vital resource as well as papers by academics Stephen Lewis and Rory McTurk, along with fascinating research by Leszek Gardeła on shield-maidens, and Heather O'Donoghue and Pragya Vohra on the Vikings in Cleveland. Works by Neil Price, Clare Downham, Gwyn Jones, Thomas Williams and Roskilde Ship Museum's Viking Ireland publication have also been very helpful sources.

Ireland seems so central in the story of Ragnar's sons, and it is a shame my beloved late gran Mary Harper (O'Neill), originally from County Wicklow, is unable to pick up a copy, but I hope she might be watching on – in-between reruns of Daniel O'Donnell concerts!

REFERENCES

Introduction

1. Waggoner, Ben (2009), *The Sagas of Ragnar Lodbrok*, Troth Publications, p.83
2. *The Sagas of Ragnar Lodbrok,* p.30
3. *The Sagas of Ragnar Lodbrok,* p.29
4. *The Sagas of Ragnar Lodbrok,* p.29
5. Carroll, Jane, Harrison, Stephen and Williams, Garreth (2014), *The Vikings in Britain and Ireland,* British Museum, p.7

Chapter 1: Brotherhoods

1. Jesch, Judith (2013), *Viking Poetry of Love and War,* British Museum, p.53
2. Brodeur, Arthur Gilchrist (translator) and Sturluson, Snorri (2011), *The Prose Edda*, CreateSpace Independent Publishing Platform, p.50–51
3. Larsen, Hanne et al (2024), *The impact of the volcanic double event in AD 536 and AD 539/540 on tree-ring growth and felling activity in Danish oak trees*, National Museum of Denmark
4. National Museum of Denmark (2024), 'Denmark was hit by humanity's biggest climate disaster, new research shows', press release (https://natmus.dk/nyhed/ danmark-blev-ramt-af-menneskehedens-stoerste-klimakatastrofe-viser-ny-forskning)
5. Price, Neil (2020), *The Children of Ash and Elm*, Penguin, pp.84–90
6. Jones, Gwyn (1968), *A History of the Vikings,* Oxford University Press, pp.60–61
7. *The Prose Edda*, p.51
8. Graslund, Bo and Price, Neil (2012), 'Twilight of the gods? The "dust veil event" of AD 536 in critical perspective', *Antiquity*, Vol 86 (No. 332), pp.428–43
9. The Viking Museum, Stockholm
10. The Viking Museum, Stockholm
11. *A History of the Vikings*, pp.145–56
12. *A History of the Vikings*, p.157
13. Magnusson, Magnus (2003), *The Vikings*, Tempus Publishing, p.16

14. Shaw, David (2016), 'Secrets of the Viking Ships', *Scandinavian Review*, p.1–21

15. *The Children of Ash and Elm,* pp.392–93

16. Jørgensen, Lise Bender (2012), *The introduction of sails to Scandinavia: Raw materials, labour and land,* in Berge, Ragnhild, Jasinski, Marek E. and Sognnes, Kalle, *N-TAG TEN: Proceedings of the 10th Nordic TAG conference at Stiklestad, Norway 2009,* BAR

17. Eleanor Barraclough (2024), 'How to Live Like a Viking', *Gone Medieval* podcast, 20 September

18. Barraclough, Eleanor (2024), *Embers of the Hands*, Profile Books, p.205

19. Clarke, Howard, Dooley, Shiela and Johnson, Ruth (2018), *Dublin and the Viking World*, O'Brien Ltd, p.30

20. *Dublin and the Viking World*, p.33

21. *A History of the Vikings*, p.192

22. 'Viking sunstone' found in shipwreck, BBC News, 6 March 2013 (www.bbc.co.uk/news/world-europe-21693140)

23. www.vikingeskibsmuseet.dk

24. Haywood, John (2015), *Northmen, The Viking Saga, 739–1241*, Head Zeus, p.77

25. Grant A. (1905), *The Early Lives of Charlemagne by Eginhard and the Monk of St Gall*, De la More Press, p.84

26. *A History of the Vikings*, p.178–80

27. Scholz, Bernard Walter and Rogers, Barbara (1970), *Carolingian Chronicles: Royal Frankish Annals and Nithard's Histories: 186,* Ann Arbor Paperbacks, p.88

28. *Carolingian Chronicles: Royal Frankish Annals and Nithard's Histories*, p.92

29. Nelson, Janet L. (1991), *The Annals of St-Bertin,* Manchester Medieval Sources, Manchester University Press, p.96

30. Gautier, Alban (2019), *Armed Bands on Both Sides of the Channel: Can We Track Individual Viking Gangs?*, Hal Open Science, hal-02132061, pp.27–38

31. Bartlett, W. B. (2019), *Vikings: A History of the Northmen*, Amberley Publishing

32. 'Armed Bands on Both Sides of the Channel: Can We Track Individual Viking Gangs?'

33. Nelleke Laure IJssennagger (2017), 'Central because Liminal: Frisia in a Viking Age North Sea World', doctoral thesis, University of Groningen, p.151

34. Stenton, Frank (1970), *Anglo-Saxon England*, Oxford University Press, p.240

Chapter 2: Ragnar Versus St Germain

1. Skre, Dagfinn and Stylegar, Frans-Arne (2004), *Kaupang, the Viking Town,* University of Oslo, p.23

2. Robinson, Charles (1921), *Anskar: The Apostle of the North, 801–65*, The Society for the Propagation of the Bible in Foreign Parts, pp.48–61

REFERENCES

3. Fordham University, 'Rimbert: Life of Anskar, the Apostle of the North, 801–865', Medieval Sourcebook, Fordham University website

4. *Anskar: The Apostle of the North, 801–865*, pp.59–61

5. *Anskar: The Apostle of the North, 801–865*, p.61

6. *Anskar: The Apostle of the North, 801–865*, p.116

7. *Anskar: The Apostle of the North, 801–865*, p.116

8. Coupland, Simon (2003), 'From poachers to gamekeepers: Scandinavian warlords and Carolingian kings', *Early Medieval Europe*, Volume 7 (Issue 1), pp.107–8

9. Sawyer, Peter (1997), *The Oxford Illustrated History of the Vikings*, Oxford University Press, p.40

10. DeSelm, Daniel (2009), *Unwilling Pilgrimage: Vikings, Relics, and the Politics of Exile during the Carolingian Era,* University of Michigan, p.149

11. Brownworth, Lars (2014), *The Sea Wolves, A History of the Vikings*, Crux Publishing Ltd, p.46

12. Migne, Jacques Paul (1844), 'On The Miracles of St. Germanus (Aimoinus Sangermanensis)', *Patrologia Latina*, Vol. 126, pp.1027–50 (wikisource.org)

13. *Unwilling Pilgrimage: Vikings, Relics, and the Politics of Exile during the Carolingian Era*, pp.149–50

14. 'On The Miracles of St. Germanus (Aimoinus Sangermanensis)'

15. 'On The Miracles of St. Germanus (Aimoinus Sangermanensis)'

16. Coupland, Simon (1999), 'The Frankish Tribute Payments to the Vikings and their Consequences', *Francia*, Vol. 26 (No.1)

17. Nelson, Janet L. (1991), *The Annals of St Bertin,* Manchester Medieval Sources, Manchester University Press, p.60

18. Joranson, Einar (1924), *The Danegeld in France*, Augustana Library Publications, No. 10, pp.33–36

19. *The Oxford Illustrated History of the Vikings,* p.37

20. *The Danegeld in France*, pp.33–36

21. 'On The Miracles of St. Germanus (Aimoinus Sangermanensis)'

22. 'On The Miracles of St. Germanus (Aimoinus Sangermanensis)'

23. *The Oxford Illustrated History of the Vikings,* pp.40–41

24. Rowe, Elizabeth (2012), *Vikings in the West: The Legend of Ragnarr Lodbrok and His Sons*, Studia Medievalia Septentrionalia, Vol. 18, pp.30–31

25. *Vikings in the West: The Legend of Ragnarr Lodbrok and His Sons*, pp.30–31

26. De Smedt, Charles, van Hooff, G., de Backer, Joseph (editors) (1883), 'Translatio S. Germani Parisiensis', *Analecta Bollandiana*, Vol. 2, pp.85–93

27. *Vikings in the West: The Legend of Ragnarr Lodbrok and His Sons*, pp.32

28. 'On The Miracles of St. Germanus (Aimoinus Sangermanensis)'

29. *Translatio Sancti Germani Parisiensis*

30. *The Annals of St-Bertin, p.61*

31. *The Annals of St-Bertin, p.129*

32. Keary, Charles Francis (1891), *The Vikings in Western Christendom, AD. 789 to AD. 888*, GP Putnam's Sons, p.199

33. Reuter, Timothy (1992), *The Annals of Fulda,* Manchester Medieval Sources, Manchester University Press, p.23

34. Cooijmans, Christian (translation 2022), 'Annales Fontanellenses', *Apardjón Journal for Scandinavian Studies*, Special Vol. II.

35. *Annals of St Bertin*, pp.60–61

36. Peter, D. R. M. (2013), 'Disorder and Warfare according to the Annals of Xanten (844–861)', *De Re Militari*, 25 June (https://deremilitari.org)

37. *Vikings in the West: The Legend of Ragnarr Lodbrok and His Sons*, p.23

38. Rau, Reinhold (1958), *Sources for the History of the Carolingian Empire II*, Darmstadt, pp.340–71.

39. Burfield, Brian (2012), 'The Invisible Enemy: Disease in Medieval Armies', *Medieval Warfare*, Vol. 2 (No. 3), pp.35–38

40. 'The Frankish Tribute Payments to the Vikings and their Consequences'

41. *The Vikings in Western Christendom, AD. 789 to AD. 888*, p.287

42. Scholz, Bernard Walter and Rogers, Barbara (1970), *Carolingian Chronicles: Royal Frankish Annals and Nithard's Histories: 186,* Ann Arbor Paperbacks, p.88, p.186

43. *Carolingian Chronicles: Royal Frankish Annals and Nithard's Histories*, p. 186

44. McTurk, Rory (1973), *Ragnarr Lodbrok in the Irish Annals*, The Seventh Viking Congress, pp.93–123

45. *Ragnarr Lodbrok in the Irish Annals,* pp.93–123

46. Hollander, Lee (1945), *Bragi Boddason the Old, The Skalds: A Selection of Their Poems, With Introductions and Notes*, The American-Scandinavian Foundation

47. Clunies Ross, Margaret (2017), 'Bragi inn gamli Boddason, Ragnarsdrápa', in Gade, Kari Ellen and Marold, Edith (editors), *Poetry from Treatises on Poetics*, Skaldic Poetry of the Scandinavian Middle Ages 3, Brepols, p.27 (https://skaldic.org)

48. 'Bragi inn gamli Boddason, Ragnarsdrápa', p. 27

49. Knell, Sydney (2013), *Exploring the Emotive versus the Scholarly: an Investigation of the Kennings in Ragnarsdrápa and Øxarflokkr,* University of Oslo, pp.21–35

50. *Viking Poetry of Love and War,* pp.14–16

51. *Exploring the Emotive versus the Scholarly: an Investigation of the Kennings in Ragnarsdrápa and Øxarflokkr*

52. Price, Neil (2020), *The Children of Ash and Elm*, Penguin, pp.301–3

53. *The Children of Ash and Elm,* pp.301–3

54. *Vikings in the West, The Legend of Ragnarr Lodbrok and His Sons*, p.184

55. *The Vikings in Western Christendom, AD. 789 to AD. 888*, p.287

56. *The Vikings in Western Christendom, AD. 789 to AD. 888*, p.287

57. *Ragnarr Lodbrok in the Irish Annals*, pp.93–123

Chapter 3: Ironside

1. Stefansson, Jon (1908–9), 'The Vikings in Spain from Arabic (Moorish) and Spanish Sources', *Saga-Book*, Vol. VI, Viking Society for Northern Research, pp.31–46

2. Farrugia, Karl (2020), *Viking Magians in Arabic Sources from al-Andalus*, University of Oslo, p.27

3. 'The Vikings in Spain from Arabic (Moorish) and Spanish Sources'

4. Aguirre, Víctor, Emanuel (2013), *The Viking Expeditions to Spain during the 9th Century*, University of Southern Denmark, p.18

5. 'The Vikings in Spain from Arabic (Moorish) and Spanish Sources'

6. Hjardar, Kim and Vegard, Vike (2019), *Vikings at War*, Casemate UK, pp 341–43

7. *The Viking Expeditions to Spain during the 9th Century*, p.71

8. 'The Vikings in Spain from Arabic (Moorish) and Spanish Sources'

9. 'The Vikings in Spain from Arabic (Moorish) and Spanish Sources'

10. Guizot, Francois (translator) (1826), *History of the Normans and Life of William Conqueror by William Jumièges*, Chez Mancel Libraire (Project Gutenberg)

11. *History of the Normans and Life of William Conqueror by William Jumièges*

12. Lunde, Paul and Stone, Caroline (2011), *Ibn Fadlan and the Land of Darkness: Arab Travellers in the Far North*, Penguin Classics, p.66–68

13. Gertz, M. C. (1917), *Chronicon Roskildense in: Scriptores Minores Historiæ Danicæ*, Vol. 1, Copenhagen (Augstana.net)

14. Rowe, Elizabeth (2012), *Vikings in the West: The Legend of Ragnarr Lodbrok and His Sons*, Studia Medievalia Septentrionalia 18, p.172

15. *History of the Normans and Life of William Conqueror*

16. Cooijmans, Christian (translation 2022), 'Annales Fontanellenses', *Apardjón Journal for Scandinavian Studies*, Special Vol. II

17. Nelson, Janet L. (1991), *The Annals of St-Bertin,* Manchester Medieval Sources, Manchester University Press, pp.82–85

18. *The Annals of St-Bertin*, p.86

19. *The Annals of St-Bertin*, pp.86–87

20. Coupland, Simon (1998), *From Poachers to Gamekeepers: Scandinavian Warlords and Carolingian Kings*, Early Medieval Europe, Volume 7 (Issue 1), pp.103–4

21. 'The Vikings in Spain from Arabic (Moorish) and Spanish Sources'

22. Pellat, Charles (1993), *Encyclopaedia of Islam*, Vol. VII, Brill, pp.941–43

23. 'The Vikings in Spain from Arabic (Moorish) and Spanish Sources'

24. 'The Vikings in Spain from Arabic (Moorish) and Spanish Sources'

25. I Gunduz et al. (2001), 'Molecular studies on the colonization of the Madeiran archipelago by house mice', Molecular *Ecology*, Volume 8 (No.8), pp.2023–29

26. 'The Vikings in Spain from Arabic (Moorish) and Spanish Sources'

27. *Vikings at War*, p.343

28. *The Annals of St-Bertin*, p.90

29. *The Annals of St-Bertin*, p.92

30. *History of the Normans and Life of William Conqueror*

31. Haywood, John (2015), *Northmen: The Viking Saga, AD 793–1241*, Thomas Dunne Books, p.171

32. Maclean, Simon (translator) (2009), *History and Politics in Late Carolingian and Ottonian Europe: The Chronicle of Regino of Prüm and Adalbert of Magdeburg*, Manchester University Press, p. 154

33. *Vikings in the West, The Legend of Ragnarr Lodbrok and His Sons*, p.59

34. Magnus, Magnusson (2003), *The Vikings*, Tempus Publishing, p.60

35. www.santiebeati.it

36. Waggoner, Ben (2009), *The Sagas of Ragnar Lodbrok*, Troth Publications, p.27

37. 'The Vikings in Spain from Arabic (Moorish) and Spanish Sources'

38. Heath, Ian (1985), *The Vikings*, Osprey Publishing, p.31

39. Holloway, Don (2021), *The Last Viking*, Osprey Publishing, pp.96–97

40. *The Viking Expeditions to Spain during the Ninth Century*, p.68

41. Scheen, Rolf (1996), 'Viking Raids on the Spanish Peninsula', *Militaria Revista de cultura military*, No. 8, p.71

42. *The Viking Expeditions to Spain during the Ninth Century*, p.71

43. Jones, Gwyn (1968), *A History of the Vikings*, Oxford University Press, pp.319–20

44. Brodeur, Arthur Gilchrist (translator) and Sturluson, Snorri (2011), *The Prose Edda*, Amazon, pp.15–26

45. Viking Museum, Stockholm

46. *History of the Normans and Life of William Conqueror*

Chapter 4: The Dark Foreigners

1. Knott, E. (editor and translator) (1958), 'A Poem of Prophecies', *Ériu*, Volume 18, pp.55–84

2. Brú na Bóinne information display

3. O'Kelly, Michael J. (1982), *Newgrange: Archaeology, Art and Legend*, Thames and Hudson, p.93

REFERENCES

4. Marr, Laura (2018), 'The Ritual Origins of the Roof-Box at Newgrange', BA thesis, Saint May's University, Halifax

5. Monaghan, Patricia (2008), *The Encyclopaedia of Celtic Mythology and Folklore*, Checkmark Publishing, p.50

6. Corpus of Electronic Texts (CELT), *Annals of Ulster*, University College Cork

7. Brú na Bóinne information display

8. *The Encyclopaedia of Celtic Mythology and Folklore*, p.457

9. Brú na Bóinne information display

10. Downham, Clare (2007), *Viking Kings of Britain and Ireland, The Dynasty of Ivarr to A.D. 1014*, Dunedin Press, p.12

11. Haywood, John (2015), *Northmen: The Viking Saga, AD 793–1241*, Thomas Dunne Books, p.136

12. Larsen, Christine-Anne (2001), *The Vikings in Ireland*, Viking Ship Museum Roskilde, p.129

13. *Northmen: The Viking Saga, AD 793–1241*, p.38

14. Doherty, Charles (2001), 'The Viking Impact on Ireland', in Larsen, Christine-Anne, *The Vikings in Ireland*, Viking Ship Museum Roskilde, p.34

15. Dumville, David (2014), 'Let's tell the bloody truth about the Vikings', *Evening Standard*, 25 February

16. Tschan, Francis J. (translator) (2002), *History of the Archbishops of Hamburg–Bremen*, Columbia University Press, p.37

17. Waggoner, Ben (2009), *The Sagas of Ragnar Lodbrok*, Troth Publications, pp.24–25

18. *The Sagas of Ragnar Lodbrok*, p.25

19. *The Sagas of Ragnar Lodbrok*, pp.34–35

20. Corpus of Electronic Texts (CELT), *Fragmentary Annals*, University College Cork

21. *Viking Kings of Britain and Ireland, The Dynasty of Ivarr to A.D. 1014*, p16

22. *Annals of Ulster*

23. Rowe, Elizabeth (2012), *Vikings in the West, The Legend of Ragnarr Lodbrok and His Sons,* Studia Medievalia, Septentrionalia 18, pp.128–29

24. *Viking Kings of Britain and Ireland, The Dynasty of Ivarr to A.D. 1014*, p.3

25. *Vikings in the West, The Legend of Ragnarr Lodbrok and His Sons*, p.129

26. 'The Viking Impact on Ireland', p.31

27. Coupland, Simon (2014), 'Holy Ground? The Plundering and Burning of Churches by Vikings and Franks in the Ninth Century', *Viator*, Volume 45 (No. 1), pp.73–98

28. Linn Marie Krogsrud (2008), *Viking Age Silver Hoards in Ireland,* University of Oslo, p.11

29. Valente, Mary (2008), *The Vikings in Ireland: Settlement, Trade and Urbanization*, Four Courts Press, p.86

30. *Northmen: The Viking Saga, AD 793–1241*, p.191
31. *The Vikings in Ireland: Settlement, Trade and Urbanization*, p.88
32. Griffiths, David (2010), *Vikings of the Irish Sea: Conflict and Assimilation*, The History Press
33. Jorgensen, Tenaya (2017), *The Scandinavian Trade Network in the Early Viking Age: Kaupang and Dublin in Context*, University of Oslo, pp.35–36
34. Tsigaridas Glørstad, Zanette (2012), 'Sign of the Times? The Transfer and Transformation of Penannular Brooches in Viking-Age Norway', *Norwegian Archaeological Review*, Volume 45 (No. 1), pp.30–51
35. *The Scandinavian Trade Network in the Early Viking Age: Kaupang and Dublin in Context*, p.36
36. Dublinia Museum display board
37. Magnusson, Magnus (2003), *The Vikings*, Tempus Publishing, p.117
38. Harrison, Stephen (2001), 'Viking Graves and Grave Goods in Ireland', in Larsen, Christine-Anne, *The Vikings in Ireland*, Viking Ship Museum Roskilde, p.63
39. Dublinia Museum display board
40. *Annals of Ulster*
41. *Annals of Ulster*
42. *Fragmentary Annals*
43. *Annals of Ulster*
44. Downham, Clare (2011), 'Viking Identities in Ireland: It's not all Black and White', *Medieval Dublin*, Volume 11, Four Courts Press, pp.185–201
45. 'Viking Identities in Ireland: It's not all Black and White'
46. Elton, Oliver (translator) (1905), *The Nine Books of the Danish History of Saxo Grammaticus*, Norroena Society, New York
47. *Annals of Ulster*
48. McTurk, Rory (1973), *Ragnarr Lodbrok in the Irish Annals*, The Seventh Viking Congress, pp.93–123
49. Mawer, Allen (1908–9), 'Ragnar Lothbrok and his Sons', *Saga-Book*, Vol. VI, Viking Society for Northern Research, pp.68–89
50. *The Nine Books of the Danish History of Saxo Grammaticus*
51. *Annals of Ulster*
52. *The Sagas of Ragnar Lodbrok*, p.80
53. Henthorn Todd, James (1867), *Cogadh Gaedhel Re Gallaibh or The invasions of Ireland by the Danes and other Norsemen*, Longmans, Green, Reader and Dyer, p.27 (Internet Achive)
54. Corpus of Electronic Texts (CELT), *Fragmentary Annals*, University College Cork
55. *Ragnarr Lodbrok in the Irish Annals*
56. Lewis, Stephen (2021), *Ragenold, Rollo and other Northmen in Franca, c.919–925*, Université de Caen Normandie and Université Bordeaux Montaigne, p.13

57. Woolf, Alex (2007), *From Pictland to Alba*, The New Edinburgh History of Scotland, p.302
58. *Fragmentary Annals*
59. *Fragmentary Annals*
60. Green, Caitlin (2015), 'A great host of captives? A note on Vikings in Morocco and Africans in early medieval Ireland & Britain', September (caitlingreen. org)
61. *From Pictland to Alba*, p.73
62. *Vikings of the Irish Sea*, p.37
63. Corpus of Electronic Texts (CELT), *Fragmentary Annals*, University College Cork
64. *Fragmentary Annals*

Chapter 5: The Great Frisian Army

1. Magnusson, Magnus (2003), *The Vikings*, Tempus Publishing, p.22
2. Stenton, Frank (1970), *Anglo-Saxon England,* Oxford University Press, p.246
3. Jones, Gwyn (1968), *A History of the Vikings,* Oxford University Press, p.198
4. Hjardar, Kim and Vegard, Vike (2019), *Vikings at War,* Casemate UK, p.49
5. Tetzner, Noah (2022), *Viking Warrior Versus Frankish Warrior*, Osprey, p.23
6. *Vikings at War,* p.53
7. Clarke, Howard, Dooley, Shiela and Johnson, Ruth (2018), *Dublin and the Viking World*, O'Brien Ltd, pp.31–32
8. Bill, Jan (2023), 'The Vikings likely brought horses and dogs with them on their voyages to England', 14 February (sciencenorway.no)
9. Loeffelmann, Tessi et al. (2023), 'Sr analyses from only known Scandinavian cremation cemetery in Britain illuminate early Viking journey with horse and dog across the North Sea'*, PLOS ONE*
10. Downham, Clare (2007), *Viking Kings of Britain and Ireland, The Dynasty of Ivarr to AD 1014*, Dunedin Press, p.64
11. Cook, Albert (1906), *Asser's Life of King Alfred*, Ginn & Company (gutenberg. org)
12. 'The Viking Great Army in Britain featuring Julian Richards and Dawn Hadley', Gone Medieval podcast, 28 February 2025
13. Woolf, Alex (2007), *From Pictland to Alba*, The New Edinburgh History of Scotland, pp.71–72
14. Stephen M. Lewis (2016), 'Rodulf and Ubba. In search of a Frisian-Danish Viking', *Saga-Book*, Vol. 40, Viking Society for Northern Research, pp.17–22
15. IJssennagger, N. L. (2017), 'Central because Liminal: Frisia in a Viking Age North Sea World', unpublished thesis, University of Groningen, p.153

16. Valente, Mary (2008), *The Vikings in Ireland: Settlement, Trade and Urbanization*, Four Courts Press, p.62

17. Bremmer Jr, Rolf (1981), 'Frisians in Anglo-Saxon England: A Historical and Toponymical Investigation', *Fryske Nammen*, Vol. 3, pp.77–78

18. Reuter, Timothy (1992), *The Annals of Fulda*, Manchester Medieval Sources, Manchester University Press, p.88

19. Harkel, Letty Ten (2013), 'A Viking Age Landscape of Defence in the Low Countries? The *ringwalburgen* in the Dutch Province of Zeeland', in Baker, John, Brookes, Stuart and Reynolds, Andrew (editors), *Landscapes of Defence in Early Medieval Europe*, Vol. 28, Brepols, pp.223–60

20. 'A Viking Age Landscape of Defence in the Low Countries? The *ringwalburgen* in the Dutch Province of Zeeland', p.238

21. 'A Viking Age Landscape of Defence in the Low Countries? The *ringwalburgen* in the Dutch Province of Zeeland', p.251

22. *Central because Liminal: Frisia in a Viking Age North Sea World*, pp.331–33

23. 'A Viking Age Landscape of Defence in the Low Countries? The *ringwalburgen* in the Dutch Province of Zeeland', pp.253–54

24. Magnusson, Magnus (2003), *The Vikings*, Tempus Publishing, p.67

25. *Vikings at War*, p.125

26. 'A Viking Age Landscape of Defence in the Low Countries? The *ringwalburgen* in the Dutch Province of Zeeland', p.242

27. Nelson, Janet L. (1991), *The Annals of St-Bertin,* Manchester Medieval Sources, Manchester University Press, p.51

28. *From Pictland to Alba*, p.71

29. Vinkenoog, Hilbert (2020), *Frisians in the Great Heathen Army*, University of Cambridge, pp.7–8

30. 'Frisians in Anglo-Saxon England: A Historical and Toponymical Investigation'

31. *Frisians in the Great Heathen Army*, p.14

32. Harper, Paul (2023), *Cerdic: Mysterious Dark Age King Who Founded England*, Pen & Sword, pp.48–69

33. Williams, Thomas (2014), *Viking Britain*, Williams Collins, pp.139–41

34. *Annals of St Bertin*, p.43

35. *A History of the Vikings*, pp.318–19

36. Bray, Olive (1908), *The Elder or Poetic Elder*, Viking Club Translation Series, Vol II, p.295 (Internet Achive)

37. *The Elder or Poetic Elder*, p.295

38. Wise, Terrence and Embleton, Gerry (illustrator) (1979), *Saxon, Viking and Norman*, Osprey Publishing, p.6

39. *Anglo-Saxon England*, pp.236–37

40. *Anglo-Saxon England*, p.233

41. Bartlett, W.B. (2019), *Vikings: A History of the Northmen,* Amberley Publishing, p.119

42. *Anglo-Saxon England*, p.246

Chapter 6: A Tale of Lagertha

1. Elton, Oliver (translator) (1905), *The Nine Books of the Danish History of Saxo Grammaticus*, Norroena Society, New York

2. Gardeła, Leszek (2021), *Women & Weapons in the Viking World, Amazons of the North*, Oxbow Books, p.23

3. *The Nine Books of the Danish History of Saxo Grammaticus*

4. Friðriksdóttir, Jóhanna (2021), *Valkyrie: The Women of the Viking World*, Bloomsbury Academic, pp.66–67

5. *The Nine Books of the Danish History of Saxo Grammaticus*

6. Chadwick, Hector (2013), *The Early Cultures of North-West Europe*, CUP, p.414

7. Jesch, Judith (2021), *Women, War and Words: A Verbal Archaeology of Shield-maidens*, Viking Special Volume 1 – Viking Wars, Centre for Viking-Age Studies and the Museum of Cultural History, University of Oslo, pp.129–38

8. *Women, War and Words: A Verbal Archaeology of Shield-maidens*, pp.129–38

9. *Women, War and Words: A Verbal Archaeology of Shield-maidens*

10. Waggoner, Ben (2009), *The Sagas of Ragnar Lodbrok*, Troth Publications, pp.21–25

11. Rowe, Elizabeth (2012), 'Vikings in the West: The Legend of Ragnarr Lodbrok and His Sons', *Studia Medievalia Septentrionalia*, Vol. 18, p.58, p.101–2

12. 'Vikings in the West, The Legend of Ragnarr Lodbrok and His Sons', pp.102–3

13. Gardeła, Leszek (2021), *Shield-maidens and Norse Amazons Reconsidered Women and Weapons in Viking Age Burials in Norway*, Viking Special Volume 1 – Viking Wars, Centre for Viking-Age Studies and the Museum of Cultural History, University of Oslo, pp.147–52

14. *Shield-maidens and Norse Amazons Reconsidered Women and Weapons in Viking Age Burials in Norway*, p.161

15. *Women & Weapons in the Viking World, Amazons of the North*, p.58

16. *Shield-maidens and Norse Amazons Reconsidered Women and Weapons in Viking Age Burials in Norway*, p.152–54

17. Dublinia Museum

18. *Women & Weapons in the Viking World, Amazons of the North*, p.33

19. *Women & Weapons in the Viking World, Amazons of the North*, p.56

20. *Women & Weapons in the Viking World, Amazons of the North*, p.71–75

21. Old Uppsala display boards

22. Viking Museum Stockholm

23. Price, Neil, et al. (2019), 'Viking warrior women? Reassessing Birka chamber grave Bj.581', *Antiquity*, Vol. 93, Issue 367, pp.181–98

24. *Women & Weapons in the Viking World, Amazons of the North*, pp.47–55

25. *Valkyrie: The Women of the Viking World*, p.60

26. *Women & Weapons in the Viking World, Amazons of the North*, p.51

27. Price, Neil (2020), *The Children of Ash and Elm*, Penguin, p.330

28. Hjardar, Kim and Vegard, Vike (2019), *Vikings at War,* Casemate UK, p.100

29. *Valkyrie: The Women of the Viking World*, pp.120–26

30. Elton, Oliver (translator) (1905), *The Nine Books of the Danish History of Saxo Grammaticus*, Norroena Society, New York

Chapter 7: The Eagle's Claws

1. Kari Ellen Gade (2017), 'Rǫgnvaldr jarl and Hallr Þórarinsson, Háttalykill', in Gade, Kari Ellen and Marold, Edith (editors), *Poetry from Treatises on Poetics*, Skaldic Poetry of the Scandinavian Middle Ages 3, Brepols, p.1001 (https://skaldic.org)

2. *The Nine Books of the Danish History of Saxo Grammaticus*

3. *The Nine Books of the Danish History of Saxo Grammaticus*

4. *The Nine Books of the Danish History of Saxo Grammaticus*

5. Rowe, Elizabeth (2012), 'Vikings the West, The Legend of Ragnarr Lodbrok and His Sons', *Studia Medievalia, Septentrionalia*, Vol. 18, p.156, p.164

6. Price, Neil (2020), *The Children of Ash and Elm*, Penguin Books, p.134

7. Thunem, Hilde (2024), *Viking Men and Trousers* (https://urd.priv.no/viking/bukser.pdf)

8. Sigfússon, Björn (1934), 'Names of Sea-Kings ('Heiti Sækonunga'), *Modern Philology*, Vol. 32, No. 2, pp.125–42

9. Reuter, Timothy (1992), *The Annals of Fulda*, Manchester Medieval Sources, Manchester University Press, pp.32–33

10. Voytovych L.V. (2016), 'Was Ragnar Lodbrok in the Rus' lands?', *Ukraine in Central and Eastern Europe*, Issue 16, pp.93–10

11. 'Vikings the West, The Legend of Ragnarr Lodbrok and His Sons', p.100

12. Breeze, Andrew (2021), *British Battles 493–937*, Anthem Press, pp.115–17]

13. Woolf, Alex (2007), *From Pictland to Alba*, The New Edinburgh History of Scotland, pp.69–70

14. Bartlett, W. B. (2019), *Vikings: A History of the Northmen,* Amberley Publishing, p.133

15. Brodeur, Arthur Gilchrist (translator) and Sturluson, Snorri (2011), *The Prose Edda*, Amazon, p.90

16. Lasota Kornelia (2021), 'Holy Serpents: Snakes in the Old Norse Worldview', *Zoophilologica*, Issue 8, pp.1–10

17. Frank, Roberta (1984), 'Viking Atrocity and Skaldic Verse: The Rite of the Blood-Eagle', *The English Historical Review*, Vol. 99, No. 391, pp.332–43

18. 'Viking Atrocity and Skaldic Verse: The Rite of the Blood-Eagle', pp.332–43

19. Stevenson, Joseph (1855), *The Historical Works of Simeon of Durham*, Seeleys, p.249 (Internet Achive)

20. www.historyofyork.org.uk

21. MacNeill, Ryan (2019), *The Great Heathen Failure: Why the Great Heathen Army Failed to Conquer the Whole of Anglo-Saxon England*, Winthrop University, pp.17–18

22. Hardy, Thomas Duffus and Martin, Charles Trice (1889), *Lestorie Des Engles Solum la Translacion Maistre Geffrei Gaimar*, HMSO, p.85–86 (Internet Achive)

23. Corpus of Electronic Texts (CELT), *Fragmentary Annals*, University College Cork

24. Cook, Albert (1906), *Asser's Life of King Alfred*, Ginn & Company (gutenberg.org)

25. *The Historical Works of Simeon of Durham,* p.654

26. Hjardar, Kim and Vegard, Vike (2019), *Vikings at War*, Casemate UK, p.58

27. Wise, Terrence and Embleton, Gerry (illustrator) (1979), *Saxon, Viking and Norman*, Osprey Publishing, pp.25–26

28. *Vikings at War*, p.168

29. *Vikings at War*, p.164

30. *Asser's Life of King Alfred*

31. Hadley, Dawn and Julian, Richards (2024), *Life in the Great Army, Raiders, Traders and Settlers*, Oxford University Press, p.37

32. Hadley, Dawn and Richards, Julian (2023), 'Beyond the D-Shaped Enclosure, Winter camps of the Viking Great Army in England', in Hedenstierna-Jonson, Charlotte and Losquiño Irene García (editors), *Viking Camps: Case Studies and Comparisons*, Routledge, pp.81–83

33. McGuigan, Neil (2015), 'Ælla and the Descendants of Ivar: Politics and Legend in the Viking Age', *Northern History*, Vol. 52, No. 1, pp.20–34

34. *The Historical Works of Simeon of Durham*, p.654

35. Clare Downham (2025), 'Ivar the Boneless', *Gone Medieval* podcast featuring, 13 May

Chapter 8: House of Munsö

1. Killings, Douglas B. and Brendan, Diane (editors) (1996), *Heimskringla: The Ynglinga Saga,* Online Medieval and Classical Library

2. Old Uppsala Museum

3. Viking Museum Stockholm

4. Old Uppsala display boards

5. Jones, Gwyn (1968), *A History of the Vikings*, Oxford University Press, pp.326–27

6. Old Uppsala display boards

7. Old Uppsala display boards

8. Guizot, Francois (translator) (1826), *History of the Normans and Life of William Conqueror by William Jumièges* (gutenberg.org)

9. Stefansson, Jon (1908–9), 'The Vikings in Spain from Arabic (Moorish) and Spanish Sources', *Saga-Book*, Vol. VI, Viking Society for Northern Research, pp.31–46

10. 'The Vikings in Spain from Arabic (Moorish) and Spanish Sources', pp.31–46

11. Elton, Oliver (translator) (1905), *The Nine Books of the Danish History of Saxo Grammaticus*, Norroena Society, New York

12. *The Nine Books of the Danish History of Saxo Grammaticus*

13. *The Nine Books of the Danish History of Saxo Grammaticus*

14. Waggoner, Ben (2009), *The Saga of Ragnar Lodbrok*, Troth Publications, p.27

15. *The Saga of Ragnar Lodbrok*, p.70

16. Rowe, Elizabeth Ashman (2012), 'Vikings the West, The Legend of Ragnarr Lodbrok and His Sons', *Studia Medievalia Septentrionalia*, Vol. 18, p.96

17. Tolkien, Christopher (1960), *The Saga of King Heidrek the Wise*, Thomas Nelson and Sons, p.61

18. *The Saga of King Heidrek the Wise*

19. Clunies Ross, Margaret (2017), 'Bragi inn gamli Boddason', in Gade Kari Ellen and Marold, Edith (editors) *Poetry from Treatises on Poetics*, Skaldic Poetry of the Scandinavian Middle Ages 3, Brepols

20. Robinson, Charles (1921), *Anskar: The Apostle of the North, 801–865*, The Society for the Propagation of the Bible in Foreign Parts, p.48, pp.65–66 (Internet Achive)

21. Nerman, Birger (1918), 'The King's Mounds on Adelsö and Sweden's Oldest Royal Lineages', *Fornvännen Journal of Swedish Antiquarian Research*, Vol. 13, pp.65–77

22. Uppsala Museum

23. Holmqvist, Wilhelm (1955), 'An Irish crozier-head found near Stockholm', *The Antiquaries Journal*, Vol. 35, No. 1–2, pp.46–51

24. Uppsala Museum

25. Forensøk website, Swedish National Heritage Board

26. Runor digital research platform, Swedish National Heritage Board and Uppsala University (https://runor.raa.se)

27. Uppsala Museum

28. Viking Museum, Stockholm

29. Troyon, Frédéric (2020), 'Björn iron side's grave field in Munsö 1846', *Fornvannen: Journal of Swedish Antiquarian Research*, Vol. 115, No. 4, pp. 260–69

30. 'Björn iron side's grave field in Munsö'

31. 'Björn iron side's grave field in Munsö'

32. Blad, Anders (1816), 'Introductory Speech', *Proceedings of the Royal Academy of Literature, History and Antiquity*, Vol. 10, Stockholm, pp.222–23

33. *The King's Mounds on Adelsö and Sweden's Oldest Royal*

34. Email correspondence with Charlotte Hedenstierna-Jonson, 10 April 2025

35. Email correspondence with Sven Kalmring, 8 July 2025

36. Nelson, Janet L (1991), *The Annals of St-Bertin,* Manchester Medieval Sources, Manchester University Press, p.104

Chapter 9: The Martyr and the Wolf

1. Lord Hervey, Francis (1907), *Corolla Sancti Eadmundi: The Garland of Saint Eadmund King and Martyr*, E. P. Dutton and Company, pp.7–59

2. Pestell, Tim (2019), *Viking East Anglia,* Norfolk Museum Service, pp.38–40; Norfolk Heritage Explorer NHER 31413, Viking Thor's Hammer (www.heritage.norfolk.gov.uk)

3. Bartlett, W. B. (2019), *Vikings: A History of the Northmen*, Amberley Publishing, p.142

4. Williams, Gareth (2023), 'Viking Camps: A Historiographical Overview', in Hedenstierna-Jonson, Charlotte and Losquiño Irene García (editors), *Viking Camps: Case Studies and Comparisons*, Routledge, p.47

5. Hjardar, Kim and Vegard, Vike (2019), *Vikings at War,* Casemate UK, p.41

6. *Viking East Anglia*, pp.38–40

7. Bray, Olive (1908), *The Elder or Poetic Elder*, Viking Club Translation Series, Vol. II, pp.35–36

8. *Viking East Anglia*, pp.39–48

9. Young, Francis (2020), *Edmund: In Search of England's Lost King*, Bloomsbury, p.50

10. *Corolla Sancti Eadmundi: The Garland of Saint Eadmund King and Martyr*, pp.7–59

11. *Corolla Sancti Eadmundi: The Garland of Saint Eadmund King and Martyr*, pp.7–59

12. *Edmund: In Search of England's Lost King*, p.60

13. Clarke, Dan, *The Mysterious 'Wolf' Burial at the Abbey of St Edmund*, Visit Bury St Edmunds website

14. *Edmund: In Search of England's Lost King*, p.61–67

15. Williams, Thomas (2014), *Viking Britain*, Williams Collins, p.123–26
16. *Edmund: In Search of England's Lost King*, p.55
17. *Viking East Anglia*, p.26
18. Stenton, Frank (1970), *Anglo-Saxon England*, Oxford University Press, p.248
19. *Edmund: In Search of England's Lost King*, p.60
20. *Viking East Anglia*, 31–32
21. Lindill, Jayne (2021), 'Suffolk's Quirky Placenames Explained', *Suffolk Magazine*, 26 May
22. Musgrove, Louis (2014), 'Thingstead, The Viking Roots of Ipswich, a personal view', *Ipswich Society Newsletter*, July 2014
23. Hadley, Dawn and Richards, Julian (2024), *Life in the Great Army: Raiders, Traders and Settlers*, Oxford University Press, pp.268–71
24. Elkwall, Eilert (1960), *The Concise Oxford Dictionary of English Place-names* (fourth edition), Oxford University Press, p.485
25. Rowe, Elizabeth (2012), 'Vikings the West, The Legend of Ragnarr Lodbrok and His Sons', *Studia Medievalia Septentrionalia*, Vol. 18, p.57
26. English Place-Name Society, 'The Survey of English Place-Names', University of Nottingham website (www.nottingham.ac.uk/research/groups/epns/survey)
27. Forester, Thomas (1853), *The Chronicle of Henry Huntingdon*, H. G. Bohnn
28. Hardy, Thomas, Duffus and Martin, Charles Trice (1889), *Lestorie Des Engles Solum la Translacion Maistre Geffrei Gaimar*, HMSO, p.93 (Internet Archive)
29. Tschan, Francis J. (translator) (2002), *History of the Archbishops of Hamburg–Bremen*, Columbia University Press, p.37
30. Waggoner, Ben (2009), *The Sagas of Ragnar Lodbrok*, Troth Publications, p.12
31. *'Vikings the West, The Legend of Ragnarr Lodbrok and His Sons'*, pp.89–90
32. Kari Ellen Gade (2017), 'Rǫgnvaldr jarl and Hallr Þórarinsson, Háttalykill', in Gade, Kari Ellen and Marold, Edith (editors), *Poetry from Treatises on Poetics*, Skaldic Poetry of the Scandinavian Middle Ages 3, Brepols, p.1001 (https://skaldic.org)
33. Friðriksdóttir, Jóhanna (2021), *Valkyrie: The Women of the Viking World*, Bloomsbury Academic, pp.22–26
34. *Valkyrie: The Women of the Viking World*, p.23
35. *Valkyrie: The Women of the Viking World*, p.23
36. *Valkyrie: The Women of the Viking World*, p.123
37. Barraclough, Eleanor (2024), *Embers of the Hands*, Profile Books, pp.182–83
38. McTurk, Rory (2006), *Kings and Kingship in Viking Northumbria,* in McKinnell, John, Ashurst, David and Kick, Donata, *The Fantastic in Old Norse Icelandic Literature*, Preprint Papers Part 2, Centre for Medieval and Renaissance Studies, pp.681–88
39. *The Sagas of Ragnar Lodbrok*, p.70
40. *Kings and Kingship in Viking Northumbria*, p.684

Chapter 10: The Fall of Alt Clut

1. www.scottishpoetrylibrary.org.uk/poem/clyde
2. Tabraham, Chris, *Dumbarton Castle Guidebook*, Historic Scotland
3. *Dumbarton Castle Guidebook*
4. Clarkson, Tim (2014), *Strathclyde and the Anglo-Saxons in the Viking Age*, John Donald, p.16
5. *Strathclyde and the Anglo-Saxons in the Viking* Age, p.16
6. Koch, John T. (2012), *The Celts: History, Life, and Culture*, Bloomsbury, pp.808–9
7. Alcock, Leslie and Alcock, Elizabeth (1990), 'Excavations at Alt Clut, Clyde Rock, Strathclyde, 1974–75', *Society of Antiquaries of Scotland Journal*, Vol. 120, p.101
8. 'Excavations at Alt Clut, Clyde Rock, Strathclyde, 1974–75', pp.113–15
9. 'Excavations at Alt Clut, Clyde Rock, Strathclyde, 1974–75', p.128
10. *Strathclyde and the Anglo-Saxons in the Viking Age*, pp.69–76
11. Email correspondence, 6 September 2024
12. Corpus of Electronic Texts (CELT), *Annals of Ulster*, University College Cork
13. Corpus of Electronic Texts (CELT), *Fragmentary Annals*, University College Cork
14. Downham, Clare (2007), *Viking Kings of Britain and Ireland, The Dynasty of Ivarr to AD 1014*, Dunedin Press, p.16
15. Woolf, Alex (2007), *From Pictland to Alba*, The New Edinburgh History of Scotland, p.110
16. 'Excavations at Alt Clut, Clyde Rock, Strathclyde, 1974–75', p.99
17. 'Excavations at Alt Clut, Clyde Rock, Strathclyde, 1974–75', p.96
18. 'Excavations at Alt Clut, Clyde Rock, Strathclyde, 1974–75', pp.109–13
19. Tetzner, Noah (2022), *Viking Warrior Versus Frankish Warrior*, Osprey, p.13
20. *Viking Warrior Versus Frankish Warrior*, p.28
21. *Fragmentary Annals*
22. *Annals of Ulster*
23. *Excavations at Alt Clut, Clyde Rock, Strathclyde, 1974–75*, pp.110–12
24. Hjardar, Kim, Vegard, Vike (2019), *Vikings at War*, Casemate UK, p.246
25. 'Excavations at Alt Clut, Clyde Rock, Strathclyde, 1974–75', pp.113-117
26. *Fragmentary Annals*
27. Glasgow City Council (2007), *Water Row, Govan, Archaeological Evaluation*, pp.8–9
28. *Strathclyde and the Anglo-Saxons in the Viking* Age, pp.70–71, pp.84–85
29. *Fragmentary Annals*
30. Buchanan, Courtney (2012), 'Scandinavians in Strathclyde: Multiculturalism, Material Culture and Manufactured Identities in the Viking Age', in Ritchie, Anna, *Historic Bute, Land and People*, Scottish Society for Northern Studies, p.27

31. Pierce, Elizabeth (2013), *The Hidden Heritage of a Landscape: Vengeful Vikings and Reckless Rustlers,* Hidden Heritage Project, University of Glasgow

32. Graham-Campbell, James and Batey, Colleen (1998), *Vikings in Scotland: An Archaeological Survey*, Edinburgh University Press, p.100

33. *Scandinavians in Strathclyde: Multiculturalism, Material Culture and Manufactured Identities in the Viking Age*, pp.21–23

34. *The Hidden Heritage of a Landscape: Vengeful Vikings and Reckless Rustlers*

35. *Dumbarton Castle Guidebook*

36. *Dumbarton Castle Guidebook*

37. Price, Neil (2020), *The Children of Ash and Elm*, Penguin, p.414

38. Holm, Poul (1986), 'The Slave Trade of Dublin: Ninth to Twelfth Centuries', Peritia, Vol. 5, p.325

39. National Museum of Ireland website

40. Valente, Mary (2008), *The Vikings in Ireland: Settlement, Trade and Urbanization*, Four Courts Press, pp.86–90

41. Clarke, Howard, Dooley, Shiela and Johnson, Ruth (2018), *Dublin and the Viking World*, O'Brien Ltd, p.57

42. Helgason, A, Hickey E, Goodacre S, Bosnes V, Stefánsson K, Ward R, Sykes B (2001), 'mtDNA and the islands of the North Atlantic: estimating the proportions of Norse and Gaelic ancestry', *American Journal of Human Genetics*, Vol. 68, pp.723–73

43. 'The Slave Trade of Dublin: Ninth to Twelfth Centuries', p.325

44. *The Vikings in Ireland: Settlement, Trade and Urbanization*, p.89

45. Reuter, Timothy (1992), *The Annals of Fulda,* Manchester Medieval Sources, Manchester University Press, p.72

46. 'The Slave Trade of Dublin: Ninth to Twelfth Centuries', p.323

Chapter 11: The Raven's Fort

1. Williams, Thomas (2013), 'The Battle of Ashdown: Victory, Battlefield, and the Language of War', *Medieval Warfare*, Vol. 3, No. 5, pp.16–20; Monsen, Erling (translator), Smith, A. H. (translator) and Snorre Sturlason (1931), *Heimskringla Or the Lives of The Norse Kings*, Heffer

2. Rasmussen, Rune (2021), 'The Nordic Raven Totem The animist roots of the Raven flag', Nordic Animism (https://nordicanimism.com/blog/the-nordic-raven-totem)

3. Brodeur, Arthur Gilchrist (translator) and Sturluson, Snorri (2011), *The Prose Edda*, Amazon, pp.35–36

4. Gaiman, Neil (2019), *Norse Mythology*, Bloomsbury, pp.107–31

REFERENCES

5. Price, Neil (2020), *The Children of Ash and Elm*, Penguin, p.97

6. *The Prose Edda*, pp.57–58

7. Jesch, Judith (2013), *The Viking Poetry of Love and War,* British Museum, p.30, p.39

8. 'The Nordic Raven Totem The animist roots of the Raven flag'

9. Waggoner, Ben (2009), *The Saga of Ragnar Lodbrok*, Troth Publications, p.32

10. Stevenson, Joseph (1855), *The Historical Works of Simeon of Durham*, Seeleys, p.487, p.654 (Internet Achive)

11. Stephen M. Lewis (2017), *Hamlet with the Princes of Denmark: An exploration of the case of Hálfdan 'king of the Danes*, Hal Open Science, hal-01943605, p.8

12. Reuter, Timothy (1992), *The Annals of Fulda*, Manchester Medieval Sources, Manchester University Press, pp.70–71

13. Berkshire Archaeology HER 02092.00.000, Burial near the engine sheds at Reading Station, Reading, Berkshire (www.heritagegateway.org.uk)

14. Hadley, Dawn and Richards, Julian (2023), 'Beyond the D-Shaped Enclosure: Winter Camps of the Viking Great Army', in Hedenstierna-Jonson, Charlotte and Losquiño Irene García (editors), *Viking Camps: Case Studies and Comparisons*, Routledge, pp.86–87

15. Cook, Albert (1906), *Asser's Life of King Alfred*, Ginn & Company (gutenberg.org)

16. *Asser's Life of King Alfred*

17. Morris, Marc (2022), *The Anglo-Saxons, A History of the Beginnings of England*, Penguin, pp.204–7

18. *The Anglo-Saxons, A History of the Beginnings of England*, p.235

19. *Asser's Life of King Alfred*

20. *The Anglo-Saxons, A History of the Beginnings of England*, p.208

21. Fleming, Robin (2011), *Britain After Rome: The Fall and Rise, 400 to 1070*, Penguin Books, p.271

22. Wise, Terrence and Embleton, Gerry (illustrator) (1979), *Saxon, Viking and Norman*, Osprey Publishing, pp.7–8

23. *Asser's Life of King Alfred*

24. Williams, Thomas (2014), *Viking Britain*, Williams Collins, p.136

25. S 288, AD 840 (Southampton), Æthelwulf, king of Wessex, to Duda, his minister; grant of 10 hides (cassati) at Asshedoune (cf. Ashdown Park in Ashbury, Berks)

26. 'The Battle of Ashdown: Victory, Battlefield, and the Language of War'

27. Knott, Peter (1990), *Alfred's Wayte*, Berkshire Old and New No. 7, Berkshire Local History Association

28. *Alfred's Wayte*

29. Heath, Ian (1983), *The Vikings*, Osprey Publishing, pp.31–32

30. 'The Battle of Ashdown: Victory, Battlefield, and the Language of War'

31. *Asser's Life of King Alfred*

32. *Alfred's Wayte*

33. *Alfred's Wayte*

34. S 564, AD 955, King Eadred to Ælfheah, his kinsman and minister; grant of 8 hides (cassati) at Compton Beauchamp, Berks, Abingdon

35. Oxfordshire HER 27677, Iron Age to Roman settlement and trackway system (www.heritagegateway.org.uk)

36. Email correspondence, 22 March 2024

37. English Place-Name Society, 'The Survey of English Place-Names', University of Nottingham website (www.nottingham.ac.uk/research/groups/epns/survey)

38. Oxfordshire HER 7329, Undated Boundary Stone (www.heritagegateway.org.uk)

39. Harper, Paul (2023), *Cerdic: Mysterious Dark Age King Who Founded England*, Pen & Sword, p.234

40. *Asser's Life of King Alfred*

41. Hardy, Thomas Duffus and Martin, Charles Trice (1889), *Lestorie Des Engles Solum la Translacion Maistre Geffrei Gaimar*, HMSO, p.93 (Internet Archive)

42. Friðriksdóttir, Jóhanna (2021), *Valkyrie: The Women of the Viking World*, Bloomsbury Academic, p.7

43. 'The Battle of Ashdown: Victory, Battlefield, and the Language of War'

Chapter 12: Warrior Bishop

1. Wise, Terrence (1979), *Saxon, Viking and Norman*, Osprey, pp 10–14

2. Gomme, E. E. C. (ed.) (1909), *The Anglo-Saxon Chronicle*, George Bell and Sons

3. Campbell, Alastair (1907), *The Chronicle of Æthelweard*, Thomas Nelson and Sons (Internet Archive), p.144. There are difficulties with Ethelward's translation of 'ferro' – Campbell and others claim this to be 'sword', but it could also be 'iron'.

4. Williams, Andy (2025), 'Bishop Heahmund, his cult and the monastic foundation at Keynsham', not yet published, Exeter University

5. S 332, AD 863 (Birenefeld). (1) Æthelberht, king of Wessex and Kent, to Æthelred, minister; grant of 9 sulungs (aratra) at Mersham, Kent, in return for 400 mancuses of gold. Latin with bounds. (2) Eadwald to St Augustine's, Canterbury; grant of land at Willesborough, Kent, Canterbury, Christ Church

6. S 342, ? AD 869 or 870 (Woodyates, Dorset). Æthelred, king of Wessex, to Ælfstan, ealdorman; grant of 5 hides at Cheselbourne, Dorset, Shaftesbury

7. Stevenson, Joseph (1855), *The Historical Works of Simeon of Durham*, Seeleys (Internet Achive), p.668

8. Higham, Nicholas J. and Martin, Ryan (2013), *The Anglo-Saxon World*, Yale University Press, pp.252–56

9. Nelson, Janet L. (1986), *Politics and Ritual in Early Medieval Europe*, Hambledon Press, p.120

10. Sneddon, Jonathan (2013), 'Mitres and maces – the medieval clergy at war', *Medieval Warfare*, Vol 3, No. 2

11. *Politics and Ritual in Early Medieval Europe*, p.124

12. Ingram, James and Giles, John Allen (1996), *The Project Gutenberg Book of the Anglo-Saxon Chronicle*, produced by Douglas B. Killings (gutenberg.org)

13. Interview with Professor Clark and Andy Williams via webcam, 22 April 2024

14. Bartlett W. B. (2021), *Vikings, A History of The Northmen*, Amberley Publishing, p.140

15. 'Mitres and maces – the medieval clergy at war'

16. Interview with Professor Clark and Andy Williams via webcam, 22 April 2024

17. S 513, AD 944 x 946, King Edmund to Æthelflæd, his queen; grant, for life, of 100 hides at Damerham and Martin, Hants, and Pentridge, Dorset; with reversion to St Mary's, Glastonbury

18. Hampshire HER 16186, Bowl Barrow N of Bokerley Dyke on Martin Down (https://maps.hants.gov.uk)

19. Elkwall, Eilert (1936), *The Concise Oxford Dictionary of English Place Names* (fourth edition), Clarendon Press, p.316

20. Lowe, Barbara (2006), 'Keynsham Abbey Excavations 1961–91 Final Report. Part II: Summary and Review', *Proceedings of the Somerset Archaeological and Natural History Society*, Vol. 149, pp.123–38

21. 'Bishop Heahmund, his cult and the monastic foundation at Keynsham'

22. Interview with Professor Clark and Andy Williams via webcam, 22 April 2024

23. Cook, Albert (1906), *Asser's Life of King Alfred*, Ginn & Company (gutenberg.org)

24. Keynes, Simon (1986), 'A Tale of Two Kings: Alfred the Great and Æthelred the Unready', *Transactions of the Royal Historical Society*, Vol. 36, pp.195–217

Chapter 13: Winter Camp

1. Skeie, Tore (2018), *The Wolf Age*, Pushkin Press, p.55

2. Dunning, Gerald and Evison, Vera (1961), 'The Palace of Westminster Sword', *Archaeologia*, Vol. 98, pp.123–28

3. Reuter, Timothy (1992), *The Annals of Fulda,* Manchester Medieval Sources, Manchester University Press, p.36

4. *The Palace of Westminster Sword*, p.157

5. *The Palace of Westminster Sword,* pp.134–55

6. Price, Neil (2020), *The Children of Ash and Elm*, Penguin, p.319

7. *The Palace of Westminster Sword*, p.157

8. Hadley, Dawn and Richards, Julian (2023), 'Beyond the D-Shaped Enclosure: Winter Camps of the Viking Great Army', in Hedenstierna-Jonson, Charlotte and Losquiño Irene García (editors), *Viking Camps: Case Studies and Comparisons*, Routledge, pp.87–89

9. Blunt, Christopher and Dolley, Michael (1959), 'The Hoard Evidence for the Coins of Alfred', *British Numismatic Journal*, Vol. 29, pp.220–47

10. Email correspondence, 23 October 2023

11. Downham, Clare (2007), *Viking Kings of Britain and Ireland, The Dynasty of Ivarr to AD 1014*, Dunedin Press, p.87

12. Hadley, Dawn and Richards, Julian (2021), *The Viking Great Army and the Making of England*, Thames & Hudson, p.93, p.110

13. Hjardar, Kim and Vegard, Vike (2019), *Vikings at War*, Casemate UK, p.90

14. Hadley, Dawn and Richards, Julian (2024), *Life in the Great Army: Raiders, Traders and Settlers*, Oxford University Press, pp.334–35

15. 'Beyond the D-Shaped Enclosure: Winter Camps of the Viking Great Army', p.80

16. *Vikings at War*, p.90–91

17. *The Viking Great Army and the Making of England*, p.112

18. *The Viking Great Army and the Making of England*, p.87, pp.105–10

19. Barraclough, Eleanor (2024), *Embers of the Hands*, Profile Books, pp.235–36

20. Gardeła, Leszek (2021), *Women & Weapons in the Viking World, Amazon of the North*, Oxbow Books, pp.53–54

21. Hadley, Dawn and Richards, Julian (2016), 'The Winter Camp of the Viking Great Army, AD 872–3, Torksey, Lincolnshire', *The Antiquaries Journal*, Vol. 96, pp.56–57

22. *The Viking Great Army and the Making of England*, pp.108–13

23. 'The Winter Camp of the Viking Great Army, AD 872–3, Torksey Lincolnshire'

24. *Life in the Great Army: Raiders, Traders and Settlers*, pp.85–86

25. *Life in the Great Army: Raiders, Traders and Settlers*, pp.85–86

26. *Life in the Great Army: Raiders, Traders and Settlers*, pp.85–127

27. Johnson, Gary and Kershaw, Jane (2024), *Viking inset lead weights: Origins, manufacture, and distribution* (https://vikingmetalwork.blogspot.com)

28. *The Viking Great Army and the Making of England*, p.97

Chapter 14: King of the Norse

1. Kruse, Arne (2017), 'The Norway to Be: Laithlind and Avaldsnes', in Cooijmans, Christian (editor) *Traversing the Inner Seas. Contacts and Continuity in and around Scotland*, Scottish Society for Northern Studies, p.200

2. Hadley, Dawn and Richards, Julian (2021), *The Viking Great Army and the Making of England*, Thames & Hudson, p.153/4

3. Biddle, Martin (2023), 'The Vikings at Repton, Wintersetl or mindesmærke – winter camp and place of memory', in Hedenstierna-Jonson, Charlotte and Losquiño Irene García (editors), *Viking Camps: Case Studies and Comparisons*, Routledge, pp.66–76

4. Biddle, Martin and Kjølbye-Biddle, B. (1992), 'Repton and the Vikings', *Antiquity*, Vol. 66, pp.36–51

5. Jarman, Catrine et al. (2018), 'The Viking Great Army in England: new dates from the Repton charnel', *Antiquity*, Vol. 92, Issue 361, pp. 183–99

6. 'Repton and the Vikings'

7. Jarman, Cat (2019), *'Resolving Repton'*, *Current Archaeology*, June

8. Corpus of Electronic Texts (CELT), *Annals of Ulster*, University College Cork

9. 'The Vikings at Repton, Wintersetl or mindesmærke – winter camp and place of memory', p.75

10. Woolf, Alex (2007), *From Pictland to Alba,* The New Edinburgh History of Scotland, p.73

11. Repton Church website

12. Corpus of Electronic Texts (CELT), *Annals of Ulster*, University College Cork; Woolf, Alex (2007), *From Pictland to Alba, 789–1070*, Edinburgh University Press, p.108–9

13. Corpus of Electronic Texts (CELT), *Fragmentary Annals*, University College Cork

14. Hjardar, Kim and Vegard, Vike (2019), *Vikings at War,* Casemate UK, p.228

15. Waggoner, Ben (2009), *The Saga of Ragnar Lodbrok*, Troth Publications, p.37

16. Downham, Clare (2007), *Viking Kings of Britain and Ireland, The Dynasty of Ivarr to AD 1014*, Dunedin Press, pp.237–77

17. Ó Corráin, Donnchadh (1998), 'Vikings in Ireland and Scotland in the Ninth Century', *Peritia*, Vol. 12, pp.296–339

18. Steffensen, Jon (1970), 'A Fragment of Viking History', *Saga-Book*, Vol. 18, Viking Society for Northern Research, pp.59–78

19. Magnusson, Magnus (2003), *The Vikings*, Tempus Publishing, p.41

20. 'The Norway to Be: Laithlind and Avaldsnes' p.198–231

21. Hadley, Dawn and Richards, Julian (2024), *Life in the Great Army: Raiders, Traders and Settlers*, Oxford University Press, pp.58–59

22. Jarman, Cat (2021), *River Kings, The Vikings from Scandinavia to the Silk Road*, Williams Collins, pp.19–26

23. 'The Viking Great Army in England: new dates from the Repton charnel'

24. 'The Gokstad Burial Mound', Museum of the Viking Age (www. vikingtidsmuseet.no)

Chapter 15: Ivar's Howe

1. Uppsala Museum display board

2. O'Donoghue, Heather and Vohra, Pragya (2014), *The Vikings in Cleveland,* Language, Myths and Finds, Vol. 4, Centre for the Study of the Viking Age, University of Nottingham, pp.21–25

3. *The Vikings in Cleveland*, pp.16–18

4. *The Vikings in Cleveland*, p.21

5. Carroll, Jane, Harrison, Stephen and Williams, Garreth (2014), *The Vikings in Britain and Ireland,* British Museum, pp.124–25

6. *The Vikings in Cleveland*, pp.16–18

7. Williams, Thomas (2014), *Viking Britian*, Williams Collins, p.252

8. Adams, Max (2017), *Alfred's Britain, War and Peace in the Viking Age*, Head of Zeus, p.119

9. Kapetanović, Nataša (2017), *The Influence of Old Norse on the English Language*, University of Osijek, pp.17–19

10. Larsen, Anne-Chrstine (2001), *The Vikings in Ireland*, Viking Ship Museum Roskilde, p.145

11. Callaway, Ewen (2015), 'UK Mapped Out by Genetic Ancestry', *Nature* (Study uses data from the Welcome Trusts' People of the British Isles study, an Oxford University project)

12. Waggoner, Ben (2009), *The Sagas of Ragnar Lodbrok,* Troth Publications, p.37

13. Yates-Hawker, Lily (2014), *Barrows in the Cultural Imagination of Later Medieval England,* Canterbury Christ Church University, p.129

14. Faulkes, Anthony (2016), *Hemings Þattr,* Thorisdal, pp.6–9

15. *Hemings Þattr*, p.34

16. *Barrows in the Cultural Imagination of Later Medieval England*, p.102

17. *The Sagas of Ragnar Lodbrok*, p.70

18. Jarman, Cat (2021), *River Kings, The Vikings from Scandinavia to the Silk Road*, Williams Collins, p.178

19. Gardeła, Leszek (2021), *Women & Weapons in the Viking World, Amazon of the North*, Oxbow Books, p.70

20. *Women & Weapons in the Viking World, Amazon of the North*, pp.95–98

21. Elkwall, Eilert (1960), *The Concise Oxford Dictionary of English Place Names* (fourth edition), Oxford University Press, p.436

22. https://opendomesday.org

23. Briddon, Richard (2015), 'Beowulf and Teesside Beowulf', Bards and Authors of North Yorkshire, 26 September, https://bardsandauthors.blogspot.com/2015/09/beowulf.html

24. Uppsala Museum

25. 'Round barrow on Boulby Cliffs known as the site of Rockcliff Beacon', Historic England website

26. Hornsby, William and Laverick John (1920), 'The British Barrows Round Boulby', *Yorkshire Archaeological Journal*, Vol. 25, p.48–52

27. Elgee, Frank (1930), *Early Man in North-East Yorkshire*, John Bellows (www.thenorthernantiquarian.org)

28. Lingrow Howe, ID 29445 (heritagegateway.org)

29. Dickinson Steve (2025), 'The King's Mound, West Cumbria', West Coast Viking Horizons Project; Manning, Jonny (2026), 'Hill could hide Viking grave of Ivarr the Boneless', 31 January (www.bbc.co.uk/news/articles/c8rm8g43x40o)

30. *Barrows in the Cultural Imagination of Later Medieval England*, p.107

Chapter 16: The Madness of Halfdan

1. Kari Ellen Gade (2017), 'Rǫgnvaldr jarl and Hallr Þórarinsson, Háttalykill', in Gade, Kari Ellen and Marold, Edith (editors), *Poetry from Treatises on Poetics*, Skaldic Poetry of the Scandinavian Middle Ages 3, Brepols, p.1001. https://skaldic.org

2. Burns, Laura (2012), 'Dogs, booze and bling: Northern Ireland's medieval shopping mall', BBC News, 25 May

3. McCormick, Finbar and Macdonald, Philip (2002/2003), *Excavations at Dunnyneill Island, Co Down*, Queen's University Belfast, pp.49–56

4. Waggoner, Ben (2009), *The Sagas of Ragnar Lodbrok*, Troth Publications, p.70

5. Reuter, Timothy (1992), *The Annals of Fulda*, Manchester Medieval Sources, Manchester University Press, p.70

6. *The Annals of Fulda*, pp.70–71

7. *The Annals of Fulda*, p.39

8. Lewis, Stephen M. (2017), *Hamlet with the Princes of Denmark: An exploration of the case of Hálfdan 'king of the Danes*, Hal Open Science, hal-01943605, pp.17–18

9. Stenton, Frank (1970), *Anglo-Saxon England,* Oxford University Press, p.242

10. Stevenson, Joseph (1855), *The Historical Works of Simeon of Durham*, pp.656–61

11. *The Historical Works of Simeon of Durham*, p.660

12. Kershaw, Jane et al. (2023), 'The Viking Great Army north of the Tyne', in Hedenstierna-Jonson, Charlotte and Losquiño Irene García (editors), *Viking Camps: Case Studies and Comparisons*, Routledge, pp.96–112

13. Corpus of Electronic Texts (CELT), *Annals of Ulster*, University College Cork

14. Noble, Gordon and Evans, Nicholas (2022), *The Picts: Scourge of Rome, Rulers of the North*, Polygon Assignment, p.251

15. *The Picts: Scourge of Rome, Rulers of the North,* p.259

16. Cook, Murray and Kilpatrick, Kelly (2024), *Old Kilmadock Doune, 2024, Season 2 Data Structure Report*

17. *The Picts: Scourge of Rome, Rulers of the North,* p.262

18. Corpus of Electronic Texts (CELT), *Annals of Ulster*, University College Cork

19. *The Historical Works of Simeon of Durham,* p.663

20. Rowe, Elizabeth (2012), 'Vikings the West, The Legend of Ragnarr Lodbrok and His Sons', *Studia Medievalia Septentrionalia*, Vol. 18, p.64, p.76

21. Downham, Clare (2007), *Viking Kings of Britain and Ireland, The Dynasty of Ivarr to AD 1014*, Dunedin Press, p.247

22. Lewis, Stephen (2025), *Rollo of Fleury: Fact or Fiction, Part I, Dudo of St Quentin's Story*, Hal Open Science, hal-05072307, pp.1–24

23. *Viking Kings of Britain and Ireland, The Dynasty of Ivarr to A.D. 1014*, p.248

24. Todd Henthorn, James (1867), *Cogadh Gaedhel re Gallaibh: The War of the Gaedhil with the Gaill Or, The Invasions of Ireland by the Danes and Other Norsemen*, Longmans, Green, Reader and Dyer, p.246

25. Bracken, Patrick (2020), *The Vikings in Ulaid*, University College Cork, p.28

26. Northern Ireland Sites and Monument Records, MRD 206:001, Holm Bay

27. Northern Ireland Sites and Monument Records, DOW 024:037, Burial in Stone Lined Grave

28. Murray Emily and Logue Paul (eds) (2010), *Battles, Boats & Bones: Archaeological Discoveries in Northern Ireland 1987–2008*, Northern Ireland Environment Agency, p.53

29. *Vikings in Ulaid*, p.22–23

30. *Annals of Ulster*

31. *Annals of Ulster*

32. Matson, Garfield (1995), 'Holmgang – Its Use, Abuse, and Fictionalization in Viking Age Norden', University of Minnesota (www.academia.edu/9102367)

33. Nelson, Janet L. (1991), *The Annals of St-Bertin*, Manchester Medieval Sources, Manchester University Press, pp.110–11

34. 'Holmgang – Its Use, Abuse, and Fictionalization in Viking Age Norden'

35. *Cogadh Gaedhel re Gallaibh: The War of the Gaedhil with the Gaill Or, The Invasions of Ireland by the Danes and Other Norsemen*, p.86

36. *Viking Kings of Britain and Ireland, The Dynasty of Ivarr to AD 1014*, pp.75–78

37. Tschan, Francis J. (translator) (2002), *History of the Archbishops of Hamburg–Bremen*, Columbia University Press, p.171

38. *The Historical Works of Simeon of Durham*, pp.664–65

39. Sichfrith was almost certainly part of the same dark foreigners' dynasty of Ivar but not linked to Ivar and unlikely to be Sigurd's son because it wasn't custom for a son to take a father's name. He was, however, not associated with Albann, as Halfdan was known, in the *Annals of Ulster*

Chapter 17: Ubbe and Cynuit

1. www.dartmoor.gov.uk/learning/dartmoor-legends/the-legend-of-the-abbots-way

2. www.dartmoor.gov.uk/learning/basic-factsheets

3. Cornish History – Stone Age to Present Day, www.cornwalls.co.uk

4. 'Gatekeepers to Heaven: religion, knowledge and power in medieval Exeter' (2023), exhibition at Royal Albert Memorial Museum Exeter

REFERENCES

5. S 1676, AD 729, Æthelheard, king of Wessex, to Glastonbury Abbey; grant of 10 hides in the valley of the river Torridge, Devon

6. S 255, AD 739 (10 April), Æthelheard, king, to Forthhere, bishop; grant of 20 hides (cassati) at Crediton, Devon

7. Probert, Duncan (2005), *Anglo-Saxons in Devon: place-name formation in Exeter's hinterland,* Society of Name Studies of Britain and Ireland Fourteenth Annual Conference, Swansea, p.4

8. Pitcher, Steve (2019), *The Origins of Early Mediaeval Settlement in North Devon,* The North Devon Archaeological Society, p.27

9. Charles-Edwards, T. M. (2013), *Wales and the Britons 350–1064.* Oxford University Press, p.494

10. Elton, Oliver (translator) (1905), *The Nine Books of the Danish History of Saxo Grammaticus*, Norroena Society, New York

11. *The Nine Books of the Danish History of Saxo Grammaticus*

12. Stephen M. Lewis (2016), 'Rodulf and Ubba. In search of a Frisian-Danish Viking', *Saga-Book*, Viking Society for Northern Research, Vol. 40, pp.5–42

13. Woolf, Alex (2007), *From Pictland to Alba*, The New Edinburgh History of Scotland, p.72

14. Nelson, Janet L. (1991), *The Annals of St-Bertin,* Manchester Medieval Sources, Manchester University Press, p.51

15. Coupland, Simon (2003), 'From Poachers to Gamekeepers, Scandinavian Warlords and Carolingian Kings', *Early Medieval Europe*, Vol. 7, Issue 1, pp.91–92

16. Reuter, Timothy (1992), *The Annals of Fulda,* Manchester Medieval Sources, Manchester University Press, p.30

17. *Annals of St Bertin*, p.112

18. 'Rodulf and Ubba. In search of a Frisian-Danish Viking', pp.9–10

19. *Annals of St Bertin*, p.180

20. 'Rodulf and Ubba. In search of a Frisian-Danish Viking', p.5

21. 'Rodulf and Ubba. In search of a Frisian-Danish Viking', pp.12–15

22. 'Rodulf and Ubba. In search of a Frisian-Danish Vikings', pp.26–31

23. Corpus of Electronic Texts (CELT), *Annals of Ulster*, University College Cork

24. Scholz, Bernhard Walter and Rogers, Barbara (1970), *Carolingian Chronicles: Royal Frankish Annals and Nithard's Histories*, Ann Arbor Paperbacks (babel. haithitrust.org)

25. *Annals of Fulda,* pp.72–73

26. Coupland, Simon (2003), 'From poachers to gamekeepers: Scandinavian warlords and Carolingian kings', *Early Medieval Europe*, Vol. 7 (Issue 1), pp.85–114

27. Rowe, Elizabeth (2012), 'Vikings the West, The Legend of Ragnarr Lodbrok and His Sons', *Studia Medievalia Septentrionalia*, Vol. 18, p.85

28. Waggoner, Ben (2009), *The Sagas of Ragnar Lodbrok*, Troth Publications, p.70

29. Smith, Albert Hugh (1936), 'The Sons of Ragnar Lothbrok', *Saga-Book*, Vol. 11 (1928–36), Viking Society for Northern Research, p.176

30. 'Vikings the West, The Legend of Ragnarr Lodbrok and His Sons', p.92

31. 'Vikings the West, The Legend of Ragnarr Lodbrok and His Sons', p.90

32. Cook, Albert (1906), *Asser's Life of King Alfred*, Ginn & Company (gutenberg.org)

33. Corpus of Electronic Texts (CELT), *Annals of Ulster*, University College Cork

34. Ingram, James and Giles, John Allen (1996), *The Project Gutenberg Book of the Anglo-Saxon Chronicle*, produced by Douglas B. Killings (gutenberg.org)

35. Clifford, Rev William (1875), *The Site of the Battle of Ethandune* (Proceedings of the Somerset Archaeological and Historical Society), Vol. 21, p.5

36. Cynwit Castle, Cannington, ID 1006225 (https://historicengland.org.uk)

37. https://oldsomerset2.wordpress.com

38. Vidal, Robert Studley (1806), 'An Inquiry Respecting the Site of Kenwith or Kenwith Castle', Society of Antiquaries of London, Vol. XV

39. Rogers, Inkerman (1948), *The Invasion of North Devon by Hubba the Dane*, Transactions of the Devonshire Association, pp.119–26.

40. Kenwith Castle 330yds (300m) SE of Kenwith, ID 1002639 (https://historicengland.org.uk)

41. Arnold, Nick (2013), 'The Site of the Battle of Cynuit 878', *Report and Transactions of the Devonshire Association*, Vol. 145, p.7–30

42. Harrison, Katie (2021), 'Northam's Two Saxon Battles', Bideford and District Archive Council

43. Breeze, Andrew (2000), 'Countisbury', in Coates, R., Breeze, A. and Horovitz, D., *Celtic Voices, English Places*, Shaun Tyas, pp.126–28

44. 'The Site of the Battle of Cynuit 878', p.6

45. www.porlockmanorestate.org

46. Earthwork defences of Countisbury Castle promontory fort, ID 1020807 (https://historicengland.org.uk)

Chapter 18: Dawn of England

1. Jesch, Judith (2013), *Viking Poetry of Love and War*, The British Museum Press, p.40

2. Ingram, James and Giles, John Allen (1996), *The Project Gutenberg Book of the Anglo-Saxon Chronicle*, produced by Douglas B. Killings (gutenberg.org)

3. Darby, H. C. and Welldon Finn (1967), *The Domesday Geography of South-West England*, pp.248–49

REFERENCES

4. Alfred's grandson Athelstan later awarded the estate to the Bishop of Exeter

5. Arnold, Nick (2013), 'The Site of the Battle of Cynuit 878', *Report and Transactions of the Devonshire Association*, Vol. 145, p.7–30; Stevenson, W. H. (1904), Asser's Life of King Alfred, Clarendon Press, p.175

6. 'The Site of the Battle of Cynuit 878', p.10–11

7. www.legendarydartmoor.co.uk/2016/03/18/marin_way

8. 'The Site of the Battle of Cynuit 878', p.10; Donn, B. (1965), Map of the County of Devon *1765 with an introduction by W. L. D. Ravenshill*, Boydell & Brewer; Gover, J. F. B., Mawer, A. and Stenton, F. M. (1932), *The Place Names of Devon*, Vols. 1 and 2, CUP

9. Parcero-Oubina, Cesar, Smart, Chris and Fonte, João (2023), 'Remote Sensing and GIS Modelling of Roman Roads in South West Britain', *Journal of Computer Applications in Archaeology*, Vol. 6, Issue 1, pp.62–78

10. Devon & Dartmoor HER MDV126834, Roman road from Crediton to Burrington Moor (www.heritagegateway.org.uk)

11. 'The Site of the Battle of Cynwit 878'. Polwhele, R. (1816), *The History of Cornwall: Civil, Military, Religious, Architectural, Agricultural, Commercial, Biographical and Miscellaneous*, Vol. 1, Law and Whittaker, p.84, p.227

12. Cook, Albert (1906), *Assser's Life of King Alfred*, Ginn & Company (gutenberg.org)

13. 'The Site of the Battle of Cynuit 878', p.3. Gaimar, Geffrei and Short, Ian (editor, translator) (2009), *Geffrei Gaimar: Estoire des Engleis: History of the English*, OUP

14. https://oldsomerset2.wordpress.com

15. 'The Site of the Battle of Cynuit 878', p.8

16. 'The Site of the Battle of Cynuit 878', p.8

17. Castle Hill Settlement, ID 1007127 (https://historicengland.org.uk)

18. 'The Site of the Battle of Cynuit 878', p.4

19. Site visits with Nick Arnold, 6 October 2023

20. 'The Site of the Battle of Cynuit 878', p.4

21. 'The Site of the Battle of Cynwit 878', p.12

22. Wise, Terrence (1979), *Saxon, Viking and Norman*, Osprey Publishing, p.9

23. *Asser's Life of King Alfred* (gutenberg.org)

24. Nelson, Janet L. (1991), *The Annals of St Bertin,* Manchester Medieval Sources, Manchester University Press, p.130

25. Site visits with Nick Arnold, 30 March 2024

26. Wright, Thomas (1850), *The Anglo-Norman Metrical Chronicle of Geoffrey Gaimar*, Caxton Society (https://oldsomerset2.wordpress.com)

27. *Asser's Life of King Alfred* (gutenberg.org)

28. Hardy, Thomas Duffus and Martin, Charles Trice (1889), *Lestorie Des Engles Solum la Translacion Maistre Geffrei Gaimar,* HMSO, p.101 (Internet Archive)

29. Rowe, Elizabeth (2012), 'Vikings in the West, The Legend of Ragnarr Lodbrok and His Sons', *Studia Medievalia Septentrionalia*, Vol. 18, pp.82–83

30. Heath, Ian (1983), *The Vikings*, Osprey Publishing, pp.49–50

31. 'Vikings in the West, The Legend of Ragnarr Lodbrok and His Sons', p.82

32. Lukman, Niels (1958), 'The Raven Banner and the Changing Ravens: A Viking Miracle from Carolingian Court Poetry to Saga and Arthurian Romance', *Classica et Medievalia*, Vol. 19, pp. 133–51

33. *The Anglo-Norman Metrical Chronicle of Geoffrey Gaimar*

34. https://oldsomerset2.wordpress.com

35. https://oldsomerset2.wordpress.com

36. Grinsell, Leslie (1970), *The Barrows of North Devon,* Devon Archaeological Society, Proceedings No. 28, p.98

37. Harrison, Katie (2021), *Northam's Two Saxon Battles,* Bideford and District Archive Council

38. Hjardar, Kim and Vegard, Vike (2019), *Vikings at War*, Casemate UK, p.33, p.46

39. 'The Site of the Battle of Cynuit 878', p.8

40. 'The Site of the Battle of Cynuit 878', p.8; Grinsell, L. V. (1970), *The Archaeology of Exmoor Bideford Bay to Bridgewater*, David & Charles

41. *The Barrows of North Devon*, p.110

42. Devon & Dartmoor HER MDV11937, Mound in the Parish of Beaford (www.heritagegateway.org.uk)

43. Gardner, Keith (1998), *The Giant's Graves: A nineteenth century discovery of human remains on Lundy*, Lundy Field Society Report, Vol. 49

44. 'The Site of the Battle of Cynuit 878', Munby, J (1982), *Domesday Book*, Vol. 4, Phillimore

45. Gaiman, Neil (2019), *Norse Mythology*, Bloomsbury, pp.183–84

46. Bray, Olive (1908), *The Elder or Poetic Elder*, Viking Club Translation Series, Vol II, p.13

47. Waggoner, Ben (2009), *The Sagas of Ragnar Lodbrok*, Troth Publications, p.83

48. Site visits with Nick Arnold, 30 March 2024

49. *Assser's Life of King Alfred*

50. *Assser's Life of King Alfred*

51. Morris, Marc (2022), *The Anglo-Saxons, A History of the Beginnings of England*, Penguin Books, p.221

52. Stenton, Frank (1971), *Anglo-Saxon England*, Oxford University Press, p.254

53. Hadley, Dawn and Richards, Julian (2025), *Life in the Great Viking Army: Raiders, Traders and Settlers*, Oxford University Press, p.334

54. Magnusson, Magnus (1970), *The Vikings,* Tempus Publishing, p.106

Chapter 19: Siege of Paris

1. Waggoner, Ben (2009), *The Sagas of Ragnar Lodbrok*, Troth Publications, p.17

2. Dass, Nirmal (2007), *The Viking Attacks on Paris, The Bella parisiacae urbis of Abbo of Saint-Germain-des-Prés,* Peeters, p.29

3. *The Viking Attacks on Paris, The Bella parisiacae urbis of Abbo of Saint-Germain-des-Prés*, p.29

4. Lewis, Stephen M. (2017), *Hamlet with the Princes of Denmark: An exploration of the case of Hálfdan 'king of the Danes*, Hal Open Science, hal-01943605, p.39

5. 'Vikings in the West, The Legend of Ragnarr Lodbrok and His Sons', p.154

6. *The Viking Attacks on Paris, The Bella parisiacae urbis of Abbo of Saint-Germain-des-Prés*, p.31

7. Donvito, F. (2015), 'Besieging an island-city: The Viking siege of Paris, 885–886', *Medieval Warfare*, Vol. 5 No. 5, pp.29–35

8. Shepphard, Si (2022), *The Viking Siege of Paris, Longships Raid the Seine, 885–886*, Osprey Publishing, p.40

9. *The Viking Siege of Paris, Longships Raid the Seine, 885–886*, p.40

10. *The Viking Attacks on Paris, The Bella parisiacae urbis of Abbo of Saint-Germain-des-Prés*, p.31

11. *The Viking Attacks on Paris, The Bella parisiacae urbis of Abbo of Saint-Germain-des-Prés*, p.31

12. *The Viking Attacks on Paris, The Bella parisiacae urbis of Abbo of Saint-Germain-des-Prés*, p.31

13. *The Sagas of Ragnar Lodbrok*, p.16

14. McTurk, Rory (2006), 'Kings and Kingship in Viking Northumbria', in McKinnell, John, Ashurst, David and Kick, Donata, *The Fantastic in Old Norse Icelandic Literature*, Preprint Papers Part 2, Centre for Medieval and Renaissance Studies, pp.681–88

15. Elton, Oliver (translator) (1905), *The Nine Books of the Danish History of Saxo Grammaticus*, Norroena Society, New York

16. *The Sagas of Ragnar Lodbrok*, p.32, p.70

17. Nelson, Janet L. (1991), *The Annals of St-Bertin*, Manchester Medieval Sources, Manchester University Press, p.128

18. *The Sagas of Ragnar Lodbrok*, p.32

19. Reuter, Timothy (1992), *The Annals of Fulda*, Manchester Medieval Sources, Manchester University Press, pp.70–71

20. Rowe, Elizabeth Ashman (2012), 'Vikings the West, The Legend of Ragnarr Lodbrok and His Son's, *Studia Medievalia Septentrionalia*, Vol. 18, p.186

21. Robinson, Charles (1921), *Anskar: The Apostle of the North, 801–865*, The Society for the Propagation of the Bible in Foreign Parts, p.14 (Internet Achive)

22. *The Annals of Fulda*, p.36

23. Lund, Niels (2008), *Scandinavia, c.700–1066*, The New Cambridge Medieval History, Part Two, CUP, p.212

24. Ingram, James and Giles, John Allen (1996), *The Project Gutenberg Book of the Anglo-Saxon Chronicle*, produced by Douglas B. Killings (gutenberg. org); Baker, John and Brookes, Stuart (2012), 'Fulham 878–79: A New Consideration of Viking Manoeuvres', *Viking and Medieval Scandinavia*, Vol. 8, pp.23–52

25. Hjardar, Kim and Vegard, Vike (2019), *Vikings at War*, Casemate UK, p.319

26. Maclean, Simon (translator) (2009), *History and politics in late Carolingian and Ottonian Europe: The Chronicle of Regino of Prüm and Adalbert of Magdeburg by Regino, Abbot of Prüm, 840–915*, Manchester University Press, pp.183–85

27. *History and politics in late Carolingian and Ottonian Europe: The Chronicle of Regino of Prüm and Adalbert of Magdeburg by Regino, Abbot of Prüm, 840–915*, p.185

28. *Annals of St Bertin*, pp.224–25

29. *Annals of St Bertin*, pp.224–25

30. *Annals of Fulda*, p.105

31. *The Sagas of Ragnar Lodbrok*, p.70

32. Peeters, Joachim (1986), 'Siegfried von Niderlant Und Die Wikinger Am Niederrhein', *Zeitschrift für Deutsches Altertum und Deutsche Literatur*, Vol. 115, No. 1, pp.1–21

33. *Annals of Fulda*, p.93

34. Cook, Albert (1906), *Asser's Life of King Alfred*, Ginn & Company (gutenberg. org); Corpus of Electronic Texts (CELT), *Annals of Ulster*, University College Cork

35. *The Annales Vedastini*, Latin Library (www.thelatinlibrary.com/annalesve dastini.html)

36. *Hamlet with the Princes of Denmark: An exploration of the case of Hálfdan 'king of the Danes*, p.38

37. Tschan, Francis J. (translator) (2002), *History of the Archbishops of Hamburg–Bremen*, Columbia University Press, p.39

38. 'Siegfried von Niderlant Und Die Wikinger Am Niederrhein', pp.1–21

39. *History and politics in late Carolingian and Ottonian Europe: The Chronicle of Regino of Prüm and Adalbert of Magdeburg by Regino, Abbot of Prüm, 840–915*, p.194

40. Palsson, Hermann and Edwards, Paul (1978), *Okneyinga Saga, The History of the Earls of Orkney*, Penguin Classics, p.26

41. Lifshitz, Felice (1998), *Dudo of Saint-Quentin's Gesta Normannorum*, ORB Online Library (https://the-orb.arlima.net)

REFERENCES

42. *Annals of St Bertin*, p.196

43. Lewis, Stephen (2025), *Rollo of Fleury: Fact or Fiction, Part I, Dudo of St Quentin's Story*, Hal Open Science, hal-05072307, pp.1–24

44. Adams, Anthony and Rigg A. G. (2004), 'A Verse Translation of Abbo of St. Germain's "Bella Parisiacae Urbis"', *The Journal of Medieval Latin*, Vol. 14, p.25

45. *The Viking Siege of Paris, Longships Raid the Seine*, p.42

46. *Vikings at War*, p.321

47. *The Viking Attacks on Paris, The Bella parisiacae urbis of Abbo of Saint-Germain-des-Prés*, p.33

48. 'A Verse Translation of Abbo of St. Germain's "Bella Parisiacae Urbis"', p.25

49. 'Besieging an island-city: The Viking siege of Paris', *885–886*

50. *The Viking Attacks on Paris, The Bella parisiacae urbis of Abbo of Saint-Germain-des-Prés*, p.33

51. *The Viking Attacks on Paris, The Bella parisiacae urbis of Abbo of Saint-Germain-des-Prés*, p.35

52. *The Viking Attacks on Paris, The Bella parisiacae urbis of Abbo of Saint-Germain-des-Prés*, p.35

53. *Vikings at War*, p.322

54. *The Viking Attacks on Paris, The Bella parisiacae urbis of Abbo of Saint-Germain-des-Prés*, p.37

55. 'A Verse Translation of Abbo of St. Germain's "Bella Parisiacae Urbis"', p.29

56. *The Viking Siege of Paris, Longships Raid the Seine*, p.48

57. *The Viking Attacks on Paris, The Bella parisiacae urbis of Abbo of Saint-Germain-des-Prés*, p.63

58. 'A Verse Translation of Abbo of St. Germain's "Bella Parisiacae Urbis"', p.29

59. *Vikings at War*, p.322

60. *The Viking Attacks on Paris, The Bella parisiacae urbis of Abbo of Saint-Germain-des-Prés*, p.43

61. *The Viking Attacks on Paris, The Bella parisiacae urbis of Abbo of Saint-Germain-des-Prés*, p.41

62. 'A Verse Translation of Abbo of St. Germain's "Bella Parisiacae Urbis"', p.35

63. *The Viking Attacks on Paris, The Bella parisiacae urbis of Abbo of Saint-Germain-des-Prés*, p.51

64. *Vikings at War*, p.46

65. *The Viking Attacks on Paris, The Bella parisiacae urbis of Abbo of Saint-Germain-des-Prés*, p.51

66. *The Viking Attacks on Paris, The Bella parisiacae urbis of Abbo of Saint-Germain-des-Prés*, pp.53–55

67. *The Viking Attacks on Paris, The Bella parisiacae urbis of Abbo of Saint-Germain-des-Prés*, pp.11–12

68. 'A Verse Translation of Abbo of St. Germain's "Bella Parisiacae Urbis"', p.38
69. 'A Verse Translation of Abbo of St. Germain's "Bella Parisiacae Urbis"', p.38
70. 'A Verse Translation of Abbo of St. Germain's "Bella Parisiacae Urbis"', p.40
71. *The Annales Vedastini,* Latin Library (www.thelatinlibrary.com/annalesve dastini.html)

Chapter 20: Warrior of the Valkyries

1. Old Uppsala Museum
2. Dass, Nirmal (2007), *The Viking Attacks on Paris, The Bella parisiacae urbis of Abbo of Saint-Germain-des-Prés,* Peeters, p.67
3. *The Viking Attacks on Paris, The Bella parisiacae urbis of Abbo of Saint-Germain-des-Prés,* p.67
4. *The Viking Attacks on Paris, The Bella parisiacae urbis of Abbo of Saint-Germain-des-Prés,* p.67
5. *A Verse Translation of Abbo of St Germain's 'Bella Parisiacae Urbis,* p.45
6. *The Viking Attacks on Paris, The Bella parisiacae urbis of Abbo of Saint-Germain-des-Prés,* pp.75–77
7. Maclean, Simon (translator) (2009), *History and politics in late Carolingian and Ottonian Europe: The Chronicle of Regino of Prüm and Adalbert of Magdeburg by Regino, Abbot of Prüm, 840–915,* Manchester University Press, p.195
8. Reuter, Timothy (1992), *The Annals of Fulda,* Manchester Medieval Sources, Manchester University Press, p.101
9. At this point, an online Latin Library translation of the *Annals of St Vaast* states *'Sigefridus rex, cuius supra meminimus, Hisam fluvium ingressus, terra et aqua iter faciens post eum cum suis'*, meaning 'King Siegfried, whom we have mentioned above, having entered the river Oise and making a journey by land and water with all his men', implying it's the same figure negotiating with Gozlin at the Paris siege. However, another translation by Steve Bivans in *Vikings War and the Fall of the Carolingians* (2017) states that Charles the Fat was 'reminded how King Sigfrid, with all his men, was advancing up the River Oise making a march by land and water', p.68
10. Donvito, F. (2015), 'Besieging an island-city: The Viking siege of Paris, 885–886', *Medieval Warfare,* Vol. 5, No. 5, pp.29–35
11. *The Annales Vedastini,* Latin Library (www.thelatinlibrary.com/annalesve dastini.html)
12. Corpus of Electronic Texts (CELT), *Annals of Ulster,* University College Cork
13. Corpus of Electronic Texts (CELT), *Chronicon Scotorum,* University College Cork

REFERENCES

14. Maunsell, William (1866), *Chronicum Scotorum: A Chronicle of Irish Affairs From the Earliest Times to AD 1135 with a Supplement, Containing the Events from 1141 to 1150*, Longmans, Green, Reader and Dyer, p.171 (Internet Archive)

15. Site visit to Leuven, 8 December 2024

16. *History and politics in late Carolingian and Ottonian Europe: The Chronicle of Regino of Prüm and Adalbert of Magdeburg by Regino, Abbot of Prüm, 840–915*, p.191

17. Bivans, Steve (2017), *Vikings War and the Fall of the Carolingians, A Critical Translation of the Annals of St-Vaast*, Shireness Publishing, p.75

18. Via Belgica website (www.viabelgica.nl/en)

19. Leuven History Group newsletter, January 2025, No. 83

20. Hjardar, Kim and Vegard, Vike (2019), *Vikings at War,* Casemate UK, p.130

21. Harkel, Letty Ten (2013), 'A Viking Age Landscape of Defence in the Low Countries? The ringwalburgen in the Dutch Province of Zeeland', in Baker, John, Brookes, Stuart and Reynolds, Andrew (editors), *Landscapes of Defence in Early Medieval Europe*, Vol. 28, Brepols, p.242

22. Schueremans, L. and Van Gemert, D. (2003), *Structural Assessment of the Medieval City Wall of Leuven,* Civil Engineering Department, KU Leuven

23. Leuven History Group presentation

24. Vanbrabant, Luc (2024), *Leuven-Louvain during the wikingtimes* (www.academia.edu/96751802)

25. Leuven History Group presentation

26. Email correspondence, 21 February 2025

27. Email correspondence, 17 January 2025

28. Lunde, Paul and Stone, Caroline (2011), *Ibn Fadlan and the Land of Darkness: Arab Travellers in the Far North*, Penguin Classics, p.48

29. Verstraeten, G. et al. (2018), *'River Landscapes in the Dijle Catchment: From Natural to Anthropogenic Meandering Rivers'*, in Demoulin, A. (editor), *Landscapes and Landforms of Belgium and Luxembourg* (World Geomorphological Landscapes series), Springer Verlag, pp.269–80

30. Vander, Linden H. (1917), 'Les Normands A Louvan (884–992)', *Revue Historique*, Vol. 124, No. 1, pp.64–81

31. *The Viking Attacks on Paris, The Bella parisiacae urbis of Abbo of Saint-Germain-des-Prés*, p.29

32. *History and politics in late Carolingian and Ottonian Europe: The Chronicle of Regino of Prüm and Adalbert of Magdeburg by Regino, Abbot of Prüm, 840–915*, p.210

33. 'Les Normands A Louvan (884–992)'

34. Leuven History Group presentation

35. Tetzner, Noah (2022), *Viking Warrior vs Frankish Warrior*, Osprey, pp.17–18

36. *Annals of Fulda*, pp.121–23

37. *Annals of Fulda*, pp.121–23

38. *Annals of Fulda*, pp.121–23

39. 'Les Normands A Louvan (884–992)'

40. Waggoner, Ben (2009), *The Sagas of Ragnar Lodbrok*, Troth Publications, pp.71–72

41. Tschan, Francis J. (translator) (2002), *History of the Archbishops of Hamburg–Bremen*, Columbia University Press, p.44

42. Logan, F. Donald (2005), *The Vikings in History*, Taylor & Francis, p.141

43. *History of the Archbishops of Hamburg–Bremen*, p.47–49

44. Nordal, Sigurður and Turville-Petre, G. (1962), *Jómsvíkinga Saga*, Thomas Nelson and Sons Ltd

45. Rowe, Elizabeth Ashman (2012), 'Vikings the West, The Legend of Ragnarr Lodbrok and His Sons', *Studia Medievalia Septentrionalia*, Vol. 18, p.200

46. Leuven History Group newsletter, January 2025, No. 83

47. *The Sagas of Ragnar Lodbrok*, pp.71–72

INDEX

A

Abbasid Caliphate, Islamic
dynasty 25, 41, 114

Abbo Cernuus, a monk of
Saint-Germain-des-Prés 200, 204,
208–16, 218, 221, 223

Abbot Eadred 161

Abbo of Fleury 37, 92, 94–95, 97, 99,
101, 167, 177

Abbott's Way 172

Adam of Bremen, eleventh century
German medieval chronicler 38, 82,
99, 102, 170, 175, 206, 224–25

Adelsö 85–86

Áed Finnilaith, the High King of
Ireland 37, 106, 167, 169

Aesir, group of Viking gods vi, 1–3,
34, 115

Agnar, son of Ragnar Lothbrok 63–64

Aimoin, author of the Translation of
St Germain 11, 13, 16

Al-Andalus, Muslim name for
Umayyad Caliphate region of
Spain 24, 28

Alba, Gaelic kingdom in Scotland 47,
110, 144, 164–65

Algeciras 24, 27, 32

Alfred the Great, king of Wessex 54,
59, 61, 97, 118–22, 125–27, 131,
135, 163, 170, 173- 74, 176, 179–80,
183, 185, 187, 189–90, 194, 198–99

Alfred's Blowing Stone 122

Alonso III, late ninth century king of
Asturias 23

Alt Clut (rock of the Clyde) 104–07,
109–11, 113, 116, 178

Áth Cliath (Dublin) 42, 45, 110, 167

Antrim 168

Antwerp 56, 219

Amlaib Conung (see Olaf the White)

Amiens 206, 218–19

Anglo-Saxon Chronicle, Old English
annals 52, 59, 61, 76, 98, 116,
126, 131, 141, 159, 185, 188,
192–93, 222

Annales Cambriae, medieval Welsh
chronicle 50, 173

Anskar, Archbishop of Hamburg and
Bremen 10–11, 85

Anulo, Danish prince 19–20

Annud, early Swedish king 85

Ari Thorgilsson, twelfth century
Icelandic scholar 22, 203

Arthgal, ninth century Alt Clut 110

Arnulf, king of East Francia 217,
221–23

Ashbury 120–23

Ashdown House 120

Aslaug, mother of Ragnar's sons vi,
63–64, 75, 99, 100, 116, 202, 224–26

Asser, Alfred the Great's
biographer 54, 74, 76, 78, 118–119,
121–22, 124–26, 131, 162, 178–80,
182, 184, 187–92, 198, 204

Asselt, scene of 882 Viking
    siege 204–06, 217, 224
Aella, king of Northumbria vi-ii, 39,
    46, 71–75, 78–80, 83–84, 100,
    116, 206
Argyll and Bute 105, 168
Armagh 41, 143
Avaldsnes 21–22, 145
Auisle, Viking ruler in Ireland 36, 40,
    106, 135
Auisle, Viking ruler at Tettenhall 135
Austria 6

B
Baghdad 25, 33, 41
Bagsecg, Viking ruler at Battle of
    Ashdown 116, 121, 124
Bangor 159
Barid, king of the fair foreigners in
    Ireland 167, 169
Bath 126
Battle of Ashdown 90, 116
Battle of Brunanburh 116, 199
Battle of Clontarf 193
Battle of Cynuit 172–73, 176, 178,
    181, 186, 188, 193, 196, 198
Battle of Edington 198–99
Battle of Ellandun 61
Battle of Guele 221
Battle of Hastings 151–52, 57
Battle of Merantun 126, 129, 131
Battle of Tettenhall 136, 170
Battle of Wilton 131, 135
Basingstoke (formerly Old
    Basing) 126
Beaford 186, 190
Bede, eighth century Northumbrian
    monk and scholar 57, 79, 106,
    119, 189
Beowulf, Old English poem 54, 86, 97,
    148, 153

Birka, Viking Age emporium in
    Sweden 2, 4, 10–11, 41, 67–68, 70,
    85–86, 88–90, 114, 136, 139–40
Bishop Heahmund, Anglo-Saxon
    bishop of Sherborne ix, 126–28,
    130–31
Bishop's Tawton 185–86
Björn Järnsidas hög, burial mound of
    Bjorn Ironside 86
Bokerley Dyke, ancient landmark 128
Boulby 148, 153–54, 157
Bradfield Nature reserve 97
Bragi Bodasson, Skaldic poet 20–21,
    84–85
Bristol 126
Brú na Bóinne (palace of the
    Boyne) 35–37, 51
Burghead fort 163
Burgundy 14, 74, 200, 216–217
Brunhild, mother of Aslaug 64,
    74–75, 99
Brussels 218
Byzantine 33, 70
Byzantine empire 33, 88, 114

C
Caedwalla, seventh century king of
    Wessex 59
Cannington Camp 177–178
Carlus, Olaf the White's son 106
Carolingian, dynasty of Frankish
    king 6, 217
Carolman II, West Francia ruler 206
Castle Hill, Iron Age hillfort 186–91,
    195–97
Ceawlin, sixth century king of
    Wessex 59
Ceccardus of Luni, a ninth century
    bishop 30
Ceowulf II, king of Mercia 136
Cerball, king of Ossory 51

Cerdic, founder of Wessex 59

Charlemagne, emperor of Francia 6–7,
204, 217

Charles the Bald, king of West Francia
and Italy 7, 11, 13, 19, 27–29, 61,
99, 169, 175, 191, 204

Charles the Fat, emperor of the
Carolingian Empire 204–06, 216–17

Chippenham 185

Chnuba, Danish king in tenth
century 224

Cináed mac Ailpín (Kenneth
MacAlpin) king of the Picts and Dál
Riata 47, 106, 164–65

Cinaed mac Conaing, ruler of
Brega 106

Cleveland 148–149, 151, 153–55,
157, 228

Cleveland Way 153–54

Clondalkin 106

Cogadh Gaedhel re Gallaibh (The War
of the Irish with the Foreigners),
twelve century Irish text 48,
167, 169

Constantine I, king of the
Picts 110–11, 143, 147, 163–65

Constantinople 33, 41, 114

Córdoba 24, 32

Cornwall 162, 173, 186

Count Pedro, ninth century Asturian
nobleman 23, 32

Count Cobbo, East Franks
diplomat 15

Countisbury hill fort 181–84, 187,
189, 194

Covent Garden 132, 134

Crediton 173, 185, 187

Creoda, sixth century king of
Mercia 59

Croydon Hoard 135

Cumbria 156

D

Dagling Dynasty 224

Dál Fiatach, ancient kingdom in
north-east Ireland 167–68

Dál Riata, ancient Gaelic kingdom 47,
104–08, 112, 164, 168

Danegeld, payment to Vikings 14

Danelaw, regions under Viking
control 57, 111, 148, 150, 199

Dartmoor 171–72, 186–87

De bellis Parisiacæ urbis (The Wars of
the City of Paris) 207

Denmark viii, 2, 4, 7–8, 12, 20, 41,
54, 56, 58, 62, 64, 67–68, 72, 84,
94, 145, 152–53, 159, 177, 192,
208, 225

Devon viii, 172–74, 178–91, 193–94,
196–99

Devonshire, Old English name for
Devon 173, 180, 194

Dinas Emrys 105

Dnieper River 41, 114

Donyarth, king of Cornwall 173

Domburg 55–56

Doomster 110

Dorestad, Viking Age emporium in
Frisia 7, 54–55, 57, 90, 160

Dorset 8, 34, 129, 185

Down 168

Downpatrick 158, 168–69

Dowth 35–36

Draupner, Odin's magical golden
ring 34

Dublin 36, 38–39, 42–46, 50, 54, 65, 102,
106–07, 109–10, 113–14, 143–45, 147,
156–57, 167, 169, 190, 217, 226

Dudo of Saint-Quentin, eleventh
century chronicler 27, 30, 208

Duke Henry of Saxony 206, 216

Dunadd, Dál Riata
stronghold 105, 112

Dunblane 107
Dunnyneill Island 158–59, 167–68
Dumbarton Castle 103–106, 112
Dumnonia, ancient kingdom in
    south-west Britain 173
Dyfed 50, 118, 178
Dyfnwal, Alt Clut king 106

E
Eadred, king of the English, tenth
    century 122
Eadwig, king of the English 123
Ealhstan, Bishop of
    Sherborne 128, 178
Eardulf, Bishop of
    Lindisfarne 161, 170
East Anglia, Anglo-Saxon
    kingdom 58, 61, 79, 92, 94, 98–99,
    102, 108, 118, 135, 141–42, 153,
    178, 197, 199, 205
East Francia (most of modern
    Germany) 8, 15, 159, 217
East Thirston 161–62
*Ecclesiastical History of the English
    People*, eighth century chronicle by
    Bede 119
Edinburgh 106
Edmund, king of East Anglia 61, 79,
    92, 94–99, 102, 118, 175, 177, 190
Egbert, ninth century king of
    Wessex 59, 61, 173, 190, 198, 199
Eirek, son of Ragnar Lothbrok 63–64,
    73
Emirate of Córdoba, Arab state in the
    Iberian Peninsula (al-Andalus) 24
Essex, Anglo-Saxon
    kingdom 58–59, 127
Ethelred, king of Wessex and brother
    of Alfred the Great 61, 74, 118,
    120–21, 123, 126–27, 129, 135,
    138, 199

Ethelred II, ruler in Northumbria 138
Ethelwulf, ninth century Wessex king,
    Alfred's father 61, 118, 120
Ethelwulf, ealdorman of
    Berkshire 118, 121
Ethlestan, king of the English 199
Eyrbyggja saga, Icelandic text 152
Eysteinn, legendary king of
    Sweden 26, 39, 64, 72, 85, 202
Eysteinn, son of Olaf the White 141,
    147, 165–69
Exeter 173, 183, 185–87, 189–90

F
Flateyjarbók, Old Norse tale 63, 151
France 6, 8, 20, 27–29, 33, 41,
    74, 158–59, 203, 205, 208, 212,
    217, 219
Fenrir, monstrous wolf in Old Norse
    mythology 60
Five boroughs, Midlands Viking
    kingdoms 57, 199
Freeborough Hill 149
Freke, wolf which accompanies
    Odin 34
Fridleif, son of Lagertha and
    Ragnar 63
Frisia 8, 34, 50, 54–57, 73, 83, 90,
    160, 175, 206, 216–18
Fimbulwinter, devastating winter in
    Old Norse mythology 1–2, 4

G
Galicia 23, 24
Galloway Viking Hoard 165
Gamla Uppsala, famous Viking
    Age archaeological site (see Old
    Uppsala)
Geoffrey Gaimar, twelfth century
    Anglo-Norman chronicler 76, 99,
    124, 176, 187–88, 192–197

Gere, wolf which accompanies Odin 34,

Germany 6–8, 16, 20, 28, 30, 54, 58, 90, 135, 158–59, 204, 206, 217, 219

Gesta Hammaburgensis ecclesiae pontificum (*Deeds of the Bishops of the Church of Hamburg*) 38

Ghent 56, 204, 219

Gibraltar 24, 31–32, 50

Glasgow 103–104, 106, 112, 149

Godafrid, late ninth century Viking ruler in Frisia 202, 204–07, 216, 224

Godafrid, late ninth century Viking ruler at Leuven 223

Godborough Castle 180

Godfred, early ninth century king of the Danes 7, 19–20, 73

Godfred, mid ninth century Viking sea king 202, 204–07, 216, 224

Gofraid, king of Lochlann 40, 48, 143–45, 167

Gokstad Ship Burial 5, 56, 192

Gorm, Viking prince at Asselt 205

Gorm the Old, tenth century Danish king 225

Gosforth 156

Govan 106, 110–11, 149

Gozlin, the Bishop of Paris 200–02, 208, 212, 216

Grand Pont, Paris 200–01, 207, 209, 212

Gualardale (Gualar Valley in Norway) 63

Gudmund, chieftain in the tenth century Iceland 65

Gudrod, late ninth century Viking ruler from Ringervike 224

Gudrod the Hunter, petty king in Old Norse sagas 145

Gunger, Odin's powerful spear 34

Guthred, king of Northumbria and probable son of Ivar 170, 217

Guthrum, leader of the Great Heathen Army 134, 161, 174, 178, 183, 185, 190, 198, 204–05, 208

Gylfi, mythical Old Norse king 1

Gwynedd 46, 50, 105, 178

H

Hakon Sigurdson, tenth century ruler of Norway 63

Halfdan the Black, father of Norway founder Harald Finehair 48, 145, 203

Harald Bluetooth, tenth century Danish king 56, 225

Harald Finehair, founder of Norway 48, 145, 203

Harald Hardrada, king of Norway 116, 151, 153, 155, 157

Harald Godwinson, king of the English 151–52, 157

Harald Klak, king of the Danes 20, 73, 175

Harald the Younger, Viking ruler in Frisia 57, 175

Hardegon, tenth century Danish king 225

Harthacnute, tenth century Danish king, possible son of Sigurd 224–25

Hastein, notorious ninth century Viking chief 27, 29–30, 32–33, 219, 225

Hattalykill, Old Norse poem 71, 100, 158

Healfdene, Viking ruler at Tettenhall, likely descendant of Ragnar's sons 135, 170

Hedeby, Viking Age emporium, formerly Denmark now Germany 7, 11, 41, 50, 54, 62, 108–109, 136, 140, 160
Heimskringla, Old Norse saga 151
Helge, late ninth century Danish king 224
Hemings Þattr, thirteenth century Icelandic saga 151, 155–56
Henry of Huntingdon, twelfth century chronicler 99, 78
Herodd, earl or king in Sweden, father of Thora 63, 71, 83
Hervarar saga, legendary thirteenth century Germanic saga 84–85, 137
Hrafnsmál, Skaldic poem 203
Hincmar, archbishop of Reins, author of Annals of St Bertin 128
Historia Normannorum (*History of the Normans*) 27
Holm Bay 167–70
Hordaland, Norway 34
Horseton Ford, ancient place name 123–24
Horm, chief of the dark foreigners 50
Horik I, king of the Danes 15–16, 18, 20, 22, 26, 51, 73, 134, 160, 203, 206, 225
Horik II, king of the Danes 26, 51, 73, 134, 160, 203, 206, 225
Houses of Parliament 132
Hugh the Abbott 200
Hugh Capet, founder of Frankish dynasty 217
Hugin (thought), raven which accompanies Odin 34, 115, 145
Humber estuary 136, 161
Hungary 6
Hunterston Brooch, archaeological find with Brittonic and Viking markings 112
Hymir, giant in Old Norse mythology 94

I
Ibn Fadlan, Arab traveller 25, 177, 220
Ibn Idhari, fourteenth century Muslim historian 23–24, 27, 31, 83
Iceland viii, 22, 63–65, 68, 114, 203
Icelandic viii, 1, 5, 48, 65, 79, 84, 100, 114, 151, 156, 169
Icknield Way 121
Île de la Cité (little island) 9, 201, 207, 211
Italy 6, 8, 32, 49, 84, 217
Imair, historical prototype of Ivar the Boneless 36, 39
Ingvar, Swedish king linked to Salme expedition 152
Ipswich 88
Islandbridge, Viking Age burial site in Dublin 45–46
Íslendingabók (*Book of Icelanders*), twelfth century 22, 203
Isle of Athelney 173
Isle of Clegg 98
Ivar's Howe, legendary burial mound of Ivar Ragnarsson 150–53, 155–56
Ivar, Viking ruler at Tettenhall likely descendant of Ragnar's sons 135

J
Jörmungandr, a sea monster from Old Norse mythology 3, 21, 60, 75, 94
Jutland, main peninsula of Denmark 7, 26, 41, 55, 58, 70, 73, 117, 159–60, 203, 205

K
Kattegat, fictional emporium in the Vikings, sea strait between Sweden and Denmark 7, 62
Kaupang, Viking Age emporium in modern Norway 41–42, 65, 114, 136, 139, 144

Kent 54, 58, 61, 127–28, 206
Kenwith Castle 180–81, 186,
Ketil Flatnose, possible ninth century
    Hebridean king 51
Keynsham Abbey 130
Keynsham 126, 128, 130–31
Kilmainham, Viking burial site in
    Dublin 44–45, 65
Kingdom of the Isles 106, 147
Kingstone Coombes 123
Kingstone Down 123
Kingstone Lisle 123
Kingstone Warren 123
Knowth, passage tombs of Brú na
    Bóinne 35–36
Kraka, Aslaug's name in
    hiding 64, 99
Krákumál, twelfth century Skaldic
    poem vi, viii, 47, 72

L
Lagertha, partner of Ragnar and
    mothers to his sons 62–64, 70–71,
    73, 84
Leuven 218–22, 223, 225
Levengrove Park 112
Lindisfarne 59, 61, 153, 161
Lingrow Howe, neolithic long
    barrow 155, 157
London 39, 61, 99, 112, 132, 134–36,
    199
Lorcán mac Cathail 36–37, the king of
    Mede (Meath) 36–37
Lochlann (also Laithlind), Viking
    kingdom later associated with
    Norway 40, 45–46, 144–45
Loch Lomond 111
Lordomani, Asturian name for the
    Vikings 23
Lothair I, emperor of Italy and Middle
    Francia 7–8, 90, 206

Løve, Viking Age archaeological site
    in Norway 65
Low Countries 7–8
Lowestoft 98
Lowther Hills 104
Louis the Blind, ruler of Provence 217
Louis the German, king of East
    Francia 7, 8, 15, 16, 27, 159,
    203–04
Louis the Pious, king of the Franks 7,
    59, 85
Lynton 181–82
Lynmouth 181–83

M
Madjus, Arab name for the
    Vikings 23–24, 31
Marden 129
Máel Sechnaill, high king of the
    Southern Uí Néill and Ireland 45,
    51, 116, 176
Máel Sechnaill, king of Southern
    Brega 116, 176, 178
Magrheb 23, 83
Massacre of Verden, Charlemagne's
    slaughter of Saxons 6
Melbrictus, early Irish king 46–47
Mercia, Anglo-Saxon kingdom 58, 79,
    136, 142, 199
Mericans, people of Anglo-Saxon
    kingdom 79, 135, 143
Middleburg 55
Middle Francia (the Low Countries and
    Italy) 7, 29, 90, 175
Midgard, the earth in Old Norse
    mythology 3, 60, 75
Midgard Serpent, a sea monster
    from Old Norse mythology
    (see Jörmungandr)
Moors, the European name for
    Muslims 24, 30, 148

Morocco 24, 27, 32, 49, 84

Moray 163

Munin (memory), raven which
   accompanies Odin 34, 115, 145

N

Navarre, small Christian kingdom in
   Spain 33

Nekor 27–28, 32–33, 49

Newgrange, passage tombs of Brú na
   Bóinne 35–37

Netherlands 7, 54–55, 176, 217, 219

Neustria, kingdom of western
   Francia 14, 205

Nordre Kjølen, Viking Age
   archaeological site in Norway 62,
   64, 70

North Yorkshire 148–53, 155, 157

Northern Uí Néill, a branch of the
   Uí Néill dynasty in north-western
   Ireland 37, 106, 169

Northumbria, Anglo-Saxon
   kingdom 48, 57, 74, 76, 78–79, 83,
   94, 102, 106, 108, 113, 118, 136,
   141, 148, 153, 159–62, 166–67,
   170, 225

Northumbrians, people of
   Northumbria 74, 76, 78, 106, 161

Norway viii, 2, 4–5, 7, 20–21, 26, 34,
   40, 43, 45–46, 48, 55–56, 62–65,
   68, 100, 112, 136, 143–45, 203, 224

Notker the Stammerer, Charlemagne's
   biographer 6

O

Obotrites, a confederation of West
   Slavic tribes 6, 20

Odda, earl of Devonshire 174, 178,
   183, 187, 190

Odin, chief Viking god vi, 3, 13, 21,
   33–34, 59–60, 81–82, 87, 92, 94,
   101, 115, 121, 145, 149, 152, 185,
   193, 197–98, 202, 220, 227

Odo, king of West Francia and count
   of Paris 200, 202, 208–09, 211,
   215–16, 219

Offa, eighth century king of
   Mercia 61, 119, 199

Olaf, early tenth century Danish king
   from Sweden 224

Olaf the White, king of Dublin and ally
   of Ivar 36, 40, 45–46, 51, 63, 103,
   106–08, 114, 116, 143–45, 147, 156,
   165, 167

Olaf Gudrodsson (Olaf Geirstad-Alf),
   Vestfold ruler from Old Norse
   saga 142

Olaf Guthfrithson, great-grandson of
   Ivar 199

Olaf Tryggvason, ninth century ruler of
   Norway 63

Old Kilmadock 164

Old Uppsala, famous Viking Age
   archaeological site 67, 81–86, 88,
   89, 92, 144

Olof, ninth century ruler in Adelsö 85, 90

Oistin (see Eystienn, son of Olaf the
   White)

Oostburg 55

Oost Sourburg 55, 56

Oslofjord 2, 42

Othenseberg, old name for Roseberry
   Topping honouring Odin 149

Oude Markt 218–19

P

Paris vii, ix, 9, 11–15, 17–20, 22,
   25–26, 29, 32, 34, 46, 47–49, 72,
   74, 90, 157, 160, 165, 199, 200, 203,
   205, 207–08, 211, 214–218, 221, 223

Penda, seventh century king of
   Mercia 59

Petit Pont, Paris 213, 218
Pictland, ancient kingdom in modern
    Scotland 47, 73, 107, 113, 143, 147,
    163–65, 178
Picts 46–47, 79, 106, 110, 113, 162–65
Pisa 30, 32
Poetic Edda, collection of anonymous
    Old Norse poems 52, 60, 87
Portland 34
Porlock Bay 182–83
Prose Edda, thirteenth century Old
    Norse text 1, 34, 74, 115
Provence 217
Pybba, seventh century king of
    Mercia 59

R
Ragnall ua Ímair, grandson of Ivar 46,
    48, 170
Ragnall from Irish Fragmentary
    Annals associated with
    Ragnar 48–50, 143
Randalin, mother of Raganr's sons
    (see Aslaug)
Ragnar's Saga (Ragnars saga
    loðbrókar), Old Norse tale vii, ix,
    30, 39, 49, 64, 75, 84, 99, 144, 150,
    157, 177
Ragnarsdrápa (a poem called The
    Long Refrain for Ragnar) 20–22,
    80, 85
Ragnhild, wife of Haldan the
    Black, possible granddaughter of
    Sigurd 203–204
Rammesburi (raven's fort), ancient
    place name near Ashbury 122–23
Rathlin Island 40
Ravenscar 155
Reading 117–119, 121, 125, 131, 134
Red Castle, eleventh century ringwork
    castle in woods in Thetford 98

Reginherus (Latin name of Ragnar at
    Paris siege) 9
Reginoldus, ninth century Viking 20
Regino of Prüm, monk and Carolingian
    chronicler 30, 204, 207, 218, 221
Repton 8, 140–43, 145, 147, 156, 161,
    165, 186, 196, 219
Reric, Slavic emporium 7
Rhodri Mawyr, the king of
    Gwynedd 178
Rhun, ninth century
    Strathclyde king 110
Ribe, a Viking Age emporium in
    southern Denmark 4, 11, 136
Rimbert, Archbishop of Hamburg and
    Bremen 10–11, 85–86, 206
River Elbe 6, 16
River Liffey 42
River Meuse 57, 206
River Parrett 178–79
River Poddle 42
River Scheldt 11, 54–56, 175, 204,
    206, 219–20
River Taw 193, 198
River Thames 134
River Torrington 191
River Trent 106, 136, 141
Robert the Quiver count of Troyes 212
Rognvald of More, earl of
    Orkney 48–49, 167
Rognvald, son of Ragnar Lothbrok 63
Rollo, founder of Normandy 207–08
Roman Britain 57
Rome 6, 9, 29, 30, 118, 164, 200
Rorik, Viking ruler in Frisia 57, 73,
    90, 160, 173, 205
Roseberry Topping 149
Roslagen 41
Rudolf, ninth century Viking, possibly
    identified as Ubbe 114, 175–76
Runswick Bay 149, 155–57

S

Sandefjord region of Norway 5

Salme ship expedition 102, 152

Saaremaa island 152

Saxo Grammaticus, thirteenth century
Danish historian viii, 22, 26, 46, 55,
62–63, 71, 73, 83, 175, 177, 202

Scandinavia vi, vii, viii, ix, 1–4, 6,
8, 10–11, 25–26, 28, 31, 37, 43,
49, 52, 56, 65, 72–73, 77, 87, 100,
111–12, 114, 139–40, 145, 149, 153,
158, 169, 199, 203–05, 210, 218, 224

Scarborough 155

Scotichronicon, fifteenth century
text 163

Scotti, Latin term for people of Ireland
and later Scotland 163–64

Seeresses, person who can perform
magic and predict the future 65

Seville 24

Shetland Islands 5

Shield Maidens, Viking warrior
women ix, 62–64

Sibilja, magical cow in the Saga of
Ragnar Lothbrok 39

Sichfrith, king of Northumbria,
possible descendant of Ragnar's
sons 170

Sichfrith mac Imair, son of Ivar 102,
204, 207, 217–18

Sicily 24, 29

Sidroc, ninth century Viking, ally of
Bjorn 24, 126

Sidroc Jr, Viking killed in Battle of
Ashdown 126

Sigfred, early ninth century Danish
prince, possible father of Ragnar
Lothbrok 19–20

Siegfried (also Sigifrid), king of the
Danes, historical archetype for
Sigurd 117, 159, 206

Siegfried, Viking ruler at Paris siege
and aftermath 200–04, 207–12,
215–218

Sigefredus (also called Siegfried),
Danish negotiator at Amiens 206

Sigfrid, Viking chieftain in
Aquitaine 203

Sigifrid, Viking leader at
Asselt 204–06, 217, 224

Sigtrygg, tenth century Danish
king 224

Sigurd Dragon Slayer, mythological
figure father of Aslaug 80, 99

Sihtric, grandson of Ivar, king of
Jorvik 170

Sihtric mac Imair, son of Ivar 170,
216, 217

Sinric, Viking leader at the siege of
Paris 216

Skjoldungatal, Danish text from the
thirteenth century viii

Sleipner, Odin's eight legged
stallion 34

Slovenia 6

Snorri Sturluson, twelfth century
Icelandic scholar 1, 21, 34, 48,
75, 81, 85, 115, 132, 144, 151–52,
215, 225

Somerset 128, 173, 178–79, 182, 184,
190, 198

Southampton 34, 61

Southern Uí Néill, branch of the Uí
Néill dynasty in the Kingdom of
Mede 45, 51

St Boniface, seventh century
monk 173

St-Germain-des-Prés, monastery in
Paris attacked by Vikings 11–12,
15, 72, 200, 218

St Patrick's Festival 106, 143

Strangford Lough 46, 167–69, 178

St Wystan's Church 140, 143, 145

Strathclyde, ancient kingdom in
     modern Scotland 79, 104, 106, 110,
     162, 181

Stockholm 10, 68, 88

Strokestown 114

Surrey 61

Sussex 58, 61, 152

Suttung, Old Norse mythological
     figure 115, 202

Sweden viii, 2, 4, 7, 8, 10, 21, 26, 41,
     62–64, 67, 70–73, 83–86, 88, 153, 224

Switzerland 6

T

Tale Of Ragnar's Sons (Ragnarssona
     þáttr), Old Norse tale viii, 26,
     83–84, 90, 101, 152, 159, 177, 203,
     205, 224, 226

Tanngnjóstr (teeth-grinder), Odin's
     goat 92

Tanngrisnir (teeth-barer), Odin's
     goat 92–93

Tawstock 186

The Annals of Fontenelle 17, 26

*The Annals of the Four
     Masters* 46–47, 176

The Annals of Fulda, ninth century
     East Frankish chronicle 17, 39, 55,
     73, 117, 159, 176, 203, 205–06, 216,
     222–24, 228

The Annals of Lindisfarne 54, 177

The Annals of St Bertin, ninth century
     Frankish chronicle 8, 13, 17,
     19, 26–30, 55, 57, 90, 128, 175,
     203–04, 208, 228

The Annals of St Vaast 206, 214,
     217, 225

The Abbey of St-Denis, located in
     Paris 12–13

The Abbey of St Genevieve 9

The Abbey of St Wandrille 17

The Annals of Ulster, medieval Irish
     chronicle 36, 40, 42, 45, 46–47, 51,
     106, 109–110, 141, 143, 163, 165,
     167, 169, 176, 178, 217

The Annals of Xanten, ninth century
     Frankish chronicle 17–18, 72, 175–76

The Chronicon Scotorum (*Chronicle
     of Scots*), twelfth century
     text 167, 217

*The Chronicon Sebastiani
     Salmanticensis*, ninth century
     text 23, 28, 31

The Dál nAraide, ancient kingdom in
     north-east Ireland 168

The dark foreigners (Dubgaill),
     Vikings associated with Ivar's
     family and descendants ix, 45, 46,
     50, 51, 143, 160, 169, 176, 178,
     204, 217

The Fair Foreigners (Finngaill), a
     group of Irish Vikings 46, 50, 167

The Fragmentary Annals of Ireland,
     eleventh century Irish text 28, 33,
     40, 46, 48–51, 76, 106, 109, 117,
     143–44, 167

The Great Heathen Army ix, 26, 30,
     40, 46, 49, 54, 57, 61, 74, 76, 79,
     83, 90, 92, 94, 98, 114, 116–117,
     121, 125, 127, 131–32, 135, 136,
     140–41, 145, 148, 155–57, 159,
     161, 167, 172, 175, 178, 184, 185,
     192, 196, 202–06, 218, 222

The Hebrides 47, 72, 106, 112, 147

The History of St Cuthbert, eleventh
     century 54, 74, 79, 163

The Isle of Man 47, 106, 110,
     152, 167

The Prophecy of Berchan, eleventh
     century Scottish text 164

The River Dyle 219–20

The Rus, Swedish Vikings who settled
  Baltic river routes 41, 72–73,
  91, 220
The Scaldingi, associated with Ivar,
  Ubbe and the Great Heathen
  Army 54, 175
The Vale of the White Horse 119
Thetford 61, 92, 95, 98–99
Thetford Castle, motte and bailey
  Norman castle and Iron Age
  settlement 61, 98
Thora, first wife of Ragnar
  Lothbrok 63–64, 70–71, 83, 90
Thor, one of the chief
  Viking gods 59–60, 63–64, 81–83,
  92–94, 99, 143
Torksey 79, 136, 138, 139,
  162, 186
Tomrair, the earl of Lochlann 46
Tostig Godwinson, deposed earl,
  brother of Harold 151, 155
Tower Hill 122–24
Tuatha Dé Danann, race of
  supernatural Irish gods 37
Twelve defenders at Paris siege 214
Turgeis, ninth century Viking in
  Ireland 44
Tynwald Day 149
Tynwald Hill 149
Tyr, Old Norse mythological
  figure 101

U
Ubbelawe, burial mound of Ubbe
  Ragnarsson 194–96
Ui Ímair dynasty (descendants of
  Ivar) 50, 147
Ulaid, Gaelic kingdom in north-east
  Ireland 158, 168–69
Ulf, the dark foreigner associated with
  Ubbe 46, 176, 178

Ulfberht, famous Frankish
  swords 222
Umayyad Caliphate, Islamic
  dynasty that ruled in the Iberian
  peninsula 24, 28, 32

V
Vestfold 7, 42–43, 55, 65, 144
Vidar, Odin's son 60
Volga River 25, 41, 114, 220
Völuspá ('Prophecy of the Seeress') 2,
  52, 60, 137
Völvas, person who can perform magic
  and predict the future 65

W
Walcheren 54–57, 175
Walichrum, Viking Age Frisian trading
  site 55
Wayland Smithy, Germanic
  mythological figure 59
Wayland Smithy, Neolithic long
  barrow 59, 120
Weathercock Hill 123–24
Weland, ninth century Viking aligned
  with the Franks 19, 169
Wessex, Anglo-Saxon kingdom 52,
  58–59, 61, 79, 116–19, 124–29,
  131, 135, 169, 173, 185, 188–90,
  198, 206
Westminster Bridge 135
West Francia (which evolved
  into France) 8–9, 11, 27, 205–06,
  217
Whitby 149, 153, 155
William of Jumièges, eleventh century
  Norman chronicler 23–27, 29–31,
  33–34, 49, 55, 72, 83, 90
William Wallace, rebel Scottish leader
  in the thirteenth century 112
Wilton 131, 135

Wimborne Minister 129
Woolleigh 188, 196

Y
Yggdrasil, world tree in Old Norse
    mythology 3, 34, 75
Ynglinga dynasty 21, 75, 81, 86,
    144, 152

York 38, 46, 49, 54, 57, 75–77, 79–80,
    90, 94, 99, 143, 148–50, 152, 157,
    160, 170, 177, 217, 226

Z
Zealand, largest island in
    Denmark 21, 26, 31, 67, 74, 99,
    175, 203